The Best
AMERICAN
ESSAYS
1994

D0969794

GUEST EDITORS OF
THE BEST AMERICAN ESSAYS

1986 ELIZABETH HARDWICK
1987 GAY TALESE
1988 ANNIE DILLARD
1989 GEOFFREY WOLFF
1990 JUSTIN KAPLAN
1991 JOYCE CAROL OATES
1992 SUSAN SONTAG
1993 JOSEPH EPSTEIN
1994 TRACY KIDDER

The Best
AMERICAN
ESSAYS
1994

Edited and with an Introduction
by TRACY KIDDER

ROBERT ATWAN,
Series Editor

HOUGHTON MIFFLIN COMPANY
BOSTON · NEW YORK 1994

ISSN 0888-3742
ISBN 0-395-69254-7
ISBN 0-395-69253-9 (pbk.)

Printed in the United States of America

AGM 10 9 8 7 6 5 4 3 2 1

Contents

Contents

Foreword

"WHERE THERE'S A WILL there's a way," an excited William Hazlitt says to himself as he hurries down Chancery Lane "about half-past six o'clock, on Monday the 10th of December, to inquire at Jack Randall's where the fight the next day was to be." The year is 1821, the city is London, and Hazlitt is pursuing his way to an out-of-town boxing match, his first fight ever. He's eager to see big Bill Neate, the raging Bristol "Bull," take on the "Gas-Man," Tom Hickman, the bravest and cruelest fighter in all of England. "I was determined to see this fight, come what would, and see it I did, in great style."

You can consult all the handbooks on literary nonfiction for all the elements of style, structure, and composition, but you'll rarely find mention of what Hazlitt just noted — *determination*. Yet its literary value is inestimable.

This year's volume of essays — the ninth in the series — is filled with determination. You can see the fight in great style. You can narrate it with equally great style. But as Hazlitt reminds us, you first have to get there. No sitting in your study with a boxing encyclopedia, no telephone interviews with experts, no electronic highway; and the travel involved takes you beyond your local library.

Such narratives can be a risky business. For one thing, the destinations are often uncertain. When Ted Conover joins up with a convoy of African truckers, he has no idea of what he'll find when they reach Rwanda. Nor does Cynthia Ozick, who doesn't usually assume the role of reporter, know what odd literary associations will result from her visit to the Louvre, where she sees "Salman Rushdie plain." In most of the essays collected here we confront worlds that exist thrillingly outside the writer's self. In fact, what makes this volume especially venturous is that most of these worlds also exist outside of the writer's control. Even when the essays concentrate on a wholly personal sphere, as Stanley Elkins's does, they confront human conditions verging on the unmanageable: "Being out of one's tree melts your watch like a Dali."

But there's an additional risk. After writing "The Fight," Hazlitt was surprised to find that people considered his eyewitness report a "vulgar thing." This wasn't simply because his story took readers into an unfamiliar subculture, but because it took them into unfamiliar prose territory as well. In other words, Hazlitt risked the unliterary; he was determined to find a way to develop an essay out of "unsuitable" material. We can see a similar determination in many of this year's essays; look at how S. Oso, Lauren Slater, and Andre Dubus III creatively confront unpromising or intractable subjects. Where there's a will there's a way.

From the narrative essays of Darcy Frey on inner-city basketball and Lucy Grealy on plastic surgery (both of which won 1994 National Magazine Awards) to the reflective performances of Nicholson Baker and John Updike, this year's volume showcases just about every type of contemporary essay: autobiographical, journalistic, critical, speculative, informative, humorous. Though their subjects range from the nuances of punctuation to the byzantine intricacies of city parking lots, what these essays have in common is their determination to take on tough assignments, to raise the difficulty level of the game.

That effort, it seems, is what finally transforms a piece of nonfiction prose into a memorable literary work. The best writers of essays or creative nonfiction seek out challenges, go for the toughest questions on the board. The challenges may spring from the demands of the assignment or of the composition — or both. The best writers of literary nonfiction resist the plodding memoir, the facile discovery of identity, the predictable opinion, or the sudden, life-altering illumination. As a great essayist, Gertrude Stein, audaciously put it, "If it can be done, why do it?"

*

The Best American Essays features a selection of the year's outstanding essays, essays of literary achievement that show an awareness of craft and a forcefulness of thought. Hundreds of essays are gathered annually from a wide variety of national and regional publications. These essays are then screened and turned over to a distinguished guest editor, who may add a few personal favorites to the list and who makes the final selections.

To qualify for selection, the essays must be works of respectable literary quality, intended as fully developed, independent essays (not excerpts) on subjects of general interest (not specialized scholarship), originally written in English (or translated by the author) for publication in an American periodical during the calendar year. Publications that want to make sure their contributors will be considered each year should include the series on their subscription list (Robert Atwan, *The Best American Essays*, P.O. Box 416, Maplewood, New Jersey 07040).

For this volume, I'd like to thank an old friend, William Vesterman, for the suggestions and encouragement he has generously offered me since the start of the series. I appreciate the assistance I received this year from Peter Krass, who helped with research and manuscript preparation. It was a great pleasure to work on this edition with Tracy Kidder, one of our truly distinguished prose writers. His immense range of human interests as well as his devotion to craft and accuracy are conspicuously present throughout this collection.

R.A.

Introduction

WE LIVE in an autobiographical age. An unusually large number of poets and novelists are writing their memoirs. Almost everyone who reports for magazines and journals uses the first person. Even academics and book reviewers begin essays with personal anecdotes, like waiters introducing themselves before getting down to business.

Contemporary critical theory lends authority to the autobiographical impulse. As every graduate student knows, only a fool would try to think or bear witness to events objectively anymore, and only an intellectual crook would claim to have done so. There's a line of reasoning that goes like this: writers ought to acknowledge that they are subjective filtering agents and let themselves appear on the page; or, in greater honesty, describe themselves in detail; or, most honest of all, make themselves their main subject matter, since one's own self is the only subject one can really know. Maybe widespread psychotherapy has made literary self-revelation popular. Certainly there are economic reasons. Editors and agents seem to think that the public's hunger for intimate true-life stories has grown large enough to include the private lives of literary figures as well as those of movie stars, mass murderers, and athletes. And the invitation to write about oneself has intrinsic attractions. The subject interests most writers. The research doesn't usually require travel or phone calls or hours in a library. The enterprise *looks* easy.

But the attempt to make one's self a character on the page invites a variety of mistakes. Paradoxically, when some people write in the first person, they feel the urge to universalize themselves. To an account of personal history or a patch of self-description, the writer appends a summarizing statement such as "By all this I mean to say that I was in denial." It is often said, in testament to the potential power of writing, that anything can be *made* interesting. But the first person beguiles some writers, and the act of writing the word "I" tends to make them forget that they have to do more than merely assert the interestingness of their experience. Unearned revelations flourish. The phrase "suddenly I realized" often stands in for the particulars of thought and observation. The writer, striving to touch the universal, experiences the revelation all by himself again.

The thoroughgoing first person is a demanding mode. It asks for the literary equivalent of perfect pitch. Even good writers occasionally lose control of their tone and let a self-congratulatory quality slip in. Eager to explain that their heart is in the right place, they baldly state that they care deeply about matters with which they appear to be only marginally acquainted. Pretending to confess to their bad behavior, they revel in their colorfulness. Insistently describing their own biases, they make it all too obvious that they wish to appear uncommonly reliable. Obviously, the first person doesn't guarantee honesty. Just because they are committing words to paper does not mean that writers stop telling themselves the lies that they've invented for getting through the night. Not everyone has Montaigne's gift for candor. Certainly some people are less likely to write honestly about themselves than about anyone else on earth.

Many of the classic works of nonfiction have been built in the first person. Needless to say, most autobiographies have been written in that mode, though Henry Adams wrote a durable book about himself in the third person, and so, in effect, did Gertrude Stein. Some writers find in the first person the likeliest means of insinuating an individuality of voice into their prose on almost any subject. But the third person, in all its varieties, has often been made to carry a strong sense of voice. The first person is a serviceable tool, but so is the third person. The writer's choice of point of view is a choice among tools, and shouldn't be made on moral grounds or for the sake of fashion, even in an autobiographical era.

Given what I've just said, the reader may wonder why almost every essay in this volume is written in the first person. It wasn't that I didn't look for notable third-person essays. In the confessional spirit of the day, I should admit that since I've written mostly in that mode myself, I was searching for some company, hoping to assemble a small third-person support group. But most of the essays that Bob Atwan sent me, and almost all of the ones that I liked best, were written in the first person. I was surprised, but, in the end, not disappointed. All of the authors represented here use the first person deftly.

I chose these essays from a group of about two hundred. I didn't have room to include all the ones I liked. I didn't take more than one essay by any one writer, but I was tempted in some cases.

Three pieces in this volume — by Ted Conover, Darcy Frey, and Mark Kramer — don't quite fit inside one traditional definition of the essay as personal reflection. They fall into a category sometimes called literary journalism. I'll call them narrative essays. These examples are all written in the first person, but none is about its writer. The "I" does not appear in all narrative essays; in all of these, the "I" is unobtrusive. Unlike many essays, these don't give the impression that the writer is thinking things over on the page, but in each of these pieces the writer addresses the reader in a personal, not a distant or institutional voice. More than most essays, these rely on reporting, but they aren't simply expository, in the manner of standard newspaper or magazine articles. The standard article presents information that a reader can use to reconstruct places, events, and people. The best narrative essays present already reconstructed worlds. They attempt to catch the reflection of human character on the page. They have underlying narratives. They deal with the big themes, and sculpt the reader's ruminations. The narrative essay deserves to be called literary. Certainly this kind of writing has a distinguished lineage. Among many others, Mark Twain, George Orwell, and Lillian Ross did some work in the form. And one can imagine James Agee or Joseph Mitchell — or for that matter the Edmund Wilson of *The American Earthquake* — in the place of Darcy Frey, hanging out with young basketball players on a Coney Island playground. Montaigne left the world and retired to his study. Writers of the narrative essay go out into the world, and then they too retire to their studies. The best narrative essays rely as heavily on the style of their writing as the best personal essays.

I've included a parody of the subject-tells-all magazine interview. This piece, by Ian Frazier, is the best commentary I've read on the subject, and certainly the funniest. For the purposes of this volume, I'll call it an essay that is cleverly disguised as a parody.

A number of these essays depend almost entirely on self-reflection. I consider them especially admirable, because I think the introspective essay is the hardest to pull off. And surely the riskiest form of literary introspection is the personal illness essay. I read several good ones, and included two. I found Lucy Grealy's essay painful and remarkably engrossing. Stanley Elkin's tale of temporary madness is a marvel. It's a vaudeville show mixed with meditation, set, as it were, in intensive care.

Many of these essays deal less with the author's life or person than with topics such as airplane flight, orangutans, *The Iliad,* the plight of Salman Rushdie, and, hilariously, the history of punctuation. In an essay about tropical plants, Jamaica Kincaid manages to say a great deal about herself while saying a great deal about many other things besides. A lot of the writers here have notably distinctive voices. Jamaica Kincaid's writing voice is one I'm sure I'd recognize in a crowd of unsigned manuscripts. Adam Gopnik uses the first person very sparingly, but the voice in his essay is strong, full of authority, intelligence, and wit, especially distinctive qualities in a contemporary essay about the fine arts. Unlike most writing on that subject, Gopnik's essay actually *describes* works of art, never resorting to the unintelligible jargon of the cognoscenti. His essay gives voice to a feeling of discomfort with the current art scene that I'd been harboring, inarticulately, for some time. I remember clearly how I felt when I finished Gopnik's essay, and indeed, all the other essays reprinted here. I felt grateful.

TRACY KIDDER

NICHOLSON BAKER

Survival of the Fittest

FROM THE NEW YORK REVIEW OF BOOKS

THE NINE BASIC MARKS of punctuation — comma, dash, hyphen, period, parenthesis, semi-colon, colon, space, and capital letter — seem so apt to us now, so pipe-smokingly Indo-European, so naturally suited in their disjunctive charge and mass to their given sentential offices, that we may forgivably assume that commas have been around for at least as long as electrons, and that while dialects, cursive styles, and typefaces have come and gone, the semi-colon, that supremely self-possessed valet of phraseology, is immutable.

But in fact the semi-colon is relatively modern. Something medieval called a *punctus versus,* which strongly resembled a semi-colon, though it was often encountered dangling below the written line, had roughly the force of a modern period; another sign that looked (in some scribal hands) exactly like a semi-colon was a widely used abbreviation for several Latin word endings — *atque* could appear as *atq;,* and *omnibus* as *omnib;.* But the semi-colon that we resort to daily, hourly, entered the picture with the first edition of Pietro Bembo's *De Aetna* two years after Columbus reached America, the handiwork of Aldus Manutius the Elder (or someone close to him) and his tasteful punch-cutter, Francesco Griffo. The mark, we are told by Dr. Malcolm Parkes, its historian, took much longer than the parenthesis did to earn the trust of typesetters: shockingly, its use was apparently not fully understood by some of those assigned to work on the first folio of Shakespeare.

And it is of course even now subject to episodes of neglect and derision. Joyce much preferred the more Attic colon, at least in

Ulysses, and Beckett, as well, gradually rid his prose of what must
have seemed to him an emblem of vulgar, high-Victorian applied
ornament, a cast-iron flower of mass-produced Ciceronianism: instead of semi-colons, he spliced the phrases of *Malone Dies* and
Molloy together with one-size-fits-all commas, as commonplace as
stones on a beach, to achieve that dejected sort of murmured
ecphonesis so characteristic of his narrative voice — all part of the
general urge, perhaps, that led him to ditch English in favor of
French, *"pour m'appauvrir":* to impoverish himself.

Donald Barthelme, too, who said that the example of Beckett
was what first "allowed him to write," thought that the semi-colon
was "ugly, ugly as a tick on a dog's belly" — but he allowed that
others might feel differently. And still the semi-colon survives, far
too subtle and useful, as it turns out, to be a casualty of modernism.
It even participates in those newer forms of emotional punctuation
called "smileys" or "emoticons" — vaguely irritating attempts to
supply a sideways facial expression at the close of an e-mail paragraph — e.g., :-) and >%-(. The semi-colon collaborates in the
"wink" or "smirk," thus — ;-).

So our familiar and highly serviceable repertoire of punctles was
a long time coming; it emerged from swarms of competing and
overlapping systems and theories, many of them misapplied or
half-forgotten. Petrarch, for example, used a slash with a dot in
the middle of it to signal the onset of a parenthetical phrase. A
percontativus, or backward question mark, occasionally marked the
close of a rhetorical question even into the seventeenth century
— Robert Herrick wrote with it. A *punctus elevatus,* resembling an
upside-down semi-colon or, later, a fancy, black-letter *s,* performed
the function of a colon in many medieval texts; when used at the
end of a line of poetry, however, it could signal the presence of an
enjambment. A nameless figure shaped like a tilted candy-cane
served to terminate paragraphs of Augustus's autobiography (A.D.
14), inscribed on his tomb. Around A.D. 600, Isidore of Seville
recommended ending a paragraph with a 7, which he called the
positura. He also advocated the placing of a horizontal dash next
to a corrupted or questionable text ("so that a kind of arrow may
slit the throat of what is superfluous and penetrate to the vitals of
what is false"), and he relied on the ancient *cryphia,* a C turned
on its side with a dot in the middle — ☺ — to be used next to

those places in a text where "a hard and obscure question cannot
be opened up or solved."

The upright letter C, for *capitulum,* developed into the popular
medieval paragraph symbol, ¶, called at times a *pilcrow* or a *paraph.*
Seventh-century Irish scribes were in the habit of using more
points when they wanted a longer pause; thus a sentence might
end with a colon and a comma (:,), or two periods and a comma
(..,), or three commas together (,,,). At the close of the twelfth
century, one of the *dictaminists,* a man named Buoncompagno,
troubled by so much irreconcilable complexity, proposed a pared-
down slash-and-dash method: a dash would mark all final pauses,
and a slash would mark all lesser pauses. It didn't take, although
the "double virgula" (//) was used to separate sentences in the
fifteenth century, and Edmund Spenser and Walter Ralegh sometimes hand-wrote with single slashes, rather than commas. A plus
sign (+) stood for a period in a few early printed books; in others,
it could set off a quotation.

Printing eventually slowed the pace of makeshift invention, forcing
out many quaint superfluities, but novel marks, and surprising
adaptations of old marks, may appear at any time. Besides smileys,
on-line services have lately given rise to the ecstatic bracket hug
of greeting: {{{{{{{{Shana!!!}}}}}}}}. Legal punctuation continues to
thrive — the ™, the ®, and the © are everywhere. (The title of
Jurassic Park is not *Jurassic Park,* but *Jurassic Park*™; likewise David
Feldman's *Why Do Clocks Run Clockwise and Other Imponderables*™.)

Especially fashionable now is the ℠, as in "Forget Anything?℠"
— observed not long ago on a triangular piece of folded cardboard beside the bathroom sink in a room at a Holiday Inn: a mark
that modifies the phrase it follows to mean, "This is not merely a
polite question regarding whether you have successfully packed
everything you require during your stay, this utterance is part of
our current chain-wide marketing campaign, and we are so serious
about asking it of you that we hereby offer fair warning that if you
or anyone else attempts to extend such a courtesy to another guest
anywhere in the hotel industry in printed or published form,
either on flyers, placards, signs, pins, or pieces of folded cardboard
positioned at or beside a sink, vanity, or other bathroom fixture,
we, the owner of this service mark, will torment and tease you with
legal remedies." Even the good old comma continues to evolve: it

was flipped upside down and turned into the quotation mark circa 1714, and a woman I knew in college punctuated her letters to her high-school friends with home-made comma-shapes made out of photographs of side-flopping male genitals that she had cut out of *Playgirl.*

Until now, readers have had to fulfill their need for the historical particulars of this engrossingly prosaic subject with narrow-gauge works of erudition such as E. Otha Wingo's sober *Latin Punctuation in the Classical Age,* or John Lennard's extraordinary recent monograph on the history of the parenthesis, *But I Digress* (1991) — a jewel of Oxford University Press scholarship, by the way, gracefully written and full of intelligence, decked out with a complete scholarly apparatus of multiple indices, bibliographies, and notes, whose author, to judge by the startling jacket photo (shaved head with up-sticking central proto-Mohawk tuft, earring on left ear, wilted corduroy jacket, and over-laundered T-shirt bearing some enigmatic insignia underneath), put himself through graduate school by working as a ticket scalper at Elvis Costello concerts. (A discussion of Elvis Costello's use of the parenthesis in "Let Him Dangle" figures in a late chapter.)

At last, however, we have *Pause and Effect,* Dr. Malcolm Parkes's brave overview: "an introduction," so he unassumingly subtitles it, though it is much more than introductory, "to the history of punctuation in the West." Not in the East, mind, or elsewhere — Arabic, Greek, and Sanskrit customs await a final fuse-blowing collation. (And according to the MLA index, there is Nanette Twine's 1984 article on "The Adoption of Punctuation in Japanese Script," in *Visible Language,* a journal that has recently done exciting things for the study of the punctuational past, to be assimilated; and, for canon-stretchers, John Duitsman's "Punctuation in Thirteen West African Languages" and Carol F. Justus's "Visible Sentences in Cuneiform Hittite.") Though his punning title promises sprightliness, Dr. Parkes — fellow of Keble College and lecturer in paleography at the University of Oxford — has produced a rich, complex, and decidedly unsprightly book of coffee-table dimensions, with seventy-four illustrative plates, a glossary, and, regrettably, no *index rerum.*

It is not an easy book to read in bed. Because of the oversized folio format, each line on the page extends an inch or so longer than usual, resulting in eye-sweeps that must take in fourteen words at a time, rather than the more comfortable ten or eleven. As his shoulder muscles tire of supporting the full weight of the open book, the reader, lying on his left side, finally allows it to slump to the mattress and assume an L-position, and he then attempts to process the text with one open eye, which, instead of scanning left to right, reads by focusing outward along a radically fore-shortened line of type that is almost parallel with his line of sight, skipping or supplying by guesswork those words that disappear beyond the gentle rise of the page. The gaps between each word narrow, hindering comprehension, although they never achieve that incomprehensible Greek ideal of page-layout called *scriptio continua,* in which the text is recorded unspaced as solid lines of letters.

And why, in fact, did the Greeks relinquish so sensible a practice as word-spacing, which even the cuneiformists of Minoan Crete apparently used? Lejeune, for one, finds this development *"remar-quable";* but even more remarquable is the fact that the pragmatic Romans had word-spacing available to *them* (via the Etruscans), in the form of "interpuncts," or hovering dots between each word (a practice successfully revived by Wang word-processing software in the 1980s), which they too abandoned in early Christian times. "For this amazing and deplorable regression one can conjecture no reason other than an inept desire to imitate even the worst characteristic of Greek books," scolds Revilo P. Oliver. Dr. Parkes, on the other hand, theorizes that class differences between readers and scribes may have had something to do with the perseverance of *scriptio continua* — a scribal slave must not presume to word-space, or otherwise punctuate, because he would thereby be imposing his personal reading of the constitutive letters on his employer. There were also, in monkish contexts, quasi-mystical arguments to be made for unspaced impenetrability: a resistant text, slow to offer up its literal meaning, encouraged meditation and memorization, sug-gested Cassian (a prominent fifth-century recluse); and the mo-ment when, after much futile staring, the daunting word-search-puzzle of the sacred page finally spaced itself out, coalescing into comprehensible units of the Psalter, might serve to remind the swooning lector of the miracle of the act of reading, which is impossible without God's loving condescension into human lan-guage and human form.

Amid all this phylogeny, Parkes does not mention, nor should he necessarily mention, the more mundane developmental fact that *scriptio continua* comes naturally to children:

DEARANDREWH
APPYBIRTHDA
YILOVEYOULO
VEALICEXXOX

Children aren't *taught* to forgo spacing; all their written models are properly spaced. Occasionally, as a concession to the recipient (or adult onlooker), they will go back and insert a virgule here and there between words for clarity. There is something so exciting about writing, perhaps, that, like barely literate five-year-olds, civilizations in the midst of discovering or rediscovering its pleasures and traditions take a while before they begin to care about casual readability — and consequently their scholars are said to study *litterae,* "letters," not words.

In part as a result of the unspaced line, pointing was viewed from the beginning as a form of ornament, as well as a means of what Parkes calls "disambiguation." Cassiodorus, the first great biblical pointillist, advised sixth-century monks to add punctuation "in order that you may be seen to be adding embellishment." Alcuin wrote Charlemagne that "*Distinctiones* or *subdistinctiones* by points can make embellishment in sentences most beautiful." Early medieval readers like Dulcitius of Aquino would decorate a work with dots and diples and paragraph marks as they read it and then proudly sign their name on the page: "I, Dulcitius, read this." Punctuation, like marginal and interlinear commentary, seems at times to have been a ritual of reciprocation, a way of returning something to the text in grateful tribute after it had released its meaning in the reader's mind.

Somewhat surprisingly, scholastic philosophy of the thirteenth and fourteenth centuries, which is, as Francis Bacon uncharitably observed, a vast and intricate cobweb spun from Aristotle, "admirable for the fineness of thread and work, but of no substance and profit," and thus ideally decorative and mannerist rather than functional, pushed by logical and disputational energy rather than pulled by truth — the sort of era, then, in which you might expect punctuation to *thrive* — turns out in fact to be a dark, sad time for *subdistinctiones*. Parkes explains that the paradigmatic nature of the scholastic manuscript, with its repetitive *queritur*s and *quaestio*s signaling to the reader precisely where he was in the formal structure of the argument, made a sophisticated punctuational tool-set unnecessary.

On the other hand, it may just be that the schoolmen, spending their days reading awful Latin translations from the Arabic of translations from the Greek, had no ear. Cicero himself disdained punctuation, insisting that the well-cadenced sentence would audibly manifest its own terminus, without the need of any mere "stroke interposed by a copyist"; but those who afterward took punctuation, and took Cicero, seriously — Cassiodorus, Isidore, Bembo, Petrarch — proved their allegiance by their virgulae: like archaizing composers who want to ensure a certain once-standard performance practice and therefore spell out every trill and every *ritenuto,* though their historical models offer only unadorned notes, these admirers could hear the implied punctuation of Ciceronian rhythm, and could in some cases duplicate his rollaway effects in their own writing, but they didn't trust their contemporaries to detect a classicizing *clausula* without the help of visual aids.

Dr. Parkes's own prose is serviceable and unprecious, if non-passerine. For those of us whose Latin never quite took flight, he has provided translations of every passage he quotes. He takes care from time to time to mention political developments as they impinge on the punctuational sphere: if some depredation or upheaval happens to have brought on "a situation hostile to grammatical culture," he says so. The puzzling thing, though, is how casual Parkes is — this eagle-eyed paleographer, who has worked so hard to "raise a reader's consciousness of what punctuation is and does"! — about his commas. Where *are* they? "Pausing therefore was part of the process of reading not copying." "Before the advent of printing a text left its author and fell among scribes." "The printing process not only stabilized the shapes and functions of the symbols it also sustained existing conventions that governed the ways in which they were employed." And: "This increase in the range of distinctive symbols also promoted new developments in usage since the symbols not only enabled readers to identify more easily the functions of grammatical constituents within a sentence but also made possible more subtle refinements in the communication of the message of a text."

Were it not for Dr. Parkes's sure-footed employment of the comma elsewhere, one might almost suspect that his was a case reminiscent of those psychotherapists who enter their profession because they sense something deeply amiss within themselves, or of those humorless people who buy joke books and go to comedy clubs to correct internal deficiencies. In a commentary accompanying a fascinating page of Richard Hooker, Parkes, or someone with whom he has shared (as he nicely says in his preface) "the burden of proofs," flouts even the sacred law of the serial comma: "The notation series for indicating glosses notes and citations in the margins, based on letters of the alphabet in sequence, was also used in the Geneva Bible of 1560."

Once, however, Parkes surprises us by unconsciously using the old-fashioned, eighteenth-century *that*-comma. It is the comma of Gibbon —

> It has been calculated by the ablest politicians, that no state, without being soon exhausted, can maintain above the hundredth part of its members in arms and idleness.

And of Gibbon's model Montesquieu, in Nugent's 1750 translation (twice) —

> Plato thanked the Gods, that he was born in the same age with Socrates: and for my part, I give thanks to the Almighty, that I was born a subject of that government under which I live; and that it is his pleasure I should obey those, whom he has made me love.

And of Burke (twice) —

> Mr. Hume told me, that he had from Rousseau himself the secret of his principles of composition. That acute, though eccentric, observer had perceived, that to strike and interest the public, the marvellous must be produced . . .

And of Burke's brilliant adversary, Thomas Paine —

> Admitting that Government is a contrivance of human *wisdom,* it must necessarily follow, that hereditary succession, and hereditary rights (as they are called), can make no part of it, because it is impossible to make wisdom hereditary.

Parkes writes, "The punctuation of the manuscript has been so freely corrected and adapted by later scribes, that it is not easy to determine whether any of the other ecphonetic signs are also by the original scribe or whether they have been added." The only other person I can think of who uses old-style *that*-commas with any consistency is Peter Brown, who, like Parkes, spends his time with Latin *quod*-clauses that have been punctuated by old German commentators. (A comma is still regularly used before a *daß*-clause in German.)

Another rarity in Parkes's book, perhaps the very first of its kind, is the occurrence of the two halves of *semi-colon* linked, not by a hyphen, but by a full-scale em-dash: *semi—colon*. This elongation could be Parkes's secret way of protesting American trends in copy-editing, which would have the noun-unit spelled without any divisive internal rule at all: *semicolon*. Truly, American copy-editing has fallen into a state of demoralized confusion over hyphenated and unhyphenated compounds — or at least, *I* am demoralized and confused, having just gone through the manuscript of a novel in which a very smart and careful and good-natured copy-editor has deleted about two hundred of my innocent tinkertoy hyphens. I wrote "stet hyphen" in the margin so many times that I finally abbreviated it to "SH" — but there was no wicked glee in my intransigence: I didn't want to be the typical prose prima donna who made her life difficult.

On the other hand, I remembered an earlier manuscript of mine in which an event took place in the back seat of a car: in the bound galleys, the same event occurred in the "backseat." *The backseat.* Grateful for hundreds of other fixes, unwilling to seem stubborn, I had agreed without protest to the closing-up, but I stewed about it afterward and finally reinserted a space before publication. ("Backseat" wants to be read as a trochee, BACKseat, like "baseball," when in reality we habitually give both halves of the compound equal spoken weight.) Therefore, mindful of my near miss with "back seat," I stetted myself sick over the new manuscript. I stetted *re-enter* (rather than *reenter*), *post-doc* (rather than *postdoc*), *foot-pedal* (rather than *foot pedal*), *second-hand* (rather than *secondhand*), *twist-tie* (rather than *twist tie*), and *pleasure-nubbins* (rather than *pleasure nubbins*).

The copy-editor, because her talents permit her to be undoctrinaire, and because it is, after all, *my* book, indulged me, for better or worse. In passing, we had a stimulating discussion of the word *pantyhose*, which she had emended to read *panty hose*. My feeling was that the word *hose* is unused now in reference to footwear, and that *panty*, too, in its singular form, is imaginable only as part of *pantywaist* or in some hypothetical L. L. Bean catalog: "Bean's finest chamois-paneled trail panty." *Pantyhose* thus constitutes a single, interfused unit of sense, greater than the sum of its parts, which ought to be the criterion for jointure. And yet, though the suggested space seemed to me mistaken, I could just as easily have gone for *panty-hose* as *pantyhose*— in fact, normally I would have campaigned for a hyphen in this sort of setting, since the power-crazed policy-makers at Merriam-Webster and *Words Into Type* have been reading too much Joyce in recent years and making condominiums out of terms (especially *-like* compounds, which can look like transliterated Japanese when closed up) that deserve semi-detachment. (Joyce, one feels, wanted his prose to look different, Irish, strange, not tricked out with fastidious Oxford hyphens that handled uncouth noun-clumps with gloved fingertips: he would have been embarrassed to see his idiosyncratic *cuffedge* and *watchchain* and famous *scrotumtightening* acting to sway US style-shepherds.) A tasteful spandex hyphen would have been, so my confusion whispers to me now, perfectly all right in *panty-hose*, pulling the phrase together scrotumtighteningly at its crotch.

I offer this personal note merely to illustrate how small the moments are that cumulatively result in punctuational thigmotaxis. Evolution proceeds hyphen by hyphen, and manuscript by manuscript — impelled by the tension between working writers and their copy-editors, and between working copy-editors and their works of reference ("I'll just go check the big *Web*," a magazine editor once said to me cheerfully); by the admiration of ancestors, and by the ever-imminent possibility of paralysis through boredom. Are the marks that we have right now really enough? Don't you sometimes feel a sudden abdominal cramp of revulsion when you scan down a column of type and see several nice little clauses (only one per sentence, of course: *Chic. Man. St.* § 5.91) set off by cute little pairs of unadorned dashes?

The nineteenth century didn't think the dash on its own was

nearly enough. Dr. Parkes ends his brief discussion of "The Mimetic Ambitions of the Novelist and the Exploitation of the Pragmatics of the Written Medium" with Virginia Woolf, so he (pardonably) avoids treating the single most momentous change in twentieth-century punctuation, namely the disappearance of the great dash-hybrids. All three of them — the *commash* , — , the *semi-colash* ; — , and the *colash* : — (so I name them, because naming makes analysis possible) — are of profound importance to Victorian prose, and all three are now (except for certain revivalist zoo specimens to be mentioned later) extinct.

Everyone used dash-hybrids. They are in Dickens, Wilkie Collins, Charlotte Brontë, and George Meredith. They are on practically every page of Trollope —

> He was nominally, not only the heir to, but actually the possessor of, a large property; — but he could not touch the principal, and of the income only so much as certain legal curmudgeons would allow him. As Greystock had said, everybody was at law with him, — so successful had been his father, in mismanaging, and miscontrolling, and misappropriating the property.

> Rapid writing will no doubt give rise to inaccuracy, — chiefly because the ear, quick and true as may be its operation, will occasionally break down under pressure, and, before a sentence be closed, will forget the nature of the composition with which it commenced.

> The novels of a man possessed of so singular a mind must themselves be very strange, — and they are strange.

They are in Thackeray —

> [. . .] the Captain was not only accustomed to tell the truth, — he was unable even to think it — and fact and fiction reeled together in his muzzy, whiskified brain.

And in George Eliot —

> The general expectation now was that the "much" would fall to Fred Vincy, but the Vincys themselves were surprised when ten thousand pounds in specified investments were declared to be bequeathed to him: — was the land coming too?

The toniest nonfictional Prosicrucians — De Quincey, Carlyle, Ruskin, Newman, Doughty — also make constant use of dashtards, often at rhetorical peaks:

It is well to be a gentleman, it is well to have a cultivated intellect, a delicate taste, a candid, equitable, dispassionate mind, a noble and courteous bearing in the conduct of life; — these are the connatural qualities of a large knowledge; they are the objects of a University: I am advocating, I shall illustrate and insist upon them; but still, I repeat, they are no guarantee for sanctity or even for conscientiousness, they may attach to the man of the world, to the profligate, to the heartless, — pleasant, alas, and attractive as he shows when decked out in them.

Pater, though he has been charged with over-sonorous purism, and is unquestionably at times a little light in his Capezios (to steal a phrase from Arsenio Hall), depends on punctuational pair-bonding to help him wrap up his terrific essay on style and his "Conclusion" to *The Renaissance.* Sydney Smith wrote that if Francis Jeffrey were given the solar system to review — Francis Jeffrey being the sour critic who said "This will never do" of Wordsworth's *Excursion* — he would pan it: "Bad light — planets too distant — pestered with comets — feeble contrivance; — could make a better with great ease." Emerson was a huge user of the semi-colash; in fact, of the fifty-two dashes in *The American Scholar,* only four, by my count, appear unaccompanied by either a semi-colon or a comma.

Hybrids become somewhat less common, though they are still easily found, after the turn of the century. Henry James employed a few in his early writing, but revised them out in the *édition de luxe* that began appearing in 1907. The 1911 *Encyclopedia Britannica,* a good test bed of Edwardian norms, resorts to them fairly frequently:

> A large screw can, however, be roughly examined in the following manner: — (1) See whether the surface of the threads has a perfect polish . . . (2) mount it between the centres of a lathe . . . (4) Observe whether the short nut runs from end to end of the screw without a wabbling motion when the screw is turned and the nut kept from revolving. If it wabbles the screw is said to be drunk.

And Edmund Gosse's 1907 *Father and Son* has a lovely comma-softened dash that can be read as a wistful farewell to a form of punctuation in its twilight:

> These rock-basins, fringed by corallines, filled with still water almost as pellucid as the upper air itself, thronged with beautiful sensitive forms

of life, — they exist no longer, they are all profaned, and emptied, and vulgarised.

They pop up here and there in Norman Douglas, early J. B. Priestley, and Cyril Connolly. J. M. Keynes used a scattering of all three forms in his 1920 *Economic Consequences of the Peace.* For instance:

> The policy of reducing Germany to servitude for a generation, of degrading the lives of millions of human beings, and of depriving a whole nation of happiness should be abhorrent and detestable, — abhorrent and detestable, even if it were possible, even if it enriched ourselves, even if it did not sow the decay of the whole civilized life of Europe.

But hybrid punctuation was doomed by then. Proust used two pre-war semi-colashes in the enormous "bedrooms I have known" sentence in the opening of *A la rehash;* Scott Moncrieff removed them in his post-war 1922 translation. (Terence Kilmartin, good man, restored the original punctuation in 1981.) The dandiest dandy of them all, Vladimir Nabokov (who, I think, read *Father and Son* just as closely as he read Proust, drawn to its engaging combination of literature and amateur naturalism), used over sixty excellent comma-dash pairings in his first and quite Edwardian English-language novel, *The Real Life of Sebastian Knight* (1941). (For example, "'A title,' said Clare, 'must convey the colour of the book, — not its subject.'") He used none at all in *Speak, Memory: The New Yorker* had sweated it out of him. In all of his later work I have noticed only one precious semi-colash: Humbert writes, "I remember the operation was over, all over, and she was weeping in my arms; — a salutary storm of sobs after one of the fits of moodiness that had become so frequent with her in the course of that otherwise admirable year!"

More precious still, to the punctuational historian, are the two instances of *reversed* commashes in Updike's early novels — one in the Fawcett edition of *The Centaur,* and one on page 22 of the Fawcett *Of the Farm:*

> As Joan comforted him, my mother, still holding the yardstick — an orange one stamped with the name of an Alton hardware store — , explained that the boy had been "giving her the eye" all morning, and for some time had been planning to "put her to the test."

This extremely rare variant form hearkens back to Forties Mencken —

> My father put in a steam-heating plant toward the end of the eighties
> — the first ever seen in Hollins Street — , but such things were rare
> until well into the new century.

And again to Proust: *"Que nous l'aimons — comme en ce moment
j'aimais Françoise — , l'intermédiaire bien intentionné qui"* etc.

But Updike, our standard-bearer, never stands up for dashtards
now. Even John Barth's eighteenth-century pastiche, *The Sot-Weed
Factor,* where they would have been right at home, doesn't use
them. (They were everywhere in the eighteenth century, too.) What
comet or glacier made them die out? This may be the great literary
question of our time. I timidly tried to use a semi-colash in a
philosophical essay for *The Atlantic Monthly* in 1983: the associate
editor made a strange whirring sound in her throat, denoting
inconceivability, and I immediately backed down. Why, why are
they gone? Was it — and one always gropes for the McLuhanesque
explanation first — the increasing use of the typewriter for final
drafts, whose arrangement of comma, colon, and semi-colon keys
made a quick reach up to the hyphen key immediately after another
punctuation mark physically awkward? Or was it — for one always
gropes for the pseudo-scientific explanation just after McLuhan —
the triumphant success of quantum mechanics? A comma is indis-
putably more of a quantum than a commash. Did the point-play
of the Dadaists and E. E. Cummings, and the unpunctled last
chapter of *Ulysses,* force a scramble for a simple hegemony against
which revolt could be measured?

The style manuals had been somewhat uncomfortable with hybrid punctuation all along — understandably so, since it interferes
with systematization. The most influential Victorian antibarbarus,
John Wilson's *A Treatise on English Punctuation,* which went through
something like thirty editions in England and America, tolerated
mixed points; indeed, later editions offered pages of exercises,
written and oral, intended to help the student refine his dexterity
with the commash. But "the unnecessary profusion of straight
lines," Wilson warned, as others had warned before him, "particularly on a printed page, is offensive to good taste, is an index of

the *dasher's* profound ignorance of the art of punctuation . . ." In *"Stops" or, How to Punctuate,* Paul Allardyce, the Edwardian successor to Wilson, was more severe: "There is seldom any reason for the use of double points." G. V. Carey, in *Mind the Stop* (1939), was unequivocal: "The combination of other stops with dashes is even less admissible than with brackets." There was a glimmer of hope in Eric Partridge's *You Have a Point There* (1953) — he advised that, yes, compound points should be used with "caution and moderation," but he had the courage to admit that "occasionally [they] are, in fact, unavoidable."

But that was 1953, in fault-tolerant England. According to the *Chicago Manual of Style* (§ 5.5), dash-hybrids are currently illegal in the U.S. In the name of biodiversity, however, I stuck a few of them in out-of-the-way places in my first novel, over the objections of the copy-editor, in 1988. I thought I was making history. But Salman Rushdie had beaten me to it, as it turned out: *The Satanic Verses,* which appeared a few months before my book, uses dozens and dozens of dashtards, and uses them aggressively, flauntingly, more in the tradition of Laurence Sterne than of Trollope. Brad Leithauser's arch, *Sebastian Knight*–like frame-narrator, in *Hence* (1989), uses many commashes; and Leithauser discussed Rushdie's "Emily Dickinsonian onslaught of dashes" in a *New Yorker* review that same year — although somehow Emily Dickinson doesn't seem quite right. But we're just playing at it now, the three of us — we aren't sincere in our dashtardy; — we can't be.

It would be nice to see Dr. Parkes or Dr. Lennard (of parenthetical fame) attempt a carefully researched socio-historical explanation of the passing of mixed punctuation. Unfortunately, a full explanation would have to include everything — Gustav Stickley, Henry Ford, Herbert Read, Gertrude Stein, Norbert Weiner, Harold Geneen, James Watson, Saint Strunk, and especially *The New Yorker's* Miss Eleanor Gould, whose faint, gray, normative pencil-point still floats above us all. And even then the real micro-structure of the shift would elude us. We should give daily thanks, in any case, to Malcolm Parkes, for offering us some sense of the flourishing coralline tide-pools of punctuational pluralism that preceded our own purer, more consistent, more teachably codified, and perhaps more arid century.

TED CONOVER

Trucking Through the AIDS Belt

FROM THE NEW YORKER

THE RED DIRT ROAD is so slick with rain that the trucks stacked along either side look as if they might simply have slid off. Pools of muddy water fill the center. All thirty or forty trucks are pointed one way: toward the border crossing a few hundred yards down the road — toward Tanzania. Most have come to this place — a Kenyan settlement called Isebania — from Mombasa, where there is a port, or from Nairobi, where there is an oil depot. The weekend has stopped their progress: the customs offices are closed. There is no traffic except for the back-and-forth of turnboys attending to a group of four semi rigs with royal-blue tractors hooked up to long white shipping containers. The trucks have punctures, as they say in East Africa, and the turnboys must repair them. And when that's done there are mechanical problems, which the turnboys must attend to as well.

The four drivers of this small convoy sip tea under the narrow wooden awning of one of the many one-room restaurants that line the road, and watch the muddy proceedings. One of the perquisites of being a driver is that the driver gets to stay clean. Each driver's turnboy is responsible for their particular truck: he maintains it mechanically, guards it at night, warms it up in the morning (in colonial days, he turned the crank that started the motor, hence "turnboy"), and even does the cooking if there's no restaurant around. The turnboys with their trucks are like Masai with their cattle, constantly attentive. When the trucks are in a group like this, the turnboys help each other out.

On my left, Malek, the driver of the truck called Fleet 10, yells to his turnboy, Stephen, to be sure to check the tubes for more than one puncture each. (The names of some of the men have been changed.) Malek then explains to me that these flats could have been avoided if the armed escort traveling with his truck from Nairobi had allowed them all to rest. Escorts, provided by the national traffic police, are required for any truck hauling valuable imported goods — electronics, for example, or tires, as in the case of Fleet 10. This is because of the likelihood of theft or ambush, even in a country with the relative stability of Kenya. The convoys of escorted trucks — up to thirty or forty of them — tend to travel at night, when traffic is light, typically setting off around 2 or 3 A.M. But the traffic police, in a hurry to arrive, sometimes push the drivers too hard. A driver like Francis, whose jumbo rig, Fleet 37, is seventy-two feet long, with a payload of three containers weighing a hundred tons, needs to go quite slowly or else make frequent stops to let his brakes and tires cool off in hilly central Kenya. But on this trip the policemen had insisted that he keep going. The result was several burst tires.

I did not arrive with the three trucks in the escorted convoy but instead joined them in a fourth truck, Fleet 19, which was carrying empty beer bottles. Such a load, Malek explains, does not qualify as protected cargo. It is unlike auto parts, imported liquor, or "clothes from your dead people."

"What?" I ask.

"Yes, you know, the clothes — the clothes they sell at markets," he says.

"But what dead people?"

"You know, the clothes they sell that have been worn by your people who now are dead — *nguo za mitumba.*"

It suddenly dawns on me. "Secondhand clothes."

"Yes!"

I see that Malek, though he is a worldly man who has traveled on three continents, does not understand the discarding of clothes that can still be worn. In other words, he does not understand the Western practice of fashion. I don't have the heart to explain it.

"Those clothes are very valuable, then?"

"Oh, yes," Malek says. He takes the sleeve of his colorful print shirt between thumb and forefinger and holds it out toward me. Green stripes in the shirt match the color of his eyes; Malek has

Arab blood. "Nice, isn't it?" (I speak with the men in English, since their English is much better than my Kiswahili, the language they prefer.)

The proprietress of the restaurant comes out to refill our cups with a pot of delicious *chai ya maziwa,* tea with milk. Refills aren't free, but everybody wants one. She then sets down the metal pot and leans against the doorjamb, and joins us in passing the time by watching the turnboys get filthy. A spider drops from a fold of her skirt and dangles above the concrete floor.

A week earlier, I had been shown around a truck stop outside Nairobi — the Athi River Weighbridge Station — by a medical doctor named Job Bwayo. In the early 1980s, when Bwayo, who also has a Ph.D. in immunology, was at the University of Nairobi researching sexually transmitted diseases among prostitutes, his subjects started showing up with the symptoms of a new disease. After AIDS had been identified, Bwayo said, "I got interested in looking at the other side of the question — there must be a vector, somebody to be spreading it. There must be a man involved. Who are these men and what do they do? And it was thought that the truck drivers who cross the continent must have some role. So we went out to see."

Truck drivers were early suspects because they not only traveled constantly but had a reputation for sleeping with the "commercial sex workers," as researchers call them, who are a feature of wayside bars and restaurants all over sub-Saharan Africa. In 1989, Bwayo, who has received grants from the University of Washington and the University of Manitoba, opened a free clinic at Athi River for the use of drivers and others in the area — mainly women from surrounding shanties.

Blood tests on his patients found that 27 percent of the drivers were HIV-positive; a later study showed that drivers coming from closer to central Africa had higher rates of seropositivity. Rwanda, for example, had a rate of 51 percent; Uganda, 36 percent; and Kenya, 19 percent. In similar studies of commercial sex workers, infection rates were found to run from 34 to 88 percent. Because AIDS is thought to have originated somewhere around the west side of Lake Victoria, in Zaire, Rwanda, or western Uganda (one theory is that it jumped to human beings from green monkeys, which carry a similar virus and are slaughtered for food in the area), and because long-distance trucking is this region's main link to the outside, it was hypothesized that truckers were unwittingly transporting the virus from central Africa to the rest of the world. Today, of the fourteen million people with HIV worldwide, more than eight million are in sub-Saharan Africa.

International aid money began to be channeled through organizations like the African Medical and Research Foundation to educate the truckers and the women they sleep with. Getting the word out was not without its problems, however. Bwayo and the drivers ruefully remember headlines such as one on the front page of a Nairobi daily announcing to a frightened nation that "Truck Drivers Spread AIDS!" This reputation became a public-relations problem for the drivers, many of whom had enjoyed for years an aura not unlike that of the American cowboy: a man of carefree mobility who traverses unknown landscapes and survives by his wits — and, in the African case, is relatively well paid besides. But in the late 1980s the drivers started to become unhappy celebrities in the annals of AIDS research. "Oh, yes, the truckers!" said Dr. O. E. Omolo, the provincial medical officer in Mombasa, when I expressed a desire to travel with some of them in order to learn about their lives. "They are true museums of disease! Chancroid, gonorrhea, syphilis, herpes, AIDS — well, the list goes on and on!"

Before the concern with AIDS, I had known of African truck drivers through brief mentions in the books of a dozen travelers who had beaten their way across Zaire, or the Sahara, or war-torn Mozambique, by hitching rides with them. Especially in the poorest or most politically unsettled countries, trucks are the only means of getting in or out, public transportation being virtually nonexistent. As travelers, it struck me, the drivers probably had no equal in Africa.

Truckers almost never drive completely across the continent, from north to south or from east to west, since the condition of roads and the politics of Africa's fifty-three countries make it easier to ship by sea. Instead, most African trucking links the middle and the margins, plying routes from the coasts to the interior and back again. The principal ports of East Africa are Mombasa and Dar es Salaam, both on the Indian Ocean south of Somalia. From there, goods travel inland to Malawi, Zambia, Uganda, Burundi, Rwanda, western Zaire, to southern Ethiopia, Somalia, and, in calmer times, to southern Sudan. The so-called Trans-African Highway is merely a network of paved roads that link Mombasa to Nairobi, to Kampala, and then to Kigali, the capital of Rwanda, or to Kinshasa, in Zaire.

Some of the biggest competitors in this business are owned by international freight-forwarding conglomerates and are European-managed. Interfreight, a German trucking firm in Dar es Salaam, and Transami, a Belgian-run concern in Mombasa, are often favored by drivers, who say they're better paying and better run. Better paying, in the case of Transami, which owns the trucks I'm with, means compensation that ranges from twenty-six hundred to three thousand American dollars a year for a driver, and, for a turnboy, between five hundred and seven hundred dollars. In a country like Kenya, whose annual per-capita income is three hundred and sixty dollars, this is good money. But to Transami managers, dealing with the huge capital costs of imported trucks, fuel, and parts — a set of new tires costs nearly fifteen thousand dollars, for example — drivers' salaries are peanuts.

Salary, however, does not necessarily constitute all of a driver's income. Wherever there are customs rules and import duties, there is money to be made getting around them. Extra fuel taken on in Tanzania, for example, can net up to a month's salary if resold on the black market in a land-locked country. Gray parrots procured in the jungles of Zaire fetch a high price back on the coast, if they make it alive. Tanzanian maize meal increases in value over 50 percent once it's smuggled into Kenya.

The four Transami trucks in Isebania will travel in a loose convoy at least as far as Rwanda. Besides Malek and Francis, who has a potbelly, wears colorful silk-screened T-shirts, and loves to listen to the news on his small short-wave radio, the drivers are Sammy, a beanpole-thin member of the Kalenjin tribe, famed for its distance runners, who sports long beatnik sideburns and begins every day with a couple of wind sprints, and Bradford, the driver of Fleet 19.

A fifty-year-old veteran of the Kenyan Army, Bradford is a soft-spoken man who is meticulous in his grooming: every day, he shaves, puts on a clean button-down shirt, and polishes his black metal-toed oxfords. Unlike Malek and many other drivers, Brad-

ford drives cautiously, which is all right with me. It is not all right
with Obadiah, the turnboy. Occasionally, as we rumble out of a
turn and onto a straightaway, Obadiah will shift restlessly in his
seat, then wave his long arms in the air, and finally say, "O.K., now
you can go faster. Faster! *Haraka-haraka!*" As the driver, however,
Bradford rules. He tells me he has not had an accident in twenty
years. He responds to Obadiah's exasperation the same way he
responds to practically any perturbation: silently, almost stonily.

Obadiah is the opposite. His liveliness, humor, and occasional
swings of mood can all be seen in his animated face and in the
way he moves. A man of thirty-four with a rangy build, he is better
educated than his driver, having completed the Kenyan equivalent
of high school. One of the things, besides my cigarettes, that
pleased him most when I joined Fleet 19 was my copies of Chinua
Achebe's *Things Fall Apart* and Ngugi wa Thiong'o's *Petals of Blood:*
he quickly borrowed and consumed both.

Fleet 19 is a white-and-blue British Leyland Landtrain. The
number 19 is roughly hand-painted in white on the big black front
bumper. Inside the cab are hand-painted the following notices: on
the dashboard, "No Smoking" and "Wear Seat Belt"; across the glove
compartment, "Speed Limit 60 Kph"; and, behind the driver's
head — the only one that Bradford and Obadiah pay any attention
to — "Engine Must Be Allowed to Run 5 Min Before Shutdown —
200 Sh. Fine." There is no radio, CB or other. The steering wheel
and a single seat are on the right; on the left is a double seat for
passengers. In between is the gearshift. The horn works from a
button on the dash. The speedometer does not work. Though the
passenger-side rear-view mirror was smashed long ago, enough
shards remain to deliver a serviceable rear view. The door it's
attached to doesn't open from the outside and can be opened only
with difficulty from the inside. The vent-window locks are broken,
but that's fine, because Obadiah and I can reach in through them
and unlock the truck if Bradford is not around with the key.
Stuffed underneath and behind the seats are all the clothes that
Bradford and Obadiah have brought on this trip, and in the
narrow slot between the seats is jammed my small duffel.

The truck is longer than an American eighteen-wheeler: the
tractor has ten wheels, and the forty-foot trailer twelve more. On
our trailer is a forty-foot container, which holds, along with a small

amount of sheet metal, a great quantity of new Belgian beer bottles bound for a brewery in Rwanda. They make a good strong beer in Rwanda, but they do not make bottles; thus, this critical import from Rwanda's former colonial master.

Though there is much to do before the reopening of the customs offices, on Monday morning, the work doesn't weigh too heavily on anyone's mind, because Kenya is the easy part of the journey. In Kenya, the roads are paved and repair facilities are close at hand, so you can traverse the country in three or four days. Communication with others, in Kiswahili or in English, is seldom difficult. Good food is available, and friends are never too far away. Traveling in convoys is nice but not essential. In Kenya, the road is known.

But at Tanzania the pavement ends, the shilling notes change from blue to red, the prices plummet. The danger quotient rises. It is like driving from Texas into Mexico. The four Transami trucks will try to travel close together. And, this being Africa, there is one major added effect: in Tanzania, the drivers and the turnboys, from multiple rival tribes and subtribes, all become Kenyans.

Obadiah, his elbow out the window, looked as hip and natural in my sunglasses as Bradford did awkward. I was sharing the glasses because the sky had cleared as we rolled away from the border, and neither had any. "Such fine goggles!" Obadiah exclaimed. "Very yellow! So nice!"

Our plunge down a hill into Tanzania was insanely bouncy. The smooth roads of Kenya had yielded to something worse than dirt: a paved road in advanced decay, its remaining islands of asphalt rising randomly to form a thousand speed bumps. For much of the afternoon, our progress varied from five to fifteen miles per hour, Bradford perspiring as he wrestled the wheel left and right, bouncing off his seat when the old pavement lifted the truck, and Obadiah wincing to think of the tires he'd have to repair. "The road is very unfair, very harsh," he said, shaking his head.

At the first town, we pulled over to await Malek, who had stayed back to avoid our dust. Next to a shop where we bought soft drinks stood the town's unusual wooden welcome sign: at the top, in Kiswahili, was a pleasant "Welcome to Tarime!" and then came a skull and crossbones and the legend "Danger — Protect Yourself. There Is AIDS Here!" Tarime, Obadiah said when we were back

on the road, had Tanzania's second-largest AIDS problem. Another afflicted locale was Mwanza, a city at the south end of Lake
Victoria, which we hoped to reach by the next night. The corner
of Tanzania that we were entering was one of the places worst hit
by AIDS in the world.

I tried to gauge Obadiah's reaction as we talked about this
situation. Four drivers he knew had probably died of the disease,
he said. But it was hard to be sure. Even if there were a way for
drivers to be tested, he explained, most drivers would probably not
want to be: "It would only make them sad to know." But this talk
did not seem to sadden Obadiah. Instead, after a while he became
philosophical. "People must die," he told me. "If they did not, the
world would be overcrowding. You could not drive. You see, when
people die, other people get their jobs. If nobody died, there
would be too many drivers." Obadiah, a smart man who was the
son of a truck driver, was probably well qualified to drive. But in
the deteriorating economy of Kenya he was not likely to be promoted anytime soon. Some turnboys were now in their forties.
Then again, if Bradford were to die . . .

I mentioned that friends of mine in the United States had died
of AIDS, and said that it was not a nice way to go.

"No, it is not," Obadiah agreed. "But there are many other ways
to die." I believe he meant that people in East Africa died of
malaria, dysentery, and truck wrecks, and, of course, he was right.
But to downplay the AIDS threat, and even to mention its positive
side, was not the reaction I had expected.

Bradford, fifty years old in a region where the life expectancy
was fifty-seven, listened to everything but said nothing.

Together, our truck and Malek's dwarfed the five or six buildings
in a village called Utegi. Sammy and Francis were somewhere
behind, but Bradford said not to worry — they would catch up in
a day or so. I was surprised when we pulled over at dusk, having
expected us to travel through the night, with Obadiah to share the
driving. But Obadiah and Bradford shook their heads. "Many bad
men in Tanzania," Bradford said, making a gun of his thumb and
index finger. "You break down at night, they shoot you."

But they had stopped at night in Kenya, too; bad men were only
part of the story. The rest, I thought, was simply that the trucking
culture they were a part of considered sleeping at night the civi-

lized thing to do. In Utegi, Bradford and Malek paid local boys a hundred shillings (twenty-five cents) each to guard the trucks overnight, and then they and I took tiny rooms in the village's only hostel, while the turnboys laid sleeping pads across their trucks' front seats.

We left in the morning for Mwanza, and Bradford said we would make it that evening if all went well. The dirt road, though seemingly empty, was full of wonders. Winding its way through tall brown brush on our left was a procession of people led by an old man with a big spear. "They are Luo, going to a funeral," said Obadiah, who was himself a Luo. The spear was "to chase away death," he explained as we passed. A few kilometers further on, where the roadway doubled as the eastern border of Serengeti National Park, we came upon baboons seated by the roadside, and soon afterward we were passed by several of the open-backed safari vehicles called "overlanders," all of them filled with white people.

"*Wazungu!*" Obadiah cried out the window, and turned to me, grinning. This was a joke, because I was already known less by my name than by the term *mzungu,* the singular of *wazungu,* which is basically Kiswahili for "gringo," with about the same hint of deprecation.

It was September, and the land, a month or two from rainy season, looked too sere to support any human life. But Africa was deceptive. Life lurked around every bend. In the seeming middle of nowhere, we saw propped up at the side of the road tall sisal bags full of charcoal. Though we had brought one bag from Kenya, to cook with, Bradford decided it would be a good idea to pick up another — prices would never be lower. We pulled over and waited. It took about five minutes for a teenage boy to emerge from the landscape of dry grass and leafless trees to discuss the price. An hour or two later, we stopped for woven bamboo mats, a sample of which hung from the only tree for miles. Bradford explained that these were good for sitting on and for sleeping on. Carved wooden stools, the truck drivers' lawn chairs, were next. Obadiah secured all the stuff to the front of the trailer.

Mwanza was not the lakeside oasis I had hoped for. A small port, it appeared to be built on a huge foundation of pink dust. We kicked up clouds of it wending through town to the filling station on its far side, over principal roads, all of them dirt. The heat was oppressive, so we rolled the windows down, and our damp bodies immediately became coated, like every two-story building in town, with a layer of pink powder, which left me looking darker and Bradford and Obadiah looking lighter.

Our destination was a lone Esso station, where we would refuel with a thousand-odd liters of diesel. Much of this was to be stored in the two main tanks of the tractor, and the rest would go into tanks fitted under the sides of the trailer. But when we arrived at the station — a single working pump at the edge of a big dirt parking lot — we discovered that trucks had been lining up there for three or four days. The station was out of fuel. Bradford, maneuvering with Obadiah's help, added Fleet 19 to the several rows of behemoths ahead of us and shut down the engine.

A few hours remained until dusk. The bamboo mats were unrolled beneath our trailer, providing a cool place to lie in the shade. In many parts of Africa, men who are friends hold hands; in a similar spirit, some of the turnboys lay with their arms across each other and snoozed. Some of the drivers sat on stools and talked. Obadiah picked up a copy of the Tanzanian weekly *Business Times* which he had found and soon came upon a news item that told of a crisis at one local factory: two top employees had died of AIDS, and the owners were having trouble finding replacements. (In Africa, it often happens that wealthier men, who can afford more prostitutes, are harder hit than poor men.)

"AIDS," Obadiah said. "It is very bad around here. This part of Tanzania, all the way to Uganda, it is the worst place in the world for AIDS. I know people who work at this factory." "UKIMWI," as the acronym reads in Kiswahili, was a word constantly on the lips of the turnboys.

Bradford and I went to buy food in the town market. He bought small bags of a number of exotic spices, and then lingered for quite a while over the apothecary stall. Nearby, several men stood next to bathroom scales; I paid to climb aboard, was told my weight, and then continued to a small shop to buy a Coke. Through the shop's glass countertop was visible a box containing perhaps a gross of condoms in plain white cellophane wrappers. The box had no markings and no brand name, which made me think it had been donated by an AIDS program. "Are they free?" I asked. "No, they are two hundred shillings," the shopkeeper replied. This sum took on meaning in the coming days, as I saw that a room for the night generally cost four hundred shillings, a woman for the night cost four hundred to six hundred shillings, a filling meal cost from eighty to a hundred and fifty shillings, and a bottled soft drink cost seventy shillings. In other words, these condoms cost a local the equivalent of seven or eight dollars apiece — a sum that would buy you a dozen in the United States.

After dropping off our groceries for the turnboys to deal with, we set about finding lodgings for the night. Malek, who said he had a local friend in whose house he could stay, offered to help us look, because he knew Mwanza. Many hotels were full, and almost all displayed AIDS warning posters in the lobby. When the only vacancy we could find turned out to be slightly expensive, I suggested to Bradford that he and I take a double and split the cost. He wasn't interested. This surprised me until, on our way down the stairs from the fifth floor, Malek loudly explained, "He wants his own room so he can take a woman!"

Bradford was typically silent, but once Malek had departed he struck back. "His friend here is just a woman," he said fiercely. "He sleeps with her every time he comes here."

It took me a while to understand that in this situation "woman" automatically signified "prostitute." Women here didn't sleep with you just for the fun of it. But the guys never used the word "prostitute." To say, in a strange town, that you were sleeping with a woman was to say it all.

Bradford and I went out on the town that night. In the near-empty bar of our hotel, we had a beer and a chat with the bartender, a woman whom Bradford seemed to like. Then, at a place lit by blue lights down a side street, we sat at the bar and drank Tanzanian beer and watered-down cognac. I noticed the care with which our waitress served us the beer — a method that all waitresses in Tanzania used. Her job wasn't just to set the bottle in front of us and rush off to the next customer. It was to place fresh glasses before us, then to set out the bottles of beer, then to wipe the dust off the necks of the long-necked bottles by putting her hand around the neck and pushing it down the bottle. (After my third beer of the night, this began to look erotic.) The waitress then tipped the glass and poured the beer. You watched while she served you; you were meant to watch.

"Which one do you like?" Bradford asked me. He was referring to the women. I nodded toward our waitress. "You can have her,

then." I lifted an eyebrow. "She likes you." I gave a little snort at
this, but knew that what he meant was that they were all available,
or probably were. Though increasingly drunk, I explained to Bradford that I was happily living with my girlfriend in New York and
wouldn't be interested in sleeping with the waitress. I took out my
wallet and showed him Margot's picture. She was sitting on her
red Schwinn Hollywood on East First Street on a hot July night,
flashing a big smile. Bradford reached into his wallet for a photograph of his wife. "She is at work," he explained. The picture
showed a middle-aged woman sitting at a large, neat desk. On it
were a telephone and a huge rubber stamp. She was not smiling;
smiling was not the custom in photographs here.

"Did you say she is your girlfriend?"

"Yes."

"Then it is fine! She is not your wife."

How to explain this? "But she is like a wife."

Bradford looked at me pityingly, as though I had chosen a very
early retirement.

I sought another approach. "Besides, you heard what Obadiah
said, right? This is one of the worst places in the world for AIDS."

Bradford agreed with me on this. "Yes, I know," he said. "To
bring that home to your wife, to then pass it on to your children
— very bad." He had a daughter and two sons, he said. He waved
his hand and shook his head. So he did understand AIDS. I felt
glad, and bought us another round.

As we entered the lobby of the hotel, I was surprised by Bradford's desire to have just one more at the hotel bar. I did not have
the stamina, and so climbed the stairs to go to bed. But the wall
between our rooms did not extend all the way to the ceiling, and
an hour or so later I awoke to the noise of whispering voices as
Bradford and someone else entered his room. The only other sound
was the rhythmic, almost ultrasonic peeping of an Abyssinian nightjar.
I listened to the little bird and I listened to Bradford, and I
wondered, Does he use condoms? In the morning, I heard a
woman speaking softly again, and as I came back from the bathroom saw her rounding the corner of our corridor, the hotel
bartender, skirt whirling behind.

Sammy and Francis and many more trucks had arrived overnight
at the Esso station, wedging themselves into any unclaimed space

in the parking lot, of which there hadn't been much to begin with, and lining the road on either side. Approximately thirty trucks were now waiting for the fuel, which, when it arrived, would be pumped out of the single pump. I took out my books and prepared for a long wait.

The drivers and turnboys chatted, smoked, drank tea, went on errands, and sat guard, some of them on mats under the trailers, some of them seated in the cabs. Obadiah took his work clothes, still mud-caked from Isebania, to the communal spigot by the Esso office and washed them by hand. Half an hour later, jeans were draped over the rearview mirrors of Fleet 19, shirts over the windows, and socks and underwear over the windshield wipers, which were flipped away from the glass. So hot and arid was it that everything dried in about fifteen minutes.

The captive drivers attracted a stream of venders, selling everything from used clothing to pencils and spare parts. What caught my eye, looking down from the cab, was slices of freshly cut pineapple being paraded by on platters on the heads of young women; the mouthwatering fruit passed by inches from my face. Malek saw me staring and bought several slices. He also bought a thick bunch of succulent, sun-warmed grapes. I had the confidence born of a month of health in unhealthy places, and my hunger for produce was so fierce that I bent my rule against it: the grapes, I concluded, might be O.K. if I just squeezed their innards into my mouth, avoiding the skins, and the pineapple should be fine, assuming it had been cut by clean hands.

Other young women we saw evidently had nothing to sell. Two joined Malek in his cab, and I thought they might be old friends of his until he gestured at them and said, "Do you like these pretty girls, Mr. Teddy?"

"Very pretty, Malek! No, thanks!"

They left after a while, Malek deciding against further involvement, but others filtered through the tall maze of trailers all day long, smiling, climbing in to have a chat, going on their way. You did not need to seek the women out.

Just as I joined Stephen, Malek's shy, retiring turnboy, to do my wash at the communal spigot, two fuel trucks drove up to the pump. All talking in the area seemed to cease as their drivers began to unreel their hoses to replenish the station's supply of diesel. The lull was followed by the roar of engines being started in anticipation of the new fuel. Within minutes, Stephen and I could no longer speak, because of the epic rumbling coming from the grand ignition. A dark cloud of smoke gathered over the compressed mass of dirty trucks. There was a generalized jostling as those nearest the pump began inching forward, and those in the rear inched after them.

Perhaps three of the thirty trucks had fueled up when, as quickly as it had started, the whole thing shut down. Obadiah had joined us by then, and I saw him sigh.

"What's going on?"

"They have shut down the electricity," he answered.

"What do you mean? Did they blow a fuse?"

"No, no, it is shut down everywhere."

He waved his arms to indicate the surrounding neighborhood. No darkened electric signs were available to corroborate his statement, but I remembered an advertisement I'd seen in the *Business Times,* announcing strategic power rationing. This was what it meant.

Delay, I was beginning to appreciate, was one of the few certainties of this life. There was the delay of breakdown and of border-crossing hours. There was the delay of refueling and the delay of bad roads. And then there were the delays that to the Africans were simply life lived reasonably; namely, twelve or more hours a day spent sleeping and resting and stopping to eat.

The drivers, because of their freedom, seemed to handle the delays better than the turnboys, who were tied down by poverty and job description. Obadiah moped, but Malek wasted no time in reverting to pleasure mode once the pump went off. "Boss! Mr. Teddy!" he called as I walked back to Fleet 19. "You will come join us? This is my friend in Mwanza!" He gestured at a shapely woman standing near him, whose dark skin was set off by a brilliant yellow dress. She wore yellow flip-flops.

"Sure," I said.

"We will be down the road. Bradford knows where."

An hour or two later, as the sun was starting to set, Bradford and I were on our way to the New Gardenia, a bright blue two-story building with a pleasant front porch set back a little from the dusty street. I had already noticed this place; it always had a good crowd. Drinking beer at a table on the porch were Malek and his friend.

"They still have rooms!" he said encouragingly. "Go inside now!"

Bradford and I walked in. The bar was full of men and women, and other women sat in upholstered chairs. Most of the lighting came from red bulbs. Bradford spoke to the bartender about rooms, and a woman appeared to show them to us.

The rooms were as rundown as the public areas were nice. On our way to the last available single, we walked through a cloud of mist from a shower stall with a broken pipe; water was hissing out loudly. The single was next door to this shower stall. The only other available room was a nearby double, with two small windows looking onto a small second-floor patio that got a lot of foot traffic, and this was more expensive. But tonight Bradford wanted to share it. The woman had us sign the register, and I puzzled over what to put under the heading "Tribe."

"Put 'Europe,'" Bradford suggested.

"Norway," I wrote, the land of my ancestors.

The flimsy door to the room was held shut by the meagerest hook; to judge from the doorjamb, the door had been kicked or pushed in two dozen times. The beds had mosquito nets, but these were badly torn. As we unpacked a few things, I noticed a thin column of tiny ants marching across my bed.

Bradford and I went out to find dinner, but I could hardly eat what looked like a delicious omelette, because of sudden stomach cramps: it was the revenge of the fruit. We returned to the New Gardenia, where my experience of the rest of the night was aural. From my bed I picked out the voices of Malek, Bradford, and Sammy amid the general laughing, squealing, and hollering from the bar. From the second-floor patio there came the occasional whispering of women and the bellowing of men. Near my head, mosquitoes buzzed faintly, seeking the holes in the netting over my bed; I lit a mosquito coil. Periodically, when the cassette tape at the bar was being changed, the amplified call to prayer from the local mosque drifted in the window. Around midnight, I was awakened by Bradford's return. Soon after that, some stupid drunk began pounding on our door and yelling, "Ishmael! Ishmael!"

"He's not here," Bradford replied in Kiswahili. "You've got the wrong room."

"Ishmael, Ishmael!" Again the pounding. Once more, I thought, and the door would fly open.

"He's not in here!"

"Ishmael!"

Finally, there came silence. Then the same voice, this time yelling through the shutters from the patio: *"Ishmael!"*

"My name is not Ishmael!" I yelled back.

By noon the next day, because of some aggressive creeping forward by Bradford, we were pumping our fuel, hoping against hope to make it by the power-off time. "If it goes off now, we can pump the rest by hand," Obadiah said. Using a hand pump that adjoined the electric one, he explained, a man (alternating with another man) could pump seven hundred liters in three or four hours. But we finished under electric power, and so did the others in our convoy. As a small truck from the national electric utility cut into the line at the pump right behind us, we had the last laugh: two minutes into the fill-up, the electricity went out on *them.*

The next night's destination was Shinyanga, and Malek was excited. He was Tanzanian by birth, he explained when we stopped for tea in the village of Mabuki, and much of his family lived in this region. We had to wait for our tea, and while Bradford washed his hands in a corner of the restaurant, Malek went on to say that he was way overqualified to be a truck driver but had been reduced to it by a confidential "controversy" in his life. "You know, I used to play guitar in a band," he said. "We played in all the clubs in Dar, all the clubs in the country. We made records! We played rock and roll, and we played *soukous.* We did everything."

I somehow knew that this was true. "But then what happened?"

Bradford returned. Malek said he would tell me later. He flirted in the local language with the young woman who brought us our tea, and finally she turned away, blushing.

"See? She would!" he told Bradford. "I asked her if she would like to pack her things now and come with us," he said to me jubilantly. He was famous in these parts, he assured me. "If someone is coming from the bush, like a monkey, he will still know me. I am like their president." Moreover, he continued, "I know all the women! They love me here!" We might stay in Shinyanga, he added, for a day or two.

"O.K.," I said. "For the women?"

"No, no. In Shinyanga, I get my parents' bless on me, then I feel much better. You cannot go through the country without stop at your parents."

Around midday, we pulled over again, in a village called Ma-

ganzo. It resembled a score of other places we had stopped in for
tea: a handful of one-story buildings set far back on either side of
the dirt highway, to give trucks plenty of maneuvering space. A
small stand of trees wilted in the sun at one end of town. As
Bradford eased the truck off the dirt road, our own wake of dust
engulfed us and the venders who besieged our convoy, climbing
up on the trucks' steps to offer us the usual bread, soft drinks, and
dried fish. Malek, increasingly animated at being back on his home
ground, beckoned for Bradford and me to follow him.

We took seats on benches in a smoky barbecue shed. Beams of
light slipped in through the slats, illuminating sides of goat hanging from hooks on the back wall. Hosts of flies jumped from the
meat to us and back again. A man with a cleaver stopped hacking
away at a beef carcass long enough to hear Malek order three skewers.
The flies landed. He started hacking again. The flies took off.

Three men already there knew Malek, and one shook his hand,
and then mine and Bradford's; the others, who were eating, offered their forearms, and we grasped them. A boy appeared with
a dish of water, and we dipped our fingers in and used a towel he
offered. A bowl of salt was set down, and a bowl of chili powder.
In the background, the skewers sizzled. The men licked their lips.
One wiped his mouth on a sleeve and began to chat with Malek
in Kisukuma, the local tongue. Malek asked me in English if I knew
that there were diamond mines nearby, and explained that the
mound of earth we had seen in the distance was part of them. The
man spoke with Malek some more and then peered behind him
and out the door. He put an oily finger back between his cheek
and lower molars and withdrew something very small. He put it in
Malek's hand. It was an uncut diamond, translucent, irregular, like
something you might find on the beach. He described it to Malek
in low tones. Malek handed me the stone and said, "He wants
twelve thousand dollars. Are you interested?" The diamond was a
little larger than the seed of a grape.

Our dish of hot goat was set in front of us, and the diamond
went back into the mouth.

Late in the afternoon, we arrived in Shinyanga. As usual, the road
had taken its toll: Malek's trailer listed to one side, and he had
turbocharger ills besides. "We might be here two or three days,
getting these fixed," he said happily.

The people of Shinyanga looked like Malek — lighter-skinned than Bradford or Obadiah, with a lot of Arab blood and sometimes blue or green eyes. Malek took Bradford and me on a walking tour of town and did, in fact, seem to know everybody. Assuming the role of host, he even installed us in a hotel costing a thousand shillings a night — two dollars and fifty cents, or more than double our usual tariff. Dinner, he announced, would be at the home of his cousin Walid. There was time before that to rest, and I bought a couple of beers for the turnboys.

Joining Obadiah and Stephen, I met Cromwel, a mechanic. Cromwel, aged twenty-nine, roamed Transami country in a radio-equipped Toyota Land Cruiser driven by a rotund "convoy leader" named Mwalimu. Mwalimu, a former truck driver, was now one of four lower-management troubleshooters who zipped from country to country attending to the mechanical breakdowns, bureaucratic snafus, and other difficulties experienced by Transami drivers. The two had caught up with us that afternoon, and would provide an escort all the way to Rwanda. Though Cromwel in a way served as Mwalimu's turnboy, he was a skilled and highly paid one. With the first beer, we talked about the trucks (of course) and the books we all were reading. Obadiah had finished the Ngugi and the Achebe and was into the Tolkien I had brought from Nairobi. He confessed he really did not care for that one. Cromwel was a fan of the thriller novelist Nelson DeMille, and was currently reading *The Charm School.*

With the second beer, the conversation turned to women and Malek's prodigious appetite. Obadiah and Cromwel debated whether it was natural to have a strong sex drive, and if so, whether you should try to control it. The terms of this talk confused me. If a strong sex drive was natural, they both indicated, one should not try to control it. But if such a drive was unnatural, one should control it. "Natural," apparently meaning God-given, was the operative concept. Was Malek's randy behavior, they asked me, natural or unnatural?

I had to shrug: I didn't know. They debated this and other matters, finally agreeing only on the perils associated with amorous pursuits.

"I tell you, my friend!" Obadiah cried, waving his hands in the air. "You are fine until you are in a bar and drinking one or two beers, and then a woman with big buttocks walks by, and — oh my God!"

At the home of Malek's cousin Walid, we were served a huge quantity of good food — chapati bread, fried fish, curried chicken stew, and lamb-and-egg pie. Afterward, over small cups of strong coffee, I asked Malek to tell me more about the controversy in his life. He turned serious, and we scooted back a little from the circle of men seated on a thin rug. In a low voice, he told me that when Tanzania invaded Uganda to unseat Idi Amin, in 1978–79, he had entered the army and become a captain in the military police. He received training in Israel and Cuba and then participated in the campaign. In its late stages, he was put in charge of some important prisoners. But, in what sounded like an admission of guilt, he said, "I made an arrangement and they escaped." The Tanzanian Army charged him with corruption. A United Nations inquiry, however, determined that the escapees were political prisoners who had been unfairly held, and arranged for Malek to receive asylum in Kenya. That was how he and his family had come to live in Mombasa, though Tanzania was home.

This tale of exile and redemption had an epic quality that made Western life, or my life, seem humdrum. He filled in more details later, in the courtyard of our hotel, but soon became distracted by a flirtation with the waitress, and by the drinks she brought. When mosquitoes started to get bad, Bradford and I turned in.

In the morning, I asked Malek how he'd done.

"Do you know the word *hanjam,* Mr. Teddy?" I did not. "It means a lot of sweet nothing. It can also mean lots of work but no pay. You understand?"

"It means you struck out."

"Yes!"

Mwalimu, the convoy leader, dispelled Malek's hope of a prolonged stay in Shinyanga by insisting that we leave by the following afternoon. Dusk found us in a market town called Kahama, whose dirt square was filled completely with about twenty overnighting trucks. A fierce old man wielding a bow and arrow and a receipt book approached, eying me suspiciously. He was the *askari,* or night guard, of the square, and his services were compulsory. Bradford and Malek anted up. Then, after some searching, Bradford, Malek, and I secured the usual sort of lodging, and within a couple of hours Bradford and I were seated in the usual sort of bar.

This one was swarming with mosquitoes. It was off a side street near our lodging and was lighted with blue fluorescent bulbs. There was a bartender, whose bar was secured against robbers by bar-to-ceiling bars, and there were two waitresses, who wore flowing blue muumuus and, over their heads, the lovely beaded scarves known locally as *kikwembe*. They did not have much to do; we were about the only customers. We sat on low couches around the far, dark end of the room and stretched out our legs around low tables in front of us. For the first time, we were able to order Primus, the Rwandan beer whose bottles we were hauling. It cost nearly as much as our room, and was quite strong. As our waitress went through the serving ritual, she bent forward. Underneath the muumuu she wore nothing.

Bradford was characteristically quiet, and things were starting to feel a bit dull when Malek entered with Sammy. Malek's appearance somehow electrified the room. It put me in mind of his earlier incarnation as a rock-and-roller. Within moments, he had made Christina, our waitress, smile, blush, and then burst out laughing with some little remark. He sat down. She returned with a drink for him. He talked to her some more. "I am discussing with her how much I will teach her sexually," he informed me. Christina's English was not so good, so he repeated the quip in Kisukuma, and she cracked up again. "She already loves you very much," he continued, to me. "She wants to do anything you want. I have told her that you are afraid of AIDS and that she must just suck. She says fine." Christina did not appear to have followed this, which was O.K. with me.

Malek and the others had by now become skilled at running interference for me with the women in bars. They explained what I felt they had come to believe — that I was overly concerned with AIDS — and they told the women not to take it personally, because this was a typical *mzungu* fear. Sometimes I would buy drinks for the women to show that it was nothing personal.

Outside, I asked Malek about exactly what went on when you paid to be with a woman. Did he wear protection?

"*Soksi?*" (That is, "socks" — slang for "condom.") "No. But I do not put it in them. I only have them suck. You are paying them, they'll do what you want." The usual price was between five hundred and a thousand shillings, he said, but since he spoke their local language they'd do it for three hundred, "and sometimes they'll even pay me."

I liked Malek, but the subject was depressing. Often the castoffs of men who had other wives and discovered that they couldn't afford them, these women had children to feed and no skills. Engaging even briefly in prostitution could mean that their village would refuse to take them back. A given evening at a truck stop provided only so many potential clients; if a woman were to displease them by insisting on condoms — well, plenty of other girls were willing. The same held true for anal intercourse, which many drivers requested.

We walked into another bar, nearer our hotel. Malek was immediately recognized by the bartender ("Everybody knows me!") and bought us a round. No sooner had he told me he needed someone for the night than a woman in a silver dress appeared and jokingly upbraided him ("She is asking why I didn't see her the last time I came through") until he calmed her down with the usual cajoling and "words to make her laugh." Also, apparently, a request for a date. Bradford, too, soon settled on a girl, and I went to bed.

In my room, I thought about a conversation I had had in the truck that day with Obadiah. He had been angry again at Bradford, this time for going too fast over bumps. We were smoking. Obadiah was also worried about AIDS. Whether his worries about the disease were preexisting or were partly brought on by me, I didn't know.

"A truck driver I know said some people don't get AIDS and some people do, and there is no reason for it," he said. "It is like the way some people have car crashes and some do not. Some get sick from smoking and many do not. It is life."

"You mean you just live with it — it's your fate."

"Yes."

"But isn't this true — that you can smoke less, drive slower, and wear a condom?"

"Yes, that is true."

"So it's not all black and white."

"No." He paused. "But life with precaution is no life."

That one I had to think about. Obadiah — who if he had been brought up as I had would probably occupy some executive position — had to spend most of his best years away from his wife and kids, and within about a fifty-foot radius of a semi rig. His pleasures were smoking and, much less frequently, beer and women. "Life with precaution" would subtract from his life the two cheaper principal pleasures — and probably all three, because of the difficulty of restraint when you had a beer in your belly and a "woman with big buttocks" on your lap. His attitude of recklessness pained me, but I found it hard to condemn him for it.

On a recent flight in Africa, I had sat next to a sixty-year-old Canadian who smoked, drank, and told me he didn't take his heart medication even though he had suffered a near-fatal heart attack the year before. This man held a doctorate in engineering. At my hotel in Nairobi, I had met a foreign correspondent for a North American daily. He was an ambitious, smart fellow who was particularly interested in the subject of AIDS because, he explained in the bar, he had slept with women all over the world. "But I'm cutting down on the fucking now, and trying just to stick to blow jobs," he said. Cutting down, it turned out, meant that he had had unprotected intercourse with "maybe six or seven" different women in the past three months. I said that that probably wasn't a good idea, and he said yeah, he knew.

The next morning, on a remote stretch of highway, Malek's truck broke down — cylinder-head problems — and by the end of the day all four big Transami trucks and Mwalimu's Land Cruiser were parked together by the side of the road. The two days that followed were like camping. The men spent a lot of time seated in circles beneath or next to a trailer, telling stories and drinking tea. A group of drivers paid a diplomatic call on the local goatherds, who lived in huts just around the bend. With a little warming up, they sold us delicious fresh milk for our tea, directed us to their well and to a muddy livestock-watering pond about a mile into the woods, in which we bathed, and even supplied us with chickens to augment those Malek kept in a wooden cage built into the underside of his trailer — emergency food, for occasions like this. In the morning, we heard the pipes of the boy goatherds, steering their goats around our encampment. At night, we climbed up on top of the containers, away from snakes, to lay our blankets out. And the turnboys, though they did not make a big deal about it, all slept with weapons at their sides, ranging from hatchets to tire irons. Their caution belied the idyllic look of the countryside.

All the work was done by the turnboys — they were kept busy

cooking (mostly chicken or goat stew and *ugali,* a chunky starch
dish, at which Obadiah excelled) — and by Cromwel, the mechanic. Replacing the *silinda hedi* was a time-consuming job for
skilled hands, and Cromwel seemed to have them. The more
covered with oil he got, the happier he seemed to be; there in
Malek's engine compartment, he had no boss but himself. Bad
cylinder heads, he explained to me, were a fairly common problem. "Transami has a shop that does nothing but recondition them
— I used to work there. But the reason these trucks break so much
is that everything in them is reconditioned. You see, we do not buy
new parts. They are costly and must be imported. We fix the old.
They last for a while, then they break again." He called out to
Stephen to pass him a *tork renchi* from the *tulboksi.*

Part of the *mzungu* mystique, I came to realize, was that the
faraway lands where people like me lived were the source of all this
machinery — of its manufacture and design. Trucking companies
there got their parts new, "factory fresh." Somebody in *mzungu*-
land actually got to drive trucks when they were new. Perhaps most
essential, I thought, taking an unexpected pride in the fact, was
that we named the trucks and named the parts.

The first afternoon, it rained, but Cromwel worked on; the truck
"bonnet" provided him with a roof, and he was so coated in oil he
looked waterproof. I sat in the cab and read and was tutored in
Kiswahili by Francis and slept. Early the second afternoon, the skies
cleared, the clothing dried, Cromwel finished, and a large hawk
landed on a snake crossing the road by the trucks. It stood there
for a long time, pecking away at the snake, as we watched from the
cabs.

Runzwewe, our last stop before Rwanda, was another collection of
small, low buildings at a crossroads in a barren landscape. All had
roofed front porches and rear courtyards and were set back far
enough for rows of trucks to park in front. We arrived in midaf-
ternoon, famished, and entered a café.

The tall, thin Somali men who ran the place wore skirts. Our
waiter spoke the menu: chicken, goat meat on rice, or beans. Most
ordered goat meat. On the wall across from us was a portrait of
Saddam Hussein; directly above our heads was an AIDS poster. It
conveyed its message graphically, showing, left to right, a man in

four phases of emaciation. He was practically dead in the last drawing; a cemetery with headstones underneath made the message clear. Mwalimu read the caption out loud — *"Utapunguza uzito kwa muda nfupi"* — and cracked a joke in Kiswahili, which I missed.

"What does it say?" I asked as the others chuckled.

"It says, 'You'll lose weight in a short time,' and I said, 'They should call it the Truck-Driver Diet.'"

Though it had clearly been drawn by an African hand, the poster carried a very Western message. The idea behind it was that a simple dose of correct information could make a huge difference in people's lives. The challenge was to print up enough posters and hang them in enough public places.

But already I could see the barriers.

"You know," Cromwel said, musing on the poster. "Some people are immune from AIDS."

I told him that was not known for sure.

"But they are not certain? Then I think it could be true!"

Francis said that he had heard many different stories about AIDS. "First, we were told the *wazungu* brought it," he said.

"*Mzungu* scientists were the first to identify it, but they think it came from here," I replied.

Francis looked at me as if to say, *Well, of course they do.* "Then they said that truck drivers brought it!" he continued. "There was a time when the women wouldn't sleep with *wazungu* or drivers. Now they will, but they want condoms with people they don't know."

"Yes," Cromwel said. "They want condoms with unmarried people. But if you talk with them and they come to trust you, then you don't have to."

"That's right," Francis agreed. "If you're married, with kids, it's much better. And if you are healthy."

"You mean looking healthy," I said. "You can look healthy but still have the virus that causes AIDS."

Though Obadiah understood this, the others were less familiar with the idea of being infected but showing no symptoms. I explained it, realizing as I did that understanding HIV infection really required a rudimentary knowledge of biology, of how infections occur — and not only an understanding of it but a belief in it, for, as they listened and I talked, I could see my words getting filed in the mental drawer labeled "Possible Explanations."

And if you did get AIDS, Cromwel added, there was always a virgin.

"What?"

"Yes, you know, if you sleep with a virgin it will often take away your AIDS," Cromwel assured me. He knew people who had done it.

I winced, and told them it wasn't true. If you slept with a virgin, you would probably just give HIV to the virgin. They didn't argue with me, but I doubt whether they believed me. Modern medicine, which I took to be a challenge to traditional beliefs, they saw as merely a complement to them. My rebuttal of every African idea about AIDS probably sounded closed-minded to them.

Stretching my legs after the meal, I was relieved to run into Obadiah by the truck. Obadiah was educated — in other words, he saw things my way. As I walked toward him, I saw him looking warily at a mentally disturbed woman weaving around the parking lot, jabbering and shouting to herself.

"She is bewitched," he whispered to me. I gave him a look of incomprehension. Was this a joke? But neither Obadiah nor any of the others tended to be ironic. "Yes, it is a spell. It happens often in these small places."

I felt despairing, and the feeling was increased by the rooms we rented. They were the worst yet. There was no light — Runzwewe had no electricity — but even in the dimming daylight the sheets were obviously dirty, and the filthy pillow had no pillowcase. Bradford said his room was the same. I rested a while and checked my watch: only 8 P.M. Maybe I could get a drink.

When I went out on the hotel porch, I could hear the faint noise of a generator and of American voices arguing: somebody had a TV. Around the trucks, it was dark, but I heard laughter on the other side and wandered over to some lantern-lit tables in front of one of the small places across the road. There a round innkeeper named Bora was joking with the drivers. They introduced me, and she continued with a story she'd been telling. It turned out that when the authorities went to the house of this man in Uganda who'd died of AIDS, they found dozens of packages of unused condoms. Ah, I thought, there's a moral here, of the right kind. But Bora went on, "And all the condoms had dates that had expired!"

Knowing murmurs circled the table, and I asked Francis to

explain. "These condoms, when they are too old, contain germs," he said. "And that's how he got AIDS."

"From expired condoms? That's ridiculous."

The woman asked Francis to translate my English. She looked hurt and offended, and replied sharply to him. "She says you should not doubt her. She knows — she is from Uganda," Francis said.

I touched her arm and tried to have Francis explain that I did not doubt her word, merely the interpretation of the facts. I could see that this was a losing day for Western medicine. I ordered a beer, quickly drained it, and returned to my bed.

The route to Rwanda took us over a brief but sudden ridge of red-soil mountains. The trucks groaned up the steep grades and whined slowly down their far sides, the drivers taking it very easy: littered at every sharp turn and at the bottom of every hill were the wrecks of trucks whose drivers had been careless. Some of the wrecks were recent and spectacular. This time, Obadiah didn't complain about Bradford's snail's pace.

Malek, as usual, drove the fastest, and soon he had the punctures to show for it. We all pulled over on a shoulder behind him as it started to rain, and the turnboys paired up to attend to the tires. Francis was the last in line. "You know what they say when you get punctures?" he asked me.

"No."

"They say you forgot to pay your girl this morning."

"So who do you suppose didn't pay today?" I asked, playing along. We had discussed this subject before, Francis explaining that with women you knew, the gift of a "compact" (cassette tape), a bottle of perfume (Francis had gestured to his underarms), a nice T-shirt, a pair of shoes, or a length of fabric was as welcome as money. "Did Malek cause this?"

Francis shrugged. "Could have been anybody," he said.

The final drop, into the river valley that marked the border, was scenic, and excruciatingly slow: the grade was 10 percent, and the drivers were hypercautious. Eventually, we rounded a bend that presented us with a view of a small Tanzanian customs station perched on the steep hillside, a compound of Rwandan customs buildings across the valley, and between them, a bridge over a wild and glorious cascade of water, identified on my map as the Chutes de Rusumo. Mist rose from the churning waters, partly obscuring dense semitropical foliage that listed toward the river from its banks. Leaving Tanzania proved to be a simple matter, but when I saw the drivers blocking their wheels and parking for the night, planning not to cross till morning, I told them I was going to walk down to the bridge and take a look.

As one, they warned me to stay. "The soldiers will shoot you," Bradford said.

When I expressed my doubts, Francis told me what had happened to another truck he had driven in Rwanda. I suddenly remembered that at the Transami office in Mombasa, Harry Hanegraaf, a white Kenyan who was the manager of land transport, had shown me a pile of snapshots of various trucking mishaps from the past two years. There were several impressive wrecks, but the most memorable was the picture of the cab of what had evidently been Francis's rig. It had been heavily sprayed with machine-gun fire and, from what I recalled, set ablaze. Francis told me that two years earlier his truck, as part of a convoy of government-escorted trucks traveling on the road west of the northern Rwandan town of Ruhengeri, had been ambushed by a squad of guerrillas. After stopping the trucks by blocking the highway with debris, the guerrillas told the drivers to run; they then looted the trucks and, to underscore their message, destroyed them.

Bradford had a way of dealing with officials that drove Obadiah crazy. "He is so stupid!" he whispered vehemently as Bradford got down from the cab to open the container for the Rwandan customs man. "He sits with a face like this" — he did a good impression of Bradford's pugnacious stare — "and pretends he doesn't understand anything. And he thinks this will work. Well, let me tell you, it doesn't work!"

All the paperwork had gone smoothly, if slowly, that morning, the drivers presenting their thick sheaves of bills of lading, export certifications, and identification documents at the single window. Around the side of the building, at the same time, Obadiah had helped me negotiate with the black-market money changers who swarmed around us in their furtive way. All that remained was to drive away.

But even with the paperwork in order, the guard who controlled the barrier gate across the road had to be dealt with. Bradford's stone-faced truculence had worked at the Tanzanian border — he had had to pay only the official duty, which Transami advanced him. But that was not going to cut it here. "You have to talk to them, to show them you are not afraid," Obadiah said, looking in his rearview mirror. "You have to compliment them, and then you have to insult them for wanting money that is not their due. Bradford does not understand this."

Bradford hoisted himself into his seat a few moments later, livid, and jerked the truck into gear. He had had to pay the guard twenty dollars, he said. "Out of my pocket! Transami should pay for this! But they pay me nothing!" Obadiah, wisely, kept quiet. Bradford was so mad that he ignored the gestures of two more soldiers, who rose to their feet as we approached, apparently signaling us to pull over. It was not until a third soldier, waving menacingly, made us understand that we were supposed to be driving on the other side of the road — in Francophone Rwanda, you drive on the right, and not on the left, as in Kenya, Tanzania, and Uganda — that Bradford veered across the tarmac, still muttering. "These people! Rwanda!"

During an afternoon of low-gear rises and drops, Bradford, the tension showing on his face, swerved and shook his fist to keep kids from grabbing rides on the trailer. He even stopped the truck, ordering Obadiah to chase them away. The reason, he said, was that kids would drop off and then cross the road without looking — many were killed this way. But I also sensed that Rwanda annoyed him in general, and that keeping kids off the truck helped him keep the country at bay.

Late the second day, we reached the hilly capital, Kigali. We passed near the modern-looking center and then continued out of town to a dingy suburb, where industry and low-grade housing were mixed. This district, Gikondo, was the home of the Magasins Généraux de Rwanda (MAGERWA), the national warehouses. In order to protect international trucks from the depredations of local thieves while they awaited customs certification and did their loading and unloading, the government had carved from a hill two huge holding yards, surrounded by red cliffs and by fences topped with barbed wire. The rear yard was for flammable loads, most of them twin-trailer petrol trucks returning from fuel depots in Tanzania and Kenya. The other was for general cargo, and we pulled up at its entrance. Obadiah dropped off with our documents as armed guards unchained the metal front gates, raised a traffic boom, and waved us in. Bradford headed for a corner of the great space where one Transami truck was already parked.

As the drivers parked their trucks, I took a walk around. The surface was not pavement but hard-packed, oil-saturated soil. A concrete building housed some fetid toilets and some overflowing sinks for washing dishes and clothes. The hundred-odd trucks in the lot were divided into national ghettos, the brand of truck varying with the nationality: the largest cluster, driven by Somalis, consisted mostly of old orange Fiats, Italy having administered parts of Somalia; the next largest consisted of Mercedes-Benz ("Benzi") trucks, operated by the big German-owned Tanzanian shipper Interfreight (Germany ruled Tanzania early in the century); trucks of Rwandan, Burundian, or Zairean registration were usually Renaults; and our vehicles, of course, a legacy of British empire, were Leyland. (One had even been used in the Falklands war, Harry Hanegraaf said.) The only other *mzungu* in the area was a vender of frozen Lake Victoria perch from Mwanza, who was selling the big fish from a refrigerated trailer.

The length of our stay in Kigali depended on the actions of two parties. Transami's sister company in Rwanda, Transintra, had to supply paperwork for the loads we were dropping off and picking up; and the MAGERWA customs personnel had to accept the paperwork. The order from Transintra to unload didn't come until the third day, Friday, and Bradford and Obadiah returned from the MAGERWA warehouses in dark moods, the container still on the trailer. There was a huge line, Bradford explained, and they didn't come close to making it to the front. And they couldn't try again until Monday.

There was more to it, Obadiah told me later, when his fury had somewhat subsided. To unload in any reasonable amount of time, you had to tip the clerks, had to tip the crane operator, had to tip the *askari* — you had to play the game. Bradford stonewalled, as usual, with the result that they got nowhere.

"I guess maybe that's the price of being honest," I suggested, looking for a positive side.

"It is not a question of honesty. He is just stingy!" Obadiah said.

Malek, Sammy, and Francis did unload, and Sammy and Francis took on new containers to take further into Rwanda and into Zaire, respectively, on Monday. In the meantime, we waited. Life in the yard had its interesting aspects, most notably the commercial ones. After we washed our shirts, boys came by to iron them. There were no electrical outlets around; the boys used portable black irons that had hot coals in an internal compartment. Venders of used clothing, *nguo za mitumba,* made the rounds night and day. Flyers advertised a showing of the film *Pretty Woman* — not in a theater, Bradford explained, but in the house of someone who had procured a VCR and a bootleg tape. Scores of venders not favored by the gatekeepers offered their wares right outside the front gate, besieging the drivers as though they were tourists emerging from a fancy hotel.

At night, the drivers and I would generally escape MAGERWA for a hotel known as the Snake. This was a nickname; on the room receipts it said "Logement Kalibu Gikondo." Except for Mwanza's New Gardenia, it was the most brothel-like of the cheap hotels we stayed at.

There were no signs. To get to the Snake, we walked up a steep road rutted by rain to the top of the Gikondo hill. Here, amid small houses, were two tall white iron gates opening onto a brick patio, the beer garden of the Snake. These gates were the sole entrance to the compound. The rooms all opened off two small courtyards farther in, past the office, and these, too, could be sealed off with iron gates. I didn't like the place at first. A drunk yelled at me as we walked through the crowded beer garden to get to the office. A crowd gathered as we registered. I was the first *mzungu* they had ever had, an unsavory-looking man in an unbuttoned shirt, who was named Alphonse, explained. He handed me a receipt and a carbon copy of it. "That one you give to the girl," he said, in French, "so that she knows what room you're in."

Another employee then asked gaily, "You want to fuck my wife?" His name was Andrew, and I think now that he was just giddy at his first chance to pander to a *mzungu,* because later he became friendly and quite helpful. The woman in question, who stood smiling, turned out to be Zairean and a great favorite of Malek's, and of course was not Andrew's wife at all. To my surprise, the room was clean and better than average: the Snake, I came to appreciate, was underpriced in the way of Las Vegas hotels, which make their real money off you in other ways.

Apart from Andrew and Alphonse, the personnel seemed to be women. They would serve you your Primus, then sit with you while you drank it. They would come to your room if you wanted, but there was no obligation — the usual arrangement. In the morning, the tiled showers had hot water — a miracle — the sun shone down on the courtyards, and the women became maids, who would sing as they washed up. There were good mirrors, each with an Afro comb hanging from a string. The Snake was a favored spot of the local military commanders, Andrew told me, and no one ever bothered you there.

Well, almost no one. As Cromwel, Sammy, and I were having a few beers the first night, a drunk guy stood up and insisted on sitting next to me. He wanted to thumb-wrestle. I consented, and each of us won a round. But then he wanted to yell loudly in my ear. He was high on something besides beer. Andrew interposed, telling him to lay off, and he did for a while; Andrew then said to me that the man had been smoking some kind of dope, and this was why he was so aggressive. Finally, escorted by my friends, I retired to my room. A while later, there was an insistent knocking at the door and then an *"Ouvrez la porte!"* I opened it. Alphonse, silk shirt unbuttoned to his waist, stood there with a young woman, who looked far more virtuous than he.

"You want?" he asked, with a big grin.

"Non, merci. Elle est très jolie, mais non. Bonsoir." I bolted my door. The knocking resumed. I ignored it.

But after that first night things calmed down. We checked out every morning, as was our custom (you never knew what the day would bring), but every night we returned, becoming regulars at the Snake.

After the convoy had spent nearly a week in the yard, however, everyone's spirits began to deteriorate. Various incidents set them back. Obadiah had a pair of jeans stolen from where he had hung them to dry over the chain-link fence. Cromwel had his flashlight *(torchi)* stolen from the Land Cruiser while Mwalimu was inside the Transintra office. MAGERWA's immigration officers, whom Obadiah had told that I was *bwana,* the boss, apparently had begun to doubt it and were looking for me. Malek started getting fevers, which reduced him to spending most of the day lying in his cab; he said it was malaria. Obadiah got diarrhea — underripe bananas, he thought. And I was with Mwalimu when he got into a fender-bender with a reckless-driving government official and had to go to the police station. There he was informed that the accident was being judged his fault.

"How could that be?" he asked.

"It would never have happened if you had not come into the country," the policeman said.

I started noticing coffins everywhere. About eight were stacked up outside a craft shop in Gikondo, and it seemed that a small funeral procession with a rough-hewn, unfinished casket held aloft passed MAGERWA every other day. Was it AIDS or the civil war? Kigali, where between 30 and 34 percent of the adults of reproductive age were infected with HIV, was the closest thing to an epicenter that the epidemic had. But at night we would sometimes hear shells exploding, and automatic-weapons fire. Then one morning a man at the Snake said he had heard on the radio that peace talks between the government and the rebels had broken off and an invasion of Kigali was imminent. I decided it might be a good time to visit the American embassy.

The center of Kigali, while more lively than the yard, was also much more frightening. Soldiers were everywhere; streets were sealed off for security reasons; a manned tank surrounded by foxholes was parked at a main intersection. I ate lunch at a restaurant overlooking the street, and stood up when everyone else did to watch a demonstration of perhaps forty people waving blue banners and singing. This, I was told by an American woman standing nearby, was not the rebel insurgency but a political demonstration by the newly constituted Social Democratic Party — one result of the simultaneous "opening" of Rwandan politics toward a multiparty system.

The marchers turned the corner and we started to sit down, but then shots were fired and people outside screamed. Demonstrators began running back down the street past the restaurant. I hastened to the door, but the American woman told me to sit down. She lived in Kigali, she said, and explained that the soldiers were very nervous. A week before, she and a friend were being interrogated on the street by a soldier when the soldier's rifle accidentally went off, sending a bullet through the narrow space between their heads. They had escaped with only a nicked ear. Today, things sounded different.

Half an hour later, she directed me to the American embassy. Officials there gave me some details about the insurgency, showed me maps, and indicated the location of the nearest rebel stronghold, about forty-five miles away.

"Is that all?"

"Well, they were here in the city two months ago," one official said. At least, they thought so: the possibility existed that the government had staged the gun battles for its own purposes.

An embassy official named Larry Richter took over, and assured me that the rumor that the talks had broken down was a result of a misunderstanding; the two sides had merely concluded the latest in a series of negotiations. Richter was candid and friendly. The shooting at lunch, an employee told him, had resulted in the death of a demonstrator — nervous soldiers had fired on the procession. He thought I had more to worry about in Gikondo, where burglars dressed as policemen were said to be entering houses and beating the occupants, and where other opposition demonstrators had been brutally attacked. He warned me to be careful, and wrote down the phone numbers of his embassy office and his residence. "Give a call if you're still here on Sunday — we play volleyball at my place," he said. I tucked the numbers into my back pocket.

A red motorbike-taxi took me back to the yard through an afternoon shower. But where the trucks had been there was only empty space. A driver who was parked next to the empty space told me that Fleet 19 had unloaded its beer bottles and been sent to a yard owned by Transintra, to take on cargo, and the driver's turnboy said he'd show me where.

We walked for an hour and entered another industrial neighborhood — this one, for better or worse, largely devoid of people. The Transintra yard had an open-air repair shop and a grassy space on which were parked Fleet 19 and another Transami truck, driven by a veteran Swahili driver named Zuberi. Resting near a brick wall in the back, slowly being absorbed by vegetation, were the components of a large building crane — engine, swivel, boom segments, everything. This was to be our load, Obadiah told me sullenly —

not the bags of coffee they had hoped to get for a quick trip back to Mombasa. The crane, bound for tiny Burundi, to the south of Rwanda, would add days to what already felt like a lengthy trip.

We talked until the sun began to set and swarms of mosquitoes wafted over from the marsh next door. Cromwel and I, it was decided, would go to the Snake to reserve rooms for all of us. Mwalimu offered to drive us over.

We alighted at the entrance to the MAGERWA yard, and Mwalimu sped away. When we had walked no more than twenty paces toward the steep hill leading to the Snake, two soldiers armed with carbines stopped us. They were dressed in fatigues, with jackboots and berets. One bore his rifle properly, with the barrel behind his shoulder, but the shorter one had his reversed, so that the barrel pointed up into the nose of anyone he spoke to. They appeared to be sixteen or seventeen years old, and both, it soon became evident, were drunk.

Thus began a fearful several-hour saga in which the soldiers, illiterate and unable to speak any language but Kinyarwanda, followed us to the Snake, harassed Alphonse and Andrew, and demanded that I surrender my passport and accompany them to an undisclosed location. That seemed like a bad idea, so I stalled, and took refuge in my room. Once, when they had left momentarily, Andrew came running in to say he'd heard that the surlier of the two planned to return and stab me. (Cromwel said it was too bad we couldn't get the soldier alone "and bash his face in.") Andrew first changed my room and later persuaded the owner of the Snake, the fattest man I had met in Rwanda, to seclude me in his personal wing of the compound. Bradford came in, too.

Several soldiers had by this point gathered at the gate to the Snake. I used the owner's phone to call Larry Richter at his home. Not long before midnight, the owner opened his door to a small, armed contingent of tall blond men from the embassy who grabbed me by either arm, brushed past the Rwandan militia, and spirited me away in a Mitsubishi Montero that had been left running at the gate.

For four days, I lay low at an embassy residence, emerging only to check on the progress of the crane loading. It was delayed, in an irony that escaped none of the drivers, by the lack of a small mobile crane needed to lift the pieces of the big one onto the trailers. Then, once everything was loaded and secured, departure was delayed again by Transintra's failure to provide a new freight manifest and other customs paperwork. In the end, we left without the paperwork, carrying only Transintra's promise to send a courier to intercept us before we made the Burundi border.

I had nothing physical to show the drivers of my ordeal — no black eye, no stitches from a stab wound. However, filling in at an embassy volleyball game, I had managed to mangle my right ring finger; it could no longer extend itself. A doctor at the game couldn't diagnose the injury but said she didn't think that the finger was broken. Seeking sympathy, I showed the injury to Obadiah, who had played volleyball at the national level in Kenya. Maybe he had seen something similar, I thought.

Obadiah looked at my hand, and then I noticed his: *he didn't even have a right ring finger.*

"A container landed on it when we were loading three years ago," he explained. "I had to miss four months of work."

For a long time, I did not worry anymore about my finger.

To fly from Kigali to Bujumbura, the capital of Burundi, takes half an hour. To drive by car usually takes five or six hours — "which tells you a lot about the road," Larry Richter had said to me. But to go by truck took us from Sunday morning to midday Wednesday, or roughly seventy-seven hours — which tells you a lot about truck driving in Africa.

By noon the second day, we had reached the remote, mountainous border. "Here is very far, very deep," Obadiah said as we parked. A river marked the actual line, with tiny settlements on either side and lush vegetation all around. We wouldn't be crossing right away — Transintra still had not caught up to us with the customs papers. Instead, we would wait at the border until the messenger arrived.

There were no lodgings, no real restaurants, and not much to do. Across the road from us was the dormitory of a small detachment of soldiers. I shied away from them, but Obadiah made friends. It was more peaceful here, he said, and the soldiers were nice. Bradford slept in the truck that night, and Obadiah and I underneath. When Obadiah slept outside, he put his shoes right next to his head, to keep them from being stolen. I did the same, and was awakened in the morning by a goat tugging on the salty, smelly leather of my cross-trainers.

Obadiah and I ended up the next evening in the small dark room of a woman who served us charcoal-broiled goat, unleavened bread, and tall glasses of a locally brewed banana wine called *urwagwa*. I had offered to buy him dinner, because I had seen his discomfort the night before when a crowd of hungry children gathered around the meal he was preparing by the side of the truck. "I cannot eat if hungry people are watching," he said, and, in fact, he hadn't. So now we were in a dark room, where hungry people couldn't see us.

We drank more *urwagwa*, and Obadiah said that it was probably what the soldiers were drinking before they hassled me — it was common in Rwanda, and cheap. I wondered as I drank if *urwagwa* normally brought on that kind of ugly response, but concluded that the general situation in Rwanda — AIDS, and a civil war that had killed tens of thousands of people and displaced nearly a million — was a more likely cause. The wine engendered a certain congeniality, and Obadiah and I sat for a long while. I had told him about some pretty *mzungu* women at the volleyball game in Kigali, and he now asked me, knowingly, if I had "made friends" with them. No, I told him, I hadn't, and he suggested, "They are worried about AIDS, like you!" No one, he assured me, could stop sleeping with people forever. "One day — after a month — they will want to do it," he said. We laughed, and he lowered his voice. "Ted," he said earnestly, "a friend of mine is sick. Are any of your pills for gonorrhea?"

What friend could it be, I wondered. And what pills were for gonorrhea? "Like penicillin?"

"Penicillin, yes, but better is amoxicillin, or tetracycline. Ampicillin, too, will work."

I was surprised to hear the names. "No, I'm sorry," I answered. "I don't have those." He didn't bring it up again for three more days, but I started wondering just how Obadiah had got gonorrhea, if that was what had happened. Gonorrhea is one of the diseases linked with a high risk of catching HIV. If Obadiah had it, that meant that even the best-educated people probably weren't using condoms. This in turn implied, of course, that they could well die, and along the way perhaps their wives and children. The impulse to lecture all the men, instead of just informing them, was practically overwhelming.

The next afternoon, the messenger arrived with the papers, and two days later we reached Bujumbura. Some of the hills en route had been extremely steep; as the convoy crawled down one, Bradford and Obadiah told me about a Transami driver who, a year before, had descended too fast, lost his brakes, and killed seven people, many of them squashed by his container; it had been filled with mattresses, and they were strewn everywhere. An ambulance rescued the injured driver moments before an angry mob of villagers would have torn him to pieces.

Bujumbura lay at the bottom of the biggest and final hill, and had a far more relaxed atmosphere than Kigali, which was in some ways its sister city. It was a city at peace. Also, it enjoyed a site on the shore of Lake Tanganyika — a wide, murky sea, across which the dark mountains of eastern Zaire were sometimes visible. Even Bujumbura's equivalent of MAGERWA was situated on the lake. From its blacktopped surface and through its high chain-link fence we could hear the lapping of water on the beach and see the tips of waving palm trees. At night, we heard the snuffling of hippos, which trundled up from the beach in search of choice garbage in the dump across the street. The sky, early in the morning, was filled with thousands of bats above a large tree half a mile away from us.

Bradford was annoyed at me for having done what I thought was a good deed — giving Obadiah a little money. "How much did you give him?" he demanded when he saw Obadiah smoking from an entire pack of cigarettes. (Turnboys normally bought them singly.) I told him half the actual amount, and he was still annoyed. "He will use it to get drunk!" he said angrily. "You should not give him money." The real problem, I figured, was that their poverty was one of the things that kept turnboys near the trucks — without money, there was really nowhere else to go — and also made them beholden to the drivers. Money was the drivers' control. I had stepped into the balance and, at Obadiah's behest, distorted it.

I had given him nine hundred Burundi francs — the equivalent of about four dollars. With a certain amount of misgiving, I watched as he left the lot with a local driver at about 4 P.M., and waited to see if Bradford's prophecy would come true. Would he just use it to get blasted? But an hour and a half later the two returned, a nice, sober spring to their steps. Obadiah had spent his remaining seven hundred francs, he told me without being asked, on a meningitis shot. Hadn't I heard? There was a big outbreak of meningitis in Burundi — two hundred people had died so far. Bus transportation between cities had been halted to try to slow its spread. I had received such a shot before coming to Africa but hadn't dreamed that I might need it. I secretly congratulated Obadiah on his caution — I hadn't known him as well as I thought.

Though the Transintra agent had visited us and promised to try to expedite things, it looked as if this were going to be another long wait. After unloading the crane, we would have to load thirty-odd tons of coffee. But first the agent would have to locate a container to put the coffee in, and he didn't know of any in the vicinity. The drivers rested, talked, slept.

The second day, Bradford offered to show me the way into town, but Obadiah pulled me aside as we prepared to leave.

"You know the gonorrhea?" he asked when we were alone. Not having heard more, I had assumed it had got better. "Well, it is much worse. You know — pus, and everything. That girl in Kigali was so very pretty, but —"

"What girl in Kigali?"

"I told you, the night the soldiers came and you gave me your key." I had tossed him my room key on the way out.

"Oh, no! That was when you got it?"

"Yes! So here is what I need — tetracycline, amoxicillin, or ampicillin." He even seemed to know the dosage in milligrams, so I had him write it all down in my notebook. And off I went.

Visiting the pharmacy put me in mind of my own health. I went by the local United States AID office, where a doctor agreed to look at my finger. By now, it was red and sore, still couldn't extend itself, and had assumed an odd gooseneck shape. He manipulated it, said he thought I'd snapped a tendon, and suggested I consult a hand surgeon.

"Can you suggest anyone locally?" I asked.

He looked at me as though I were joking. The country didn't have x-ray machines with the definition needed to diagnose my injury, he said, much less a specialist. "But maybe in Nairobi," he added. I thanked him and returned to the lot.

Obadiah was thrilled to see the packets of amoxicillin capsules I had picked up for him. "Oh, you are such a nice *mzungu!*" he exulted. Then I handed him another purchase from the pharmacy — a small package of Prudence condoms, price twenty Burundi francs, or less than a dime. "Next time, use these," I said, in a mock man-to-man tone. Looking at the box, he didn't know what they were. "Open it," I said. He pulled out the four cellophane-wrapped condoms. He still didn't know what they were. "You don't know?" They didn't look any different from condoms you would buy anywhere. I opened one and removed the latex circle.

At last, there was a sigh of recognition. "Oh, yes."

Obadiah had finished reading a well-thumbed Perry Mason mystery, *You Find Him, I'll Fix Him,* and left it for me. I lay on my side and opened the paperback to a small card that he had used as a bookmark. On it was a paragraph in his handwriting: "Short, fat, and built like a barrel, but all the same the best description I can give her is that she reminded me of Mussolini in her size, same ruthless, jutting jaw, dark complexion . . ." This was not, I would later confirm, a passage copied from the book. Obadiah admitted sheepishly that he had written it while he was sitting, bored, in the yard that afternoon. He said the Perry Mason book had inspired him, and so had the way I was always writing things down. I told him he should write the whole book.

The winds the first night had been hot, but dry and strong enough to keep us cool. This second night, though, the breeze slowed and reversed direction; humid air from the lake poured in and soon had us soaked. It also brought a huge quantity of mosquitoes. Everyone started slapping himself and pulling a blanket or a shirt over his head, despite the swelter. Though my malaria medication was supposed to be good, it wasn't fail-safe, so I reached into my bag and dug out mosquito repellent. Because this was the dry season, I had hardly used repellent up to this point; tonight would be a test. Others gathered around as they saw me slathering on the pungent lotion.

"What medicine is that?" Obadiah asked.

"Mosquito repellent," I said matter-of-factly, passing some to him. He asked for directions. "You've never used it?" He shook his head.

The others, waiting their turn, regarded the little red bottle with such amazement that I felt like Aladdin demonstrating my lamp. Only Zuberi looked on with any recognition. "We used this in the Sudan," he said to me. "In the army."

I felt a prick in my shoulder and reached back to slap it. The action left a stain of blood on my white shirt. Shit, I thought — it was one of the few "confirmed hits" I'd had since coming to Africa. And this was moments after applying the repellent. No precaution, I supposed, was a hundred percent foolproof. Under the trucks, even with the lotion, there was still a lot of swatting going on. One unlucky mosquito bite, I thought, trying to take the drivers' point of view, could perhaps be likened to one unlucky fuck: you'd probably already had it, and what was the incremental risk of just one more? I wondered if what had been called Africa's fatalism wasn't just a reasonable response to the fact that there was only so much you could do.

I left three days later. That morning, a crowd of people had gathered on the beach of Lake Tanganyika, across the road from the truck yard. Obadiah was among them. He had an uneasy look on his face as I approached. There at his feet, water lapping over its bloated limbs, lay a corpse that had just washed up. "He was a sailor on the lake," Obadiah reported. "They say he fell overboard three days ago when he was drunk." I had never seen a drowned man before. He was gray, and very dead. Nobody touched him.

The crane had still not been unloaded — "Some of these shippers use our trucks to store things for free," Bradford explained — and I had caught my bad finger on some clothing and further torn something inside it. We guessed that it could be another ten days before the truck left Burundi (it turned out to be even longer). I said my goodbyes, traded addresses, took orders for presents. Obadiah and Bradford walked me to a taxi stand, and I left for the airport.

I made it to Mombasa in a day; Bradford and Obadiah's return trip took three weeks. Bradford's truck and Zuberi's, I later learned from Transami, reached home without incident; they left Bujumbura two weeks after I did, and in the provincial town of Gitega they each loaded about thirty-five tons of coffee packed in sisal bags, like our charcoal. Other trucks from the convoy returned earlier and later. Sammy was back from Ruhengeri, Rwanda, on the twenty-third of October, soon enough to receive a promptness incentive payment (fifteen dollars). Francis didn't return from Goma, Zaire, until the twelfth of November. And Malek had some-how managed to break down again in Shinyanga, and would be there a while. I knew that would make him happy.

I had several questions to ask Harry Hanegraaf, of Transami, among them details of a story I had heard when we were waiting at the MAGERWA yard in Kigali. A turnboy of Zuberi's had died there two years before, of malaria, Zuberi had told me. Malaria, of course, is endemic to the area, and everyone suffers bouts of it; women and children sometimes die of it, but grown men seldom do. Since Zuberi's English was worse than my Kiswahili, I had had to collect this story secondhand and had heard many versions. What, I asked Hanegraaf, had really happened?

Hanegraaf said the turnboy had been dead several days when drivers brought him to the Kigali hospital from Gisenyi, on the Zaire border. The body was so decomposed, the morgue there claimed, that it could not be put in cold storage; instead — and this outraged the drivers — it was left outdoors. Transami dis-patched a truck to recover the body but, realizing the awful shape it was in, finally paid to fly the corpse to Mombasa. ("It's Africa," Hanegraaf said, explaining the expense. "The family refused to allow the remains to be buried in Kigali.") The family came for the corpse at company headquarters, and the casket it had been shipped in was buried at the back of the yard. ("Nobody here would touch it.") Of course, no autopsy was done — who would ever pay for such a thing? — but Hanegraaf had an opinion about the death which differed from Zuberi's. "That turnboy didn't die of malaria," he said. "He died of AIDS."

DAVID DENBY

Does Homer Have Legs?

FROM THE NEW YORKER

I HAD FORGOTTEN. I had forgotten the extremity of its cruelty and tenderness, and, reading it now, turning *The Iliad* open anywhere in its 15,693 lines, I was shocked. A dying word, "shocked." Few people have been able to use it seriously since Claude Rains said "I'm shocked, *shocked* to find that gambling is going on in here" as he pocketed his winnings in *Casablanca*. But it's the only word for excitement and alarm of this intensity. The brutal vitality of the air, the magnificence of ships, wind, and fires; the raging battles, the plains charged with terrified horses, the beasts unstrung and falling; the warriors flung face down in the dust; the ravaged longing for home and family and meadows and the rituals of peace, leading at last to an instant of reconciliation, when even two men who are bitter enemies fall into rapt admiration of each other's nobility and beauty — it is a war poem, and in the Richmond Lattimore translation it has an excruciating vividness, an obsessive observation of horror that causes near-disbelief.

> Idomeneus stabbed at the middle of his chest with the spear, and
>   broke the bronze armour about him
> which in time before had guarded his body from destruction.
> He cried out then, a great cry, broken, the spear in him,
> and fell, thunderously, and the spear in his heart was stuck fast
> but the heart was panting still and beating to shake the butt end
> of the spear.
>
> (XIII, 438–44)

If I had seen that quaking spear in a shopping-mall scare movie, I would have abandoned the sticky floors and headed angrily for the door. Exploitation and dehumanization! Teenagers never *read* any-thing — that's why they love this grisly movie trash! Yet here is the image at the beginning of Western literature, and in its most famous book.

The quivering spear was hair-raising, though there were even more frightening images: eyeballs spitted on the ends of spears and held aloft in triumph, a blade entering at the mouth "so that the brazen spearhead smashed its way clean through below the brain in an upward stroke, and the white bones splintered." Homer records these mutilations with an apparent physical relish that can suddenly give way to bitter sorrow (this is one way the images differ from those in horror movies) and a yearning for ordinary life, a yearning expressed with just a phrase, a caress of nostalgia that he slips into the description of the mesmerizing catastrophe before us. The exultant violence is shot through with the most profound dismay. The Greeks, camped outside the walls of Troy, are far from home; but home, and everything lovely and proper and comfort-ing that might happen there, is evoked in heartbreaking flashes. There is the case of

> Simoeisios in his stripling's beauty, whom once his mother
> descending from Ida bore beside the banks of Simoeis
> when she had followed her father and mother to tend the
>   sheepflocks.
> Therefore they called him Simoeisios; but he could not
> render again the care of his dear parents; he was short-lived,
> beaten down beneath the spear of high-hearted Aias,
> who struck him as he first came forward beside the nipple
> of the right breast, and the bronze spearhead drove clean through
>   the shoulder.
> He dropped then to the ground in the dust, like some black poplar.
>   (IV, 474–82)

The nipple of the *right* breast. Homer in his terrifying exactness tells us where the spear comes in and goes out, what limbs are severed; he tells us that the dead will not return to rich soil, that they will not take care of parents, receive pleasure from their young wives. His explicitness has a finality beyond all illusion. In the end, the war (promoted by the gods) will consume almost all of them, Greeks and Trojans alike, sweeping on year after year, in battle after battle — a mystery in its irresistible momentum, its profoundly absorbing moment-to-moment activity and overall meaninglessness. First, one side drives forward, annihilates hundreds, and is on the edge of victory. Then, a few days later, the other side recovers, often inspired by some god's trick or phantasm — a prod to the sluggish brain of an exhausted warrior — and *that* side advances and carries all before it. When the poem opens, this movement back and forth has been going on for more than nine years.

The teacher, a small, compact man, about sixty, walked into the room and wrote some initials on the board:

> WASP
> DWM
> WC
> DGSI

While most of us tried to figure them out (I had no trouble with the first two, made a lame joke to myself about the third, and was stumped by the fourth), he turned, looked around the class, and said ardently, almost imploringly, "We've only got a year together." His tone was pleading and mournful, that of a lover who feared he might be thwarted. There was an alarming pause. A few students, embarrassed, looked down, and then he said, "This course has been under attack for thirty years. People have said" — he pointed to the top set of initials — "the writers were all white Anglo-Saxon Protestants. It's not true, but it doesn't matter. They've said they were all dead white males. It's not true, but it doesn't matter. That it's all Western Civilization. That's not quite true, either — there are many Western civilizations — but it doesn't matter. The only thing that matters is this."

He looked at us, then turned back to the board, considering the initials DGSI carefully, respectfully, rubbing his chin. "Don't Get Sucked In," he said at last. "Don't get sucked in by false ideas. You're not here for political reasons. You're here for very selfish reasons. You're here to build a self. You create a self; you don't inherit it. One way you create it is out of the past. Look, if you find *The Iliad* dull or invidious or a glorification of war, you're right. It's a poem in your mind; let it take shape in your mind."

Another pause, and I noticed the girl sitting next to me, who had wild frizzed hair and a mass of acne, opening her mouth in panic. Others were smiling. They were freshmen — sorry, *first-year students* — and were not literature majors, necessarily, but a cross-section of students, and therefore future lawyers, accountants, teachers, corporate executives, TV producers, doctors, computer programmers, poets, layabouts. They were taking Humanities: Masterpieces of European Literature and Philosophy — or Lit Hum, as everyone calls it — which is one of the two famous required core-curriculum courses at Columbia College. Lit Hum, which has been around since the late 1930s, is a standard "great books" course: it begins with Homer (both *The Iliad* and *The Odyssey*) and includes works by Sappho, the Greek dramatists, Thucydides, Plato, Aristotle, Virgil, the biblical writers, Augustine, Dante, Boccaccio, Montaigne, Shakespeare, Cervantes, Descartes, Goethe, Austen, and Woolf. The other required core-curriculum course is Contemporary Civilization, or C.C., which was devised in 1919. C.C. is an introduction to political and social theory and follows a similar trajectory, beginning with Plato and Aristotle and including Descartes, Locke, Rousseau, Kant, Hegel, Marx, Nietzsche, and Freud, and ending with whomever the individual instructor wants to use to bring things up to the present.

Lit Hum and C.C. are, in brief, precisely the kind of core courses in the literature, philosophy, and political thought of the West that have come under increasing attack in recent decades as "Eurocentric," "hegemonic," and, in general, inappropriate for a country whose population is made up of people from many places besides Europe — descendants of enslaved Africans and of American Indians, for instance. Such political attacks have had the effect of strengthening the drift of the sixties, when many universities, under pressure from student demands for more choice, retained the courses only as electives — which has meant, in practice, that Americans could graduate from a good college without having ever read the Bible, a play by Shakespeare, or a word of philosophy. In recent years, several universities that still required a course in the Western classics (most notoriously, Stanford) have modified the reading lists to include works from Latin America, Africa, and Asia, a move that threatens to turn the course into a pleasantly antinomian mishmash of traditions.

Columbia, though, despite some criticism from within the university, has preserved its core curriculum largely intact. A few women and minority authors were added to the reading lists in the early eighties, but both Lit Hum and C.C., and also two half-year courses in the art and music of the West, are still required of all undergraduates. And the college retains the form of the courses — as intensive seminars for young students. There are no lectures; Lit Hum and C.C. are taught entirely in sections, which might be led by anyone from a full professor, tenured for decades, to a fourth-year graduate student trying to make some money while writing her dissertation. Standing at the beginning of the student's college career, Lit Hum and C.C. were intended to provide an introduction to literary and intellectual study and a first glimpse of some of the leading values and debates of the West. Certain works have been so influential in the culture of the West that no one should graduate from college without reading them — that is the official rationale for the courses. The unofficial and unspoken rationale is "now or never" — that is, grab the students and make them read Sophocles, Kant, and Mill before those students disappear into their major subjects and specialized reading.

As a freshman at the college in 1961, I had taken Lit Hum and C.C. myself and had enjoyed them a good deal. I then largely forgot about them, as one forgets most college courses one takes; exactly how the books had remained in my mind, as a residue of impressions and a framework of taste and sensibility, and even action, I could not say. Having forgotten them as *courses,* I was amazed to discover, in the middle and late eighties, that such seemingly innocent selections of Western classics, and the Western "canon" in general, were coming under increasing fire from "the cultural left" in the universities, especially from a variety of feminist, Marxist, and African-American scholars. "As someone recently remarked," Carolyn G. Heilbrun, a former Columbia professor, wrote in the *Times* last year, "great-books courses teach young men to be warriors the first semester, priests the second; an exaggeration, but a small one." Most attacks, however, were not in this donnishly jocular vein. A typical radical critique of "the canon" denounced the list of books, and the standards by which such books were made classics, as "intellectual property" that had been first frozen as "timeless values" and then passed on from the ruling class of one era to that of the next. The books, in other words, were in some way tainted by their association with power.

A furious counterattack, of course, had also been mounted in the eighties, and the intellectual right, including such public officials as William Bennett and Lynne Cheney, had responded by maintaining that the classic works of the West possessed an almost redemptive political value — that studying the great works would preserve us from communism or anarchy or authoritarianism, or whatever barbarians were at the gates.

Reading here and there in this debate, I had been overtaken by an increasing sense of unreality. Almost no one, I noticed, appeared to be discussing the books themselves. Instead, the books had become a largely featureless abstraction, a weapon in an ideological war. What, I wondered, did one get out of actually reading a representative list of classics such as those in Columbia's core curriculum? What actually went on in the classroom? Could the books, grouped this way, really be as wicked as the cultural left — or as boring as the cultural right — was making them sound?

In the fall of 1991, thirty years after first entering Columbia, I went back to the university, sat in classes, and began to read the books of the two courses again. But how would I read them? That is, under the aegis of what method? The university literature departments, in their recent devotion to "theory," had so professionalized the act of reading that by 1987 the deconstructionist J. Hillis Miller (formerly of Yale) could remark that in the academy "a resistance to theory is in fact a resistance to reading." In response to this extraordinary statement, one should not make the mistake of underestimating the role played by earlier versions of today's literary theoreticians — medieval Schoolmen, say — in keeping the great works alive. But surely the books included in courses like Columbia's were originally composed not for academics but for the instruction or pleasure of ordinary educated readers. And so I wanted to see if I could read them again as I had read them once and as the eighteen- and nineteen-year-old students at Columbia were reading them now — unarmed, without benefit of the elaborate critical or historical framework that in so many American universities is now considered necessary mediation. "Contextualization," it's called.

"The women in *The Iliad*," the teacher was saying, "are honor gifts. They're war booty, like tripods. Less than tripods. If any male reading this poem treated women on campus as chattel, it would be very strange. I also trust you to read this and not go out and hack someone to pieces."

Ah, a hipster, I thought. He admitted the obvious charges against the course in order to minimize them. And he said nothing about transcendental values, supreme masterpieces of the West, and the rest of that. *We're here for selfish reasons.* The voice was pleasant but odd — baritonal, steady, but with traces of mockery garlanding the short, definitive sentences. The intonations drooped, as if he were laying black crape around his words. A hipster wit. He nearly droned, but there were little surprises — ideas inserted in the corners, a sudden expansion of feeling. He had sepulchral wit, like one of Shakespeare's solemnly antic clowns.

I remembered him well enough: Edward Tayler, professor of English. I had taken a course with him twenty-eight years earlier (he was a young instructor then) — not Lit Hum but a course in seventeenth-century metaphysical poetry — and I recalled having been baffled as much as intrigued by his manner, which definitely tended toward the cryptic. He liked to jump around, keep students off balance, hint and retreat; I learned a few things about Donne and Marvell, and left the class with a sigh of relief. In the interim, he had become famous as a teacher, and he was now the sonorously titled Lionel Trilling Professor in the Humanities — the moniker was derived from Columbia's most renowned English professor and critic, a great figure when I was there thirty years ago.

"The hermeneutic circle," he was saying. "That's what Dilthey called it. You don't know what to do with the details unless you have a grip on the structure, and at the same time, you don't know what to do with the structure unless you know the details. It's true in life and in literature. The hermeneutic circle. It's a vicious circle. Look, we have only a year together. You have to read. There's nothing you'll do in your four years at Columbia that's more important for selfish reasons than reading the books of this course. You're making a self. Read the books and see what version of them appears in your mind."

Could they become selves? From my position at one side of the classroom, I sneaked a look. The men sat with legs stretched all the way out, eyes down on their notes. Some wore caps turned backward. They were eighteen. In their T-shirts, jeans, and turned-around caps, they had a summer-camp thickness, like counselors just back from a hike with the ten-year-olds. *Give me a beer.* The women, also in T-shirts and jeans, many with their hair gathered at the back with a rubber band, were more directly attentive; they looked at Professor Tayler, but they looked blankly.

"Look, keep a finger on your psychic pulse as you go," he said, finishing up. "This is a very selfish enterprise."

By the time the action of *The Iliad* begins, the deed that set off the whole chain of events — a man making off with another man's wife — is barely mentioned by the participants. Paris, a prince of Troy, visiting the house of the Greek king Menelaus, took away, with her full consent, Helen, the king's beautiful wife. Agamemnon, the brother of the cuckold, then put together a loose federation of kings and princes, whose forces voyaged to Troy and laid siege to the city, intending to punish the proud inhabitants and reclaim Helen. But after nine years the foolish act of sexual abandonment that set the whole cataclysm in motion has been virtually forgotten. By this time, Helen considers herself merely a slut, and Paris, more a lover than a fighter, barely comes out to the battlefield. When he does come out, and he and Menelaus fight a kind of duel, the gods muddy the outcome, and the war goes on. After nine years, the war itself is causing the war.

It is almost too much, an extreme and bizarre work of literary art at the very beginning of Western literary art. One wants to rise to it, taking it full in the face, for the poem depicts life at its utmost, a nearly ceaseless activity of marshaling, deploying, advancing, and fleeing, spelled by peaceful periods so strenuous — the councils and feasts and games — that they hardly seem relief from battle. Reading the poem in its entirety is like fronting a storm that refuses to slacken or end. At first, I had to fight my way through it; I wasn't bored, but I was rebellious, my attention a bucking horse unwilling to submit to the harness. It was too long, I thought, too brutal and repetitive, and, for all its power as a portrait of war, strangely distant from us. Where was *Homer* in all this? He was everywhere, selecting and shaping the material; but he was nowhere a palpable presence, a consciousness, and for the modern reader his absence was appalling. No one tells us how to react to the brutalities or to anything else. We are on our own. Movie-fed, I wasn't used to working so hard, and as I sat on my couch at home, reading, my body, in daydreams, kept leaping away from the soft seat and into the bedroom to sink into bed, or to the kitchen, where I would open the fridge. Mentally, I would pull myself back, and eventually I settled down and read and read, though I remained out of balance and sore for a long time.

Other men may have more active recollections — scoring a goal, kissing a girl at the homecoming game, all that autumn-air, pocket-flask Scott Fitzgerald stuff — but my sweetest memory of college is on the nuzzling, sedate side. At the beginning of each semester, I would stand before the books required for my courses, prolonging the moment, like a kid looking through a store window at a bicycle he knows his parents will buy for him. I would soon possess these things, but the act of buying them could be put off. Why rush it? The required books for each course were laid out on shelves in the college bookstore, and I would stare at them a long time, lifting them, turning the pages, pretending I didn't really *need* this one or that, laying it down and then picking it up again. If no one was looking, I would even smell a few of them and feel the pages — I had a thing about books as physical objects, and I was happy when I discovered that Edmund Wilson, my idol, also had strong feelings about the feel and size of a book.

It wasn't just reading that excited me but the *idea* of reading the big books, the promise of enlargement, the adventure of strangeness. The love of reading has within it a collector's passion, the desire to possess: I would swallow the whole store. Reality never entered into this. The difficulty or the tedium of the books, the droning performance of the teacher, the blanking out of my own attention in a post-midterm swoon — none of this mattered at the moment of anticipation, which was renewed each term. I might have spent most of the previous semester in a self-absorbed funk, but I roused myself at the beginning of the new semester for the wonderful ritual of the bookstore. Each time I stood there, I saw myself serenely absorbing everything, though I was such an abominably slow reader, chewing until the flavor was nearly gone, that I never quite got around to completing the reading list of any course.

And so it has been ever since. Walking home from midtown Manhattan, I am drawn helplessly to a bookstore — Coliseum Books, at Broadway and Fifty-seventh, will do — where I will buy two or three books, which then, often enough, sit on my shelves for years, unread or partly read, until finally, trying to look something up, I will pull one or another out, bewildered that I have it. I like to *own* them: I had grown into a book buyer but not always a book reader — a boon to the book trade, perhaps, but not a boon to myself.

Reading, after eating and sex one of the most natural, central, and satisfying of all acts, had, amazingly, become a vexed experience. I read a great deal, sometimes I read all day long, but most of the stuff was journalism, essays, criticism, or novels that had been adapted into movies and that I needed to check on before writing my weekly movie reviews for a New York magazine, or books by writers whom I never missed (Philip Roth, Saul Bellow, John le Carré) and whose work seemed less like something new than a reacquaintance with trusted friends. But what did I *read?* I mean read seriously? Reading *Swann's Way* was a rapturous experience not likely to be succeeded by the rest of *Remembrance of Things Past.* To read anything as densely, lusciously detailed as Proust, you have to set aside a special time, at least ninety minutes of quiet, and though there are people I know who get up early to read Proust, or even a decent new American novel, I couldn't get myself up early, and if I could I would make coffee and read the *Times* in peace before the boys hit the kitchen. My wife, whose life was certainly as disrupted and jangled as mine, still read a great deal, book after book, sometimes plowing straight through an author's entire work. But I no longer had the concentration or the discipline for serious reading; I had lost the habit of just falling into something, the way real readers do, devouring it on the bus, in the tub, at a lunch counter. Movies more than satisfied my desire for trash, but when I picked up a serious book my concentration wandered after twenty pages. My rhythm had changed. I was a moviegoer, a magazine reader, a CNN watcher. Following a breaking story on CNN, I would watch updates at certain points during the day, then pick up the story again when a car alarm woke me in the middle of the night, then catch the dénouement in the morning. This business of being "informed" could be almost nightmarish: if you stayed with a story long enough, you began to feel as if you were a ball rolling over and over, or the hands of a clock coming back to the same point.

Going back to school would force me to read the whole shelf in the bookstore. In going back, I would not be searching for my youth — a ghoulish thought. Youth, I now saw, was the most over-praised time of life. Not only was it wasted on the young; it was a waste, period. When you're young, you can't enjoy power or watch your own kids playing, and the money you spend mostly belongs to your parents. I hated being young and relished being middle-aged (more than you were supposed to, more than most people would admit), but I longed for, well, another *chance,* another time spent reading seriously, another shot at school. I longed to submit myself to something greater than my career.

At the age of forty-eight, I stood in front of the shelves in Columbia's bookstore, at Broadway and 115th Street — a larger and better-lit place than the old store from my day, which was so tightly packed that one never got away from that slightly sweet smell that new books have. I was absurdly excited. There they were, the books for the Lit Hum and C.C. courses: the two thick paper-back volumes of Homer; the elegant Penguin editions of Aeschylus and Hobbes, with their black borders and uniform typeface; the rather severe-looking academic editions of Rousseau and Locke, all business, with no designs on the covers or backs, just the titles, and, within, rows of rather ugly-looking type — they were as densely printed as law books. I was thrilled by the possibility that they might be *difficult.* I would read, I would study, I would sit with teenagers.

How can a book make one feel injured and exhilarated at the same time? What's shocking about *The Iliad* is that the nobility and the cruelty of it seem inseparable, like the good and evil twins of some malign fantasy who together form a single unstable and dangerous personality.

Western literature begins with a quarrel over booty between two arrogant pirates. At the beginning of the poem, the various tribes of Greeks who have assembled before the walls of Troy are on the verge of disaster. Agamemnon, their leader and the most powerful of the kings, has kidnapped from a nearby city and taken as a mistress the daughter of one of Apollo's priests, and the god has retaliated by bringing down a plague on them. A peevish, bullying king, unsteady in command, Agamemnon, under pressure from the other leaders, angrily gives the girl back to her father. But then, demanding compensation, he takes the concubine of Achilles, his greatest warrior. Achilles is so outraged by this bit of plundering within the ranks that he comes close to killing Agamemnon, a much older man. Restraining himself, Achilles retires from combat, praying to his mother, the goddess Thetis, for the defeat of his own side; he then sits in his tent playing a lyre and "singing of men's fame" as his friends get cut up by the Trojans.

Can Achilles really be the first hero of our literature? He seems a fool, an infantile narcissist. The first word of the poem is *mnin* — in old Greek, "rage" or "wrath." Homer means Achilles' rage, the kind of rage that has an element of divine fury in it and destroys armies and breaks cities. But to us Achilles' anger seems less divine than egotistical. His war booty has been stolen by another man. Is not the immense size of his anger almost absurdly out of proportion to its cause? Yet Achilles dominates the poem even as he withdraws; his moody self-preoccupation is part of what makes him fascinating. He creates an aura: we understand something of who he is from Marlon Brando's glamorously sullen performances in his youth. A greater destiny flows from Achilles' angry will than from the settled desires of simpler men.

He is very young, perhaps in his early twenties, fearless, tall, fleet-footed, strong, a compound of muscle and beauty with so powerful a sense of his own precedence that he is willing to let the war go badly when his honor is sullied. The Trojans, led by their stalwart, Hector, kill many Greeks and come close to burning the Greek ships and cutting off their retreat. Hoping to stem the tide, Achilles' tentmate and beloved friend Patroclus enters the battle. He wears Achilles' armor, and in that armor — as a substitute for Achilles — he is slain by Hector.

Achilles' withdrawal now comes to an end. Enraged, inconsolable, he prepares at last to enter the battle. (We are deep into the poem, and we have not yet seen him fight.) The sky darkens, the underworld nearly cracks open. Huge forces, unstoppable, move into place. Achilles begins to fight, expelling his anguish in a rampage. As Book XXI opens, he is driving the Trojans back toward Troy:

> But when they came to the crossing place of the fair-running river
> of whirling Xanthos, a stream whose father was Zeus the immortal,

there Achilleus split them and chased some back over the flat land
toward the city, where the Achaians themselves had stampeded in
  terror
on the day before, when glorious Hektor was still in his fury.
Along this ground they were streaming in flight; but Hera let fall
a deep mist before them to stay them. Meanwhile the other half
were crowded into the silvery whirls of the deep-running river
and tumbled into it in huge clamour, and the steep-running water
sounded, and the banks echoed hugely about them, as they
  out-crying
tried to swim this way and that, spun about in the eddies.
As before the blast of a fire the locusts escaping
into a river swarm in air, and the fire unwearied
blazes from a sudden start, and the locusts huddle in water;
so before Achilleus the murmuring waters of Xanthos
the deep-whirling were filled with confusion of men and of horses.

But heaven-descended Achilleus left his spear there on the bank
leaning against the tamarisks, and leapt in like some immortal,
with only his sword, but his heart was bent upon evil actions,
and he struck in a circle around him. The shameful sound of their
  groaning
rose as they were struck with the sword, and the water was reddened
with blood. As before a huge-gaping dolphin the other fishes
escaping cram the corners of a deepwater harbour
in fear, for he avidly eats up any he can catch;
so the Trojans along the course of the terrible river
shrank under the bluffs. He, when his hands grew weary with killing,
chose out and took twelve young men alive from the river
to be vengeance for the death of Patroklos, the son of Menoitios.
These, bewildered with fear like fawns, he led out of the water
and bound their hands behind them with thongs well cut out of
  leather,
with the very belts they themselves wore on their ingirt tunics,
and gave them to his companions to lead away to the hollow ships,
then himself whirled back, still in a fury to kill men.

(XXI, 1–33)

Homer didn't have to tell his listeners that the leather thongs,
tightening as they dried, would cut into the skin of Achilles' Trojan
captives. Nor did he have to explain why Achilles, both the noblest
and the cruelest of the heroes, later kills a Trojan warrior, an
acquaintance, who begs for mercy at his knees. They would not

have praised Achilles, or anyone else, for withholding his sword in battle.

The American reader comes from a society that is nominally ethical. Our legal and administrative system, our presidential utterances, our popular culture, in which TV policemen rarely fail to care for the victims of crime, are swathed in concern. Since many Americans believe that our society is actually indifferent to hardship, it is no surprise that irony and cynicism barnacle our attitudes toward public life. By contrast, the Greek view was savage, but it was offered without hypocrisy. Accepting death in battle as inevitable, the Greek and Trojan aristocrats of *The Iliad* experience the world not as pleasant or unpleasant, or as good and evil, but as glorious or shameful. Homer offers a noble rather than an ethical conception of life. You are not good or bad. You are strong or weak, beautiful or ugly, conquering or vanquished, favored by the gods or cursed.

Academic opponents of courses in the Western classics are constantly urging readers to consider "the other": the other cultures, odd to Western tastes, that we have allegedly trampled or rendered marginal, and also the others who are excluded or trivialized within our own culture — women, people of color, anyone who is non-white, non-male, non-Western. But here, in *The Iliad,* written perhaps in the eighth century B.C., is something like "the other": a race of noble barbarians, stripping corpses of their armor and reciting their genealogies at one another during huge feasts and even on the field of battle. Kill, plunder, bathe, eat, offer libations to Athena — what do we have to do with these ancient pirates of the eastern Mediterranean? They address each other with elaborate ceremony, boasts, and threats of violence. Here was "the other," and right at the beginning of our tradition.

From where I sat, on the steps of Low Library, watching them walk around the Columbia campus on the second day of school, the students looked serious, a bit gloomy, and tense. The recession was still on, the tuition was a fortune (about twenty-three thousand dollars, including room and board), and even though many of them received aid, they probably needed more money. They had spent the summer working, I would bet. Anyway, Columbia students never did look too healthy. In my day, the college was heavily populated with city Jews and Italian-Americans, bookish, sallow young men (like me), preoccupied with Sartre and Kafka and Beethoven and the Modern Jazz Quartet, and we smoked — unfiltered cigarettes, mostly, in the Bogart imitation fashionable in the early sixties. We weren't the only students, of course. In fact, we were a minority, my friends and I — English and history majors heading for careers in law, teaching, and journalism — but we had created our own snobbish version of Columbia, which centered on such famous writers (and fairly recent students) as Allen Ginsberg and Jack Kerouac, and such English teachers as Trilling and his chief disciple, Steven Marcus. There were also the students I thought of as Ivy League boys — noble oarsmen, I called them, who had a haughty but depressed air about them, as if they were disappointed not to be at Princeton. I was prejudiced against them, not only because their manners were different from ours but because they were so often in good shape. Now the male students were generally in better physical shape; they almost all had some muscle tone (infra dig among intellectual students in 1961).

More important, the students weren't all males anymore: women had been admitted in 1982 and now made up half the college. And the size of the minority population had grown. Walking into another Lit Hum section the first week of the semester (I was sampling different approaches), I had nodded to a few students, and then a few more, and had suddenly realized that the class was utterly unlike the ones I had sat in thirty years earlier. In this class of twenty-two first-year students, there were exactly four white males. The students were from Europe, India, Singapore. O America! They were from everywhere. But why was I so surprised? Did I *want* a predominance of white males in the class? In my memory of Lit Hum thirty years ago, half the men sat glumly through the required course, regarding it grouchily as an onerous way station along the road to serious work in physics, history, or chemical engineering. Few words escaped their lips, though they would emit a low whistle of disapproval when an exam was announced. I was not sure I missed them much. Still, an old-grad memory bank had been jolted. If you are a man over forty, you simply do not realize, until you walk into a classroom, how pluralistic American university education has become.

On the first day of the other required great-books course — Contemporary Civilization — I heard a youthful assistant professor of

history, Anders Stephanson, ask a puzzled class if they would agree
that the statement "John F. Kennedy was killed on November 22,
1963," could be called "objective." When most of them murmured
yes, he pointed out that the date was a convention and that "a
whole series of hegemonic processes" accounted for telling time
according to the Christian calendar and not, say, the Chinese or
Jewish calendar; and that the books of the C.C. course — the Bible,
Descartes, Kant, Mill, et al. — similarly followed the "material development" of Western Europe, the domination of Europe.

So there, I thought, I've heard it, and in my first C.C. class.
Nothing could be called objective, nothing could be taken as
natural or universal — not even a date. Such was a principal conviction of the "cultural left," the academic insurgents eager to
destroy the certainty of Westerners that their ideas and institutions
embodied a universal norm. The reading list, however traditional,
was the result of an arbitrary process. That the books had survived
for so long was proof not of their universality but of the opposite
— that they were part of a tradition that had triumphed *politically*.
Stephanson didn't even call them "books." He used the standard
new-academic word "texts," which has a deromanticized, disillu-
sioned sound. The texts "represent a condensation of a certain way
of putting education before students and saying what is culture
and what isn't," he said. "It isn't an innocent list." This notion that
lists were not innocent was central to attacks on "the canon." Such
lists reeked of exclusion. "The teaching of literature *is* the teaching
of values," Henry Louis Gates, Jr., wrote in 1990. "Not inherently,
no, but contingently, yes; it is — it has become — the teaching of
an aesthetic and political order, in which no women or people of
color were ever able to discover the reflection or representation
of their images, or hear the resonances of their cultural voices."
Gates was arguing not for the dissolution of the traditional canon
but for its enlargement to include those missing voices. Many
others went much further, however — into a kind of philosophical
attack on the hierarchies of judgment which produced lists of
classics in the first place. Such lists (and not just Columbia's)
amounted to a unitary, or almost unitary, sensibility and set of
values, which elected itself as central, even universal, in an endless
process of self-confirmation, rather like a club that insisted on the
superiority of its own members while refusing to recognize the
qualities of anyone else. What was presented in this tradition as

"universal" (so the argument went) actually represented no more than the experience and the drive to power of a single group. Universality was not only a false claim, a mystique and an imposture; it was political in its intentions and effects. "The canon," far from being a mere anodyne collection of remarkable works, was a key element in the "hegemony" of white Euro-American males, a disguised ideological spearhead of such Western modes, good and bad, as individualism, market capitalism, imperialism, racism, and sexism.

Professor Stephanson, it turned out, agreed with the radical analysis but not with the radical solution. He saw no reason that a society should not inculcate in its élites the society's leading values. If Tayler, in his Lit Hum section, was saying, "These books will form you," Stephanson was saying, "These books have been *selected* to form you." Yet, as I sat there, I felt not dismay but something like a warming swell of pride. The idea was almost titillating. *We* were the objects of this immense historical process that had been going on since the flowering of Greek literature.

"Think shape, how it's put together, rather than what the characters feel or don't feel," Professor Tayler was saying in the second meeting of the class. "*The Iliad* is not a simple glorification of war; something else is happening here. And the something else requires an epic reading."

Enough initials; this was the real thing, the nuts and bolts of literary analysis. He was working with the class on the structure of the huge poem, getting them to see large, overall movements and then smaller movements and patterns within limited blocks, giving them a handle on the sprawling text which suddenly began to seem not nearly so sprawling. Tayler could be called a historian of ideas, but when he dealt directly with a text he used a method derived from the New Criticism — the dominant approach in the teaching of literature in my days as an undergraduate. New Criticism had actually become rather rare, and Tayler was attempting to do something that some would now regard as impossible or delusional — to let the text "speak for itself."

He didn't simply tell the students what he wanted, of course. Imploring and urging, he pulled it out of them, asking leading questions, dropping hints, making them read aloud passages that had no apparent connection, passages spaced far apart in the poem. At times, the class stalled, and he retreated from his point, literally stepping backward and letting his head drop for a moment before approaching from another angle, like a guerrilla force making tentative forays through the jungle. Eventually, he would coax them out of hiding and surround them.

Trapped, a student spoke.

"Um, because Achilles calls this guy he's, y'know, about to kill, 'Friend'?"

The students stumbled a lot, speaking in broken fragments. Some of them would start and then trail off or just stare blankly when Tayler called on them, and suddenly, even though I knew he wasn't going to call on me, my palms began to sweat and I looked down at my notebook, because I didn't always know the answer, either, and school, *school*, came flooding back — a time when I often didn't know the answer. Even worse, he was the kind of teacher who kept a student on the spot, trying to rattle the kid's brain until the answer, lost in the bottom drawers of sloth and forgetfulness, suddenly fell out — something I always hated, because in that situation my brain would usually lock up. Fortunately, he seemed to understand that there was no point in just waiting. When a student went into lockup, he would move away to someone else, or he would take what the student had said, however minimal, and play with it, enlarging it so it made some kind of sense, and then weave it together with the three or four intelligible words that someone *else* had said; and soon these two half-mute students, still flushed with embarrassment, were described as *building* something together, or even as having a full-fledged "disagreement." Which was funny, since neither of them was aware of having said much of anything. Sometimes, emboldened by Tayler's magic tricks, the students would begin talking and actually become the rabbits he had pulled out of the hat. He began as a con artist and ended up holding the class by its ears.

Why was structure so important? The class was a little ragged, but he kept working at it, jumping all over the poem. Would he tie together all the loose ends? Suspense gathered in the spaces between his summarizing remarks. He worked on, say, five books of the poem at a time, getting the students to see a recurring pattern of oaths, truces, duels, and feasts, and after an hour or so (the class met for two hours twice a week) they were beginning to do it without much prodding: they were finding the symmetries — "ring composition," he called it — in which chunks of structural elements returned in the poem but with the elements in reverse order. Then, suddenly, he went to the board and drew something.

"What's this?"

"Cat," said a student named Hurewitz.

"Yeah. And" — Tayler made a new drawing — "Hurewitz, what's this?"

"Rat," said Hurewitz.

"*Rat?* Hurewitz, *c'mon!*"

"Oh, um . . . pig!"

"Yeah. Pig. See, your cultural baggage is novels, movies, and TV; you're used to reading for characters and psychological development. So you can recognize the cat. But if your cultural baggage doesn't let you see the squiggle on the tail, you're lost, you're still lapping milk instead of heading for the trough. This poem isn't a novel." He crossed out the cat. "It's a piggy epic. In all these instances, I've been asking you to look at the squiggle on the tail — asking you to look at a mind that works differently. It's an epic — it works by circles and symmetries. Look, it's a poem about wrath, about a special kind of wrath. Achilles drops out and sits sulking in his tent for days. So what's all this other stuff doing there — the battles and the other heroes? We study all these minor heroes and these patterns because they exemplify different aspects of the heroic code. Then we understand what Achilles means, because he violates the code."

Smiles broke out, relief. The mystification was over — for the time being.

"Intellectual thumbscrews have been applied, and I'm sorry. I apologize for it. What I've been trying to do is to teach you how to read the older works of art. You have to read something from another culture. There's no psychology in this poem, no conflict between free will and determinism, no subjective and objective. It's an epic — all foreground. See, it's not a random collection of battles: each part gets its emotional counterpart later. As soon as you get used to it, you can get rid of me, which will be a relief to you. You get rid of me, and you get you."

Suddenly, everyone looked up. How would that happen?

The formal approach, I could see, was Tayler's defense against banality. He mentioned the contemporary resistance to reading *The Iliad.* There had been a time in the late eighties at Columbia when the yearly prospect of reading the poem in Lit Hum had been greeted by a chorus of dismay from some of the younger faculty. It was a poem that oppressed women and glorified war, and it had an infantile hero, and so on. I smiled to myself, because I was thinking some of this myself, and without the benefit of critical theory. Tayler didn't say so in so many words, but I gathered that his opinion was that any idiot could see those things, and you could see them and think you were saying something, while never seeing what the epic poem *was* about. By appropriating it to some modern perception of class, power, gender — none of which much applied to Homer — you made the poem meaningless. The older classics, he implied, would not live if the books were turned into a mere inadequate version of the present.

I got that part, but I still didn't see how studying the poem formally was going to reveal the students to themselves. Did he mean it, or was it just a conceit? Because if he did mean it, it was a tremendous promise — and a frightening one. Did they want to be mucked around with so openly — the girl just out of high school, with long straight hair and a serene way about her; the big guy from California with his legs sprawled out; the Korean boy who said little to anyone but was awfully polite? As for me, the last thing I had wanted at eighteen was to be revealed to myself. And at forty-eight? Maybe it was too late.

There was a logic at the heart of the argument against "the canon" which some outsiders found bizarre. Take the situation of women students, for instance. For thousands of years, women generally had been denied higher education and also discouraged from heroic composition in literature, philosophy, painting, and so on. But if until, say, about the seventeenth century this infamous double prohibition had caused women in the West to produce little of superlative value — or little of superlative value which has survived — how could this disaster be used as an argument *against* women's now studying the masterpieces of the past? For women had gained full access to the universities at last. Shouldn't they use it, in part, to study what earlier women had been forced to study on their own or not at all? In *A Room of One's Own,* written in 1929, Virginia Woolf had spoken again and again about how it would take not just financial independence but generations of education, and the work of many minor writers, to produce great literature by women. First, women needed to get into the libraries and universities; they needed a thorough grounding in the great work of the past. But wasn't the cultural left — by suggesting that women were in some way "oppressed" by reading works that didn't "represent" them — in effect discouraging women yet again, this time with the highest motives, from studying the works that Woolf thought they needed to read? And wasn't the same underlying logic at work in the insistence that minorities newly admitted into the university should read work that "represented" them, rather than the classic works that their parents had had no chance to read?

Columbia did not accept that logic. It rejected the notion that the reading list of either Lit Hum or C.C. should represent the ethnic and gender composition of the students taking the courses. Representation wasn't the issue. In an opening-day C.C. section taught by Professor Wim Smit — a Dutch-born history professor and then the head of the C.C. program — the question of black writers and black representation had been raised, with some heat, by a black woman student. "Where were *my* people while all this was going on?" she asked. "We were *there.*" And Smit, sighing slightly, had said, "They were *there,* but they weren't part of the influence on America. Has Chinese political thinking influenced American political thought? Our free-market economy led to, and molded, our individualistic thinking. African community organization has led to a very different way of thinking — the ideology of community-based organization."

Smit's argument for sticking to the classics, then, was historical *influence.* America's principal institutions — its political and economic system, its language, its jurisprudence, its moral imperatives — were derived from England and Western Europe as filtered through the Founding Fathers and the early political, religious, and intellectual leaders. The C.C. reading list represented the evidence of history, a judgment offered without regard to the feelings of blacks, Latinos, Asians, Native Americans, or the many others who had played a large role in the actual building of the country, its railroads, cities, farms, and so on — without regard to anyone who had created its folk culture, its popular speech and humor and music, rather than its legal and market institutions.

In part, Smit was free to make his case for an unchanged C.C. because the university, recognizing the force of such complaints as the black student's, had taken action outside the course. In 1988, Columbia agreed that the two great-books courses, as well as the required courses in Western art and music, might induce a limited and complacent perspective. The college therefore decided to add what it called at the time "the extended core" — the further requirement that all undergraduates take either two half-year courses in another culture (say, Modernist Thought in the Arab World or Latin-American Literature in Translation) or one culture course and a course in contemporary issues (say, Introduction to Gender, Development, and Empowerment or Disease in Modern History). In 1991, the compromise struck many students that I spoke to as a fair one, though the rubric "extended core" rankled some minority students, who felt that it had the sound of an afterthought. By the spring of 1992, the college had changed the name of the requirement to "Cultures and Issues." Columbia had adroitly satisfied both traditional and reformist constituencies, keeping its core curriculum intact while requiring students to look across borders.

When the Greek and Trojan warriors in *The Iliad* fall, they go down heavily, slowly, like great oaks, with all their lineages, stories, lands, and animals crashing down with them. The slaughter is huge but never impersonal. You feel each death freshly, as a blow; you never go numb. Everything in the poem has remarkable weight and consequence, even the warriors' boasts. The men address one another formally, recounting the family honors and triumphs: the spears taken from fallen enemies; the shields, helmets, and corselets, all taken "in the pride of their shining." Genteel modern taste forbids boasting (a winner never boasts), but the Homeric vaunting has a far different flavor from, say, two Mafia dons comparing turf. The shining helmets would not be so valuable if the men who wore them had not been of heroic quality. Glory is possible everywhere: it is the helmets in the *pride* of their shining.

Nor is Homer ever indifferent to the ceremonies attendant on behavior or possessions. He insists on the fitness of things. Calling this a "heroic code" doesn't capture the prescriptive and celebratory force of it. Feasting and acts of warfare and of sacrifice to the gods can be performed properly in only one way — superbly, with utmost effort and lavish skill and maximum exposure to failure. Again: nothing could be further from our world. The absence of pity was only the first shock. The second came slowly and was perhaps more a frightened realization than a shock: the splendor of *The Iliad*, the magnificence of earth, air, and weather and the clash of arms, would not be fully possible if the ethical component ruled the poem. Physical exultation blazes out, untrammeled. It is not a humanist work, and it can't be made into one (though many have tried). When I understood this — and Tayler helped a lot — I stopped fighting the poem. I relaxed; I began to enjoy it, though my attention still wandered away. Imps of distraction invaded my paradise. They came unbidden, summoned by some charge of energy in the poem which would draw from my unconscious a daydream or a series of daydreams — I was a warrior, forging mighty prose — and then I would snap out of it and five minutes had passed, a little pocket of time gone forever.

Surely my concentration was patchier than it once was. As a teenager, I had sat on my bed in my parents' apartment in New York, looking up from my book only to study the pattern of woolen threads in the thick afghan lying on the bed. Green, brown, green, brown . . . and then back to Dickens or Tolstoy. I can no longer *submit* to fiction in that way; I read and stop, read and stop, a train halted by obstacles on the track, bad weather, power failures. Everyone complains that young people, growing up on TV, movies, and rap music, lack the patience for a long, complex narrative, and yet as a child I had not watched much television, and the same thing had happened to me in middle age. Had all the movies I'd seen in the last thirty years broken the circuits, sending the lines helter-skelter? A gloomy idea, for if it's true, my thoughts, such as they were, were doomed to incompleteness, haplessly shifting perspectives, manic intrusions. Snurfling gremlins were moving the furniture around. My thoughts were mediated.

But could movies really be the culprit? My moviegoing friends did not complain of poor concentration. Anyway, with two kids running around, a clever wife, and multiple jobs, I had more to think about than I had had at eighteen. A much larger experience was now casting up its echoes. Perhaps daydreaming was not simply wasted time but an elaboration, a sort of disguised commentary from the deep. Perhaps it was a relief from the ferocity of the poem, too.

How can a man who stays out of the action through many days (and many thousands of lines), angrily keeping to his tent as friends and enemies die, remain the hero of an epic? The answer to this question suggests why *The Iliad,* for all its frightening strangeness, its violence and barbarity, will not easily yield its place or its predominance at the beginning of our literary tradition.

The crux of the poem comes in Book IX, well before Achilles reenters the war. As the Trojans wait at their night fires, ready to attack at dawn, the Greeks, now in serious trouble, send three ambassadors to Achilles with promises of gifts. Tripods, cauldrons, horses, gold, slave women, one of Agamemnon's daughters as a future bride, and even the return of Achilles' slave mistress, whom Agamemnon swears he has never touched — what more can Achilles ask for? According to the warrior code that they all live by, he should take the gifts and return to battle. His honor had been assaulted; now it has been satisfied.

Achilles' initial answer, a staggering Shakespearean speech of a hundred and twenty-two lines, composed in shifting planes of thought and emotion, sounds unlike anything else in the poem, for it shows a man struggling to say what has never been said, or even imagined, before that instant. If the other warriors all hold forth with the awareness of family traditions, honors, trophies, and plunder supporting their words, he speaks only for himself:

> For as I detest the doorways of Death, I detest that man, who
> hides one thing in the depths of his heart, and speaks forth another.
> But I will speak to you the way it seems best to me: neither

do I think the son of Atreus, Agamemnon, will persuade me,
nor the rest of the Danaans, since there was no gratitude given
for fighting incessantly forever against your enemies.
Fate is the same for the man who holds back, the same if he fights
   hard.
We are all held in a single honour, the brave with the weaklings.
A man dies still if he has done nothing, as one who has done much.
Nothing is won for me, now that my heart has gone through its
   afflictions
in forever setting my life on the hazard of battle.
For as to her unwinged young ones the mother bird brings back
morsels, wherever she can find them, but as for herself it is suffering,
such was I, as I lay through all the many nights unsleeping,
such as I wore through the bloody days of the fighting,
striving with warriors for the sake of these men's women. . . .
                                   Of possessions
cattle and fat sheep are things to be had for the lifting,
and tripods can be won, and the tawny high heads of horses,
but a man's life cannot come back again, it cannot be lifted
nor captured again by force, once it has crossed the teeth's barrier.
                           (IX, 312–27; 405–09)

The hero turns out to be a hero after all. Achilles' rage, which
had seemed almost infantile, a narcissistic wound at most — he
had lost his war booty, his slave mistress, to Daddy — has had the
remarkable effect of stunning this haughty young man into a new
conception of war. Suddenly, he is groping toward an idea of honor
that doesn't depend on the bartering of women and goods or on
the opinions that men have of one another's prowess. "We are all
held in a single honour. . . . A man dies still if he has done
nothing, as one who has done much." For the greatest warrior in
the world, that is a devastating admission. From our point of view,
Achilles has jumped forward to a private, or even spiritual, sense
of worth: honor is a matter between a man and Zeus or between
a man and himself, and in the end, no one can be compensated
for the death of another; the worth of life is immeasurable. When
you read this speech against the behavior and the speeches of the
other heroes (as Tayler did with his class), you see that Achilles
has come close to breaking with the honor/shame code of Homer's
warrior society. He has made an attempt, not always successful, to
reach consciousness itself, the consciousness that (for a modern
reader) has been missing from the poem.

The first hero of consciousness can go only so far; his revolt is incomplete. After Patroclus is slain, Achilles' wrath turns into personal rage at Hector, Patroclus' slayer, and he goes on a rampage (as we've seen), killing everyone in sight; he sacrifices the twelve young men taken in the river, pushes the Trojan army back into the city, and finally kills Hector, whose body he drags around for days. Sleepless and unappeasable, unreachable, he has gone mad with grief.

Now, in the complacent, "humanist" reading of *The Iliad,* Achilles achieves completeness as a hero at the end of the poem. He gives Hector's body back to the great warrior's father — Priam, the king of Troy. In the scene of Priam's supplication of Achilles, in Book XXIV ("I have gone through what no other mortal on earth has gone through; I put my lips to the hands of the man who has killed my children"), one of the most moving things in all literature, Achilles attains compassion (so the reading goes) and is ready to die. Homer ends the poem with the burial of Hector, but we know that Achilles has chosen glory and an early death rather than a comfortable middle age in the safety of his father's land. His character improved, Achilles gives up cruelty and rejoins the community, and will die as a hero fulfilled.

But this is too pat; it's Sunday-school stuff, or perhaps a Lit Hum reading from fifty years ago. If that were all the poem added up to — the maturing of an arrogant young man — one could more easily agree with those people ready to give *The Iliad* a rest. But it isn't so. Rage such as Achilles', once awakened, cannot be silenced, for it takes on a new cruelty, the cruelty of thought: the questions he asks about war and death remain unanswered in the poem, because they cannot be answered. *The Iliad,* for all its vaunting glory, remains in tension with itself, questioning, and even subverting, its own ethos, and it leaves one profoundly uneasy. I felt relief and also a kind of awe when it ended. Could this be the same work that some had castigated as a mere insensible celebration of war? Surely that reading was a mistake, even a malicious mistake. Achilles knows he will attain immortal renown as a hero, yet he's the only one who takes the measure of death. One imagines him at the end of the poem as still inconsolable and unconsoling, still raging somewhere outside the walls. The written civilization of the West begins with a hero who both embodies and questions the nature of civilization as it was then constituted.

*

A white male and a bourgeois, a man who was reared on the culture of the West, I am not an imperialist, exactly, but I write from within the walls of the imperium and enjoy its protections. Seen from the outside, or by the cultural left, that is my identity. But only as seen from outside. For how could identity defined by race, gender, and class (the cultural left's inescapable trinity) account for the use that any of us make of the cards we've been dealt? Or for the way we feel about our own experience? And so, as I was finishing *The Iliad*, I remembered — I now remembered — that at eighteen, as a freshman reading both core-curriculum courses, I had been dismayed by Homer's war poem. A young man suffering the self-conscious torments of eighteen, I measured the difference between myself and Homer's heroes, and I was not happy about it. I was overawed by physical courage and by the poem's grandeur, which I experienced as a taunt.

In the interim, I had become a middle-class New York householder and father. I now enjoyed thick walls, fitted cotton sheets, and Pellegrino water on the dinner table; and when I read *The Iliad* again it troubled me in a different way. The poem's amoral magnificence, the unhoused splendor of air, feasts, and fire, resounded with the savage celebration of physical joy, whose excesses — once the shock wore off — became almost completely intoxicating. Which left one, at the very least, with a considerably diminished satisfaction in sheets and Pellegrino water. Middle-class life was no more than a pleasant compromise compared with

> As when along the thundering beach the surf of the sea strikes
> beat upon beat as the west wind drives it onward; far out
> cresting first on the open water, it drives thereafter
> to smash roaring along the dry land, and against the rock jut
> bending breaks itself into crests spewing back the salt wash;
> so thronged beat upon beat the Danaans' close battalions
> steadily into battle, with each of the lords commanding
> his own men.
>
> (IV, 422–29)

I don't mean to imply that *The Iliad*'s power can be measured by the distress it causes a single middle-class reader. A great work of art is likely to be subversive of almost anyone's peace. *The Iliad* contests most of our current ideas about what is right and wrong, what is true, what is heroic, and, finally, what is human.

If the West enjoys a moral advantage over other cultures, the advantage lies in placing a high value on the experience of being unsettled. It esteems self-criticism perhaps as much as self-confirmation, and as I walked out of Tayler's last class on *The Iliad,* watching the students race down the stairs ahead of me, I wondered how the students' future experience of the Western "canon" could possibly conform to the most dire descriptions of the cultural left. And how could the rest of the books, if they were anywhere near as disturbing as *The Iliad,* serve as William Bennett's bulwark against disorder? My experience left me dismayed by the use both left and right were making of "the canon." Was Columbia's — or anyone's — version of the Western classics likely to be a monolith that either simply crushed or "empowered"? Or would the books appear to the students as a porous, unstable tradition, in which the works turned out to be at odds with one another, or even at odds with themselves — less a devouring beast than a snake that twists, writhes, folds back on itself, and occasionally bites its own tail?

ANDRE DUBUS III

Tracks and Ties

FROM EPOCH

YEARS LATER, when I was twenty-six, she said in the *New York Times* you would tie her naked and spread-eagled on the bed, that you would take a bat to her. She said you'd hit her for any reason. But in Haverhill, Massachusetts, you were my best friend, my brother's too. I was fifteen and you two were fourteen and in 1974 we walked the avenues on cold gray days picking through dumpsters for something to beat off to. We'd beat off to anything, though I was shy about it and couldn't do it just anywhere.

One February morning we skipped school and went downtown. It was ten or eleven degrees and the dirty snow piled along both sides of River Street had become ice; the air made my lungs hurt and our noses, ears, and fingers felt burned, but you wore your faded blue jean jacket with the green magic marker peace signs drawn all over it. You wore sneakers and thin fake denim pants that looked more purple than blue. It was so cold I pulled the rubber band from my ponytail and let my hair down around my neck and leather-jacketed shoulders. Your hair was long too, brown and stringy. My brother, barely fourteen, needed a shave.

We had a dollar between us so we sat in a booth at Vahally's Diner and drank coffee with so much milk and sugar in it you couldn't call it coffee anymore. The Greek man behind the counter hated us; he folded his black hairy forearms across his chest and watched us take our free refills until we were giddy with caffeine. You went for your seventh cup and he yelled something at you in Greek. On the way out you stole two dollars someone had left on their check under a sugar shaker.

You paid our way on the city bus that was heated and made a loop all the way through town, along the river, up to the Westgate shopping center, then back again. We stayed on it for two hours, taking the loop six times. In the far rear, away from the driver, you took out your black-handled Buck knife and carved a peace sign into the aluminum-backed seat in front of you. For a while I looked out the window at all the red brick factory buildings, the store-fronts with their dusty windows, bright neon price deals taped to the bottom and top. Barrooms on every block. I probably thought of the high school algebra I was flunking, the gym class I hated, the brown mescaline and crystal meth and THC my sister was selling. The bus was warm, too warm, and more crowded than before. A woman our mothers' age sat in her overcoat and scarf in the seat in front of you both. Her back was to you and I'm sure she heard you laughing but she didn't see my brother hunched forward in his seat, jerking back and forth on his penis and coming in no time, catching it all in his hand. I think I looked away and I don't remember what he did with it.

After the bus, we made our way through the narrow factory streets, most of the buildings' windows covered with gray plywood, though your mother still worked at Schwartz's Shoe, on the fifth floor, when she wasn't drinking. We walked along the railroad tracks, its silver rails flush with the packed snow, the wooden ties gone under. And we laughed about the summer before when we three built a barricade for the train, a wall of broken creosote ties, an upside-down shopping cart, cinder blocks, and a rusted oil drum. We covered it with brush, then you siphoned gas from a Duster behind Schwartz's and poured it on. My brother and I lit it, air sucked by us in a whoosh, and we ran down the bank across the parking lot into the abandoned brewery to the second floor to watch our fire, to wait for the Boston & Maine, to hear the screaming brakes as it rounded the blind curve just off the trestle over the river. But a fat man in a good shirt and tie showed up at the tracks, then a cop, and we ran laughing to the first floor where we turned on the keg conveyor belt, lay on it belly-first, and rode it up through its trap door over and over.

As we made our way through town it began to snow. My brother and I were hungry, but you were never hungry; you were hawny, you said. One morning, as we sat in the basement of your house and passed a homemade pipe between us, your mother upstairs drunk on Kappy's vodka and Pepsi, singing to herself, you said: "I'm always hawny in the mawnin'."

My brother and I laughed and you didn't know why, then you inhaled resin on your next hit and said, "Shit man, the screem's broken."

"The *what?*"

"The screem. You know, the *screem*. Like a screem door?"

By the time we reached the avenues the snow had blanketed the streets. There were two sisters on Seventh who lived in the projects that always had motorcycles in front of them, and trash, and bright-colored babies' toys. Trish and Terry were older, sixteen and seventeen and so skinny their breasts looked like prunes beneath their shirts, but they had dark skin and long hair and sometimes, if they were high, they'd suck you. But there was a day party on the first floor of their building, and it had only been two weeks since Harry Wright and Kevin McConigle, rent collectors for Fat Billy, both twenty-three or -four, beat us up, you and me, just walked us out of a pot party we were both quiet at, walked us off the front porch into the mud then kicked and punched us until they were through. So we kept walking, heading for a street close to the highway where we knew three girls who would fuck if you had wine and rubbers, though after the wine they didn't mention the rubbers.

On Cedar Street, cars spun out snow as they drove from the curb or the corner store. You let out a yelp and a holler and went running after a Chevy that had just pulled away, skidding slightly as it went. You ran low, bent over so the driver wouldn't see you, and when you reached the back bumper you grabbed it and squatted on your sneakers, your butt an inch or two from the road. And you skied away, just like that, the snow shooting out from under the wheels of the car, out from under your Zayre Department Store sneakers, blue exhaust coughing out its pipe beside you.

In the spring and summer we hopped trucks. A mile from the highway was a crosswalk on Main with a push-button traffic signal pole that we three leaned against until a truck came along and one of us pressed the button to turn red. I was the decoy that day, for a white refrigerator truck from Shoe City Beef. It stopped at the line, and I crossed the street jerking my head like a chicken to keep his attention from the mirrors while you two ran around to the back and climbed up on the foot-wide iron ledge at the bottom of its rear doors. As soon as I got to the sidewalk I heard the driver shift from neutral to first, heard him give it the gas. I waited for a car to drive by from the opposite direction, then I ran out into the street behind the truck, which was only shifting up to second. You and my brother stood on the ledge waiting, smiling, nodding your heads for me to hurry. I reached the ledge just as the truck moved into higher gear and I grabbed the bolt lock on its back doors and pulled myself up, the truck going faster now, shifting again, dipping and rattling through a low spot in the road. You both held an iron handle on opposite sides of the door so I stayed down, gripping the bolt lock with both hands, sitting on the ledge.

A car horn behind us honked and the driver, some man who combed his hair to the side like a teacher, shook his head and honked his horn again. You gave him the finger and we laughed but it was a scared laugh because the truck wasn't slowing down as it got to the gas stations and Kappy's Liquor near the highway, it was speeding up. Before, we'd jumped off into the grass of the highway ramp, but now we couldn't; he took the turn without leaving third gear and you yelled: "He *knows!* He friggin' *knows!*" My brother wasn't smiling anymore, and he stuck his head around the corner and let the growing wind hit him in the face, run through the hair on his cheeks as he squeezed the handle with both hands and I wanted to stand, to get my feet on something solid, but there was no room and now the driver was in fourth gear, heading north on 495, going fifty, then sixty, then sixty-five. He moved to the middle lane and I tried not to look down at the zip of the asphalt a foot beneath my dangling boots, but it was worse looking out at the cars, at the drivers looking at us like we might be a circus act they should catch sometime. Some honked as they passed so I looked up at you, at the side of your face as you looked around the corner, the June wind snapping your hair back past your forehead and ears, your mouth open in a scream I could barely hear. You smiled and shook your head at my brother then down at me, your brown eyes wet from the wind, your cheeks flushed in a satisfaction so deep I had to look back at the cars behind us, at the six or seven I was convinced would run me over one after the other, after my fingers failed. Miles later, at the tollbooths of the New Hampshire line, the truck slowed to a stop and we jumped off exhausted, our fingers stiff, and thumbed home.

That fall you went to the trade school, my brother joined me at the high school, and I saw you six years later in an all-night store in Monument Square. I was buying cigarettes for my college girlfriend. She waited in the car. It was winter. The floor was dirty with people's slush and mud tracks, the overhead light was fluorescent and too bright, and I was waiting my turn at the register when I saw you, watching me, smiling as you walked up. You carried a carton of ice cream and a quart of Coke. I had on a sweater and a jacket but you wore only a T-shirt, green Dickie work pants, and sneakers. You were taller than me, lean, and your young black mustache and goatee made you look sinister until you started talking in that high voice that hadn't changed since you'd told us you were hawny in the mawnin'. You said you were living down on the avenues, that you were getting married soon. I said congratulations, then I was at the counter asking for a pack of Parliaments and you touched me on the shoulder, said to say hi to my brother. I said I would. At the door I glanced back at you and watched you dig into your front pocket for crumpled bills. You nodded and smiled at me, winked even, and as I left the store, the cold tightening the skin on my face, I remembered the time your mother went to visit her sister in Nebraska for a whole month. I could never understand why she went alone, why she'd leave her family like that to go off for a visit. Then my mother told me it was detox she went to, some twenty-eight-day program in Boston. When I told you I knew, you laughed and said, "Nah," but you swallowed twice and walked away to do nothing in particular.

Six months after I saw you in the store my brother and I got invitations to your wedding. We didn't go.

Four more years and you were dead.

I heard about it after you were buried. They said your wife stabbed you in the back. That was it; she stabbed you. But a year later I was behind the bar at McMino's Lounge and Fat Billy's son, Bill Jr., told me what really happened, that you were cooked, always thinking your wife was cheating on you, always beating her up.

That night you ran outside off the porch to go kill the guy you thought she was fucking. This was down on one of the avenues, behind the projects, and you took the trail in back of your house. But your wife opened your black-handled Buck knife and chased after you, screaming. She was short and small, barely five feet, and just as you reached the weeds she got to you and drove it in low, sinking the blade into your liver, snipping something called the portal artery. You went down without a sound. You curled up in a heap. But your wife spent four hours at a neighbor's house crying before they called anyone, and then it was the cops, and you were gone.

I served Bill Jr. another White Russian and for a second I felt sure it was him she went to that night, and I thought about hitting him for not making a faster call, but I felt no heat in my hands, no pull inside me. And I've always hated woman beaters. Part of me thought you got what you deserved. I left Bill Jr. to finish his too-sweet drink.

The following winter I was living in New York City, in a one-room studio with my girlfriend. It was late on a Sunday morning and we both sat with our feet up on the couch reading the *New York Times*. Outside our barred window snow fell on parked cars, on the sidewalk and street. I got tired of the movie section and picked up a story about three women in prison, all there for the same reason, for killing the husbands who beat them. And your wife was one of them; they gave her full name, *your* name. They wrote how she chased you outside and stabbed you. They described the town you both lived in as economically depressed, once a thriving textile town but no more. I lowered the paper and started to tell my girlfriend all about you, but she and I weren't doing so well, both past wanting to hear anything extra about each other, so I pulled on my boots and jacket and went walking. I crossed Third Avenue and Second and First. A car alarm went off in front of some Chinese laundry. I stuck my hands in my pockets and wished I'd worn a hat. I passed an empty basketball court, then I waited for the traffic on FDR Drive and walked the last block to the East River. To my right and left were bridges over to Queens. Though from where I stood I could see only the backs of warehouses, dry weeds five feet tall, then the gray river, swirling by fast.

The snow had stopped and I started walking along the cobblestone walk. One morning I skipped school and cut through back yards to your house. I didn't know your mother was home from Nebraska and I almost stepped back when she answered the door. She'd dyed her brown hair black, she wore sweatpants and a sweater, she had a cold sore on her bottom lip, and she'd gained weight, but she smiled and kissed me on the cheek and invited me in. The small kitchen was clean and warm. It smelled like coffee and cinnamon rolls. She put one on a napkin and handed it to me. I thanked her, and while I chewed the sweet buttery bread, she lit up a cigarette and asked about my mother. Then you came downstairs in just your jeans, no shirt, your chest pale and thin, your nipples pink, and your mother rushed over and kissed and hugged you like you'd been gone and just gotten home. And you didn't pull away, you hugged her back, and when your eyes caught mine, you lowered your face into the hair at her shoulder, and kept hugging.

STANLEY ELKIN

Out of One's Tree

FROM HARPER'S MAGAZINE

LIKE MANY PEOPLE I do my life by the numbers, or if not my life exactly, then at least my personal habits — the small, secret hygienes no one, not my wife, not my children, is privy to. Each day I brush from left to right and top to bottom as if I were reading my teeth. I shave the right side of my face before the left. I lather my privates three times and follow the invented, customized rituals of my morning shower with all the formality and inflexibility of a coronation.

Breakfast is another story. Breakfast is prescriptive. No one, I mean, invents breakfast. Juice precedes cereal precedes eggs precedes coffee as fixed and inevitably as scissors cuts paper, paper covers rock, rock smashes scissors. These are the social certainties, public as law, and stand in relation to those secret hygienes in about the same way as classical music does to jazz.

So there are the known, predictable orbits of the mathematical sky and the unique, personal ones of self revolving about self like inspired, hidden riffs of superstition — the snowflake variables of a private mythology. Only more dutied and orthodox than any verity. When sink comes to swim, for show not for blow is always the first thing off the boat.

How is it, then, that in mid-April 1991, I forgot how to shower? Forgot, that is, not only the first-this, then-thats of the drummed-in drill of my by-the-numbers life, or even just the function of water or the meaning of soap, but what I was doing there, on the bath bench, behind the shower curtains, why I was naked?

Joan found me. I was staring into the porcelain soap-crèche built into the tile wall.

"Stanley?" she says she said. "Stanley?"

And in truth, I remember her alarm, how helpless and anxious and concerned she was, how distressed at what must have appeared to her a sort of disappearing act on my part, some escape caper, the now-you-see-'ems-now-you-don'ts of self and identity, this, well, Houdini-ization of the will.

She tried to talk me through my shower like someone in a control tower, and when that didn't work she bathed me herself. I was so out of it it couldn't have mattered that she didn't lather my privates three times.

What I'm about to relate is a mixture of what I remember and what I've been told happened; something I suppose, like one's earliest memories — life as martini, one part fact to three parts hearsay and legend. Most, even that to which I'd swear, is probably filtered through the blown circuits of confusion and madness and is, I suppose, artful forgery, rigged document, a knocked-off passport of the soul. Which don't mean there's not a lot left over that ain't genuine article, what I speak from the charmed, temperate, still waters of vestigial, holy sanity, the bespoke calm of my axeless, even-steven heart.

Here, in rough chronology (because a sidebar of the loony, whacko condition is what it does to time, how much more disorienting it is to one's clocks than all the psilocybins on all the floors of all the forests in the world; being out of one's tree melts your watch like a Dali), is what happened.

On the day of my Japanese shower I went to my word processor and, for the life of me, couldn't open the store, couldn't, I mean, remember how to break into my bubble machine. Calls to Al Lebowitz, who talked me into buying it, and to Sid Wolff, who sold it to me, availeth not. When I distressed to my wife she pointed out I hadn't worked in two weeks anyway. This was impossible. I'm crippled, not lazy. All I can do is work. If I hadn't been working, what *had* I been doing? Had I been reading?

"You can't process information, you haven't even been reading the paper."

"Impossible. Why are you doing me this way? Ain't this March?"

"It's the middle of April."

And, indeed, the leaves on one's trees out one's windows were green! What had happened to the fledgling spring? How had I lost such a humongous fortnight? She told me, well, she told me I'd gone nuts, and what I'd been doing, she said, was sit on the side of my bed, zapping TV channels with the remote control.

This is complicated. We don't have cable. We have cable-*ready*. There are, on our remote-control wand, buttons for over a hundred possible TV stations, plus a menu of about a dozen lozenges for a variety of functions that, when pressed, superimpose on our only twenty-five-inch screen yellow information: not only the ordinary day, time, and A.M./P.M. variations but displays for STEREO, SAP, MONO, TV, CATV, HRC; for adjusting color; for modulating sound. Now Newton's third law of thermodynamics is, or ought to be if it isn't, that though the radio may crackle or the lights flicker and dim during an electrical storm, they normally recover without so much as blowing a fuse, whereas time settings and other displays on one's VCR and TV are knocked all cock-a-hoop. I don't know why this is. I'm merely an observer of phenomenon, I don't undertake to explain it.

Except, as they say, there's method to madness. It's late March, recall. It's early April. It's the season of wild nights and murderous rains. Channel 30 is where channel 87 — if we had channel 87 — ought to be; channel 24 is in the low 100s. On KETC I'm locked into the SAP mode, which informs over and over that I've reached a service on my TV that provides auditory descriptions for the visually impaired. The public service announcer says that if I wish to disengage and return to normal programming I should refer to my owner's manual. My wife has told me I don't process information, I can't read a paper, what would I do with an owner's manual?

So I sit on the side of the bed in my underwear with my remote control in my hand, lost in some electronic rapture, a chap lost in SAP, pushing the lozenges, frantically trying to get back to normal programming but discovering instead disembodied voices on 18 and images busting up on the Home Shopping Network, which until this wild spring I didn't even know I got, color draining from the dissolving aura of zircons and faux pearls, all the bleeding gems and wavering, disappearing shards of matter being sold at so-much-the-carat twenty-four hours a day. Having put by the driving, mainstream signals of your ABCs and NBCs and CBSs, I'd given myself over to all the dot-driven snows and statics and esoteric bands and the voices of a Christian zealotry on 18, which I'd also never received before on my receiver and which, by reason of the very absence of image, might be that much more the manifest signal of invisible God.

This, *this* is how I spent my time, that humongous lost fortnight of the breaking winter and leaps-and-bounds spring.

Until, I mean, the morning of my hands-on cleansing, the day Joan had had it with me, the day she turned me in.

I spent first grade in a hospital room in Chicago, did a year in bed in the Michael Reese Hospital for a deep strep throat in the pre-penicillin dark ages when the treatment for strep was high dosages of radium delivered two or three times weekly for a year. I had a heart attack when I was thirty-seven. Three or four times I've been hospitalized for kidney stones, three or four more for the collapse of my left lung. And once, for a short time, I was blind. But now I see. In 1972, in England, I was diagnosed for multiple sclerosis. In '76 I started to use a cane, in '79 a foot brace, in 1989 I went onto a walker, in 1990 I moved into a wheelchair. In 1985 I had quintuple heart bypass surgery, three years later they went back in and gave me a quadruple. That same year I had an endarterectomy and a second heart attack. Other than a couple of trips to the hospital for pneumonia and one for congestive heart failure, that's about the size of it, the story of my life, healthyhood-wise. As you can see, I'm one of the fortunate few who has Blue Cross by the balls.

I reel this stuff off out of neither pride nor self-pity. Pride? What's to be proud? But what's to be ashamed, either? None of my diseases was ever an embarrassment to me. Humiliating, yes, but never embarrassing.

Only the madness. Only the time I was out of my tree, off my rocker, around my bend.

Because to me, *for* me, it's only the personal that's personal. Broken bones are nothing. Pain is merely troubled matter, the double-dealing of the sensories. Why, pleasure is more disgraceful — the naked, revealed, oh Jesus's! oh God's! oh Christ's! and O yes Yes *YES!* of frictive, sexual heat. A case, if you want to know, of nobody's business but your own, private as property, proper as privacy.

Maybe because madness has no shame, maybe because it blows one's cover and offers, ipso facto, a kind of mind's mooning, the mooning of the mind. Because it's below the belt of restraint and dignity and goes around all hours like an autobiography with its fly open. Difficult to deal with as a drunk.

But really because one only *thinks* one's shy, and autobiography, if it ain't just one man's peacockeyed name-droppings, is finally the most arduous, rigorous, punishing form there is, as hard to work close up as the magician's best trick. No. I withdraw the analogy. The magician's best trick is to save his secrets. No. I retract the retraction. Because the absolutely splendid, world-class, A-number-one aces magician would be the one who not only performed his tricks for you but delivered up their secrets as well. I daresay no genuine autobiography has ever been written. No one, however kind, charactered, or gracious, could afford such generosity. Decorum is the natural enemy of autobiography. By its very nature, a perfectly true autobiography might cut against but must finally break its blade on the diamond-hard grain of the superego because, though scissors cuts paper, paper covers rock, and rock smashes scissors, decorum is, strictly speaking, life's ultimate weapon. At its most daring, and maybe even at its best, all autobiography is "authorized," a striptease with the pasties or G-string that covers the mind left on. Left on, too, is some final, ultimate, impenetrable eighth veil, the nasty hoard in the secret cellar.

I offer inside info from the season of my madness, nest gossip, tidbits from one's vacated tree.

But before I do — didn't I tell you autobiography is striptease? — here's where the disclaimer goes, the fine print, the warning label, the crossed fingers, the just-kiddings, the take-it-all-backs.

Prednisone, a dehydrogenated analogue of cortisone, is an anti-inflammatory agent used, but used sparingly, in the treatment of multiple sclerosis. It gives the patient strength, greater flexibility, and a wider range of motion. As best as I can recall, the usual course of treatment — one starts off with the highest dosage, 60 or so milligrams for the first week, say, then gradually tapers down, to 40 milligrams for the next few days, then 30 for a few more, then 20, then 10 every other day for a week, then 5 for a while, then $2\frac{1}{2}$ every other day for maybe four days, then cold turkey. I don't *really* remember, I'm talking ballpark, but by the ordinary weights and measures a patient is on the stuff for perhaps a month, possibly a little less. Now, a side effect of prednisone is a feeling of well-being. Well, why not? One has energy, one functions better, one forgets one's deficits, one may even feel the curse has been lifted, that summer is a-cummin in, that one has been cured. Can one get an amen, somebody?

I *love* my doctors. There was this one guy, this neurologist who lived in the hood and who not only made house calls and refused to charge me but pretty much permitted me whatever I wanted whenever I wanted it, prednisonewise.

Now, another side effect of the drug is that if you don't come off it by Cinderella's sensible curfew it can make you very crazy. Right up to the very point, for example, where one morning you're sitting on what you don't even know is your bath bench in what you don't even recognize is your bathroom and your wife comes along and makes a scientific diagnosis: "You've gone nuts."

I'd been on 60 milligrams a day for maybe seven weeks.

So that's the disclaimer. I lay this fig leaf over my character. Prednisone did it. Mechanical failure, not pilot error.

Now for the juicy parts.

You mustn't think my mind was a blank during those twenty or so minutes when I lost the meaning of water and the function of soap. Not a bit of it. It had never been so occupied. Thoughts chased each other like cars in a cops and robbers. With just that sense, too, of reckless urgency, of all pedal-to-the-metal, high-speed abandon, a no-fault world of bump, crunch, smash-oops-boom, and over the cliff. I lay awake at night flipping the channels of my attention, my ideas — if you can call terror an idea — careening from one disaster to the next, worrying the fates of my wife and kids and myself like beads.

Though chiefly, ultimately, myself.

Against a wall in our hallway, beyond the bedroom and across from the bath, is a bookcase high as a door and wide as a desk. On its shelves are not only all the books I've ever written along with their British editions, and all the books I've written that have been translated, and all my paperbacks, and all the essays, introductions, and prefaces I've done, and all the anthologies in which my work has appeared, and the magazines, anthologized or not, in which it *first* appeared, and the interviews I've given, and the articles, chapters, and books about my work, and recordings of all the times I've been on the radio, and the six or seven videos, mostly PBS but some community access too, in which I've been featured, but also, with the exception of the phone books, all the places my name has ever been mentioned. I call these shelves the Wall of Respect, and I swear I put them together, piece by piece like a narcissistic Lego, when I was perfectly sane!

So chiefly, ultimately, myself. The neutrinos, particles, quarks, and atoms of Self bouncing around and off the walls of my head like bumper cars. And what I was wondering, no, thinking, no, deciding, when Joan came along was that that bookcase out there like a kind of wallet shtupped with identity, overflowing with oeuvre, with all the birth certificates, driver's licenses, passports, and credit cards of my Being, was fraudulent, counterfeit, not *my* work at all. A wall of respect indeed, hanging there, painted like a flat in a play. I kept asking her.

"Did I write these books?"

"Of course you did."

"No, really. Did I?"

"Yes."

"All of them?"

"Certainly."

"How do you know?"

"I'm your wife. We're married. I saw you write them."

"I don't *think* I wrote them."

"Oh, Stanley," she said, "don't do this to me."

"Did I *really* write them? Please tell me. You don't have to lie."

Joan called the neurologist. It was the prednisone. She says she'd called him a few days earlier to tell him I was losing it and asked if I should still be on 60 milligrams a day. She said she'd been giving me only 40 milligrams since she'd spoken to him. But I don't remember any of this. As I don't really remember those two lost weeks of my life when I wasn't working.

What I *do* remember is how unhappy I was, what I *do* remember is obsessing over those books and wondering whether I'd written them and suspecting down deep, but not down all that deep, that I hadn't.

And just here, to whatever credit redounds to my character in all this, and — more later — not much does, is the shining hour of my madness. That though I was concerned, and more than concerned, about having stripped from me the very only thing in the world I did well, the deepest regret I reserved for my students, for having misrepresented myself to them as a writer. Who'd never written a book. I was a charlatan, mountebank, a clown on velvet. I was so unhappy. How could I face them? Knowing about myself what I knew about myself. Though, oddly, it never occurred to me to doubt that I was a professor, that I taught writing to grad students and supervised their theses. It never crossed what I had left of my mind that I didn't teach it well. Only that I'd been faking, strutting, swaggering, swanking; only that I'd put on, shammed, affected, made up; only that I'd been this mincing, unforgivable fop of façade.

So I struck my bargains.

"All right," I told Joan, "if I didn't write all of them, did I write any? Did I write two? One? Have I ever been published?"

"You're crazy. You're crazy and you're driving me crazy. You can't stay here. You've got to go where they can take care of you," she said.

Joan doesn't go in much for humoring a chap. But in a way, it was the kindest thing she could have told me. If I was really crazy, then at least there was a chance I had published.

That night doctors would be coming to see me. My free neurologist. That tender, let-'em-eat-prednisone, good, house-calling soul. Another doctor, a stand-in cardiologist pal. Because it wasn't only Blue Cross and HMO Partners and Major Medical I had by the balls but a lot of just interested, board-certified reserves. The cardiologist was brought in because I'd put a call through to his wife. (Because here's where some of that more-later-so-devastating-to-my-good-name comes in.) They wanted crazy, I'd give them crazy! Screw loose I'd give them, o'erthrown mind, demented, non compos, starkers and crackers, batty and bent.

A point I'm trying to make about autobiography is that it puts one under the obligation of restraint. It's one thing to shame one's own devils, quite another to intrude on the rights of others. I'm not so brave — or rude — that I will name her for you. The cardiologist's wife will be the cardiologist's wife, and that call I put through, though, word of honor, I don't remember the details or, by my troth, even the gist, I've a pretty good sense of the drift.

The cardiologist and the cardiologist's wife have a lovely daughter, the subject of my mad, John Aldenish call to the cardiologist's wife. She would have been a senior in high school in the spring of '91. I would have been a senior citizen. I think the phone call — I really *have* repressed it — must have been a heavy-breathing job, a sort of no-load 900-number number. I've a vague memory — I do, I do, but even if I recalled the conversation verbatim I wouldn't give it to you, the self-imposed gag order of the shamed, autobiographical heart — of what I said. Breasts had to be in it, cold cuts and haunches, the body's meats and delicatessen.

But I misrepresent myself. "Heavy breathing" won't serve as the proper trope for that call. I was too manic, gay; almost, I think, charming. This is my memory of my memory, but I think it must be so. I was trying to wow folks with my raving, remember. Yet I could be wrong. Like someone riding a crisis, I slipped in and out of lunacy all day. In a lucid moment I called the cardiologist's wife to apologize. I raved all right. When I asked her to tell me what I'd said she was too embarrassed and shrugged it off. She couldn't have been nicer. Dancing on eggs with the dirty old man. Really. She *couldn't* have been nicer. She couldn't have made me feel more like an asshole. It turned out she'd phoned the cardiologist and put him on notice we'd had conversation. I called him, and *he* wouldn't say what I'd said. Him, a *doctor,* a guy you don't know where his hands have been!

And my own daughter, Molly, the law student, the apple of my eye, for I'd called her too, sharing, filling her in, giving *her* a piece of my mind! (Me, who takes it all back, the statistics skeptic, who never believed — believes? — in the inflated incidence of rape, date rape, child abuse, incest; not even, for that matter, in the improbable acrobatics and high yoga of the *Kamasutra* or any of sexuality's farcical outlandishness; i.e., aphrodisiacs, spells, romantic love, and fatal attractions, or, when you come right down to it, never put all that much faith in the kinky — cross-dressers, spankers and spankees, leather lingerie; closed doors even, what goes on behind, or even in the mostly normal congress between consenting adults.) Shocking my daughter black-and-blue with my fouled thoughts, who'd always been this reserved daddy, prudish even, who not only didn't entirely approve when her friends came over to swim and sunbathe but who immediately went back into the house when they did.

"Please," I asked more than a year after the mere minute or so of the anatomical obloquy I'd subjected her to, "I'm writing an essay about those days, I have to know."

"I can't tell you, Daddy," Molly said.

"Please."

"I can't," she said, "I won't. Not guilty by reason of insanity, Daddy."

Only in the head of the "interested" party is less really more. Only, to use the case before us, in the mad guy's, only, I mean, in mine. The reader wants facts and figures — what the president knew and when he knew it. Add to this one's righteous reticence and you see the further impossibility of autobiography. A disinterested observer takes you further. I've an example.

Besides my medical records, which I've not taken the trouble to obtain and which, in the event, would account merely for the period from April 19 to April 24 when I was in the hospital, the only objective written report of my behavior that exists comes from the May 15–21 issue of the *Riverfront Times*, one of those local — one might even say provincial — free papers that pop up in cities of a certain size. My novel *The MacGuffin* had just come out, and publishers being what they are and midlist authors what *they* are, Simon & Schuster, which wouldn't spring for an ad, sprang instead for a long-distance call to set up an interview with the *Riverfront Times*. It took place sometime during that lost spring and gives a sense of what I was like:

> When I showed up at Elkin's gray brick house . . . the author was slumped at the kitchen table in his wheelchair. His wife . . . was fixing breakfast. "Use your spoon," she told her husband, waiting for him to finish a bowl of cereal.
>
> Instead, Elkin hoisted the bowl and slurped the dregs. Joan put half a grapefruit in front of him. Elkin lifted the grapefruit to his face with his hands and chomped into it.
>
> He tore a chunk of flesh out with his teeth. Juice dripped down his chin and onto his fingers. As he swallowed, Elkin winced. He fixed his eyes on me.
>
> "Go ahead," he said. . . .
>
> The whole thing went poorly. Elkin answered each question with one or two words. "Please, let's get on with it," he'd say, again and again, as if enduring a dental procedure. At one point, he sighed mournfully.

"These are such *old* questions."

His wife interrupted once. Stanley had been taking prednisone for his multiple sclerosis, Joan said; sometimes it made him confused. "I can see by the look in his eyes that it's happening right now." Elkin looked at her with a mild half-smile, then at me. . . .

Packing up, I told him that I hoped he felt better soon. A lot of people want more stories from Stanley Elkin, I said.

"There won't be *many* more," he said, his tone rising. "Because I am going to die!"

What counts in the account are my table manners, my truculence, Joan's protectionism; what counts is my wild *cri de coeur*—all details, effects really, it would be impossible to render in *my* first person. The power of reportage, the force of fiction, is the credulity given to *witness*. The "I" may certainly provide witness but not, I think, or not as effectively, to its own traumas.

Cut to the personal, cut to the interior life.

I *despise* madness. The mad, in literature as in life, are too flighty. They are not a dependable people. They are too operatic. They come on too strong. You can't take them anywhere. They give a telethon for mental health, I change the station.

On the evening of the day of my Japanese shower, the night my circuit-riding neurologist came calling, it was maybe nine o'clock. I'd finished the supper Joan brought up on a tray for me to eat on the small table by the side of my bed while I pounded the numbers on the remote control searching for the lost chord when I heard the doorbell ring. Joan opened the door for the doctor. I could hear them murmuring in the downstairs hall. Hurriedly, I took off my shirt and placed it in my soup bowl. I stripped off my boxer shorts and carefully laid them on my dinner plate like a garnish across the chewed bones and uneaten veggies. I regarded the arrangement critically and, inspired, turned my shorts inside out. As I've said, I was trying to make an impression.

"How are you?" he asked.

"I've gone for a nut case. I'm goofy, I'm daft, there's bats in my belfry. I'm cuckoo for Cocoa Puffs."

Really, if you want to know, I was quite amusing, the way, I suppose, someone tipsy might feel, or high on dope. I ran down for him what I recalled of the events of my day. Indifferent to my spirited account, Doc made his neurological passes over me. ("Which is sharper, this or this?" "Close your eyes. Am I bending your toe up or down?" "Squeeze my hand as hard as you can." "Hold up your arm, don't let me pull it down.") While I blathered on about my emotions, how no matter how hard I squeezed my memory, I couldn't exactly tell what I'd said in those phone calls, he pronounced me not appreciably weaker than when he'd last seen me. Or pronounced to Joan, making eye contact with Joan in a different part of the room, as he'd avoided looking at me — well, that shirt in that soup; well, those inside-out shorts in my supper — even during all the special olympics of our hand-to-hand combat.

Until, to get his attention, I accused him of making eyes at my wife, of trying, in front of his very patient, to seduce the patient's very wife.

It was, finally, my primary-care physician who admitted me to the hospital the next day, the one guy I actually paid, or paid in those ten- and twenty-dollar copayments like a kind of medical scrip.

A funny thing happened on the way to the funny farm (the General Medicine floor, but autobiographers must sometimes make up in attitude what they lack in credential). It was determined that my son, Bernard, would take me to the hospital in his truck. "Lick my dick!" I screamed at him when he came into the room for me.

Something must be made clear here. I'm trying to be as faithful as I can to the fossil record. I wasn't trying to be charming, amusing. This has more to do with those phone calls, I think, a holdover from loose screw and o'erthrown mind, still sprinkling bona fides over my condition like those croutons of laundry on my supper. Because madness, *in which I did not believe,* shouldn't be taken on faith! I suppose I thought I had to act out, I suppose I thought that's what I was doing, though it became quite clear enough quite soon enough that all that was the furthest thing from my mind, that I, whoever I was, had never been further from that mind myself, that I was out of my tree for true, doing some terrible, perilous, arduous, solo migration across the vasty deeps, terrains, and moods of the world.

Another funny thing that happened on the way to the funny farm was this:

In Admitting, turned out in these days of aggressive competition for the sick man's dollar like a lobby in an expensive, gorgeous hotel, I was taken over by an odd euphoria. I was in the *hospital,* I told Bernie and Joan. I was in the *hospital,* I told the hotel clerk

who registered me. And tried to explain how safe I felt, that just
by passing through those glass doors I'd somehow entered some
zone of health, arrived at sanctuary, beyond the reach of disease,
out of harm's way, immortal, restored. I won't swear to this, but I
think I warned them about the risks of returning home. There be
lions, there be dragons, I cautioned like the old cartographers.

More data from the front lines.

I'm told by Bernie that just after I was put into my hospital bed
(the sides of which rise like a crib's) I had to use the plastic urinal;
that I couldn't get my penis into it; that the nurse bent over and
did it for me; and that when she did I touched her breasts. And
perhaps having a screw loose is as apt and scientific a definition of
insanity as any Freud ever came up with. Coming undone, I mean,
man's works exposed and lying about like the gears, springs, and
studs of a watch. Because by ordinary I'm — was — a shy man, a
repressed, not-quite-confident-enough fellow who can't sit on a
toilet if he hears so much as a radio playing beyond the bathroom
door, who (look up the phone logs — all that bawdy talk, the
impure mind and limerick heart; how it unmans one; reveals that
nubbin of sin that sits at the bottom of one's being like the irritant
in a seed pearl) was returned now to all the warm and schluffy
campfires of the womb, to all-spent, suck-thumb, lick-tit lassitude.
Or one phase of madness anyway. Because lunacy has as many
phases as the moon it's named for. It ain't *all* peaches and cream,
I'm here to tell you.

Soon after Bernie and Joan left me I explored the appurte-
nances and appointments of my environment (quite like a child
in an upper berth on a train, say) — to the extent it was possible,
I mean, hobbled as I was by the multiple sclerosis, which pinned
me to my hospital bed and made me reliant on bedpans and nurses
who on doctor's orders transferred me into chairs on which I
didn't want to sit because there was nothing to do in them. It was
more convenient to take my meals in bed, where all I had to do
was push away my tray with its uneaten food and fall back upon
my pillows in some hara-kiri of boredom.

I'd been wrong. The world beyond my window was the zone of
health. Out there, in the city's brown and rust and cream apartment blocks, within their mysterious rooms, was whatever of sanctuary, immortality, and restoration there was. *Here* be the dragons,
beasts, and lions! Just *here*, on this floor of the General Medicine

in this queer zoo of virus and microbe, bacteria and germ, among all the poisoned sprats of blain and tumor. And I had this strange and terrible insight: that hospitals were apartment blocks of disease, and knew in brain and knew in bone that you didn't get out of them alive. They were way stations between where you lived and where you went to be buried, though I hadn't realized madness could kill. Prednisone, shmednisone, I was going to die, and it no longer seemed I had anyone by the balls. I tried to call Joan with the news but couldn't remember my number.

Who'd had no trouble getting my messages through yesterday (or whenever it was), all those terrible broadsides and communiqués from the glands, but who'd entered a new phase, passing over with a madman's skill from one obsession to another with the ease of a terrorist crossing a border. Into the business of fixed ideas now, not hallucination — hallucination came later — but wacky, pointless, almost comic conviction. (Though connected, I see now, to those first compulsive experiments with the remote control, the twelve or so days at home when I cruised television's invisible lanes looking for — what, a signal?) I became convinced that the TV that angled down from brackets on the wall and intruded into the hospital room like a sort of stuffed electronic trophy *got* cable, wasn't merely cable-ready like mine at home but the real McCoy, that all that was required to activate it was for someone to come in and turn a key.

I rang for a nurse.

The nurse explained how the patient operated the set right from the bed. I *knew* all that, I told her, but this particular set got cable and it was up to the hospital to activate it. She examined the set. She was unfamiliar with this feature, she said, she'd send up an engineer. Believe me when I say I lived for the time when the engineer would come and free up my set, but it never happened. I tried to call the engineer myself, but since I couldn't work the phone I had to ring for the nurse to call him for me. She handed me the phone and I explained the problem. They'd get to me as soon as they could, the engineers said.

But they never did. I stayed on their case — the nurses'. As each shift changed I'd bring them in and go over it with them. When they stopped coming when I called I flashed my call button and shouted *"Stat!"* at them over the intercom. *"Code blue! Code blue!"* I yelled at them.

(And here a caveat to the autobiographer. Joan just read this part. It was never cable I believed they were keeping from me, it was stereo sound. She's right. I remember. One's a terrible source for one's autobiography.)

It was at about this time that I was visited by the three angels. Customized, cut to the cloth of their venue, got up as nurses, I mean, but angels, no mistake. I remember only the sweetest, smartest, most beautiful of them, could at the time have described her for a police artist's sketch, but now if I tried, I would only be stretching. The immediacy of her presence is gone, her immanence, and all that remains is some bland vision, the girl from Ipanema, the girl of your dreams, the sweetheart of Sigma Chi, Laura on a train that is passing through.

The other two, though lovely, were harpies by comparison. They were, all three, my trio of comforters, though I've no memory of what they said. All I know for sure is that they told me the truth about myself. All I know for sure is that they made me cry. It may have been all that head-on confrontational all-fouled soul's sweet masochism, character's dark skinny that breaks your heart. They *could* have been harpies, my angels, sent out to sting, singling one out in the very air beyond one's tree.

"Go back, go back," they may have warned.

Difficult to say. For I did *not* go back. Couldn't make a move while my physicians, like alchemists, fiddled with my medications, giving Mellaril (for psychosis) with one hand while they took prednisone away (in jots and incremental tittles) with the other. And, at bedtime, a light seasoning of Halcion, Valium, to see me through my wired nights. (Which they never did.) Shooting for *mens sana in corpore sano*. But never, *in corpore sano* at least, getting it right. What a piece of work is man. This one anyway. Who lost his angels but never recovered strength, flexibility, range of motion. *What* a piece of work is man! Though I'll tell you something. Rotten health for lost angels ain't entirely a bad tradeoff. Which is what you *don't* get in the *Riverfront Times* or the *New York Times*, 'cause this part isn't witness, it's testimony!

Though I'm getting ahead.

Back in the General Medicine strange things were happening. I'll give examples. I lump them together because that's how they seem in my head now, all time lines blurred, melded.

I didn't suffer visitors gladly. Entertaining is hard work, paying attention is. To tell the truth, I didn't much enjoy even Joan's visits, nor, in fact, did she. (Though I was furious when she wasn't there or came later and later each day only to leave earlier and earlier. It's a myth we don't want to be pitied. We *flash* our suffering, guys like me. We eat pity up like dessert.) Anyway, I must have been on one of those lightning, transitory highs that came over me once in a while in the General Medicine. Joan was already there when three friends, Steve Zwicker, Naomi and Al Lebowitz, came into my room. I was delighted to see them and had this remarkable perception. Seized by the fetching sight of their symmetry, I bolted upright.

"*My God,*" I exclaimed at them, "*you're all wearing glasses! Steve's wearing glasses! Naomi's wearing glasses! Joan! Al's glasses are on a chain round his neck!* Even *I'm* wearing glasses!"

"Naomi isn't wearing glasses," Joan said.

"Maybe contacts?"

Without a word, without so much as looking at each other, as if on some secret cue of the blood, my three pals began this sort of soft-shoe sidelong out of the room. They looked exactly like the last three dancers in a chorus line disappearing into the wings.

"They didn't even say goodbye," I said.

"They didn't even say hello," Joan said.

And once, at two or three in the morning, attempting to reach the engineers, I actually managed to get a call through to Security and tried to explain to *them* about cable, the key, that the engineers wouldn't come, and that I was going to take my life, that I'd pull the IVs from my arms and stick the needles into my neck, my ears. And Security came lickety-split and nurses stayed with me all night. And then they decided — Joan, Security, the nurses, and doctors — I would have to be watched. (Though I didn't mean it, though all I intended was to get somebody's attention, to let them know the high priority I put on cable. Hey, I was new to madness. Did I know that the one thing you must never say — because, God knows, they'd let me say everything else! — is that you're a potential threat to yourself or to others?)

Which is when they brought in my minders. The minders. The minders were neither registered nor practical nurses. They were, well, *minders,* ancient hobgoblins of the custodial, as far a cry from my three angelic visitors as you could get.

Mostly they knit, or dozed in an armchair near the air-condition-ing vents — it was high April now — wrapped in their sweaters, except for one woman, the only one I have a distinct impression of, as I have a distinct impression of the sweetest, most beautiful angel, who was, in fact, her earthen Calibanesque equivalent, a toothless, feral old hag whose eyes glowed in the dark like a fox's. All night she chewed on herself, making a sound as if she were kissing her gums, and looked, I remember (nuts or not, this isn't an impression), exactly like the comedienne Moms Mabley. I could hear her snoring, but whenever I looked at her she stared unblink-ingly out at me from her old yellow eyes.

"What you want? You want your urinal?"

"Yes."

She would wash my penis. Of all the people in the hospital who touched me — the technicians, the nurses, and aides — she's the only one who never wore gloves.

"Put your wanky in there."

I finished.

"You finished?"

"Yes."

"Take out your wanky."

She washed it again.

"You have strange rules," I told her.

"I ain't crazy."

And one time I heard her snoring but when I opened my eyes hers were open too. As hard as I could, I threw the heavy telephone at her head. It dropped loudly, harmlessly to the floor. My wrecked range of motion, my fucked flexibility. She snorted at me. She kissed her gums. Maybe, like the angels, she was also telling me to go back, go back.

Which I was trying to do now.

Because what I feared most — this would have been the last, the final phase — was shrinks' rounds. It was a teaching hospital. Maybe half a dozen students doing their psychiatric rotation. Coming by each morning, taking turns, popping their devastating questions. Do you know where you are, do you know why you're here, can you tell us the date, the vice president's name? Take nine from thirty-two, add seven to a hundred seventeen.

So I *must* have been trying. To go back, go back, get back in my tree. Cramming my senators, what the state capital is, sweating my address, sweating my phone number, the names of my kids. As if I were practicing for prelims, my thesis defense. Doing the difficult algebras of the daily and functional. Eschewing wise guy, smart aleck, class clown. Eschewing obsession. (I can't say when, but gradually, over the course, in time, it did not occur to me I did not write my books.)

Only to pick up another obsession, even more humbling. That I had been crazy, out of my mind. And had misplaced, when I was getting to an age when I could least afford it, almost an entire spring. Couldn't get over it, the irony of having contracted the single disease I most despised. Learning a hard lesson, the hardest, that sanity is a privilege, not a right.

I was discharged from the General Medicine on the twenty-fourth of April. I had spent only five nights there and part of six days, but they were the worst, most difficult, most agonizing days and nights of my life. Nor did I leave with a clean slate. This wasn't any amazing grace that had happened to me. It wasn't a case of I once was lost but now I'm found, was blind but now I see. It would be a month or more before I satisfactorily processed information again, though I was writing letters two weeks after going home, answering mail that had accumulated during the almost two months I'd been away. A slow process, it sometimes took me a day to write two letters, trying to explain myself, what had happened to me, for if the time I'd been out of my tree had been the worst I'd ever known, it was also the most interesting, and I couldn't let it go.

I was taking my own showers again, weaker without the pred-nisone, so weak Joan had to walk behind me, holding my hips, pushing at the backs of my shoes as I kicked myself along on the walker on the way to the bathroom. Where, when I emerged, I could see the bookcase with whatever I'd written and what had been written about me, and which I now understood, because the duty of one's life is to see it clearly, was not a monument to my mind at all, those shelves no wall of respect so much as the jerry-built benches and bleachers of ego.

Which is where the catch comes in, the trap of the literary, that final adjustment, meaning filtering chaos, fine-tuning madness, panning the random for value and ends.

LOUISE ERDRICH

Skunk Dreams

FROM THE GEORGIA REVIEW

WHEN I WAS FOURTEEN, I slept alone on a North Dakota football field under the cold stars on an early spring night. May is
unpredictable in the Red River Valley, and I happened to hit a
night when frost formed in the grass. A skunk trailed a plume of
steam across the forty-yard line near moonrise. I tucked the top of
my sleeping bag over my head and was just dozing off when the
skunk walked onto me with simple authority.

Its ripe odor must have dissipated in the frozen earth of its
winterlong hibernation, because it didn't smell all that bad, or
perhaps it was just that I took shallow breaths in numb surprise. I
felt him — her, whatever — pause on the side of my hip and turn
around twice before evidently deciding I was a good place to sleep.
At the back of my knees, on the quilting of my sleeping bag, it trod
out a spot for itself and then, with a serene little groan, curled up
and lay perfectly still. That made two of us. I was wildly awake,
trying to forget the sharpness and number of skunk teeth, trying
not to think of the high percentage of skunks with rabies, or the
reason that on camping trips my father always kept a hatchet
underneath his pillow.

Inside the bag, I felt as if I might smother. Carefully, making
only the slightest of rustles, I drew the bag away from my face and
took a deep breath of the night air, enriched with skunk, but clear
and watery and cold. It wasn't so bad, and the skunk didn't stir at
all, so I watched the moon — caught that night in an envelope of
silk, a mist — pass over my sleeping field of teenage guts and glory.
The grass in spring that has lain beneath the snow harbors a sere

dust both old and fresh. I smelled that newness beneath the rank tone of my bag-mate — the stiff fragrance of damp earth and the thick pungency of newly manured fields a mile or two away — along with my sleeping bag's smell, slightly mildewed, forever smoky. The skunk settled even closer and began to breathe rapidly; its feet jerked a little like a dog's. I sank against the earth, and fell asleep too.

Of what easily tipped cans, what molten sludge, what dogs in yards on chains, what leftover macaroni casseroles, what cellar holes, crawl spaces, burrows taken from meek woodchucks, of what miracles of garbage did my skunk dream? Or did it, since we can't be sure, dream the plot of *Moby-Dick*, how to properly age parmesan, or how to restore the brick-walled, tumbledown creamery that was its home? We don't know about the dreams of any other biota, and even much about our own. If dreams are an actual dimension, as some assert, then the usual rules of life by which we abide do not apply. In that place, skunks may certainly dream themselves into the vests of stockbrokers. Perhaps that night the skunk and I dreamed each other's thoughts or are still dreaming them. To paraphrase the problem of the Chinese sage, I may be a woman who has dreamed herself a skunk, or a skunk still dreaming that she is a woman.

In a book called *Death and Consciousness*, David H. Lund — who wants very much to believe in life after death — describes human dream-life as a possible model for a disembodied existence:

> Many of one's dreams are such that they involve the activities of an apparently embodied person whom one takes to be oneself as long as one dreams. . . . Whatever is the source of the imagery . . . apparently has the capacity to bring about images of a human body and to impart the feeling that the body is mine. It is, of course, just an image body, but it serves as a perfectly good body for the dream experience. I regard it as mine, I act on the dream environment by means of it, and it constitutes the center of the perceptual world of my dream.

Over the years I have acquired and reshuffled my beliefs and doubts about whether we live on after death — in any shape or form, that is, besides the molecular level at which I am to be absorbed by the taproots of cemetery elms or pines and the tangled mats of fearfully poisoned, too-green lawn grass. I want some-

thing of the self on whom I have worked so hard to survive the
loss of the body (which, incidentally, the self has done a fairly
decent job of looking after, excepting spells of too much cabernet
and a few idiotic years of rolling my own cigarettes out of Virginia
Blond tobacco). I am put out with the marvelous discoveries of
the intricate biochemical configuration of our brains, though I
realize that the processes themselves are quite miraculous. I understand that I should be self-proud, content to gee-whiz at the
fact that I am the world's only mechanism that can admire itself.
I should be grateful that life is here today, though gone tomorrow,
but I can't help it. I want more.

Skunks don't mind each other's vile perfume. Obviously, they find
each other more than tolerable. And even I, who have been in the
presence of a direct skunk hit, wouldn't classify their weapon as
mere smell. It is more on the order of a reality-enhancing experience. It's not so pleasant as standing in a grove of old-growth red
cedars, or on a lyrical moonshed plain, or watching trout rise to
the shadow of your hand on the placid surface of an Alpine lake.
When the skunk lets go, you're surrounded by skunk presence:
inhabited, owned, involved with something you can only describe
as powerfully *there.*
    I woke at dawn, stunned into that sprayed state of being. The
dog that had approached me was rolling in the grass, half-addled,
sprayed too. The skunk was gone. I abandoned my sleeping bag
and started home. Up Eighth Street, past the tiny blue and pink
houses, past my grade school, past all the addresses where I had
baby-sat, I walked in my own strange wind. The streets were wide
and empty; I met no one — not a dog, not a squirrel, not even an
early robin. Perhaps they had all scattered before me, blocks away.
I had gone out to sleep on the football field because I was afflicted
with a sadness I had to dramatize. Mood swings had begun, hor-
mones, feverish and brutal. They were nothing to me now. My
emotions had seemed vast, dark, and sickeningly private. But they
were minor, mere wisps, compared to skunk.

I have found that my best dreams come to me in cheap motels.
One such dream about an especially haunting place occurred in
a rattling room in Valley City, North Dakota. There, in the home

of the Winter Show, in the old Rudolph Hotel, I was to spend a weeklong residency as a poet-in-the-schools. I was supporting myself, at the time, by teaching poetry to children, convicts, rehabilitation patients, high-school hoods, and recovering alcoholics. What a marvelous job it was, and what opportunibes I had to dream, since I paid my own lodging and lived low, sometimes taking rooms for less than ten dollars a night in motels that had already been closed by local health departments.

The images that assailed me in Valley City came about because the bedspread was so thin and worn — a mere brown tissuey curtain — that I had to sleep beneath my faux fur Salvation Army coat, wearing all of my clothing, even a scarf. Cold often brings on the most spectacular of my dreams, as if my brain has been incited to fevered activity. On that particular frigid night, the cold somehow seemed to snap boundaries, shift my time continuum, and perhaps even allow me to visit my own life in a future moment. After waking once, transferring the contents of my entire suitcase onto my person, and shivering to sleep again, I dreamed of a vast, dark, fenced place. The fencing was chain-link in places, chicken wire, sagging X wire, barbed wire on top, jerry-built with tipped-out poles and uncertain corners nailed to log posts and growing trees. And yet it was quite impermeable and solid, as time-tested, broken-looking things so often are.

Behind it, trees ran for miles — large trees, grown trees, big pines the likes of which do not exist on the Great Plains. In my dream I walked up to the fence, looked within, and saw tawny, humpbacked elk move among the great trunks and slashing green arms. Suave, imponderable, magnificently dumb, they lurched and floated through the dim-complexioned air. One turned, however, before they all vanished, and from either side of that flimsy-looking barrier there passed between us a look, a communion, a long and measureless regard that left me, on waking, with a sensation of penetrating sorrow.

I didn't think about my dream for many years, until after I moved to New Hampshire. I had become urbanized and sedentary since the days when I slept with skunks, and I had turned inward. For several years I spent my days leaning above a strange desk, a green door on stilts, which was so high that to sit at it I bought a barstool upholstered in brown leatherette. Besides, the entire Northeast seemed like the inside of a house to me, the sky small and oddly lit, as if by an electric bulb. The sun did not pop over the great trees for hours — and then went down so soon. I was suspicious of Eastern land: the undramatic loveliness, the small scale, the lack of sky to watch, the way the weather sneaked up without enough warning.

The woods themselves seemed bogus at first — every inch of the ground turned over more than once, and even in the second growth of old pines so much human evidence. Rock walls ran everywhere, grown through and tumbled, as if the dead still had claims they imposed. The unkillable and fiercely contorted trees of old orchards, those revenants, spooked me when I walked in the woods. The blasted limbs spread a white lace cold as fire in the spring, and the odor of the blossoms was furiously spectral, sweet. When I stood beneath the canopies that hummed and shook with bees, I heard voices, other voices, and I did not understand what they were saying, where they had come from, what drove them into this earth.

Then, as often happens to sparring adversaries in 1940s movies, I fell in love.

After a few years of living in the country, the impulse to simply *get outside* hit me, strengthened, and became again a habit of thought, a reason for storytelling, an uneasy impatience with walls and roads. At first, when I had that urge, I had to get into a car and drive fifteen hundred miles before I was back in a place that I defined as *out*. The West, or the edge of it anyway, the great level patchwork of chemically treated fields and tortured grazing land, was the outside I had internalized. In the rich Red River Valley, where the valuable cropland is practically measured in inches, environmental areas are defined and proudly pointed out as stretches of roadway where the ditches are not mowed. Deer and pheasants survive in shelter belts — rows of Russian olive, plum, sometimes evergreen — planted at the edges of fields. The former tall-grass prairie has now become a collection of mechanized gardens tended by an array of air-conditioned farm implements and bearing an increasing amount of pesticide and herbicide in each black teaspoon of dirt. Nevertheless, no amount of reality changed the fact that I still *thought* of eastern North Dakota as wild.

In time, though, *out* became outside my door in New England. By walking across the road and sitting in my little writing house — a place surrounded by trees, thick plumes of grass, jets of ferns, and banks of touch-me-not — or just by looking out a screen door or window, I started to notice what there was to see. In time, the smothering woods that had always seemed part of Northeastern civilization — more an inside than an outside, more like a friendly garden — revealed themselves as forceful and complex. The growth of plants, the lush celebratory springs made a grasslands person drunk. The world turned dazzling green, the hills rode like comfortable and flowing animals. Everywhere there was the sound of water moving.

And yet, even though I finally grew closer to these woods, on some days I still wanted to tear them from before my eyes.

I wanted to *see*. Where I grew up, our house looked out on the western horizon. I could see horizon when I played. I could see it when I walked to school. It was always there, a line beyond everything, a simple line of changing shades and colors that ringed the town, a vast place. That was it. Down at the end of every grid of streets: vastness. Out the windows of the high school: vastness. From the drive-in theater where I went parking in a purple Duster: vast distance. That is why, on lovely New England days when everything should have been all right — a fall day, for instance, when the earth had risen through the air in patches and the sky lowered, dim and warm — I fell sick with longing for the horizon. I wanted the clean line, the simple line, the clouds marching over it in feathered masses. I suffered from horizon sickness. But it sounds crazy for a grown woman to throw herself at the sky, and the thing is, I wanted to get well. And so to compensate for horizon sickness, for the great longing that seemed both romantically German and pragmatically Chippewa in origin, I found solace in trees.

Trees are a changing landscape of sound — and the sound I grew attached to, possible only near large deciduous forests, was the great hushed roar of thousands and millions of leaves brushing and touching one another. Windy days were like sitting just out of sight of an ocean, the great magnetic ocean of wind. All around me, I watched the trees tossing, their heads bending. At times the movement seemed passionate, as though they were flung together in an eager embrace, caressing each other, branch to branch. If there is a vegetative soul, an animating power that all things share, there must be great rejoicing out there on windy days, ecstasy, for trees move so slowly on calm days. At least it seems that way to us. On days of high wind they move so freely it must give them a cellular pleasure close to terror.

Unused to walking in the woods, I did not realize that trees dropped branches — often large ones — or that there was any possible danger in going out on windy days, drawn by the natural drama. There was a white pine I loved, a tree of the size foresters call *overgrown*, a waste, a thing made of long-since harvestable material. The tree was so big that three people couldn't reach around it. Standing at the bottom, craning back, fingers clenched in grooves of bark, I held on as the crown of the tree roared and beat the air a hundred feet above. The movement was frantic, the soft-needled branches long and supple. I thought of a woman tossing, anchored in passion: calm one instant, full-throated the next, hair vast and dark, shedding the piercing, fresh oil of broken needles. I went to visit her often, and walked onward, farther, though it was not so far at all, and then one day I reached the fence.

Chain-link in places, chicken wire, sagging X wire, barbed wire on top, jerry-built with tipped-out poles and uncertain corners nailed to log posts and growing trees, still it seemed impermeable and solid. Behind it, there were trees for miles: large trees, grown trees, big pines. I walked up to the fence, looked within, and could see elk moving. Suave, imponderable, magnificently dumb, they lurched and floated through the dim air.

I was on the edge of a game park, a rich man's huge wilderness, probably the largest parcel of protected land in western New Hampshire, certainly the largest privately owned piece I knew about. At forty square miles — 25,000 acres — it was bigger than my mother's home reservation. And it had the oddest fence around it that I'd ever seen, the longest and the tackiest. Though partially electrified, the side closest to our house was so piddling that an elk could easily have tossed it apart. Certainly a half-ton wild boar, the condensed and living version of a tank, could have strolled right through. But then animals, much like most humans, don't charge through fences unless they have sound reasons. As I soon found out, because I naturally grew fascinated with the place, there were many more animals trying to get into the park than out, and they couldn't have cared less about ending up in a hunter's stew pot.

These were not wild animals, the elk — since they were grained at feeding stations, how could they be? They were not domesticated either, however, for beyond the no-hunt boundaries they fled and vanished. They were game. Since there is no sport in shooting feedlot steers, these animals — still harboring wild traits and therefore more challenging to kill — were maintained to provide blood pleasure for the members of the Blue Mountain Forest Association.

As I walked away from the fence that day, I was of two minds about the place — and I am still. Shooting animals inside fences, no matter how big the area they have to hide in, seems abominable and silly. And yet, I was glad for that wilderness. Though secretly managed and off limits to me, it was the source of flocks of evening grosbeaks and pine siskins, of wild turkey, ravens, and grouse, of Eastern coyote, oxygen-rich air, foxes, goldfinches, skunk, and bears that tunneled in and out.

I had dreamed of this place in Valley City, or it had dreamed me. There was affinity here, beyond any explanation I could offer, so I didn't try. I continued to visit the tracts of big trees, and on deep nights — windy nights, especially when it stormed — I liked to fall asleep imagining details. I saw the great crowns touching, heard the raving sound of wind and thriving, knocking cries as the blackest of ravens flung themselves across acres upon indifferent acres of tossing, old-growth pine. I could fall asleep picturing how, below that dark air, taproots thrust into a deeper blankness, drinking the powerful rain.

Or was it so only in my dreams? The park, known locally as Corbin's Park, after its founder, Austin Corbin, is knit together of land and farmsteads he bought in the late nineteenth century from 275 individuals. Among the first animals released there, before the place became a hunting club, were thirty buffalo, remnants of the vast Western herds. Their presence piqued the interest of Ernest Harold Bayne, a conservation-minded local journalist, who attempted to break a pair of buffalo calves to the yoke. He exhibited them at county fairs and even knit mittens out of buffalo wool, hoping to convince the skeptical of their usefulness. His work inspired sympathy, if not a trend for buffalo yarn, and collective zeal for the salvation of the buffalo grew until by 1915 the American Bison Society, of which Bayne was secretary, helped form government reserves that eventually more than doubled the herds that remained.

The buffalo dream seems to have been the park's most noble hour. Since that time it has been the haunt of wealthy hunting enthusiasts. The owner of Ruger Arms currently inhabits the stunning, butter-yellow original Corbin mansion and would like to buy the whole park for his exclusive use, or so local gossip has it.

For some months I walked the boundary admiring the tangled landscape, at least all that I could see. After my first apprehension, I ignored the fence. I walked along it as if it simply did not exist, as if I really were part of that place which lay just beyond my reach. The British psychotherapist Adam Phillips has examined obstacles from several different angles, attempting to define their emotional use. "It is impossible to imagine desire without obstacles," he writes, "and wherever we find something to be an obstacle we are at the same time desiring something. It is part of the fascination of the Oedipus story in particular, and perhaps narrative in general, that we and the heroes and heroines of our fictions never know whether obstacles create desire or desire creates obstacles." He goes on to characterize the Unconscious, our dream world, as a place without obstacles: "A good question to ask of a dream is: What are the obstacles that have been removed to make this extraordinary scene possible?"

My dream, however, was about obstacles still in place. The fence was the main component, the defining characteristic of the forbidden territory that I watched but could not enter or experience. The obstacles that we overcome define us. We are composed of hurdles we set up to pace our headlong needs, to control our desires, or against which to measure our growth. "Without obstacles," Phillips writes, "the notion of development is inconceivable. There would be nothing to master."

Walking along the boundary of the park no longer satisfied me. The preciousness and deceptive stability of that fence began to rankle. Longing filled me. I wanted to brush against the old pine bark and pass beyond the ridge, to see specifically what was there:

what Blue Mountain, what empty views, what lavender hillside, what old cellar holes, what unlikely animals. I was filled with poacher's lust, except I wanted only to smell the air. The linked web restraining me began to grate, and I started to look for weak spots, holes, places where the rough wire sagged. From the moment I began to see the fence as permeable, it became something to overcome. I returned time after time — partly to see if I could spot anyone on the other side, partly because I knew I must trespass.

Then, one clear, midwinter morning, in the middle of a half-hearted thaw, I walked along the fence until I came to a place that looked shaky — and was. I went through. There were no trails that I could see, and I knew I needed to stay away from any perimeter roads or snowmobile paths, as well as from the feeding stations where the animals congregated. I wanted to see the animals, but only from a distance. Of course, as I walked on, leaving a trail easily backtracked, I encountered no animals at all. Still, the terrain was beautiful, the columns of pine tall and satisfyingly heavy, the patches of oak and elderly maple from an occasional farmstead knotted and patient. I was satisfied, and sometime in the early afternoon, I decided to turn back and head toward the fence again. Skirting a low, boggy area that teemed with wild turkey tracks, heading toward the edge of a deadfall of trashed dead branches and brush, I stared too hard into the sun, and stumbled.

In a half crouch, I looked straight into the face of a boar, massive as a boulder. Cornfed, razor-tusked, alert, sensitive ears pricked, it edged slightly backward into the convening shadows. Two ice picks of light gleamed from its shrouded, tiny eyes, impossible to read. Beyond the rock of its shoulder, I saw more: a sow and three cinnamon-brown farrows crossing a small field of glare snow, lit by dazzling sun. The young skittered along, lumps of muscled fat on tiny hooves. They reminded me of snowsuited toddlers on new skates. When they were out of sight the boar melted through the brush after them, leaving not a snapped twig or crushed leaf in his wake.

I almost didn't breathe in the silence, letting the fact of that presence settle before I retraced my own tracks.

Since then, I've been to the game park via front gates, driven down the avenues of tough old trees, and seen herds of wild pigs and elk meandering past the residence of the gamekeeper. A no-hunting zone exists around the house, where the animals are almost tame. But I've been told by privileged hunters that just beyond that invisible boundary they vanish, becoming suddenly and preternaturally elusive.

There is something in me that resists the notion of fair use of this land if the only alternative is to have it cut up, sold off in lots, condominiumized. Yet the dumb fervor of the place depresses me — the wilderness locked up and managed but not for its sake; the animals imported and cultivated to give pleasure through their deaths. All animals, that is, except for skunks.

Not worth hunting, inedible except to old trappers like my uncle Ben Gourneau, who boiled his skunk with onions in three changes of water, skunks pass in and out of Corbin's Park without hindrance, without concern. They live off the corn in the feeding cribs (or the mice it draws), off the garbage of my rural neighbors, off bugs and frogs and grubs. They nudge their way onto our back porch for catfood, and even when disturbed they do not, ever, hurry. It's easy to get near a skunk, even to capture one. When skunks become a nuisance, people either shoot them or catch them in crates, cardboard boxes, Havahart traps, plastic garbage barrels.

Natives of the upper Connecticut River valley have neatly solved the problem of what to do with such catches. They hoist their trapped mustelid into the back of a pickup truck and cart the animal across the river to the neighboring state — New Hampshire to Vermont, Vermont to New Hampshire — before releasing it. The skunk population is estimated as about even on both sides.

We should take comfort from the skunk, an arrogant creature so pleased with its own devices that it never runs from harm, just turns its back in total confidence. If I were an animal, I'd choose to be a skunk: live fearlessly, eat anything, gestate my young in just two months, and fall into a state of dreaming torpor when the cold bit hard. Wherever I went, I'd leave my sloppy tracks. I wouldn't walk so much as putter, destinationless, in a serene belligerence — past hunters, past death overhead, past death all around.

IAN FRAZIER

The Frankest Interview Yet

FROM THE NEW YORKER

A: I was having sex. I had had sex previously, found that I enjoyed
it, and so was having it again. With a sexual partner, I screwed all
over the floor. Orgasms were multiple for the both of us. I took a
lover, also. Plus I had a tryst with a fellow in the shower room of
the old Grand Avenue Y. I turned an empty office at work into a
snuggery, and made use of it. I became proficient not only in
standard English, but also in tavern English. I cursed like a sailor
or sometimes like a navvy. I mixed obscenities with profanities at
will when the spirit moved me, using anatomical and physiological
terms, inferences of parentage, and blasphemies. When called
upon, I could turn the air blue.

Oral sex.

See what I mean? I did not (and do not) shrink from explicit
language. If you are shocked, or perhaps are feeling ambivalent
about what I am saying, good. Sexual practices should be more
open, and no one knows this better than I. When the young
shopgirls in their sheer blouses and blank faces come ankling into
the elevator, my expression turns unmistakably sensual. I simply
drip with sex. It oozes from my every pore, which I like, and they
do, too. And when I see a strapping young hoss of a guy the
experience is remarkably similar. I wiggle like a streetwalker and
go right up to him and say, "Hello, my name is Mr. Bascom." I
garden in the near-nude in the residential community where I live.
I put on a pair of coveralls only when the weather is chilly or I'm
doing landscaping. If my neighbors are offended, they shouldn't
be. I have an excellent, heavyset body. We are all deeply sexual
beings.

I met a young woman with a criterion figure and bedroom eyes at a sales event the other day. I mentally undressed her, then re-dressed her. She noticed the pertinacious quality of my stare and asked, "What are you looking at, Mr. Johnsberry?" I mumbled a pleasantry and looked away. She knew as well as I did that if we wanted, we could screw. I could tell she was appraising me, wondering what I'd be like in the sack, and if I was a swordsman. I wouldn't have been at all surprised if she had a mental image of me bare-butt naked. So much the better. I informed her that my name was Mr. Bemis, and that I would very much enjoy her company in my hotel suite later in the evening. We began chatting. The sexual tension, undercurrents, and electricity in the air were so thick you could have seen them, while our colleagues leered at us with a casual knowingness.

Her name was Ms. Buxbaum, and Christ, what a great lay she turned out to be! After the obligatory postcoital cigarette, I immediately went to church and confessed my sins and was shriven for them, the peace of divine forgiveness filling me as I bent over the prayer rail in my fellow congregants' holy, homely scent of soap and dry-cleaned wool and Sunday shoe polish. By the renewed light of the high chancel windows I signed my name, Mr. Randsworthy, in the registry. Then it was back to the hotel. My lover at the time was a male nurse, and you know how nurses are. He was lithe, sloe-eyed, and rather matter-of-fact about sex, as are many young men who work in hospitals. We discovered a mutual pursuit that gave us enormous pleasure: screwing our heads off.

Yes, I believe in lap dancing. Far from censuring it, I wholeheartedly encourage it as a healthy outlet. At the end of a long day, with my colleagues Mr. Pixley, Mr. Simpkins, et al., I often spend a few wickedly relaxing hours at a small club I know of where lap dancing is done. To have a well-built entertainer of either sex clad in little more than thong, pasties, and/or black bow tie sit in one's lap and gyrate has a marvelous effect. In this, of course, my views come into direct conflict with those of many. I believe that opposition to lap dancing is a destructive holdover from the Puritans, and have argued my point on a number of occasions, even with members of my own family — my children, and their spouses or companions. By now they know enough not to expect moralizing pabulum from me.

The children's mother, Ms. Frampton, and I had great sex

throughout our long marriage and, quite candidly, before, when we were just a couple of randy college kids shacking up. In those days, Johnson (my pet name for my or any penis) could become an ivory wand virtually at command and achieve orgasm in just a few penile thrusts. Then, as now, I wore painted-on trousers with stirrups at the cuffs to pull them down even tighter, and my fiancée, Ms. Samples, did the same. We acquired a reputation on campus for unashamed and forthright behavior, which I have maintained ever since. All the kids except Gary know the time, place, and erotic circumstances of their conception, and are stronger for it. All the kids except Gary can tell you the particulars, thus freeing themselves and others from prudery and cant. When I heard that Gary was having problems at school, I flew up on the shuttle first thing the next morning, met with the dean, Mr. Bentley, had sex, and thrashed out the whole situation. The following term, Gary's marks were back up where they belonged. Neither I, Gary's mother, nor his probable biological dad ever spared any effort with Gary, which is why I find some of his recent remarks unsubstantiated.

From the point of view of one who has spent the balance of his life pursuing vigorous sexual intercourse and sport-screwing, I can say that public attitudes have changed for the better. I give people like myself credit for this. How easy it would have been for me and my contemporaries to continue the backstairs bundling and fondling and frottage that characterized earlier times. But I am an avowed hedonist and sensualist, whose lasting legacy will be more of the same. I don't care how the future may judge me, Mr. Spradlin, as long as it acknowledges that I chased after anything in a skirt or trousers and mounted and was mounted freely. The sexual response is a pleasure given by God, in most cases. To deny this is to deny a natural desire to hear about my sex life and the sex lives of thousands of other businesspeople no different from ourselves.

DARCY FREY

The Last Shot

FROM HARPER'S MAGAZINE

RUSSELL THOMAS PLACES his right sneaker one inch behind the three-point line, considers the basket with a level gaze, cocks his wrist to shoot, then suddenly looks around. Has he spotted me, watching from the corner of the playground? No, something else is up: he is lifting his nose to the wind like a spaniel, he is gauging air currents. He waits until the wind settles, bits of trash feathering lightly to the ground. Then he sends a twenty-five-foot jump shot arcing through the soft summer twilight. It drops without a sound through the dead center of the bare iron rim. So does the next one. So does the one after that. Alone in the gathering dusk, Russell works the perimeter against imaginary defenders, unspooling jump shots from all points. Few sights on Brooklyn playgrounds stir the hearts and minds of the coaches and scouts who recruit young men for college basketball teams quite like Russell's jumper; they have followed its graceful trajectory ever since he made varsity at Abraham Lincoln High School, in Coney Island, two years ago. But the shot is merely the final gesture, the public flourish of a private regimen that brings Russell to this court day and night. Avoiding pickup games, he gets down to work: an hour of three-point shooting, then wind sprints up the fourteen flights in his project stairwell, then back to the court, where (much to his friends' amusement) he shoots one-handers ten feet from the basket while sitting in a chair.

At this hour Russell usually has the court to himself; most of the other players won't come out until after dark, when the thick humid air begins to stir with night breezes and the court lights come on. But this evening is turning out to be a fine one — cool and foggy. The low, slanting sun sheds a feeble pink light over the silvery Atlantic a block away, and milky sheets of fog roll off the ocean and drift in tatters along the project walkways. The air smells of sewage and saltwater. At the far end of the court, where someone has torn a hole in the chicken-wire fence, other players climb through and begin warming up.

Like most of New York's impoverished and predominantly black neighborhoods, Coney Island does not exactly shower its youth with opportunity. In the early 1960s, urban renewal came to Coney Island in the form of a vast tract of housing projects, packed so densely along a twenty-block stretch that a new skyline rose suddenly behind the boardwalk and amusement park. The experiment of public housing, which has isolated the nation's urban poor from the hearts of their cities, may have failed here in even more spectacular fashion because of Coney Island's utter remoteness. In this neighborhood, on a peninsula at the southern tip of Brooklyn, there are almost no stores, no trees, no police; just block after block of gray cement projects — hulking, prisonlike, and jutting straight into the sea.

Most summer nights an amorphous unease settles over Coney Island as apartments become too stifling to bear and the streets fall prey to the gangs and drug dealers. Options are limited: to the south is the stiff gray meringue of the Atlantic; to the north, more than ten miles away, are the Statue of Liberty and the glass-and-steel spires of Manhattan's financial district. Officially, Coney Island is considered a part of the endless phantasmagoria that is New York City. But on nights like these, as the dealers set up their drug marts in the streets and alleyways and the sounds of sirens and gunfire keep pace with the darkening sky, it feels like the end of the world.

Yet even in Coney Island there are some uses to which a young man's talent, ambition, and desire to stay out of harm's way may be put: there is basketball. Hidden behind the projects are dozens of courts, and every night they fill with restless teenagers, there to remain for hours until exhaustion or the hoodlums take over. The high-school dropouts and the aging players who never made it to college usually show up for a physical game at a barren strip of courts by the water known as Chop Chop Land, where bruises and minutes played are accrued at a one-to-one ratio. The younger kids congregate for rowdy games at Run-and-Gun Land. The court there is short and the rims are low, so everyone can dunk, and the only pass ever made is the one inbounding the ball. At Run-and-Gun, players stay on the move for another reason: the court sits just below one of the most dreaded projects, where Coney Island's worst hoodlums sometimes pass a summer evening "getting hectic," as they say — tossing batteries and beer bottles onto the court from apartment windows fifteen stories above.

The neighborhood's best players — the ones, like Russell, with aspirations — practice a disciplined, team-driven style of basketball at this court by the O'Dwyer projects, which has been dubbed the Garden after the New York Knicks' arena. In a neighborhood ravaged by the commerce of drugs, the Garden offers a tenuous sanctuary. A few years ago, community activists petitioned the housing authority to install night lights. And the players themselves resurfaced the court and put up regulation-height rims that snap back after a player dunks. Russell may be the only kid at the Garden who practices his defensive footwork while holding a ten-pound brick in each hand, but no one here treats the game as child's play. Even the hoodlums decline to vandalize the Garden, because in Coney Island the possibility of transcendence through basketball is an article of faith.

Most evenings this summer I have come to the Garden to watch Russell and his friends play ball. The notion that basketball can liberate dedicated players like these from the grinding daily privations of the ghetto has become a cherished parable, advanced by television sportscasters, college basketball publicists, and sneaker companies proselytizing the work ethic and $120 high-tops. And that parable is conveyed directly to the players at the Garden by the dozens of college coaches who arrive in Coney Island each year with assurances that even if a National Basketball Association contract isn't in the cards, a player's talent and tenacity will at least reward him with a free college education, a decent job, and a one-way ticket out of the neighborhood. But how does this process actually unfold? And what forces stand in its way? How often is basketball's promise of a better life redeemed? It was questions like these that drew me to this court, between Mermaid and Surf avenues.

"Just do it, right?" I glance to my left and there is Corey Johnson, smiling mischievously, eyes alight. He nods toward the court — players stretching out, taking lay-ups — and it does, in fact, resemble a sneaker commercial. "Work hard, play hard, buy yourself a pair of Nikes, young man," Corey intones. Corey is a deft mimic and he does a superb white TV announcer. "They get you where you want to go, which is out of the ghet-to!" He laughs, we shake hands, and he takes up an observation post by my side.

Corey is Russell's best friend and one of Lincoln High's other star seniors. He, too, expects to play college ball. But he specializes in ironic detachment and normally shows up courtside with his Walkman merely to watch for girls beneath his handsome, hooded eyes. Tonight he is wearing a fresh white T-shirt, expertly ripped along the back and sleeves to reveal glimpses of his sculpted physique; denim shorts that reach to his knees; and a pair of orange sneakers that go splendidly with his lid — a tan baseball cap with orange piping, which he wears with the bill pointing skyward. From his headphones come the sounds of Color Me Badd, and Corey sings along: *I — wanna — sex — you — up* . . . He loops his fingers around the chicken-wire fence and says, "I tell you, Coney Island is like a disease. Of the mind. It makes you lazy. You relax too much. 'Cause all you ever see is other guys relaxing."

Although a pickup game has begun at the basket nearest us, Russell still commands the other. As the last light drains from the sky, he finishes with three-pointers and moves on to baby hooks: fifteen with the left hand, fifteen with the right; miss one and start all over again. Corey smiles at his friend's hair-shirt discipline. Russell, it is hoped, will play next year in the Big East, one of the nation's top college conferences, in which Seton Hall, St. John's, Georgetown, Syracuse, and others compete. Russell is six foot three, 180 pounds, with a shaved head and a small goatee that seems to mean business. Last spring the Lincoln team, with Russell leading the way, won the New York City public-school championship in a rout at Madison Square Garden that was broadcast citywide on cable TV. But one can never predict what may happen to Russell, because, as Corey observes, "Russell is Russell." I can guess what this means: Russell lives in one of the neighborhood's toughest projects, and misfortune often seems to shadow him. Last year a fight between Russell and his girlfriend turned violent. Terrified that his college scholarship had just been replaced by a stiff prison term, Russell climbed to the top of one of Coney Island's highest buildings. It took almost half an hour of reasoned talk by his high-school coach and members of the Sixtieth Precinct to bring him back from the edge.*

Russell may be tightly wound, but no Coney Island player can avoid for long the agonizing pressures that might bring a teenager with his whole life ahead of him to the edge of a roof. Basketball newsletters and scouting reports are constantly scrutinizing the players, and practically every day some coach shows up — appraising, coaxing, negotiating, and, as often as not, making promises he never keeps. Getting that scholarship offer is every player's dream — in anticipation, no one steps outside in Coney Island without a Syracuse cap or a St. John's sweatshirt. But in reality only a handful of the neighborhood's players have ever made it to such top four-year programs; most have been turned back by one obstacle or another in high school. Others who have enrolled in college never saw their dream to completion. The list is grim: there was Eric "Spoon" Marbury, who played for the University of Georgia but never graduated, and ended up back in Coney Island working construction; his younger brother Norman "Jou-Jou" Marbury, who lost his scholarship to highly ranked Tennessee because of academic problems in high school; and now David "Chocolate" Harris, a talented player who never even graduated from high school. He dropped out of Lincoln after his freshman year and became a small-time drug dealer. Earlier this summer police found him in an abandoned lot, his hood pulled over his head and a bullet through his skull. He was seventeen. Some of the players warming up at the Garden have written on the tongues of their sneakers, CHOCOLATE: R.I.P.

The orange court lights have come on now, displacing the encroaching darkness. Two players on either end of the court climb the fence and sit atop the backboards, hanging nets — a sign that a serious game is about to begin. Suddenly a ferocious grinding noise fills the air. It gets louder and louder, and then a teenage

* Some New York City newspapers withheld Russell's name when reporting this incident. In keeping with the practice of withholding the names of minors involved in suicide threats or attempts, I have changed Russell's name and the name of his mother in this article. No other names have been altered.

kid riding a Big Wheel careers onto the court. He darts through the playground crowd, leaving a wake of pissed-off players, then hops off his ride and watches it slam into the fence. "Ah, yes, Stephon Marbury," Corey says dryly, "future of the neighborhood."

Stephon — Eric and Norman Marbury's kid brother — is barely fourteen, has yet to begin high school, but already his recruiting has begun. At least one college coach is known to have sent him fawning letters in violation of National Collegiate Athletic Association rules; street agents, paid under the table by colleges to bring top players to their programs, have begun cultivating Stephon; and practically every high-school coach in the city is heaping him with free gear — sneakers, caps, bags — in an attempt to lure him to his school. At first glance, Stephon doesn't look like the future of anything: he's diminutive, barely five foot nine, with the rounded forehead and delicate features of an infant. He sports a stylish razor cut and a pierced ear, and the huge gold stud seems to tilt his tiny bald head off its axis. Caught somewhere between puberty and superstardom, he walks around with his sneakers untied, the ends of his belt drooping suggestively from his pants, and half a Snickers bar extruding from his mouth.

With Stephon here, Corey wanders onto the court. Russell, too, is persuaded to give up his solo regimen. Basketball, it is commonly said, is a game of pure instinct, but the five-on-five contest that begins here is something else. Corey and Stephon are cousins, and Russell is as good as family — the three of them have played together since they were in grade school. They seem to move as if the spontaneous, magical geometry of the game had all been rehearsed in advance. Stephon, the smallest by far, is doing tricks with the ball as though it were dangling from his hand by a string, then gunning it to his older teammates with a series of virtuoso no-look passes: behind-the-back passes, sidearm passes, shovel passes. Corey is lulling defenders with his sleepy eyes, then exploding to the basket, where he casually tosses the ball through the hoop. Russell is sinking twenty-footers as if they were six-inch putts.

The game has just begun when a crowd starts to form: sidelined players, three deep, waiting their turn. A prostitute trolling for clients. A drunk yelling maniacally, "I played with Jordan, I played with Jabbar. They ain't shit. And neither are *you!*" A buffed-out guy in a silk suit and alligator shoes arrives, swigging from a bottle of Courvoisier. An agent? A scout? The crowd gives him elbow room. A couple of teenage mothers with strollers come by; they get less elbow room.

Basketball is so inextricably woven into the fabric of Coney Island life that almost everyone here can recite a complete oral history of the neighborhood's players. People remember the exact scores of summer tournament games played at this court ten years ago, or describe in rapturous detail the perfect arc that Carlton "Silk" Owens put on his jumper before he was shot in the elbow in 1982. Dog-eared copies of a ten-year-old University of Georgia catalogue with a picture of Spoon Marbury playing with future NBA great Dominique Wilkins get passed around like samizdat.

Russell, Corey, and Stephon are the natural heirs to this vaunted tradition. But this is a complicated business: given the failures that have preceded them, the new crew is watched by the neighborhood with a certain skittishness, a growing reluctance to care too deeply. Yet Coney Island offers its residents little else on which to hang their pride. So the proceedings here take on a desperate, exalted quality, and by unspoken agreement the misfortunes of bygone players are chalked up to either a lack of will or plain bad luck — both of which make possible the continuance of hope. Silk didn't go pro, it is said, "because that was the year they cut the college draft from three rounds to two." Another player, the explanation goes, had that pro game, went to the hoop both ways, "but he was done in by a shyster agent."

Still, the suspicion lingers that something larger and less comprehensible may be at work. Ten years ago, the Long Island City projects in Queens produced New York's best players, but the drug industry and the collapse of that neighborhood into violence, broken families, and ever-greater poverty put an end to its dynasty. In recent years the torch has passed to Coney Island, which struggles to avoid a similar fate.

It's past midnight now, and the ambient glow of Manhattan's remote skyscrapers has turned the sky a metallic blue. Standing courtside, we can see only the darkened outlines of the projects, looming in every direction, and the shirtless players streaking back and forth, drenched in a pool of orange light. For Russell, Corey, and Stephon, the hard labor of winning their scholarships lies ahead; for now this game is enough. Corey, sprinting downcourt, calls out, "Homeboy! Homeboy!" Standing under his own basket, Stephon lets fly with a long, improbable pass that Corey somehow manages to catch and dunk in one balletic leap. The game is stopped on account of pandemonium: players and spectators are screaming and staggering around the court — knees buckling, heads held in astonishment. Even Mr. Courvoisier loses his cool. Stephon laughs and points to the rim, still shuddering fearfully from its run-in with Corey's fists. "Yo, cuz," he yells. "Make it bleed!" Then he raises his arms jubilantly and dances a little jig, rendered momentarily insane by the sheer giddy pleasure of playing this game to perfection.

September

Abraham Lincoln High School is a massive yellow-brick building of ornate stonework and steel-gated windows a few blocks north of the boardwalk. As Coney Island has deteriorated, so has Lincoln High, though the school itself sits about a mile from the projects at the end of Ocean Parkway, a stately, tree-lined boulevard. Across the parkway are Brighton Beach and several other Jewish neighborhoods, but the kids from those areas are usually sent elsewhere for their education, as Lincoln has become, little by little, a ghetto school for the projects.

A malaise has set in at Lincoln, as it has at so many inner-city public schools. Students regularly walk in and out of class, sleep at their desks, throw projectiles through doorways at friends in the hall. In the teachers' cafeteria, conversation often reverts to pension plans and whether the 2,500 Lincoln kids are as bad as last year or worse. The first day I dropped by, there was much commotion because the locker of a student was found to contain a handgun. On my second visit, the weapon in question was a six-inch knife. After one student was sent to the hospital with a neck wound requiring forty stitches, even some of the most peaceable kids began carrying X-Acto knives for protection.

Spectators at games in the New York Public School Athletic League (PSAL) are often frisked at the door by guards with metal detectors. Still, incidents occur. In the middle of the 1982 semifinals, between Alexander Hamilton and Ben Franklin, an off-duty security guard chased a knife-wielding fan directly onto the court and put a gun to his head while the crowd and players ran screaming for the exits. And then there is that ritual of basketball in the urban public schools: the pregame *passeggiata* of the neighborhood's drug dealers. During warm-ups in certain gyms, the steel doors will swing open and slowly, conspicuously, daring the security guards to stop them, the dealers will make their entrance, signaling to friends in the bleachers while strolling around the court draped in leather, fur, and several pounds of gold.

Into this chaos walk the college coaches — pinstriped and paisley-tied, bearing four-color photos of sold-out college arenas and statistics on how many games their teams play on national television. Usually they precede their visits by dropping the players brief notes, like the one from a Fordham coach to a Lincoln player describing how one of the college's basketball stars became rich beyond his wildest dreams. "This could be you someday," the coach wrote. "See how Fordham can change your life?" The coach signed off with the salutation, "Health, Happine$$, and Hundred$."

Most of the coaches are leery of Corey right now; he spends too much time with girls, and despite his intelligence, his grades are among the worst on the team. Stephon is, as far as the NCAA rules are concerned, off-limits for the next three years. So they come to see Russell. In the first week of school, Wichita State, St. Bonaventure, and the University of Delaware have paid him visits. After school today he sits down with Rod Baker, the head coach at the University of California at Irvine.

"My apologies for not coming to see you before, but the fact is one of our players just dropped out and suddenly we need another guard." Coach Baker is a trim, handsome black man wearing a natty blue suit, tasseled loafers, and a gleaming gold NCAA ring. "And the first person we thought of was Russell Thomas. I'm not bullshitting you. Frankly, I think you're an impact player, a franchise player. Five years from now, I wouldn't be surprised if people were saying, 'Remember when Russell Thomas came in and changed the fortunes of Cal-Irvine?'" Baker runs a finger down each side of his well-groomed mustache. Russell smiles uncertainly.

"Now let me tell you about California. Ever been there?" Russell shakes his head. "Well, you're gonna think you died and went to heaven. I'm serious. What is it today — seventy degrees? Nice and sunny? In California this is a shitty day in December. That's the God's truth. And the other thing about going to school on the West Coast . . ." Baker looks down, allows himself a moment to collect his thoughts, then looks up at Russell. "Everybody's got certain things they want to get away from in their past." How on earth does Baker know about Russell's incident on the roof? "In California, Russell, you can get away from that, from all the stuff that brings you down in Coney Island. At Cal-Irvine you can be whoever you really want to be."

After Coach Baker leaves, Russell and I walk out to the football field behind the school, a lovely, tree-lined expanse of green in an otherwise barren urban setting. It's one of those crystalline September afternoons, with fall in the air but the sun pulsing down on the aluminum bleachers where we sit with the last warmth of summer. (Weather like this may ruin a Californian's day, but in Brooklyn this is as good as it gets.) "I was impressed with Coach Baker. I felt he was definitely leveling with me," Russell declares. "But I'm going to wait and see. Hear what they all have to say. Then decide. Try not to be pressured. Just take it one day at a time." Russell's initial comments after a recruiting session often mimic the solemn coach-speak to which he is subjected every day. So many people — high-school and college coaches and freelance street agents — want a piece of Russell and try to influence where he will sign that it often takes him a while to locate his own thoughts. "They say it's the second-biggest decision I gotta make in my life — after I pick my wife." He looks around the field, swatting imaginary flies. "But I'm doing good, I'm handling it." He locates some gum on the bottom rung of the bleachers, picks it free, rolls it between two fingers, and flips it onto the grass. "It's normal to be confused, right?" Now the elastic of his right sock receives his complete attention as he performs a series of micro-adjustments to get the folds just right. "That's only human, isn't it?" He takes one more look around and, finding nothing else to distract him, falls silent.

The recruiting circus has been a fact of life for Russell and his friends ever since they were in junior high. Directly across the street from Lincoln sits William Grady Tech — another power-house PSAL team — and the two schools compete zealously for the pool of talent coming out of the Coney Island projects. Lincoln players often refer to Grady as "the best team money can buy." Grady players claim that Lincoln tries to lure them away with sneakers and promises to "pass them along" in their classes. Coaches at both schools deny such allegations, but it is a fact that thirteen-year-old Coney Island athletes are encouraged to shop for high schools the way the seniors pick colleges — according to which school will give them the most playing time, the best chance to win a city title, and the exposure to get recruited to the next level.

The pressure of playing basketball in Coney Island affects Russell in mysterious ways. One time last year he snuck out the back door of the locker room to avoid a postgame team meeting, leaving everyone wondering whether he was angry at himself for his performance or angry at his teammates for not passing him the ball. Probably both. This year, knowing how much is at stake, Russell has struggled to change. He does this in small ways. Over the summer he told me he was planning a new image for himself. I waited to see what he meant. The first day of school he arrived wearing penny loafers, just like the coaches. The next day, building from the bottom up, he had added pleated pants. Then suspenders. A paisley tie. Finally he topped off the look with a pair of nonprescription wire-rimmed glasses — "because they make you look educated. You know, the professor look."

But today Russell seems agitated in the old way, restless with an emotion he can't identify. "You know, I used to say that I couldn't wait to be a senior," he says. "But I got to worry about classes, the season, recruiting, the SATs. That's *a lot* of pressure." According to NCAA rules, students who want to play sports at a four-year, Division I school, those with the nation's top athletic programs, must enter college having maintained at least a 70 average in high school and having received a combined score of 700 on the math and verbal sections of the SATs — the last an insurmountable obstacle to many black players with poor educations and little experience taking standardized tests. Failing that, a player must earn a two-year degree at a junior college before moving on to a four-year school. Many Division I coaches, however, refuse to recruit junior-college players, considering them damaged goods. So players who don't go directly to a four-year school often never get to play top college ball or earn their bachelor's degrees.

The first time Russell took the SATs, he received a combined score somewhere in the mid-500s. (You receive 400 points for signing your name.) This year he gave up his lunch period to study, and lately he's been carrying around a set of vocabulary flash cards, which he pulls out whenever there isn't a basketball in his hands. By dint of tremendous effort, Russell had also brought his average up to 78 — the highest on the team. These are extraordinary developments for someone whose schooling over the years has been so bad that he had never, until recently, finished a book or learned the fundamentals of multiplication, even as he was being called upon to answer reading comprehension and algebra questions on the SATs. "I used to think there were smart people and dumb people, but that's not true," Russell says forcefully. "Everybody's got the same brain. They say a human mind can know a thousand words — it's like a little computer! But you got to practice." He pauses. "But how come it's always the guys who don't study who get their 700s? Seems like the guys who work hard always get screwed. But oh, well."

From across the football field, the chants and cries of cheerleading practice travel toward us with perfect clarity. Russell shades his eyes with his hands and watches a tumble of cartwheels. "It's nice out here, isn't it? All the trees and everything? Out where I live there's nothing but total corruption and evilness, drugs and stolen cars. All my friends be getting arrested, shot at . . ." It is not too much to say that basketball saved Russell. In junior high he was trouble, sometimes leaving home for long stretches to hang out on the streets with his friends. But he was spotted playing ball in the parks by one of Lincoln's unofficial recruiters, who persuaded him to enroll. In high school he gained confidence and won the hearts of teachers who admired his efforts while growing increasingly appalled by what he had never been taught. Now after school, while certain of his classmates walk over to Brighton Beach to hold up pensioners at gunpoint, Russell goes straight home, takes his vitamins, does his push-ups, and combs through college recruiting brochures until bedtime. His dream is not to become a pro, he tells me, but "to graduate college, start me a nice little family, and get me a nice little job as a registered nurse."

Russell has begun throwing his things into his gym bag: books, towel, basketball. Something still bothers him, though, and he keeps going back to it, like a tongue to a broken tooth. "You know, I look at all these players, like Silk and Jou-Jou. They're *way* better than me, and look what happened to them: Jou-Jou lost his scholarship, Silk never graduated. This recruiting business, man, it's *scary*. But Coach Baker — for some reason he made me feel secure, like he'll take good care of me, like I'm part of the family." Russell, so effusive about other matters, almost never mentions his own family. All I know is that his father moved away when Russell was young, leaving his mother to raise him and his two younger sisters. I can't help wondering if it isn't doubly hard for Russell to resist all the high-powered coaches who recruit him because he has lived most of his life without a father.

Russell's new girlfriend, Terry, comes into view across the field. She waves to us and starts walking toward the bleachers. "Now that girl is *smart!*" Russell exclaims. "She got an 88 average!" A cloud has just shifted in Russell's mood and the sun has reappeared. "She got a *nice* family, too. They even got their own house. One of these days I'm going to marry that girl." Russell started seeing Terry not long after the incident with his previous girlfriend. All of Russell's friends were thrilled to see him involved with someone so pretty and levelheaded; Terry's friends thought she was crazy. But she stuck by Russell, and recently he announced to his teammates that he would wear a small blue ribbon — Terry's favorite color — on his uniform this season. This, too, was part of the new Russell.

Terry is still a good fifty yards away. Russell puts his hand on my arm confidentially. "You know what happened to me last year, with that business on the roof?" This is the first time he's mentioned it to me. "I really thought my career was shattered. But you know, I see now it was good for me. I been through certain things other teenagers haven't. I learnt that part of success is failure, having hard times smack you in the face, having to go without having." Still gripping my arm, Russell looks me in the eye and says, "I'm gonna get my 700 and go Division I. Trust me. You know why? I've come too far, worked too hard already."

This is what this whole basketball business is about, isn't it? By playing ball and playing by the rules, a kid like Russell is saved from the streets — saved too from that unshakable belief in his own insignificance — and set on a path that could change his life.

Terry is almost upon us now. Russell licks his fingertips and cleans a smudge off the top of his loafer. Then he takes a precautionary whiff of each armpit and, finding the results tolerable, shakes my hand and runs off to meet his girl.

October

"Come on, Russell — we're jetting!" Stephon places his hand against the back of Russell's bald head and flicks it hard to make the skin sting.

"Damn, Stephon, stop sweating me! Can't you see I'm talking to my girl?" When Russell gets upset, his voice jumps to a higher register. *"Can't you see I'm talking to my girl?"* Stephon mimics. Russell tries to ignore him. He whispers something in Terry's ear, gives her a kiss, then slings his book bag over his shoulder and marches toward the locker room. The last class bell has rung, disgorging hundreds of students into the Lincoln corridors. Stephon lingers in the crowd and leans in close to Terry. "You know, when Russell goes to college, I'm next in line."

Terry is almost as tall as Stephon, and for an instant I think she's going to hit him. But she says, "You got *some* mouth," and walks away.

Stephon does not suffer from the usual array of adolescent insecurities, but why should he? As a freshman, he arrived at Lincoln already a legend, and his performance later today, during the season's first official practice, will do nothing to lower his profile. Hopes for this year's team are running so high that everyone gathers in the gym to see for himself: students, teachers, other coaches, and a reporter for *Newsday* who will cover the team all season.

And the players do not disappoint. All of them have improved since I saw them in August. Russell, once a stationary jump shooter, is shooting off the dribble, driving with authority to the hoop. For years, Russell had gotten a rap for "playing white" — taking a lay-up when he could have dunked. "No one thinks I can dunk 'cause I never dunked in public," he told me over the summer. "But between you and me, I dunk in the park all the time — when no one's looking." I was tempted to ask if this was a riddle (is a dunk really a dunk if no one is around to see it?), but Russell wasn't smiling. "I'm going to dunk this year. Trust me." And he does. At practice, Russell drives the lane and goes straight over Corey for an emphatic jam. The whole place erupts — guys are chanting his name, yelling, "He flushed it *good!*" Russell, ignoring the cheers, walks over to me and grips my shoulder. "See, it's all part of the plan," he says. "Just like the shoes." Now what the hell does *that* mean?

As for Corey, he seems to have added an extra cylinder for the coming season. At six foot one, Corey is so fast he doesn't even bother to fake; he just wastes his man on the first step and springs into the air as if coming off a trampoline. "Do the 360!" someone yells from the bleachers and Corey obliges, performing a gyrating dunk. "Statue of Liberty!" comes the next request, and Corey takes off near the foul line, soars toward the basket, and then — legs split, arm extended, ball held high like a torch — throws down a thunderous, backboard-rattling jam. Corey knows how to work a crowd, sometimes too well. Last year, in one of the season's crucial games, Corey was all alone under the basket, tried a fancy lay-up, and blew it. The coaches rose to their feet, howling in rage. Corey jogged downcourt shrugging, palms turned toward the ceiling. "Relax, guys," he said, nonchalance itself. "It's just *basketball.*"

And then there is Stephon. He is making his debut as a high-school player today, but he takes the court as he always does — ever confident, leaning forward onto the balls of his feet in happy antici-pation, arms jangling at his sides. "Mission day," he announces with a clap. "Time to get busy." Within moments he is making quick work of his competition, stunning the crowded, noisy gym into a reverential silence. Here he is, out by the three-point line. He does a stutter step to freeze the defense, then drives the lane. En route, he encounters the team's six-foot-seven center in midair, so he changes direction, shifts the ball from right hand to left, and sinks a reverse lay-up. I hear one of the coaches mutter, "Holy shi — ," not even finishing the thought because here Stephon is again, off to the left. He drives, sees too many bodies in the paint, and pulls up for a jumper. He is way out of position, his lithe body still floating toward the basket, so he calculates his velocity, takes a little something off the ball, and banks it gently off the glass.

"Jesus, this kid's the real thing! Do you realize Stephon could

keep us in TV tournaments for the next four years?" Bobby Hartstein, head coach of the Lincoln team, sounds overjoyed — and
vastly relieved. Lincoln has had great players before, but never a
virtual child prodigy like Stephon. All summer long, Coach Hartstein held his breath as other schools tried to lure his incoming
star with promises of a starting position and a guaranteed supply
of his favorite sneakers. One Brooklyn coach presented Stephon
with a new uniform and treated him and his father to a series of
extravagant dinners. A coach in the Bronx was rumored to have
offered cash up front. But Lincoln had the edge. Stephon's three
older brothers — Eric, Donnie, and Norman — had all starred
at the school. And to close the sale, Hartstein made Stephon
an extraordinary offer: the forty-two-year-old coach promised the
fourteen-year-old player that he'd turn down any college coaching
offer to personally shepherd Stephon through high school.

After practice the players all tumble down the school's front steps.
Stephon walks up to me and says, "Take me to Mickey D's. I'm
hungry. I could eat three Big Macs. You got any cash?" I've already
agreed to drive Russell and Corey home, so I tell Stephon to hop
in. "This is your ride?" Stephon stares slack-jawed at my ten-year-old
Toyota. "When I get to college, I'm gonna get me a white Nissan
Sentra — that shit is *milk!*"

"Just get in the damn car," Russell says. In the last few weeks,
some schools that had recruited Russell aggressively in September
have backed off, and Russell is taking it hard. No sooner had
Russell made up his mind to sign with Cal-Irvine than Coach Baker
called to say they were no longer interested — the guard they
thought was leaving decided to come back. Meanwhile, other
schools seem convinced that Russell won't ever pass his SATs.
(Coaches somehow learn of Russell's test scores before he's even
had time to show them to his mother.) With every school that
courts and then abandons him, Russell goes through the full cycle
of infatuation, falling in love, rejection, and recuperation; each
time he survives with a little less of the spirit to forge on with the
school year. Stephon wants the front seat of my car, but Russell says
gruffly, "Six foot three gets the front. Five foot nine gets in back."
Corey wisely stays out of it. He puts his Walkman on, pops the
hatch, and climbs in the far back, draping his legs over the bumper.

Autumn is arriving quickly this year. For weeks now the sky has been a study in gray, and the trees along Ocean Parkway are already bare. On the drive to McDonald's we splash through piles of fallen leaves. "If you crash and I get injured, Coach is gonna kill you," Stephon advises me. Then he announces, to no one in particular, "When I go to college, I'm going to Syracuse or Georgia Tech."

"How come?" I ask.

"Because at Syracuse you play in front of 32,820 people every home game — it's crazy-loud in there," he says, meaning the Syracuse Carrier Dome. "And because Georgia Tech knows how to treat its point guards." Stephon is no doubt thinking of Kenny Anderson — the player he is most often compared with — who left Georgia Tech after his sophomore year to sign a five-season, $14.5 million contract with the NBA's New Jersey Nets. Anderson's salary is a figure Stephon knows as precisely as the seating capacity of the Carrier Dome.

Driving along, we pass beneath the elevated tracks over Stillwell Avenue, where four of New York City's subway lines come to an end. The Coney Island peninsula begins here; beyond the tracks are the projects. Few store owners will risk doing business out there, and the McDonald's near Stillwell is the last outpost of junk food before the streets plunge into the shadow of the high-rises. We order our food to go and pile back into my car. Stephon, hungrily consuming his first burger, wedges himself between the two front seats in order to speak directly into his friend's ear. "So, Russell. What are they offering you?" Russell snatches his head away and stares out the window. "You mean you're just gonna sign?" Stephon goes on. "And then when you get to campus and see all them players driving those nice white Nissan Sentras, what are you gonna say to yourself? 'Oh well, I guess they got them from their *mothers*'?"

We ride along in hostile silence. As we drive down Mermaid Avenue toward the projects, the trees, shops, and pedestrians become scarcer, block by block. During the urban-renewal years, the city knocked down storefronts all along this stretch, but it abandoned much of its commercial redevelopment plan after moving tenants into the projects. Now the only signs of life along some blocks are the drunks leaning against the plywood of boarded-up buildings and the mangy dogs scavenging vacant lots.

Russell says, "By the way, Stephon, the NCAA does *not* allow players to get cars."

"Ha! You think the NCAA gives a fuck about *cars?*" Stephon, still with his head next to Russell's, gives a shrill little laugh. "Why do you think the best players go where they go? 'Cause the schools promise to take care of them and their families. They say the magic word: *money.*"

It's no secret where Stephon gets his head for business. Last summer, while I was watching Stephon play ball, his father, Donald Marbury, approached me. "You the guy writing about Lincoln?" he asked. "And you haven't even interviewed Mr. Lincoln himself?" We shook hands, and when I told him how much I wanted to speak to him, a sly smile crossed his creased and handsome face. "Well, in that case I expect there will be some gratuities for me and my family." I must have looked surprised because Mr. Marbury snapped angrily, "Oh, come on now! If it weren't for me and my boys, Lincoln wouldn't even be worth writing about!"

The Marbury story *is* a good one, though it may never be written to the father's liking. After starring at Lincoln, Eric went on to play for the University of Georgia, but he failed to graduate before his scholarship ran out and was now back in Coney Island. Donnie, the second son, displayed even greater promise, but he didn't have a 70 average in high school and had to do time at two junior colleges. After two years, he moved on to Texas A&M, where he led the Southwest Conference in scoring. But he too never graduated and was passed over in the college draft; now he's out in Utah, at another college, trying to finish his degree. Then came Norman. If ever Coney Island had produced pro material, it was he. The first public-school player in New York ever to be named all-city three years in a row, Norman was a dazzler — fast, strong, with a deadly outside shot and the ability, on drives to the basket, to take on the largest foes. He had his pick of top programs and eventually signed with Tennessee, which had assured him that if he chose their school, he could still attend for free even if he didn't make 700; he would simply have to sit out his freshman season, as the NCAA rules require. But in the summer of 1990, just weeks before he was set to leave for Knoxville, he came up 40 points short of 700 on his final SAT attempt. Tennessee broke its promise and withdrew its offer. Norman, Coney Island's finest product to date, packed his bags for a junior college in Florida. (He now plays for a Salt Lake City junior college.)

For years Donald Marbury had watched his boys fall short. Now he was down to his last — and most talented — son. "You want information, I expect that you will have the money to pay for it," he said to me last summer. I told him that wasn't possible and he shrugged dismissively. "I'm not like all them other Coney Island guys — too stupid to know the value of what they're sitting on." He tapped his brow. "This is a business — ain't nothing but. And if I don't receive satisfaction, I will take my business somewhere else."

Among the coaches who are now recruiting Stephon, it is said, as one did recently, that Donald Marbury "just won't stop dining out on his son's talent." As for Stephon, the coaches complain that he's a player always looking to "get over," to take advantage of any situation. But how *should* they act? The entire basketball establishment has been trying to buy Stephon for years: summer-league teams pay his way to tournaments around the country (last summer found him in Arizona); street agents take Stephon into the Nets' locker room for chats with the pros; basketball camps give him wardrobes full of free gear; and coaches are constantly laying on hands and giving him awkward little hugs, hoping to win his affection.

And the Marbury family knows only too well, from witnessing the fates of Eric, Donnie, and Norman, how abruptly the coaches will withdraw their largess. So the Marbury policy, as Stephon explains it to Russell in my car, has become quite simple: "If you don't ask, you don't get. Like if I wasn't getting my burn" — his playing time — "here at Lincoln? I'd be up and out with quickness."

By the time I reach the tag end of the peninsula, where Corey, Russell, and Stephon live, everyone has finished his burgers and fries, and I swing by their buildings to drop them off. It's not yet 6 P.M., but the drug dealers are already out. Russell spots a kid he used to play with at the Garden loping down the street with a rangy gait and his Georgetown cap on backward. "Look at him. Just doing the same ol' same ol'. Shoot 'em up. Bang bang." Dealers and players make up the principal social groups among young men in Coney Island, although there's cross-pollination, with washed-up players joining the gangs and dealers disrupting games to show off their playground moves. One major difference, however, is that the dealers own white Nissan Sentras whereas players like Stephon just talk about them.

Russell, Corey, and Stephon have never been involved with the gangs, but that leaves them broke most of the time, with few options for making money besides hawking sodas on the board-walk during the summer. It's hard work, lugging a case of Cokes from the nearest supermarket a mile away, then selling them one by one in the blazing heat. For their trouble, they usually get a summons from the police. Later on those summer evenings, when the athletes start their workouts, the dealers often gather at the sidelines to jeer. "They ain't doing nothing with their lives, so they don't want you to be doing nothing either," Russell explains. He climbs out of my car with a pile of SAT review books under his arm. "Man, I hate Coney Island. After I get to college, I'm *never* coming back. Until then, boys" — he gives us a weary salute — "I'm staying inside."

I drive down the block to drop off Stephon and Corey. They live on the fourth and fifth floors of the same building, directly over the Garden. After leaning into the window to slap my hand, Stephon starts walking with that King Marbury stride toward his building. I watch as he swaggers across the deserted playground, trailing his hand along the jungle gym. All the guys drinking their afternoon beers call out to him as he goes by.

I've spent some time in Stephon's building, and it's not the most pleasant place to come home to after a long practice. It's fourteen stories high and the elevator never works. The long halls stink of urine, and the dark stairwells, where the dealers lurk, echo with the low rumble of drug transactions. The apartment doors don't even have numbers on them, though they must have at one time be-cause just outside the Marburys' apartment someone has scrawled violently across the wall, I WANNA FUCK THE GIRL IN 3B CAUSE SHE SUCKS DICK GOOD.

Everyone is hoping that Stephon will keep his head together as his notoriety grows throughout his high-school career and that, more to the point, he or his father won't accept some "gratuity" that raises the interest of the NCAA enforcement division. Given the family's circumstances, however, and the lessons they have learned about how this recruiting game is played, one can hardly blame Stephon and his father for wanting theirs — and wanting it now.

November

Heading toward Thanksgiving, Lincoln could not have asked for greater success. The team was undefeated, making headlines in all the major New York City dailies, and had received an invitation to play in San Diego in a Christmas tournament of the country's top high-school teams. Lincoln didn't just win its games, either; the team routed its opponents by such lopsided scores that opposing coaches often shook their heads and remarked, "Those guys were *high-school* players?" Russell was scoring at will — in the team's first scrimmage he turned in an outrageous forty-six-point performance, missing only three of twenty-four field-goal attempts, then kept to that pace for the next several games. *The Hoop Scoop,* a recruiting newsletter, ranked him the sixth best player in New York City, and he earned an honorable mention in the magazine *Street & Smith's* nationwide basketball roundup.

Meanwhile Stephon was getting his burn, and then some. He started the season's first game (fifteen points, twelve assists) and every one thereafter. *New York Newsday,* under a half-page picture of the Lincoln team holding their smiling young point guard in their arms, announced the beginning of "the era of Stephon Marbury." Scouting reports were giving Stephon their top rating, and an assistant from Providence College showed up in Coney Island to watch Stephon practice one day, waving discreetly to the freshman — violating the intent, if not the letter, of NCAA rules designed to protect underclassmen from recruiters. "It's never too early to start showing interest," the coach whispered. Word of Stephon's prowess even reached a TV production company, which contacted Stephon about making a commercial, though when the NCAA informed the Marburys that accepting a fee might violate its rules, his father declined.

Off the court, however, there were some unwelcome developments. Stephon was working hard in his classes, hoping to break the pattern of academic failure set by his brothers, but his teachers were noticing that his book reports rarely included a period or a capital letter — not a good omen for the verbal portion of the SATs. As for Russell, he was scoring well on practice SAT exams, but when test day arrived he would panic and forget all his last-minute cramming, shaking his faith that hard work would eventually win the day. Years of bad schooling are coming back to haunt Russell just when he needs his education the most. Leaving the school building now, he looks exhausted, defeated, like a sullen factory worker at the end of a long shift.

Russell took the SATs yet again last weekend. Terry was planning to treat him to a celebratory dinner after the test. As we walk down the school steps, I ask how his date went. "I dissed her good. You should have seen it. Tell him, Corey." Corey says nothing, so Russell goes on. "She came up to me all nice and sweet, and I said, 'Get out of my sight! Don't bother me no more!'"

I'm stunned by this development. The last time I saw them together, Terry was sitting on Russell's lap in study hall, feeding him a bagel bite by bite. "What were you fighting about?"

"I don't know. I guess I was just in a bad mood because of the SATs." Russell drapes his arm over my shoulder. "Never let a girl see you sweat. Didn't your mother ever tell you that?" Russell emits a peculiar mirthless laugh. I look at Corey. He shrugs and traces a circle around his temple with his index finger.

The days are getting shorter now. By the time practice is over, the sun has long since dropped into its slot behind the Verrazano Narrows Bridge and the sky at twilight is covered with brooding clouds. Corey's older brother Willie owns a barbershop just off Flatbush Avenue in central Brooklyn, twenty minutes away. After practice Russell, Corey, and Stephon like to hang out there, and I usually give them a lift on my way home. As we drive past the brightly lit bodegas and rice-and-beans joints on Flatbush Avenue, fires rage out of metal drums, circled by hooded men trying to keep warm. Corey looks out the window and says in a high, fragile voice, "Oh, no. I just *hate* it when the Negroes wear those hoods. Scary! Oh! So scary!" Everyone laughs and Corey lifts his own hood over his head. He knows that when he too walks around like that, cops will stop him and pedestrians will turn away from him in fear. "Only in America," he says.

I have yet to hear Corey talk much about colleges, so I ask him where he wants to play. "Oh, I'm thinking about some southern schools: Florida State, North Carolina, maybe Virginia. I hate it when it gets sharp and brisk out like this. My one rule is, I won't go anyplace where I got to wear one of them Eskimo coats." Corey's recruiting hasn't even begun, but he's already established the proper hedonistic frame of mind.

"Still got to pass those SATs," Russell warns.

"I'm not scared," Corey replies. "I do well on tests. Anyway, this should be our year to relax."

"That test is *hard*," says Stephon from the back seat. "I looked at it once and almost fainted. I read somewhere that David Robinson got a 1300. Is that possible?"

"I heard there are players who get other guys to take the test for them," Russell says. "How do they get away with that? Find someone who looks like them?"

This is not a good sign. One of Russell's friends at Grady, who had scored lower than he on practice tests, suddenly got his 700 and signed with a top program. Some Lincolnites have begun wondering whether Grady players are using stand-ins to take the test.

The NCAA and the college basketball industry have done much soul-searching in recent years over the SAT requirement, as well they should. A combined score of 700 may not seem like a terribly rigorous standard, but given the quality of the Lincoln players' schooling, it's not surprising that they don't know a synonym for *panache* or how to make the most of what they do know; they've never been told, for example, to avoid guessing and answer only the questions they're sure of — the kinds of test-taking tips suburban kids learn on their first day in a Stanley Kaplan review course. Russell's school average, now over 80, says a lot more about his determination to succeed, but that alone will get him nowhere.

Business is brisk tonight at Willie's shop — either that or a lot of guys are using the place to keep warm. Willie and his partner are cutting with dispatch and still a half-dozen guys are hanging out. Willie keeps a basketball in the shop that everyone passes around while watching sitcom reruns on the TV. It's a homey place: taped to the mirrors are photos of the Johnson clan — Corey, Willie, and their six siblings. (The Johnsons are one of the only intact families I know in Coney Island: the father lives at home and all the children out of high school have jobs.) A T-shirt commemorating Lincoln's championship last year is pinned to the wall, next to a painting of Jesus, a bust of Nefertiti, and four portraits of Martin Luther King. Willie has also slapped up an assortment of bumper stickers: MORE HUGGING, LESS MUGGING and TO ALL YOU VIRGINS ... THANKS FOR NOTHING. Outside, darkness has fallen like a black curtain against the shop window, but inside Willie's it's bright and warm.

Corey, whistling the theme song to *The Andy Griffith Show*, grabs a razor and stands next to Russell, trimming his right sideburn. (When Russell began dressing for success this season, Corey would remain in the locker room to troubleshoot in case Russell hit any snags knotting his tie.) Corey asks him what's going on with Terry, and Russell admits he's not really angry at her; he's just worried she'll get distant with him if he shows how much he likes her. "What if she decides she don't want to be with me?" he says unhappily. "I would take that hard."

"You just got to tease her a little, is all," Corey says. He moves behind Russell to trim his neck hairs. "Like, instead of kissing her on the lips, kiss her on the nose. Then kiss her on the eyebrow. Give her a kiss on the ear. Before you know it, she'll be beggin' you, 'When you gonna kiss me on the *lips?*'" Corey laughs and laughs, enjoying his own good advice — he knows it's been thoroughly market-tested. Most Coney Island kids feel utterly lost outside their neighborhood, but Corey goes club-hopping in Manhattan, and every time he shows up for a game — no matter where in the city it is — some girl in the bleachers is calling out his name. His shrewdness on a variety of topics — dating, churchgoing, cooking, writing poetry — has earned him the nickname "Future," because, as Russell once explained, "Corey's a future-type guy, crazy-smart, a walking genius. There are no limits to what he can do."

One day in study hall, I watched Corey sitting in the back, bent over his desk, while all around him his classmates wreaked havoc, throwing spitballs and jumping from desk to desk. At the end of the period I asked what he had accomplished and he handed me a poem about life in Coney Island that ended, "A place meant for happiness, sweet love and care — / Something any human desires to share. / Yet it seems to haunt instead of praise / The foundation and center of our bitter days."

When I had finished reading, Corey said to me, "I'm going to be a writer — you know, creative writing, poetry, free-associative stuff. I just play ball to take up time." Corey was tremendously prolific, dashing off a new poem for every girl he met. But having successfully merged his twin passions — writing and romance — he never left time for his homework. He did the assignments he liked, ignored the rest, and, though he never caused trouble in class, had a 66 average and was one failed test away from losing his high-school eligibility. Already Division I coaches had identified him as a gifted player whose grades could be his undoing.

Corey is standing in front of Russell, evening his sideburns. He says, "But whatever you do with Terry, just don't bust inside her. That almost happened to me." Across the room, I hear Willie Johnson snort with disapproval. Willie is cutting Stephon's hair, but mostly he's been keeping a weather eye on his brother. "Corey's smart, but he's stupid too," Willie says to me. "You know what I mean? In junior high, he was a virgin with a 90 average. Now he's got a 65. You tell me." I laugh, but Willie says, "No, I'm *serious*, man. I try to talk to him. I say, 'Don't you want to go to college? Don't you know you got to sacrifice for things you want?'" Willie is clipping Stephon's hair with growing agitation, and Stephon has sunk low in his chair, hoping to avoid a scalping. "At home Corey's on the phone all night, talking to girls. I say, 'You got a personal problem? Just tell me.'"

Willie is speaking in code now. What he's hinting at is the Johnson family's fear that Corey will get one of his girlfriends pregnant. In Coney Island, girls and the distractions of friends represent such a threat to a college career that the neighborhood's talented athletes are often urged to give up the rights and privileges of adolescence and attend a high school far from home. They will be lonely, but they will stay on the straight and narrow. Corey's older brother Louis took this strategy one step further, going into seclusion at an all-boys school, then spending an extra year at a prep school that serves as a sort of academic rehab clinic for basketball players. Not coincidentally, he passed his SATs and became the first of the six Johnson boys to make it to a Division I program, the University of Buffalo.

Louis was so dedicated to his craft that he would practice his shot under the Garden lights until 4 A.M. Everyone wishes Corey were equally single-minded. But Corey's sensibility is too quirky for that, and therein lies a danger. If Corey lived twenty-five miles north, in, say, Scarsdale, he'd play the offbeat writer whose poor grades earn him a four-year sentence at Colgate, to be served while his classmates all go Ivy. But Corey fools around in an arena where there are no safety schools or safety nets. All of which presents a sad bit of irony: inner-city kids are always accused of doing nothing but throwing a ball through a hoop. Then along comes someone like Corey who takes pleasure in a million other things. (When the Lincoln team runs wind sprints on the outdoor track, Corey gladly takes the outside lane so he can run his hands through the canopy of leaves above his head.) In Coney Island, however, you ignore your basketball talent at great risk — athletic scholarships being significantly easier to come by than those for ghetto poets.

By the time Russell and Corey submit themselves to Willie's shears, it's already late, so I agree to drive them home. All three are tired, and we ride along in a rare moment of quiet. Finally, Russell turns to me and says, "What do you know about Rob Johnson?"

Oh boy.

Johnson is a street agent, a middleman, a flesh peddler. He makes his living getting chummy with high-school players and then brokering them to colleges for a fee — though the coaches who pay it swear they've never heard of him. Lately, Johnson has become entangled in an NCAA investigation, but it hasn't kept him from showing up regularly at the Lincoln gym — a tall black man with an enormous gut, Day-Glo Nikes, and a thick gold chain around his wrist. After practice, he lingers around the players, offering to drive them home or take them to the movies — a particularly appealing figure to broke and fatherless kids like Russell.

"Has Rob offered to be your agent?" I ask. Russell looks out the window and says, "He called me last night. Said he liked the way I played. *A lot.*" I tell Russell he might want to check out Rob's reputation, but Russell says, "It don't matter. I've decided to sign with South Carolina. They really want me." Having announced this unexpected decision, Russell pulls out a paper bag with his customary after-practice snack: a plain bagel and a carton of Tropicana.

"You should visit before you make up your mind," Corey advises. He's stretched luxuriously across the back seat.

"But I already know I want to go there," Russell says between mouthfuls.

"Russell, you've never been outside Coney Island! How the hell are you gonna know? Look" — Corey lowers his voice and tries to speak in tones of unimpeachable reasonableness — "Russell, say you're going to marry someone. You going to marry the first girl you sleep with? No. Of course not. You're going to look around, see what the other girls can do for you, and *then* make your decision. Same with colleges. You got to go up there and have a careful look around."

"Nobody can make me take visits if I don't want to."

Corey laughs. "Nobody's gonna *make* you do anything. But you might as well let them show you a good time. Let them wine you and dine you. When my recruiting starts, I'm going to have me some fun."

Russell, having finished his snack, balls up the paper bag and tosses it out the window with an air of finality: "I don't want to be wined and dined."

As much as he hates Coney Island, Russell has never lived anywhere else, and he often fears that his dark complexion (Corey and Stephon are lighter-skinned) will get him into trouble outside his home turf. That may explain why he doesn't want to take any visits. But something else is up. Corey notes this and changes strategy. "What's your reason? You got to have a reason."

"I'm not like everybody else," Russell replies.

"Yes," Corey says slowly. "This is true."

"Look, all the best players sign in the fall. Only the scrubs wait until spring."

"I'm not telling you to sign in the spring," Corey says. "I'm just saying you change your mind every day."

"I'm telling *you*, Corey, I'm having a great season. And when those schools that lost interest in me come back in the spring, I'm gonna be, like, 'Too late, *sucka!*' I'm gonna be throwing it all year! Tomahawk jams!" Russell starts thrashing about in the front seat, dunking his orange-juice carton into the ashtray of my car, and now I finally get it — that his decision to dunk in public, like his policy of wearing nice shoes, and now his intention to sign abruptly at a school he's never seen, is Russell's way of propping up his identity, of seizing some measure of control, now that he has realized how easily exchangeable he is for a player with better test scores. Recruiting may be the most important thing in Russell's life, but to the coaches it's just a yearly ritual.

"Man, you are one *crazy* nigger!" Corey says. "I'm not talking about dunking! I'm talking about whether you should sign at some school you never even seen in your life!"

"Don't matter. It's my decision. And part of growing up is learning to live with your decisions. Even if it turns out to be a nightmare."

"But why?"

"Don't push me, Corey." Russell's voice has begun to rise up the scale.

"But *why?*"

"Because I don't want to talk about it."

"That's not a reason."

"BECAUSE I HATE ALL THIS FUCKING RECRUITING!" Russell screams. "All right?"

Corey leans back against his seat, defeated. "Okay, well, at least that's a reason."

December

Coney Island never looks quite so forlorn as it does just before Christmas. The amusement park is shuttered, the boardwalk littered with broken glass and crack vials. The cold weather has swept the streets clean of everyone but the most hardened criminals. At night, Christmas lights blink on and off from the top floors of the projects, but few people are around to enjoy them. No one simply passes through Coney Island on the way to somewhere else.

Tonight, Russell and I walk into the deserted lobby of his building and he says, his eyes cast down by shame, "Welcome to the old ghetto." Russell's building is identical in design to the one in which Corey and Stephon live, just a block away — an X-shaped slab of concrete rising fourteen stories into the air. I have always assumed it was no better or worse than theirs. But Russell assures me that looks are deceiving. By the way he peers around the elevator door before getting in, I believe him.

Upstairs, his family's apartment is tiny: a living room, kitchenette, and two bedrooms. His mother has one bedroom, Russell and his two younger sisters share the other. It's Russell's room, though: basketball posters cover the walls from top to bottom and trophies crowd the floor.

I notice that Russell is wearing a new ring on his finger and I ask if it's from Terry. He doesn't answer. Instead he says, "Want to see some pictures of Terry and me?" He pulls out a scrapbook filled with newspaper clippings about himself and the Lincoln team. Stuffed in the back is a pile of snapshots. "We been together for a long time," he says wistfully. "All those days last summer, picnics, all the stuff we used to do. Maybe someday — way, way off in the future — we'll get married." We're still looking at the photos when Russell hears a key in the front door. He grabs the pictures from my hand and shoves them back in the scrapbook, snapping it shut just as his mother walks through the door.

"You come home right after practice?" she asks anxiously. He nods, and she smiles in my direction. "Russell thinks I'm overprotective, but I have to know where he's at. If he's at practice or at Willie's, okay. But just hanging out on the street? No!" She plunks down a bag of groceries on the kitchen table and lets out a long sigh. The neighborhood's only supermarket is fifteen blocks away. "This is a hard neighborhood, *wicked*, nothing but drugs out there," says Mrs. Thomas. "Most of Russell's friends are just wasting their lives. You've got to have a strong and powerful will not to go in that direction."

Joyce Thomas certainly has that. She is tall and thin like Russell, and moves around her apartment with fierce efficiency. A burst of what sounds like gunfire erupts outside, but Mrs. Thomas doesn't react. "I always tell Russell, it takes that much" — she spreads two fingers an inch apart — "to get into trouble, and that much" — now two hands shoulder-width apart — "to get out of it." She looks over to her son, but he has vanished from the room. "So far Russell's okay." She raps twice on her kitchen table. "So far."

I start to say something, but Mrs. Thomas cuts me off. "When Russell messes up, I knock him out. I *do*. I tell him, 'Don't you dog me, boy, I'm all you got!'" She is looking at me forcefully, without blinking. "I don't care how big he is or how much ball he plays, I'll put a ball in his head!"

Russell reappears, this time with his Walkman on and a strange, stricken look on his face. He starts to sing aloud to a slow love song coming from his Walkman — though all we can hear, of course, is Russell's crooning.

Suddenly Mrs. Thomas takes in a breath. Looking at Russell, she says, "Did you do it?" Russell keeps on singing, so Mrs. Thomas picks up his hand and examines the ring. "Terry gave it back to you?"

He slides the headphones around his neck. "I took it back," he says. His voice is clotted.

"How did it go?"

He can't think of anything to say. Finally he murmurs, "She was real sad."

Mrs. Thomas doesn't stir. The apartment is quiet, except for the refrigerator's hum. Russell has begun to turn inward and the next words he utters seem to reach us from a great distance. "She was crying, hanging on to my leg, saying, 'Don't go, don't go.'"

"Now don't you worry about Terry," Mrs. Thomas says matter-of-factly. "She'll be all right. You just watch out for *yourself.*"

"I'm real sad, too," he says quickly, and now I can see him struggling not to cry.

"Don't be. How long were you together — five, six months? That's not so hard to get over." Mrs. Thomas turns briskly toward her groceries and begins to unpack. Russell stands stock-still in the middle of the living room staring at his feet.

She glances over at me. "I explained to Russell, 'You want friends? Fine. But I don't want you attached to *anyone.* You will go to college alone, and so will Terry.'" Russell can't bear to hear his mother's words, so he puts on his Walkman and begins his tone-deaf accompaniment. "A girl like Terry could make him do something stupid. He gets carried away. He's very emotional, you know." She speaks with seeming indifference, though it's not hard to hear what lies beneath it: a desperation to get Russell away from Coney Island that is so great she will take away from him the one most stabilizing influence in his life, at a time when he seems to need it the most. "Russell got a second chance on this planet," she says, referring to Russell's suicide threat, "and *no one* gets that! *No one!*" She stares at me again, this time with such intensity that I have to fight the urge to look away. "He's got a lot of decisions ahead of him. Important decisions. *Business* decisions. Without that scholarship, he's nothing. *Nothing!*" Mrs. Thomas looks to her son to gauge his reaction, but Russell has checked out completely. He's turned his Walkman up to full volume, and he's singing as loud as he can.

A few nights later, Russell, Stephon, Corey, and I are all in my car, making the usual rounds to Willie's. Stephon announces that he's going to get an X shaved into the back of his scalp. Russell is considering a center part like Larry Johnson's, the star of the Charlotte Hornets. As we approach the barbershop Corey says, "Don't be wasting time, all right?" When I ask why, he tells me a gang from a nearby project has been roaming lately. Last week a woman was hit by a stray bullet right outside the shop, so they all want to get their cuts and be gone.

To me, Coney Island's desolate project walkways and stairwells have always seemed more threatening than the raucous street life here along Flatbush Avenue. And, in fact, the few Lincoln players who live "across town" — Flatbush or Crown Heights or East New York — won't be caught dead in the Coney Island high-rises ever since one of them spent the night at Corey's apartment and someone blew up a car right outside his window. But I am given to understand that in the patchwork of highly distinct neighborhoods that make up Brooklyn, a group of black teenagers will always be at risk outside their own turf. Wherever they go, the three are always scanning to see who might be coming up to them. One of their teammates was shot in the hand a few months ago. Another classmate was stabbed at a party recently; he's still in intensive care. "Something's happening, boy, every day, every day," says Russell.

As planned, they're in and out of Willie's in a flash and happy to be heading home in my car. Russell has been unusually quiet all evening. When I ask if something is bothering him, he tells me his mother has forbidden him to speak to me anymore. Apparently, she doesn't think it wise for him to talk to a reporter while his recruiting hangs in the balance. I tell Russell that this story won't appear until he's already off to college, but he says, "You don't understand. My mother's *crazy!*"

Stephon pipes in with some advice for me. "Just greet her at the door and hit her with a hundred. She'll change her mind." He snickers knowingly. "She's no different than my father. He wants to make sure he gets some loot." Lately, Mr. Marbury has been threatening to keep Stephon from talking to me unless I cut him a deal.

At first I think Stephon is missing the point — that Mrs. Thomas's suspicion of me and her desperation to get Russell out of Coney Island are entirely different from Mr. Marbury's demand for money. But Corey sees the connection: "Damn," he says, "your parents must have had a hard life."

"Still do," Stephon replies. "Your father got himself a whole plumbing business. My father and Russell's mother got nothing." Stephon looks at me out of the corner of his eye and says, "You're thinking, *What a bunch of niggers,* right?"

The word just hangs in the air. I can't think of a thing to say. Over the last five months, I realize, I have tried to ignore our racial differences in an attempt at some broader understanding. Stephon's comment may be his way of telling me that understanding *begins* with race. "You got to think like a black man," he goes on, "got to learn how to say, 'Fuck it, fuck everybody, *fuck the whole damn thing.*' Now *that's* life in the ghetto."

"It's true!" Russell exclaims, his mood improving for the first time all evening. "My mother *is* a nigger! She's a black woman who does not give a damn."

"Man, I'm *tired* of all this shit!" Stephon slams his hands down hard on his book bag. "Somebody's *got* to make it, somebody's *got* to go all the way. How come this shit only happens to us Coney Island niggers?" He shakes his head wildly and laughs. "My father and Russell's mother — yeah, they're crazy, but it's about time there was a little something for the niggs."

"Something for the niggs!" Russell repeats the line with a hoot. "Yeah, Steph! Time to get outspoken!"

"You got it," Stephon says, and laughs again. Then Corey joins in. And they're all three whooping and slapping their knees — laughing at their parents and also, I imagine, at the absurdity of this whole situation.

Here they are, playing by all the rules: They stay in school — though their own school hardly keeps its end of the bargain. They say no to drugs — though it's the only fully employed industry around. They don't get into trouble with the NCAA — though its rules seem designed to foil them, and the coaches who break the rules go unpunished. They even heed their parents' wishes — and often pay a stiff price.

Of course none of them is perfect: Russell panics about his SATs and the choices he must make, and has trouble owning up to it; Corey won't apply himself and kids himself into thinking it won't matter; Stephon has — what shall we call it? — an attitude that needs some adjustment. But they operate in an environment that forgives none of the inevitable transgressions of adolescence and bestows no second chances.

Which makes this process of playing for a scholarship not the black version of the American dream, as some would suggest, but a cruel parody of it. In the classic parable you begin with nothing and slowly accrue your riches through hard work in a system designed to help those who help themselves. Here you begin with nothing but one narrow, treacherous path and then run a gauntlet of obstacles that merely reminds you of how little you have: recruiters pass themselves off as father figures, standardized tests humiliate you and reveal the wretchedness of your education, the promise of lucrative NBA contracts reminds you of what it feels like to have nothing in this world.

Jou-Jou, Silk, Chocolate, Spoon, Spice, Ice, Goose, Tiny, T, Stretch, Space, Sky: all of them great Coney Island players, most of them waiting vainly for a second chance, hanging out in the neighborhood, or dead. And here come Russell, Corey, and Stephon in my car, riding down Mermaid Avenue in the bone chill and gloom of this December night, still laughing about "the niggs," hoping for the best, and knowing that in this particular game failure is commonplace, like a shrug, and heartbreak the order of the day.

Epilogue: Winter 1993

In the spring of 1992, near the end of his senior year, Russell signed with Philadelphia's Temple University, whose team in recent years has regularly been among the nation's top twenty. But on his final SAT attempt, his score went down and Temple withdrew its scholarship offer. Rob Johnson brokered Russell into a Texas junior college known on the street as a "bandit" school, where his teammates seemed to carry more guns than school-books. Desperately unhappy, Russell transferred after a week to a junior college near Los Angeles. There, this past winter, he was averaging twenty-six points per game and hoping that after two years he would be recruited by a four-year school and earn his degree.

Corey fell short of a 700 on his SATs by ten points. He planned to spend a year at a prep school to brush up on his academics but filed his application for financial aid too late. He went to another junior college in Texas. Away from his girlfriends, Corey earned four B's and two A's in his first semester. He hopes to move on to a four-year school himself.

Stephon is now in his sophomore year. In the summer of 1992, he was among the four youngest players invited to the Nike all-American camp, an all-expenses-paid jamboree in Indianapolis for the 120 top high-school stars in the country. His play, before every Division I coach in the country, looked like a highlight film. Now four inches taller and dunking the ball, he is dominating the PSAL and should have his pick of top programs in his senior year, provided that he can score 700 on the SATs and that neither he nor his father violates any recruiting rules.

And at the Garden, some of Coney Island's elders have organized nighttime shooting drills for the neighborhood's schoolchildren — eight years old and up — to prepare them for the road ahead.

ADAM GOPNIK

Death in Venice

FROM THE NEW YORKER

IN THE FIRST WEEKS of June this year, the path of an art-minded American through Europe was as fixed and as well-worn as a medieval pilgrim's. People were going either from the Titian show, in Paris, down to the Biennale, in Venice, or from the Biennale up to the Titian show, with a little detour along the way in either direction to visit the Marcel Duchamp retrospective at the Palazzo Grassi, on the Grand Canal. Those of us who were trying to be exquisitely judicious about the *Venus and Adonis* at the Grand Palais were, a week later in Venice, trying to remain exquisitely judicious while looking at Damien Hirst's *Mother and Child Divided* — a cow and calf that have been slaughtered, bisected lengthwise, and pickled in formaldehyde in clear-glass cases. (Hirst, a kind of Pugsley Addams version of Jeff Koons, is an English artist who had previously worked mostly in sharks; for this international occasion, he moved up the evolutionary ladder.) The lesson this pilgrimage produced — at least, on the well-trodden center-right of the path — was just as predictable. The Titian show was a triumph, the Biennale was not, and the man to blame for the descent was Duchamp, who had made arbitrariness respectable in art. ("It is unmistakably the ghost of Marcel Duchamp that looms large over the proceedings," one critic wrote in the first week of the Biennale. "Here is a whole generation that has been led to believe that simply to have an idea, any idea, is enough.")

I've just returned from my own version of this pilgrimage, and it seems to me that the peculiar badness of this year's Biennale has to do less with a decline of "standards" than with the increasing stranglehold on art of an international manner — a process whose mechanics are illuminated, in an odd way, by the Titian exhibition. The trouble with contemporary art isn't that anything goes; it's that the same thing keeps going, on and on and on. The world may be coming apart at the seams, but the avant-garde has never been so united. As a consequence, contemporary art has lost its sense of mischief, its eccentricity, and its compulsion toward the margins — exactly its Duchampian virtues. Instead, it has settled into an international formula, a High Morbid Manner that is likely to survive as the signature style of our *fin de siècle*.

You need to lack historical consciousness to get indignant about this. All revolutionary art eventually produces a manner. You just have to hope that when the dust has settled you'll get a grand manner instead of a small one. The point of the Titian show should have been to demonstrate exactly how a truly grand manner gets made. It failed to do this, because of a series of technical and intellectual incompetences. Badly hung, horrifically lit, with slovenly scholarly standards and an unilluminating catalogue, the show was remarkable mostly as a successful act of cultural intimidation. It loomed over its visitors, genielike, and frightened them into praise. Of course, it contained a half-dozen great paintings — but no more than that. Anyone hungry for an education in Titian would have been better off going directly to Venice to see the *Presentation of the Virgin*, at the Accademia, and the *Assumption*, at the Frari. For that matter, a long weekend spent on Amtrak's Northeast Corridor, with stops to visit the *Rape of Europa*, in Boston, the two Titians at the Met, and *The Annunciation*, in Washington, would have been about as good.

Short on masterpieces from the Master's hand, the show depended for its existence on the idea of a Golden Age of Titianesque painting — on a sentimental notion of Titian as the presiding genius of a happy isle of artists. In fact, Titian's historical accomplishment was to deprovincialize (or, if you prefer, deracinate) Italian painting. Titian sits at a pivot point in the history of art — the moment when it became a commodity produced for the international market. Titian helped turn painting from a local, bespoke operation into a mail-order business, presiding over the transformation that took art from its dependence on neighborhood churches and guilds and made it into décor for the absolutist

European courts. He worked for and accepted titles from the big powers in Europe, including the emperor Charles V. This ambition made Titian, who had a long working life — he claimed to be ninety-nine the year he died — a very rich man, the first artist tycoon. Almost single-handed, he invented the Grand Master life-style, from the palazzi to the literary cheerleaders. His influence on his contemporaries and followers therefore had little of the modest, artisanal spirit of, say, Carpaccio or Bellini. Rather, it was formulaic — or, at least, arrogant and dictatorial. When a genuine original showed up at the studio, Titian kicked him out; this is what he is said to have done, for example, to the young Tintoretto, who admired Titian but nevertheless took his revenge by pointedly sending a posse of Titianesque blondes tumbling down into Hell, pearls and all, in his *Last Judgment*. You don't have to be a religious fanatic to feel that he had a point. Lovers of Venetian art as different as Mary McCarthy and John Ruskin have come to feel that Titian was almost a traitor to the Venetian Republic, what with his toadying to the pope and the Spanish emperor, and that he foreshadowed the Baroque not just in his spiraling, cursive compositions but in a certain sleazy readiness to grant that the end of art was to sell, and to sell anything, including sex and religion.

Still, if there was a formula, it was a resplendent one; the very least you ought to have had is a good-looking show. But the Titian show looked better in the catalogue than on the walls. The trouble began with the space it was hung in. For all the *grands projets* that the French have launched in the past twenty years, Paris still lacks a first-class temporary exhibition space. (The Louvre's, down in the basement, is far too small; the Musée d'Orsay's, up in the rafters in that most dysfunctional of all modern museums, is far too mean.) So "Le Siècle de Titien" — to give the Titian show its full, Avenue of the Americas name — had to be held, like the Seurat show two years ago, in the Grand Palais, the vast Right Bank greenhouse-like exhibition hall left over from the World's Fair of 1900. The Grand Palais, to work at all, needs to have a second, makeshift museum built inside it — a cellblock inside the green-house. (It's as if New York had to house its Old Master shows in the Trylon and the Perisphere.)

Worse, the "story line" of the show was muddled by the absence of a major picture by Giovanni Bellini — Titian's predecessor as the supreme Venetian painter, and the originator of much of Titian's attack and style (and an incomparably greater and more profound artist). The organizers tried to make up for this absence by leaning very heavily on the work of Titian's other teacher, Giorgione — a far more glamorous and *recherché* figure than Bellini. Giorgione (the name just means Big George) is one of the great mystery men in art. Though his career, which fell between the careers of Bellini and Titian, lasted hardly more than a decade, he is usually credited with having stocked the entire property room of poetic, secular painting as it endured for the next three hundred years — everything from the misty landscape to the happy picnic to the sleeping nymph. But the number of uncontested autograph pictures from his hand is small, and the amount of speculation large. When word got around that the Titian organizers had assembled a room of eighteen solid-gold Giorgiones, it seemed incredible.

And remained so. The Giorgione on view in Paris was an unconvincing artistic personality. In this Giorgione, there were at least four different artists at work, and one of them — the author of some really ghastly oversized heads of musicians making faces — didn't even look particularly Venetian. The three or four true, breathtakingly beautiful Giorgiones (or, at worst, near-Giorgiones) were crowded by a dozen unconvincing and ugly pictures. To be fair, the problems that confront a curator trying to mount a show like this are huge. You cannot ask the National Gallery of Smolensk to lend you its Giorgione and then send it back to Smolensk no longer a Giorgione — not if you hope to get another loan from Smolensk. Doubtful cases have to be hung as if they were certain cases. Yet there was no need to muddy these waters at all; the Giorgionesque is inherently more interesting than Giorgione. What Giorgione actually painted is by now an insoluble issue. But what Giorgione invented is not mysterious at all. Suddenly, around 1500, in Venice, a new set of subjects enters art, and a new way of portraying them. A new style makes itself felt, which is neither quite like early Titian nor at all like the late Bellini. You have only to look at one of the few uncontested Giorgiones — *The Tempest,* at the Accademia, in Venice — to get it: the lightning-lit scene; the ability to render not only the way the people look but the weather around them; the lulling, contemplative softness; the broad, enigmatic faces caught in soft light. Giorgione is one of those artists who invent a manner so seductive that it instantly leaps out of their work to become the manner of an entire epoch. The influence *is* the accomplishment. The fact that after five hundred years the trained eye still can't be sure what in early Titian is Titian and what is Giorgione is not the problem; it's the point.

But having invented an isolated, unconvincing Giorgione, the organizers of the show insisted on maintaining this narrow, old-fashioned monographic approach. Within each picture bay at the show, there were plenty of paintings to look at, mostly by lesser Venetians (of whom Lorenzo Lotto and Dosso Dossi take the prize, in a slow field), but relatively few mint Titians. Looking at them, one came to feel that it was not Victorian piety alone that made Ruskin believe, in the end, that Titian was a man of dubious artistic virtue. Titian is inarguably a great painter, but of all the inarguably great painters he had the least interesting mind. The reverence for the concrete world that makes the painting of Carpaccio and Bellini one of the heights of human achievement was driven out by Titian. What takes its place — elbows it out, inch by glorious inch of pneumatic flesh — is a manner. A big manner, to be sure, even a great manner, but a manner all the same: huge, unreal nymphs, noble saints, elevated souls pursuing elevated subjects.

Titian's mature style is, with Raphael's and Michelangelo's, one of the pillars of the Grand Manner properly so called — that set of elevated, generalized, idealized, coercive formulas that kept its grip on painting in Europe for three hundred years. Modern art was, in essence, a century-long revolution against that manner, and it's hard for anyone who loves the modern tradition not to have ambivalent feelings as he watches that manner being constructed: the suffocatingly unreal language of elevated gesture; the compositions pointing inexorably toward the dramatic climax; the unreal, vegetable beauty of the women and the unreal, noble action of the men; the elimination of anything that is there simply for its own sake. The radiant love for the actual in the highest Venetian painting is in Titian replaced by a rhetoric. You feel the whole soulless Baroque machinery of martyrdoms and Ascensions coming just around the corner. Even the portraits, for all their marriage of polish and immediacy, have in them the first whisperings of the kind of flunkydom that leads directly to van Dyck. Confronted by the endless reaches of high-minded painting at the Grand Palais, one longs for the great, thoroughly *Venetian* Titian of the *Presentation of the Virgin,* in the Accademia, where the imperturbable little girl is trailed by a kind of mummers' parade of Venetian life, each egg and each inch of particular silk registered with as much delight as the major, necessary characters are — a picture where a certain democracy of vision still seems solidly in place.

In the exhibition, there are only two real masterpieces from Titian's hand: the *Danaë,* from Madrid, and the *Flaying of Marsyas,* from Czechoslovakia. The *Danaë* is one of the great erotic pictures, all the more impressive because Titian is honest here about a subject that must have been close to his heart — the near relation of ecstasy and money. It shows a nymph having an orgasm as she is struck by a shower of gold coins. It ought to be a hopelessly cheap subject, but it becomes a riveting picture, largely because in it Titian gave up his usual nymph type for a figure taken right off a Michelangelo tomb, and the combination of Michelangelesque power and Titianesque delicacy makes for something genuinely crazy and sublime. (The *Danaë* benefits, too, from the girl's still having her original face; the faces of some of Titian's Venuses look as though they've been heavily restored; at least, that is the most charitable explanation of their insipid, oddly nineteenth-century, Lillian Russell character.)

The best thing about Titian is his brushwork; even when he's empty, he's dazzling. But this is just where the awkwardness of the exhibition was most apparent. Most of the paintings were so badly overlit that you had to approach them at an oblique angle to see them at all, and the paint surface itself disappeared. A couple of years ago, when the *Flaying of Marsyas* hung in the National Gallery in Washington, it was exquisitely underlit. By dimming the room so that the silvers and the violet light of the picture became, in effect, the ambient light, the curators made the painting come alive in all its horror and loveliness; it had the dim fascination of a half-remembered nightmare. In Paris, the same picture was lit head on, and so its middle range became unintelligible. What you saw was mostly glare, with a few figures protruding on either side.

In the end, the real lesson to be drawn from "Le Siècle de Titien" is pleasingly insular and chauvinistic. For all the attacks on their

virtue, honor, and probity, American museums, particularly the
Metropolitan and the National Gallery, have, over the past quar-
ter-century, become incomparably more expert at putting on large
Old Master shows than any other museums in the world. Standards
of installation (and of scholarship: the catalogue in Paris is mostly
a recap of old connoisseurship, combined with some redistribu-
tion) at our two national museums are so much higher than they
are anywhere in Europe that European Old Master shows these
days look merely old-fashioned. Now that the great American
museums seem to be coming to the end of their high period, slain
by the double blows of multiculturalism and a changing tax code,
we may at last be able to appreciate what they did. That's probably
the way it is with all Golden Ages. It isn't until they're over that
you recognize them.

The Venice Biennale is a constant occasion of hypocrisy — hypocrisy motivated in part by journalists' guilt. The amount of invective
the show regularly receives is almost directly proportional to the
pleasure you get from going to Venice. You can't turn a corner in
Venice without wanting to drop to your knees in gratitude, so it
seems almost indecent to tell the truth, which is that no amount
of bad or depressing art can really alter the joy of being there.
Nonetheless, this Biennale is a terrible show, but terrible in more
memorable and more poignant ways than might at first seem to
be the case. Though the show is a misery, it's not a mess. Americans
have been so preoccupied by the debate over "politicized" art that
we haven't noticed that that art is really just a tiny subsection of a
new, full-blown, one-size-suits-all-moods international style.
    The emergence of that uniform style is the more remarkable
because everybody associated with the Biennale tried to do everything they could to keep a single style from emerging. Faced with
organizing the first Biennale since the breakup of the old political
blocs, the Italian curator Achille Bonito Oliva, who is the overseer
of the show, realized that the familiar system of national pavilions
in the Giardini, where the bulk of the Biennale is held — a system
that has been in place for most of this century — looked dated.
So he encouraged each nation to include in its pavilion some work
by artists who happened to belong to another nation. (The Aperto
— the junior-varsity version of the Biennale which is held around

the corner, in the Arsenale, showed, as it always does, a roundup of contemporary art.) This was a nobly antitribal idea, and didn't need to be intellectualized. But to defend it he employed two new ideas — that a spirit of "transnationalism" had already appeared in art, and that this style had been produced by an open-minded, free-spirited, museum-wandering "cultural nomadism."

The trouble is that all the nomads seem to have gone to art school at the same oasis. The number of things young artists are encouraged to make, or do, seems remarkably limited and stereotyped. There are Macedonian site sculptors, Slovenian practitioners of Fluxus-type conceptualism, Danish minimalists, Chinese appropriation artists. Walk through even the distant pavilions out on the edges of the Giardini and you feel that you have explored these issues of gender and identity before. The situation seems, in a way, nearly medieval: a fragmented, disordered, and increasingly tribalized world, bound together by a lingua franca of official art. The eeriest instance of this standardization occurs in pictures by Li Shan, from China, which use the Warholian imagery of Mao — the winsome, silk-screened Pop icon — as a figure in what seems sincerely meant to be paintings about the actual experience of Maoism.

Among the national pavilions, the repetitiveness looks a little like the doings of an international cartel of the avant-garde. The familiar figures from every Documenta and Carnegie in memory pop up again, only this time in unexpected countries, like basketball players with doctored transcripts being shifted from one junior college to another. Hans Haacke, for instance, a thoroughly New York artist, represents Germany, along with, of all people, the Korean video artist Nam June Paik. The Hungarians asked another New York artist, Joseph Kosuth, to show them how to do one of his installations: the walls of their pavilion are covered with improving slogans and clippings taken from other people's writings. Some of the shufflings from country to country are rote, some touching. The seventy-one-year-old Romanian artist Damian, who has lived since the forties in Paris, represents his native land with two of his signature columns. In the past, these have been wooden columns set on a heroic diagonal and tethered to a kind of handmade gantry — folk-art Saturn 5s. A new one, though, is dead prone — finished.

Of the big-name exhibitions, by far the most talked about and successful was Haacke's for Germany, which managed to get its work done economically. Haacke took a pneumatic drill to the marble floor of the German pavilion, breaking it up into a thousand rough fragments, and then hung a sign reading "Germania" on the back wall and invited the spectators in to walk on the ruins. The sound of hard-shod feet on the rubble echoed as though in the ghost of a larger hall. As a theatrical piece of Piranesian sublime, it was very effective. But Haacke is not happy to let you stumble around in a ruin without telling you exactly what moral purpose you are stumbling around for, and in accompanying commentary he made clear his own view of the significance of the piece. Hitler, it seems, had visited the Biennale in 1934 (a photograph from this visit hung at the entrance to the pavilion), and it seems to be Haacke's thesis that the line running from Hitler's annexation of the Beaux Arts to the current corrupt relationship between art and power is pretty straight. The art world, Haacke believes, is part of the "consciousness industry," and he, with his hammer, is its Luddite. This analysis is typical of the innocence of so much art-world politics. Only someone who has never actually seen an industry can imagine that the art world — with its small-scale, speculative, boom-and-bust economy, its discoveries and outrages — is one. An industry produces a standardized product for a more or less reliable mass market of consumers. The art world is not an industry. It isn't even a business. It is a carnival with a casino attached.

Or it was a carnival, anyway; now it looks more like a morgue. For if there is a single stylistic tic that fills both the pavilions and the work of the younger artists in the Aperto, it is the display of images of death, decay, and violence. Damien Hirst's bisected cow and calf is only the most immediately creepy of these gestures. Jean-Pierre Raynaud tiled the French pavilion with thousands of unvarying images of a skull; the American artist Andres Serrano's piece is actually called *The Morgue* and shows huge photographs of corpses; the Japanese Kohdai Nakahara displays a lifelike model of a mutant in front of a "module for floating" (two huge flesh-colored tanks, in which, presumably, the mutation took place); Marco Brandizzi offers a precise description of the procedure (and effects) of an electrocution; the American group TODT offers a war machine: a high-tech motorcycle armed with rockets and spears and machine guns — a prop for a Schwarzenegger movie. Bodies rot, faces are filled with maggots, surgical instruments and examination tables are on display.

Other than death, the set subject is sex. There's a lot of genital imagery in the show, including a Benetton ad by Toscani that lays out more than a hundred different, exquisitely printed closeups of crotches. But even here the arrangement is utterly clinical; formally, it has the same unbroken, drumbeat rhythm as the Raynaud skulls, and has the same benumbing effect. Other sexually explicit pieces are aggressively nasty, like Kiki Smith's wax models of a mom sucking on her own breast while her son sucks his own member, or like Sean Landers's video of himself engaged in affectless masturbation. (In lieu of a wall label, he supplies some of his own writings, which include the thought "I have way more self respect than you'll ever imagine possible from somebody who writes such horrid dribble.")

A little of this art has a specific political point to score, but most of it is vaguely, generally apocalyptic. It isn't hard to spot the stylistic sources, near and distant. The complaint has been entered that no single artist emerged into his or her majority at this exhibition, as, say, Robert Rauschenberg and Jasper Johns did in Biennales past. Actually, the emergence of the Morbid Manner at the Biennale had a great deal to do with the work of a single world-class artist. He just didn't happen to be in the show. The immediate model for almost all the grimmest work — for the macabre fragment, the tortured videos, the cryptic neon signs, even the simple idea of assembling a lot of morbid bits and pieces in a darkened room — is the art of the American Bruce Nauman: he emerged at this Biennale as by far the most influential artist working today. It is Nauman's mood — the sense of building memorials-in-advance to an apocalypse whose causes are ill-defined but whose inevitability is grimly certain — that dominates the exhibition. This is doubly ironic, since the much-talked-of point of Nauman's work was to deny a signature style; what has happened instead is that each style Nauman has left behind has become a series of building blocks for someone else — an alphabet.

What Nauman really offers young artists, albeit in a compressed, laconic form, is a newly refitted kind of Surrealism, and if there is a revelation that this Biennale offers about "postmodern" art in the last decade of the century, it is the triumph of academic Surrealism. Anyone walking through the Biennale would have no idea that not very long ago it was taken for granted that the central achievement of modern art was abstract painting. (I counted only two abstract artists in the whole exhibition, and one, from Iceland, had so much national modesty as to be practically invisible.) But no one would have any trouble seeing that a movement must have once swept through this century's art which put a premium on gruesome fragments, strangled expression, displaced objects, the celebration of the strange, and the upturning of the sexually taboo. (It's all wrong to see anything of Duchamp in this. As the show at the Palazzo Grassi reminded us, Duchamp was a comic poet of the tangible, with a lighthearted insistence on *things* for their own sake.)

And so it's also probably inevitable that the two older stars of this Biennale, Francis Bacon and Louise Bourgeois — even though they have been singled out as the humane exceptions to the glut of mannerism — are in fact the great-grandparents of the Morbid Manner: they represent academic Surrealism at its most accomplished. Bacon, who is the subject of a special retrospective, organized by David Sylvester at the Museo Correr, leaves the overwhelming impression that he spent his life in a battle with the urge to make his own misery into a universally applicable melodrama. The difference in poetic intensity between his pictures of the 1950s, with their little, Audenesque figures — smeared faces in violet suits and knit ties — crowded in little rooms, and his later, more famous, formalized popes and other screamers, with their unintentional cartoon look and their forced, theatrical pathos, seems now more marked than ever before. No painter was more moving or frightening when in touch with the particular, and none fled the particular quite so desperately, or sometimes so showily.

Bourgeois, who, at eighty-two, has been selected to represent the United States, is a more complicated case. Her story is familiar: she worked in relative obscurity for many years, showing her work to no one, and eventually created a style of her own — a collection of stage sets filled with repressed, obscure, sexual imagery. For the Biennale, she has created, most memorably, three "cells": little rooms filled with the paraphernalia of torture and remorse —

guillotine blades, fragmented porcelain hands, fences, glass wombs, and laconic inscriptions.

Bacon and Bourgeois are masters of the Morbid Manner, but even in their hands it remains a manner. Both, for all the sustained emotional pressure they can achieve, are remarkably "elevated." The work isn't about some particular pain but about Pain. Bacon is a very *remote* artist; so is Bourgeois. This remoteness is both the armor of their work — what keeps it from dating or becoming trivial — and the armor's chink. Bacon is full of the messiness of death but has very little of the messiness of life. Place him beside, say, a genuine Expressionist like Max Beckmann, and how much more *personal* Beckmann seems — how much more rooted in a landscape (or cityscape) and an autobiography and a set of facts. Place Bourgeois beside an eccentric visionary like Joseph Cornell, and how fixed her imagery seems. Both belong to the tradition of rhetorical pathos, and the difference between rhetoric and poetry is that in rhetoric what matters most is the verbs and in poetry what matters most is the nouns. (Looking at Bellini, you see instantly each string on each angel's lute; looking at late Titian, you see the way things rush into each other; the only question is what the stock figures are going to do next.) The thingness, the inventory of objects, in both Bacon's and Bourgeois's work is fairly stereotyped and familiar: the agonized posture that stands for suffering; the blobby biomorphic forms that stand for sexuality. What makes them work is the way the familiar nouns are put together. The grand received themes of the Freudian century — sexual thrall, suffering, the animal nature of human life — come out in a measured, stately, chiseled, and magisterial form.

But at least Bacon and Bourgeois demonstrate that in its higher reaches the Morbid Manner can produce major art. When the rhetoric breaks down into mere stuttering and repetition, as in so much of the Biennale, the only interesting question is not whether it works (it doesn't) but what makes people believe that it matters. Anyone can see that the Morbid Manner offers, if not the spirit of the age, then at least the mood of the moment. A detached, distanced, oddly smiling presentation of violence — a *pageantry* of violence — is, as every evening's television and every summer's big movie demonstrates, as much the popular fashion as the avant-garde one. (The gaze that the new art suggests was first fixed in the popular imagination, I suppose, by a pop moment: by the famous opening of *Twin Peaks* — that new kind of ghostly, frozen, remote look at death and suffering. The affectlessness that everyone used to decry in the movies had passed from the characters to the camera.)

In both its popular and its highbrow forms, the new cult of violence always justifies itself with some pious reference to the responsibilities of realism: the young artists are obsessed with death and violence because the world has become so fatal. That's the apparent argument of the Aperto, which is devoted to the theme of "Emergency." The Morbid Manner is, officially, an alternative to the "old" — that is, late eighties — culture of irony. But in the Aperto, just as in a pop movie like, say, *Batman Returns,* the violence has nothing "real" about it; it's too distanced, too remote, too *patterned* for that. Looking at a Damien Hirst, you don't think that it's a terrible thing that cows are killed; you just register a dull shock of disgust and confusion at someone's having killed this cow. The presentation is so antiseptic and enclosed — so presentational — that it doesn't easily attach itself to any other feeling. The violence in the work of Hirst or Serrano is, like the violence in *American Psycho,* so self-consciously "obsessional," so ripped away from any context of value, or even any feeling, however perverse, that it acts as a barrier to reality rather than as a window on it. The violence comes out of the prop room rather than the street.

A cult of violence has always been part of modernism, of course, but in the past it's been practiced as a protest against a merely formal aestheticism. The Biennale this year marked the moment when the cult of violence itself finally became a kind of formal aestheticism. This had less to do, I suspect, with the response of art to something outside it — the world has always been a fatal place — than with the formal paralysis of late modernism. Violence becomes an obsession of academic art, because it's the easiest way — sometimes the *only* way — of making something happen to stock material. Violence in art is a measure not of contact with reality but mostly of the opposite. (Virtuosos like Delacroix and Rubens are the masters of horror; Manet is almost unduly fastidious when he kills someone off.)

Of course, that kind of formal paralysis, the constant recycling of the past, seems part of pop culture now, and has similar effects.

Tim Burton and Damien Hirst are on the same wavelength. When you're working within entirely banal cartoon genres, just as when you're working within a vocabulary where all the formal decisions were made long ago, about all you can hope to do to make it memorable — to make it *count*— is to make it scary. The shock of the new, which for most of the century could reside as much in a black square as in a slit eyeball, isn't available any longer. It's not possible to shock anymore by being new. The only way to shock is by being shocking. The difference between the cult of violence in, say, *Un Chien Andalou* and the cult of violence at this year's Biennale is a lot like the difference between, say, *King Kong* and *Jurassic Park*. Monsters used to eat people for a reason; now they just eat people. The cult of violence has become, throughout our culture, self-propelled and self-perpetuating.

Of all the rumors and gossip that swept through Venice during the opening of this year's Biennale, the oddest was that Thomas Krens, the director of the Guggenheim, had somehow acquired, as a new Guggenheim annex, the Dogana — the customs house that extends from the Church of the Salute to the little spinning figure of Fortune that may be the only successful work of kinetic art on record. What made the story strange was that no one who told the story knew, or would say, exactly what Krens would put inside. The institutional momentum of modernism is by now mostly independent of its art, and is pretty much self-sustaining. And yet the myth of the wholeness of modernism persists — the belief that culture and civilization are continuous. One changes, and then the other changes, too. Civilization, the manners and social habits of real people living in the real world, and culture, the formal objects that people make and teach one another to admire, are still thought to be simple, interchangeable expressions of each other. Make a new kind of picture, and you make a new kind of life.

For the first half of the century, the mistake lay in treating culture as though it were the key to civilization — in thinking that the world could be remade the way you made art. Now the mistake is to treat civilization as though it were the key to culture — to believe that by adopting the right political attitudes, annexing the right buildings, and carrying on the right kind of "discourse" you will somehow produce new languages of form. But the space between the culture of modernism (the things it makes) and the civilization of modernism (the life it offers) has become so vast that nobody can any longer honestly believe that one changes the other. If you keep pretending that making art makes everything else happen, you're going to be led into the delusion that making something else happen is the same as making art. There's nothing to regret about giving up this myth. If you're realistic about it, you can actually like art for what it does, instead of demanding that it do the hundred things that it does poorly or not at all. Art changes the world by being art; after you've made some, there's more art in the world. That's enough.

The trouble is that if you're unrealistic about this — and right now being unrealistic about it is what the art world encourages — you end up with bad news at both ends. The manners of the art world become identical with the meanings of art, and at the same time the meanings of art become so prefabricated that they become a manner. All that is left to the institutions is an extension of the old receptacles, and all that is left to the artists is an inflation of the old effects. The Morbid Manner is therefore likely to see out the century — partly as an affectation, partly as an expression of genuine disaffection, and partly as a disappointed response to the knowledge that the civilization of modernism conquered the world just at the moment when the culture had lost most of its power to intervene.

STEPHEN JAY GOULD

Cordelia's Dilemma

FROM NATURAL HISTORY

WHILE GONERIL AND REGAN jockey for their father's wealth by
proclaiming their love for him in false and fulsome tones, Lear's
third daughter, Cordelia, fears the accounting that her father will
soon demand: "What shall Cordelia do? Love, and be silent . . .
since, I am sure, my love's more ponderous than my tongue."

Lear then forces Cordelia into this game of ever more elaborate
professions of love: "What can you say to draw a third more opulent
than your sisters?" When the honorable Cordelia, refusing to play
falsely for gain, says nothing, Lear cuts her off from all inheritance,
proclaiming that "nothing will come of nothing."

Lear's tragic error, which shall lead to blinding, madness, and
death, lies in not recognizing that silence — overt nothing — can
embody the deepest and most important meaning of all. What, in
all our history and literature, has been more eloquent than the
silence of Jesus before Pilate, or Saint Thomas More's date with
the headsman because he acknowledged that fealty forbade criticism of Henry VIII's marriage to Anne Boleyn, but maintained,
literally to the death, his right to remain silent and not to approve?

The importance of negative results — nature's apparent silence
or nonacquiescence to our expectations — is also a major concern
in science. Of course, scientists acknowledge the vitality of a negative outcome and often try to generate such a result actively — as
in trying to disprove a colleague's favored hypothesis. But the
prevalence of negative results does pose an enormous, and largely
unaddressed, problem in the reporting of scientific information.
I do not speak of fraud, cover-up, finagling, or any other manifes-

tation of pathological science (although such phenomena exist at a frequency that, in all honesty, we just do not know). I refer, rather, to the all too wonderfully human love of a good tale — and to our simple and utterly reasonable tendency to shun the inconclusive and the boring.

The great bulk of daily scientific work never sees the light of a published day (and who would wish for changes here, as the ever-increasing glut of journals makes keeping up in one's own field impossible and exploration of others inconceivable?). Truly false starts are deposited in circular files — fair enough. But experiments fully carried forth and leading to negative results end up, all too often, unpublished in manila folders within steel-drawer files, known only to those who did the work and quickly forgotten even by them. We all know that thousands of novels, considered substandard by their authors, lie in drawers throughout the world. Do we also understand that even more experiments with negative results fill scientific cabinets?

Positive results, on the other hand, tell interesting stories and are usually written up for publication. Consequently, the available literature may present a strongly biased impression of efficacy and achieved understanding. Such biases, produced by the underreporting of negative results, do not only permeate the arcana and abstractions of academic science. Serious, even tragic, practical consequences often ensue. For example, spectacular medical claims for the efficacy of certain treatments (particularly for chronic and fatal illnesses like cancer and AIDS) may be promulgated after a single positive result (often obtained in a study based upon a very small sample). Later and larger studies may all fail to duplicate the positive results, effectively disproving the value of the treatment. But these subsequent negative results often appear only in highly technical journals read by more restricted audiences and, as nonstories, do not so readily attract the attention of the media — and people may continue to squander hope and waste precious time following useless procedures.

Statistics often get a bum rap in our epithets and editorials. But I am both a champion and a frequent user of statistical procedures, for the science exists largely to identify and root out hopes and misperceptions falsely read into numerical data. Statistics can tell us when published numbers truly point to the probability of a negative result, even though we, in our hopes, have mistakenly conferred a positive interpretation. But statistics cannot rescue us when we hide our nonlights under a bushel (with apologies to Matthew 5:15) — that is, when we only publish positive results and consign our probable negativities to nonscrutiny in our file drawers.

I had thought about this problem a great deal (especially when writing *The Mismeasure of Man*), but I had not realized that this special sort of bias had both a name and a small literature devoted to its weighty problems, until I came upon a paper by Colin B. Begg and Jesse A. Berlin entitled "Publication bias: a problem in interpreting medical data" (*Journal of the Royal Statistical Society*, vol. 151, 1988, pp. 419–63).

Begg and Berlin begin their paper with a wonderful quotation from Sir Francis Bacon (*The Advancement of Learning*, 1605) on the tendency to publish only positive results that tell good stories:

> For as knowledges are now delivered, there is a kind of contract of error between the deliverer and the receiver; for he that delivereth knowledge desireth to deliver it in such form as may be best believed, and not as may be best examined; and he that receiveth knowledge desireth rather present satisfaction than expectant inquiry.

Begg and Berlin then cite several documented cases of publication bias. We can hardly doubt, for example, that a correlation exists between socioeconomic status and academic achievement, but the strength and nature of this association represent important information for both political practice and social theory. A 1982 study by K. R. White revealed a progressively increasing intensity of correlation with the prestige and permanence of the published source. Studies published in books reported an average correlation coefficient of 0.51 between academic achievement and socioeconomic status; articles in journals gave an average of 0.34, while unpublished studies yielded a value of 0.24. Similarly, in a 1986 article, A. Coursol and E. E. Wagner found publication bias both in the decision to submit an article at all and in the probability of its acceptance. In a survey of outcomes in psychotherapy, they found that 82 percent of studies with positive results led to submission of papers to a journal, while only 43 percent of negative outcomes provoked an attempt at publication. Of papers submitted, 80 percent reporting positive outcomes were accepted for publication, versus only 50 percent of papers claiming negative results.

My favorite study of publication bias is the book-length *Myths of Gender* by Anne Fausto-Sterling, a unique and important contribution to the literature of feminism for this reason. In tabulating claims in the literature for consistent differences in cognitive and emotional styles of men and women, Fausto-Sterling does not deny that genuine differences often exist, and in the direction conventionally reported. But she then, so to speak, surveys her colleagues' file drawers for studies not published, or for negative results published and then ignored, and often finds that a great majority report either a smaller and insignificant disparity between sexes or find no differences at all. When all studies, those not published as well as those published, are collated, the much-vaunted differences often devolve into triviality. Natural history, after all (as I have argued so often), is preeminently a study of relative frequency, not of absolute yeses or noes. If a claim based on published literature states that "women in all studies strongly . . ." — and the addition of unpublished data changes that claim to "in a minority of studies, a weak effect suggests that women . . ." — then meaning is effectively reversed (even though positive outcomes, when rarely found, show a consistent direction.)

For example, a recent favorite in pop psychology (although waning of late, I think) has attributed different cognitive styles in men and women to the less lateralized brains of women (less specialization between right and left hemispheres of the cerebral cortex). Some studies have indeed reported a small effect of greater male lateralization; none has found more lateralized brains in women. But most experiments, Fausto-Sterling found, detected no measurable differences in lateralization — and this is the dominant relative frequency (even in published literature) that should be prominently reported, but tends to be ignored as "no story."

Publication bias is serious enough in its promotion of a false impression based on a small and skewed subset of the total number of studies. But at least the right questions are being asked and negative results can be conceptualized and obtained — even if they then tend to be massively underreported. But consider the far more insidious problem closer to Cordelia's dilemma with her father: what if our conceptual world excludes the possibility of acknowledging a negative result as a phenomenon at all? What if we simply can't see, or even think about, a different and meaningful alternative?

Cordelia's plight is a dilemma in the literal sense — a choice between two equally undesirable alternatives: she either remains honorable, says nothing, and incurs her father's wrath; or she plays an immoral game to dissemble and win his affection. She tumbles into this plight because Lear cannot conceptualize the proposition that Cordelia's silence might signify her greater love — that nothing can be the biggest something.

Cordelia's dilemma is deeper and more interesting than publication bias, as we glimpse the constraining role of neurological, social, and psychological conditioning in our struggle to grasp this complex universe into which we have been so recently thrust. Publication bias is only a guard at the party door giving passage to those with the right stamp on their hands. At least the guard can see all the people and make his unfair decisions. Those rejected can gripe, foment revolution, or start a different party. The victims of Cordelia's dilemma are "unpersoned" in the most Orwellian sense. They are residents in the last gulag in inaccessible Siberia, the last outpost of Ultima Thule. They are not conceptualized and therefore do not exist as available explanations.

These two forms of nonreporting have different solutions. Publication bias demands, for its correction, an explicit commitment to report negative results that appear less interesting or more inconclusive than the "good story" of positive outcomes. The solution to Cordelia's dilemma — the promotion of her nothing to a meaningful something — cannot be resolved from within, for the existing theory has defined her action as a denial or nonphenomenon. A different theory must be imported from another context to change conceptual categories and make her response meaningful. In this sense, Cordelia's dilemma best illustrates the dynamic interaction of theory and fact in science. Correction of error cannot always arise from new discovery within an accepted conceptual system. Sometimes the theory has to give first, and a new framework be adopted, before the crucial facts can be seen at all. We needed to suspect that evolution might be true in order to see variation among individuals in a population as the dynamic stuff of historical change and not as trivial or accidental deviation from a created archetype.

I am especially interested in Cordelia's dilemma, and its resolution by using new theories to promote previously ignored phenom- ena to conceivability and interest, because the "main event" of my early career included an example that taught me a great deal about the operations of science. Before Niles Eldredge and I proposed the theory of punctuated equilibrium in 1972, the stasis, or non- change, of most fossil species during their lengthy geological lifespans was tacitly acknowledged by all paleontologists, but almost never studied explicitly because prevailing theory treated stasis as unin- teresting nonevidence for nonevolution. Evolution was defined as gradual transformation in extended fossil sequences, and the over- whelming prevalence of stasis became an embarrassing feature of the fossil record, best left ignored as a manifestation of nothing (that is, nonevolution).

My own thesis adviser had mastered statistics in the hopes of detecting a subtle gradualism that was not visually evident in fossil sequences. He applied his techniques to some fifty brachiopod lineages in Silurian rocks of the Michigan Basin, found no evi- dence for gradual change (but stasis in all lineages with one ambiguous exception), considered his work a disappointment not even worth publishing, and left the field soon thereafter (for a brilliant career in another domain of geology, so our loss was their gain).

But Eldredge and I proposed that stasis should be an expected and interesting norm, and that evolution should be concentrated in brief episodes of branching speciation. Under our theory, stasis became interesting and worthy of documentation — as the norm that rare events of change disrupt. We took as the motto of punc- tuated equilibrium: stasis is data. (One might quibble about the grammar, but I think we won the conceptual battle.)

Punctuated equilibrium is still a subject of lively debate, and some (or most) of its claims may end up on the ash heap of history, but I take pride in one success relevant to Cordelia's dilemma: our theory has brought stasis out of the conceptual closet. Twenty-five years ago, stasis was a nonsubject — a "nothing" under prevailing theory. No one would have published, or even proposed, an active study of lineages known not to change. Now such studies are routinely made and published, and we have a burgeoning litera- ture to document the character and extent of stasis in quantitative terms.

Punctuated equilibrium is a theory about the origin and history of species. That is, the stability of individual species represents the "nothing" that our theory emphasized to attract the attention of researchers. A different kind of "nothing" permeates, and also biases, our consideration of the next most inclusive level of evolutionary stories — the history of phyletic bushes, or groups of species sharing a common ancestry: the evolution of horses, of dinosaurs, of humans, for example. This literature is dominated by the study of trends — directional changes through time in average characteristics of species within the bush. Trends surely exist in abundance, and they do form the stuff of conventional good stories. Brain size does increase in the human bush; and toes do get fewer, and bodies bigger, as we move up the bush of horses.

But the vast majority of bushes display no persistent trends through time. All paleontologists know this, but few would ever think of actively studying a bush with no directional growth. We accept that the history of continents and oceans presents no progressive pattern most of the time — "the seas come in and the seas go out" in an old cliché of geology teachers from time immemorial. But we expect life's bushes to grow toward the light, to tell some story of directional change. If they do not, we do not feature them in our studies — if we even manage to see them at all. We cannot accept for life the preacher's assessment of earthly time (Ecclesiastes 1:9): "The thing that hath been, it is that which shall be; and that which is done, is that which shall be done; and there is no new thing under the sun."

Yet we must study bushes with no prominent directional change if we are to gain any proper sense of the full range and character of life's history. Even if we believe (and I will confess to holding this conventional bias myself) that trends, however rare, are the most interesting of phyletic phenomena — for they do supply the direction that makes evolution a pageant rather than a tableau — we still need to know the relative frequency of nonprogressive evolution, if only to grasp the prevailing substrate from which rare trendiness builds interesting history. How can we claim to understand evolution if we only study the percent or two of phenomena that construct life's directional history and leave the vast field of straight-growing bushes — the story of most lineages most of the time — in a limbo of conceptual oblivion?

I see some happy signs of redress, as paleontologists are now beginning to study this higher-order stasis, or nondirectional history of entire bushes. An excellent and path-breaking case has just been published by Ann F. Budd and Anthony G. Coates in our leading trade journal, *Paleobiology* (vol. 18, 1992, pp. 425–46): "Nonprogressive evolution in a clade of Cretaceous *Montastraea*-like corals." Budd and Coates state their aim in their introduction, and I could not agree more:

> Just as the study of stasis within species has facilitated understanding of morphologic change associated with speciation, we show that study of nonprogressive evolution offers valuable insight into how the causes of trends interact and thereby produce complex evolutionary patterns within clades [evolutionary bushes], regardless of their overall direction.

Montastraea is a genus of massive colonial reef-building corals, still important in our modern faunas (many readers undoubtedly have a chunk of *Montastraea* on their mantelpieces). Budd and Coates studied the earlier history of the *Montastraea* bush during the long span of Cretaceous time — some 80 million years' duration, and representing the last period of dinosaurian domination on land. They found little evidence of directional change, but rather a story of oscillation within a range set by minimal and maximal size of corallites (individual coral animals within the colony). At one end, "large-corallite" species (3.5–8.0 mm in diameter) are more efficient in removal of sediment and tend to be more common in regions of turbid water; at the other end, "small-corallite" species (2.0–3.5 mm in diameter) tend to dominate in clearer waters near the reef crest. In addition, large-corallite species tend to feed actively on small planktonic animals, while small-corallite species derive more nutrition directly from the zooxanthellae (photosynthetic algae) that live symbiotically within their tissues.

Budd and Coates conjecture that corallite diameters may be held within these limits by some ecological or developmental constraint at the low end (implying that still smaller corallites could neither develop nor function adequately) and by a limit to the number of septa at the high end. (Septa are the radiating series of plates that form the skeletal framework for a corallite. The "astraea" in *Montastraea* refers to the star-shaped pattern of these radiating septa in cross-section.) The size of corallites might be limited if new septa could not form beyond a certain number — although this argument is frankly speculative. If such constraints limit the domain of corallite form, and if each end enjoys advantages in different environments always available in some parts of the geographic range, then evolution might just oscillate back and forth, with no persistent directional component through time.

Budd and Coates found just such an oscillation, hence their well-chosen title of "nonprogressive evolution." They divided the Cretaceous into four intervals and then traced the pattern of species changes through these times (most of their long paper presents technical details of defining species and inferring genealogical connections among them). They found that the transition from interval one to interval two featured a differential production of small-corallite species from large-corallite ancestors and a southward spread of the bush's geographic range. "Limited speciation and stasis" then predominated within intervals two and three. Later, between intervals three and four, large-corallite species tended to radiate from small-corallite ancestors as the bush became restricted in range to the Caribbean. The end, in other words, did not leave the bush very different from its beginnings — the seas came in and the seas went out, and *Montastraea* oscillated between prevalence of small- and large-corallite species within its restricted range. And so it goes for most groups in most long segments of geological time — lots of evolutionary change, but no story of clear and persistent direction.

I do feel the force of Cordelia's dilemma as I write these words. Budd and Coates's article inspired me to write this essay. Yet my description of their results occupies only a small portion of this text, because nondirectional evolution doesn't provide the stories that stir our blood and incite our interest. This is the bias of literary convention that we must struggle to overcome. How can we interest ourselves sufficiently in the ordinary and the quotidian? Nearly all of our life so passes nearly all the time (and thank goodness for that, lest we all be psychological basket cases). Shall we not find fascination in the earth's daily doings? And how can we hope to understand the rarer moments that manufacture history's pageant if we do not recognize and revel in the pervasive substrate?

No one has illustrated the dilemma better than Cordelia and

Lear themselves, in their last appearance as prisoners in Act 5, Scene 3. They are about to be taken away, and Lear, through the veil of madness, speaks of forthcoming time in jail, made almost delightful by the prospect of telling stories in the heroic and directional mode:

> Come, let's away to prison: . . . so we'll live,
> And pray, and sing, and tell old tales, and laugh
> At gilded butterflies, and hear poor rogues
> Talk of court news; and we'll talk with them too,
> Who loses and who wins, who's in, and who's out;
> And take upon's the mystery of things,
> As if we were God's spies: and we'll wear out
> In a walled prison, packs and sects of great ones
> That ebb and flow by the moon.

Sean O'Casey said that "the stage must be larger than life," for how can we make adequate drama from the daily doings of shopping, eating, sleeping, and urinating (in no particular order). If this be so, then our biases in storytelling augur poorly for an adequate account of life's real history, for how shall we ever promote the "nothing" that surrounds us to adequate fascination for notice and documentation? But then, one of O'Casey's countrymen solved this problem in the greatest novel of the twentieth century. James Joyce's *Ulysses* treats one day in the life of a few ordinary people in 1904, yet no work of literature has ever taught us more about the nature of humanity and the structure of thought. May I then close with a kind of literary sacrilege and borrow the famous last line of *Ulysses* for a totally different purpose. Molly Bloom, in her celebrated soliloquy, is, of course, speaking of something entirely different! But her words make a good answer to a pledge we should all take: shall I promise to pay attention to the little, accumulating events of daily life and not treat them as nothing against the rare and grandiose moments of history? "yes I said yes I will Yes."

LUCY GREALY

Mirrorings

FROM HARPER'S MAGAZINE

THERE WAS A LONG PERIOD of time, almost a year, during which I never looked in a mirror. It wasn't easy, for I'd never suspected just how omnipresent are our own images. I began by merely avoiding mirrors, but by the end of the year I found myself with an acute knowledge of the reflected image, its numerous tricks and wiles, how it can spring up at any moment: a glass tabletop, a well-polished door handle, a darkened window, a pair of sunglasses, a restaurant's otherwise magnificent brass-plated coffee machine sitting innocently by the cash register.

At the time, I had just moved, alone, to Scotland and was surviving on the dole, as Britain's social security benefits are called. I didn't know anyone and had no idea how I was going to live, yet I went anyway because by happenstance I'd met a plastic surgeon there who said he could help me. I had been living in London, working temp jobs. While in London, I'd received more nasty comments about my face than I had in the previous three years, living in Iowa, New York, and Germany. These comments, all from men and all odiously sexual, hurt and disoriented me. I also had journeyed to Scotland because after more than a dozen operations in the States my insurance had run out, along with my hope that further operations could make any *real* difference. Here, however, was a surgeon who had some new techniques, and here, amazingly enough, was a government willing to foot the bill: I didn't feel I could pass up yet another chance to "fix" my face, which I confusedly thought concurrent with "fixing" my self, my soul, my life.

*

Twenty years ago, when I was nine and living in America, I came home from school one day with a toothache. Several weeks and misdiagnoses later, surgeons removed most of the right side of my jaw in an attempt to prevent the cancer they found there from spreading. No one properly explained the operation to me, and I awoke in a cocoon of pain that prevented me from moving or speaking. Tubes ran in and out of my body, and because I was temporarily unable to speak after the surgery and could not ask questions, I made up my own explanations for the tubes' existence. I remember the mysterious manner the adults displayed toward me. They asked me to do things: lie still for x-rays, not cry for needles, and so on, tasks that, although not easy, never seemed equal to the praise I received in return. Reinforced to me again and again was how I was "a brave girl" for not crying, "a good girl" for not complaining, and soon I began defining myself this way, equating strength with silence.

Then the chemotherapy began. In the seventies chemo was even cruder than it is now, the basic premise being to poison patients right up to the very brink of their own death. Until this point I almost never cried and almost always received praise in return. Thus I got what I considered the better part of the deal. But now it was like a practical joke that had gotten out of hand. Chemo-therapy was a nightmare and I wanted it to stop; I didn't want to be brave anymore. Yet I had grown so used to defining myself as "brave" — i.e., *silent* — that the thought of losing this sense of myself was even more terrifying. I was certain that if I broke down I would be despicable in the eyes of both my parents and the doctors.

The task of taking me into the city for the chemo injections fell mostly on my mother, though sometimes my father made the trip. Overwhelmed by the sight of the vomiting and weeping, my father developed the routine of "going to get the car," meaning that he left the doctor's office before the injection was administered, on the premise that then he could have the car ready and waiting when it was all over. Ashamed of my suffering, I felt relief when he was finally out of the room. When my mother took me, she stayed in the room, yet this only made the distance between us even more tangible. She explained that it was wrong to cry *before* the needle went in; afterward was one thing, but before, that was

mere fear, and hadn't I demonstrated my bravery earlier? Every
Friday for two and a half years I climbed up onto that big doctor's
table and told myself not to cry, and every week I failed. The two
large syringes were filled with chemicals so caustic to the vein that
each had to be administered very slowly. The whole process took
about four minutes; I had to remain utterly still. Dry retching
began in the first fifteen seconds, then the throb behind my eyes
gave everything a yellow-green aura, and the bone-deep pain of
alternating extreme hot and cold flashes made me tremble, yet
still I had to sit motionless and not move my arm. No one spoke
to me — not the doctor, who was a paradigm of the cold-fish
physician; not the nurse, who told my mother I reacted much more
violently than many of "the other children"; and not my mother,
who, surely overwhelmed by the sight of her child's suffering,
thought the best thing to do was remind me to be brave, to try
not to cry. All the while I hated myself for having wept before the
needle went in, convinced that the nurse and my mother were
right, that I was "overdoing it," that the throwing up was psycho-
somatic, that my mother was angry with me for not being good or
brave enough.

Yet each week, two or three days after the injection, there came
the first flicker of feeling better, the always forgotten and gratefully
rediscovered understanding that to simply be well in my body was
the greatest thing I could ask for. I thought other people felt this
appreciation and physical joy all the time, and I felt cheated
because I was able to feel it only once a week.

Because I'd lost my hair, I wore a hat constantly, but this fooled
no one, least of all myself. During this time, my mother worked in
a nursing home in a Hasidic community. Hasidic law dictates that
married women cover their hair, and most commonly this is done
with a wig. My mother's friends were now all too willing to donate
their discarded wigs, and soon the house seemed filled with them.
I never wore one, for they frightened me even when my mother
insisted I looked better in one of the few that actually fit. Yet we
didn't know how to say no to the women who kept graciously
offering their wigs. The cats enjoyed sleeping on them and the
dogs playing with them, and we grew used to having to pick a wig
up off a chair we wanted to sit in. It never struck us as odd until

one day a visitor commented wryly as he cleared a chair for himself, and suddenly a great wave of shame overcame me. I had nightmares about wigs and flushed if I even heard the word, and one night I put myself out of my misery by getting up after everyone was asleep and gathering all the wigs except for one the dogs were fond of and that they had chewed up anyway. I hid all the rest in an old chest.

When you are only ten, which is when the chemotherapy began, two and a half years seem like your whole life, yet it did finally end, for the cancer was gone. I remember the last day of treatment clearly because it was the only day on which I succeeded in not crying, and because later, in private, I cried harder than I had in years; I thought now I would no longer be "special," that without the arena of chemotherapy in which to prove myself no one would ever love me, that I would fade unnoticed into the background. But this idea about *not being different* didn't last very long. Before, I foolishly believed that people stared at me because I was bald. After my hair eventually grew in, it didn't take long before I understood that I looked different for another reason. My face. People stared at me in stores, and other children made fun of me to the point that I came to expect such reactions constantly, wherever I went. School became a battleground.

Halloween, that night of frights, became my favorite holiday because I could put on a mask and walk among the blessed for a few brief, sweet hours. Such freedom I felt, walking down the street, my face hidden! Through the imperfect oval holes I could peer out at other faces, masked or painted or not, and see on those faces nothing but the normal faces of childhood looking back at me, faces I mistakenly thought were the faces everyone else but me saw all the time, faces that were simply curious and ready for fun, not the faces I usually braced myself for, the cruel, lonely, vicious ones I spent every day other than Halloween waiting to see around each corner. As I breathed in the condensed, plastic-scented air under the mask, I somehow thought that I was breathing in normality, that this joy and weightlessness were what the world was composed of, and that it was only my face that kept me from it, my face that was my own mask that kept me from knowing the joy I was sure everyone but me lived with intimately. How could the other children not know it? Not know that to be free of the fear of taunts and the burden of knowing no one would ever love you was all that anyone could ever ask for? I was a pauper walking for a short while in the clothes of the prince, and when the day ended I gave up my disguise with dismay.

I was living in an extreme situation, and because I did not particularly care for the world I was in, I lived in others, and because the world I did live in was dangerous now, I incorporated this danger into my secret life. I imagined myself to be an Indian. Walking down the streets, I stepped through the forest, my body ready for any opportunity to fight or flee one of the big cats that I knew stalked me. Vietnam and Cambodia, in the news then as scenes of catastrophic horror, were other places I walked through daily. I made my way down the school hall, knowing a land mine or a sniper might give themselves away at any moment with the subtle metal click I'd read about. Compared with a land mine, a mere insult about my face seemed a frivolous thing.

In those years, not yet a teenager, I secretly read — knowing it was somehow inappropriate — works by Primo Levi and Elie Wiesel, and every book by a survivor I could find by myself without asking the librarian. Auschwitz, Birkenau: I felt the blows of the capos and somehow knew that because at any moment we might be called upon to live for a week on one loaf of bread and some water called soup, the peanut-butter sandwich I found on my plate was nothing less than a miracle, an utter and sheer miracle capable of making me literally weep with joy.

I decided to become a "deep" person. I wasn't exactly sure what this would entail, but I believed that if I could just find the right philosophy, think the right thoughts, my suffering would end. To try to understand the world I was in, I undertook to find out what was "real," and I quickly began seeing reality as existing in the lowest common denominator, that suffering was the one and only dependable thing. But rather than spend all of my time despairing, though certainly I did plenty of that, I developed a form of defensive egomania: I felt I was the only one walking about in the world who understood what was really important. I looked upon people complaining about the most mundane things — nothing on TV, traffic jams, the price of new clothes — and felt joy because I knew how unimportant those things really were and felt unenlightened superiority because other people didn't. Because in my fantasy life I had learned to be thankful for each cold, blanketless night that I survived on the cramped wooden bunks, my pain and despair were a stroll through the country in comparison. I was often miserable, but I knew that to feel warm instead of cold was its own kind of joy, that to eat was a reenactment of the grace of some god whom I could only dimly define, and that to simply be alive was a rare, ephemeral gift.

As I became a teenager, my isolation began. My nonidentical twin sister started going out with boys, and I started — my most tragic mistake of all — to listen to and believe the taunts thrown at me daily by the very boys she and the other girls were interested in. I was a dog, a monster, the ugliest girl they had ever seen. Of all the remarks, the most damaging wasn't even directed at me but was really an insult to "Jerry," a boy I never saw because every day between fourth and fifth periods, when I was cornered by a particular group of kids, I was too ashamed to lift my eyes off the floor. "Hey, look, it's Jerry's girlfriend!" they shrieked when they saw me, and I felt such shame, knowing that this was the deepest insult to Jerry that they could imagine.

When pressed to it, one makes compensations. I came to love winter, when I could wrap up the disfigured lower half of my face in a scarf: I could speak to people and they would have no idea to whom and to what they were really speaking. I developed the bad habits of letting my long hair hang in my face and of always covering my chin and mouth with my hand, hoping it might be mistaken as a thoughtful, accidental gesture. I also became interested in horses and got a job at a rundown local stable. Having those horses to go to each day after school saved my life; I spent all of my time either with them or thinking about them. Completely and utterly repressed by the time I was sixteen, I was convinced that I would never want a boyfriend, not ever, and wasn't it convenient for me, even a blessing, that none would ever want me. I told myself I was free to concentrate on the "true reality" of life, whatever that was. My sister and her friends put on blue eye shadow, blow-dried their hair, and spent interminable hours in the local mall, and I looked down on them for this, knew they were misleading themselves and being overly occupied with the "mere surface" of living. I'd had thoughts like this when I was younger, ten or twelve, but now my philosophy was haunted by desires so frightening I was unable even to admit they existed.

Throughout all of this, I was undergoing reconstructive surgery in an attempt to rebuild my jaw. It started when I was fifteen, two years after chemo ended. I had known for years I would have operations to fix my face, and at night I fantasized about how good my life would finally be then. One day I got a clue that maybe it wouldn't be so easy. An older plastic surgeon explained the process of "pedestals" to me, and told me it would take *ten years* to fix my face. Ten years? Why even bother, I thought; I'll be ancient by then. I went to a medical library and looked up the "pedestals" he talked about. There were gruesome pictures of people with grotesque tubes of their own skin growing out of their bodies, tubes of skin that were harvested like some kind of crop and then rearranged, with results that did not look at all normal or acceptable to my eye. But then I met a younger surgeon, who was working on a new way of grafting that did not involve pedestals, and I became more hopeful and once again began to await the fixing of my face, the day when I would be whole, content, loved.

Long-term plastic surgery is not like in the movies. There is no one single operation that will change everything, and there is certainly no slow unwrapping of the gauze in order to view the final, remarkable result. There is always swelling, sometimes to a grotesque degree, there are often bruises, and always there are scars. After each operation, too frightened to simply go look in the mirror, I developed an oblique method, with several stages. First, I tried to catch my reflection in an overhead lamp: the roundness of the metal distorted my image just enough to obscure details and give no true sense of size or proportion. Then I slowly worked my way up to looking at the reflection in someone's eyeglasses, and from there I went to walking as briskly as possible by a mirror, glancing only quickly. I repeated this as many times as it would take me, passing the mirror slightly more slowly each time until finally I was able to stand still and confront myself.

The theory behind most reconstructive surgery is to take large chunks of muscle, skin, and bone and slap them into the roughly appropriate place, then slowly begin to carve this mess into some sort of shape. It involves long, major operations, countless lesser ones, a lot of pain, and many, many years. And also, it does not always work. With my young surgeon in New York, who with each passing year was becoming not so young, I had two or three soft-tissue grafts, two skin grafts, a bone graft, and some dozen other operations to "revise" my face, yet when I left graduate school at the age of twenty-five I was still more or less in the same position I had started in: a deep hole in the right side of my face and a rapidly shrinking left side and chin, a result of the radiation I'd had as a child and the stress placed upon the bone by the other operations. I was caught in a cycle of having a big operation, one that would force me to look monstrous from the swelling for many months, then having the subsequent revision operations that improved my looks tremendously, and then slowly, over the period of a few months or a year, watching the graft reabsorb back into my body, slowly shrinking down and leaving me with nothing but the scarred donor site the graft had originally come from.

It wasn't until I was in college that I finally allowed that maybe, just maybe, it might be nice to have a boyfriend. I went to a small, liberal, predominantly female school and suddenly, after years of alienation in high school, discovered that there were other people I could enjoy talking to who thought me intelligent and talented. I was, however, still operating on the assumption that no one, not ever, would be physically attracted to me, and in a curious way this shaped my personality. I became forthright and honest in the way that only the truly self-confident are, who do not expect to be rejected, and in the way of those like me, who do not even dare to ask acceptance from others and therefore expect no rejection. I had come to know myself as a person, but I would be in graduate school before I was literally, physically able to use my name and the word "woman" in the same sentence.

Now my friends repeated for me endlessly that most of it was in my mind, that, granted, I did not look like everyone else, but that didn't mean I looked bad. I am sure now that they were right some of the time. But with the constant surgery I was in a perpetual state of transfiguration. I rarely looked the same for more than six months at a time. So ashamed of my face, I was unable even to admit that this constant change affected me; I let everyone who wanted to know that it was only what was inside that mattered, that

I had "grown used to" the surgery, that none of it bothered me at all. Just as I had done in childhood, I pretended nothing was wrong, and this was constantly mistaken by others for bravery. I spent a great deal of time looking in the mirror in private, positioning my head to show off my eyes and nose, which were not only normal but quite pretty, as my friends told me often. But I could not bring myself to see them for more than a moment: I looked in the mirror and saw not the normal upper half of my face but only the disfigured lower half.

People still teased me. Not daily, as when I was younger, but in ways that caused me more pain than ever before. Children stared at me, and I learned to cross the street to avoid them; this bothered me, but not as much as the insults I got from men. Their taunts came at me not because I was disfigured but because I was a disfigured *woman*. They came from boys, sometimes men, and almost always from a group of them. I had long, blond hair, and I also had a thin figure. Sometimes, from a distance, men would see a thin blonde and whistle, something I dreaded more than anything else because I knew that as they got closer, their tune, so to speak, would inevitably change; they would stare openly or, worse, turn away quickly in shame or repulsion. I decided to cut my hair to avoid any misconception that anyone, however briefly, might have about my being attractive. Only two or three times have I ever been teased by a single person, and I can think of only one time when I was ever teased by a woman. Had I been a man, would I have had to walk down the street while a group of young women followed and denigrated my sexual worth?

Not surprisingly, then, I viewed sex as my salvation. I was sure that if only I could get someone to sleep with me, it would mean I wasn't ugly, that I was attractive, even lovable. This line of reasoning led me into the beds of several manipulative men who liked themselves even less than they liked me, and I in turn left each short-term affair hating myself, obscenely sure that if only I had been prettier it would have worked — he would have loved me and it would have been like those other love affairs that I was certain "normal" women had all the time. Gradually, I became unable to say "I'm depressed" but could say only "I'm ugly," because the two had become inextricably linked in my mind. Into that universal lie, that sad equation of "if only . . ." that we are all prey to, I was sure that if only I had a normal face, then I would be happy.

The new surgeon in Scotland, Oliver Fenton, recommended that I undergo a procedure involving something called a tissue expander, followed by a bone graft. A tissue expander is a small balloon placed under the skin and then slowly blown up over the course of several months, the object being to stretch out the skin and create room and cover for the new bone. It's a bizarre, nightmarish thing to do to your face, yet I was hopeful about the end results and I was also able to spend the three months that the expansion took in the hospital. I've always felt safe in hospitals: they're the one place I feel free from the need to explain the way I look. For this reason the first tissue expander was bearable — just — and the bone graft that followed it was a success; it did not melt away like the previous ones.

The surgical stress this put upon what remained of my original jaw instigated the deterioration of that bone, however, and it became unhappily apparent that I was going to need the same operation I'd just had on the right side done to the left. I remember my surgeon telling me this at an outpatient clinic. I planned to be traveling down to London that same night on an overnight train, and I barely made it to the station on time, such a fumbling state of despair was I in.

I could not imagine going through it *again,* and just as I had done all my life, I searched and searched through my intellect for a way to make it okay, make it bearable, for a way to *do* it. I lay awake all night on that train, feeling the tracks slip beneath me with an odd eroticism, when I remembered an afternoon from my three months in the hospital. Boredom was a big problem those long afternoons, the days marked by meals and television programs. Waiting for the afternoon tea to come, wondering desperately how I could make time pass, it had suddenly occurred to me that I didn't have to make time pass, that it would do it of its own accord, that I simply had to relax and take no action. Lying on the train, remembering that, I realized I had no obligation to improve my situation, that I didn't have to explain or understand it, that I could just simply let it happen. By the time the train pulled into King's Cross station, I felt able to bear it yet again, not entirely sure what other choice I had.

But there was an element I didn't yet know about. When I returned to Scotland to set up a date to have the tissue expander inserted, I was told quite casually that I'd be in the hospital only three or four days. Wasn't I going to spend the whole expansion time in the hospital? I asked in a whisper. What's the point of that? came the answer. You can just come in every day to the outpatient ward to have it expanded. Horrified by this, I was speechless. I would have to live and move about in the outside world with a giant balloon inside the tissue of my face? I can't remember what I did for the next few days before I went into the hospital, but I vaguely recall that these days involved a great deal of drinking alone in bars and at home.

I had the operation and went home at the end of the week. The only things that gave me any comfort during the months I lived with my tissue expander were my writing and Franz Kafka. I started a novel and completely absorbed myself in it, writing for hours each day. The only way I could walk down the street, could stand the stares I received, was to think to myself, "I'll bet none of them are writing a novel." It was that strange, old, familiar form of egomania, directly related to my dismissive, conceited thoughts of adolescence. As for Kafka, who had always been one of my favorite writers, he helped me in that I felt permission to feel alienated, and to have that alienation be okay, bearable, noble even. In the same way that imagining I lived in Cambodia helped me as a child, I walked the streets of my dark little Scottish city by the sea and knew without doubt that I was living in a story Kafka would have been proud to write.

The one good thing about a tissue expander is that you look so bad with it in that no matter what you look like once it's finally removed, your face has to look better. I had my bone graft and my fifth soft-tissue graft and, yes, even I had to admit I looked better. But I didn't look like me. Something was wrong: was *this* the face I had waited through eighteen years and almost thirty operations for? I somehow just couldn't make what I saw in the mirror correspond to the person I thought I was. It wasn't only that I continued to feel ugly; I simply could not conceive of the image as belonging to me. My own image was the image of a stranger, and rather than try to understand this, I simply stopped looking in the mirror. I perfected the technique of brushing my teeth without a mirror, grew my hair in such a way that it would require only a quick, simple brush, and wore clothes that were simply and easily put on, no complex layers or lines that might require even the most minor of visual adjustments.

On one level I understood that the image of my face was merely that, an image, a surface that was not directly related to any true, deep definition of the self. But I also knew that it is only through appearances that we experience and make decisions about the everyday world, and I was not always able to gather the strength to prefer the deeper world to the shallower one. I looked for ways to find a bridge that would allow me access to both, rather than riding out the constant swings between peace and anguish. The only direction I had to go in to achieve this was to strive for a state of awareness and self-honesty that sometimes, to this day, occasionally rewards me. I have found, I believe, that our whole lives are dominated, though it is not always so clearly translatable, by the question "How do I look?" Take all the many nouns in our lives — car, house, job, family, love, friends — and substitute the personal pronoun "I." It is not that we are all so self-obsessed; it is that all things eventually relate back to ourselves, and it is our own sense of how we appear to the world by which we chart our lives, how we navigate our personalities, which would otherwise be adrift in the ocean of *other* people's obsessions.

One evening toward the end of my year-long separation from the mirror, I was sitting in a café talking to someone — an attractive man, as it happened — and we were having a lovely, engaging conversation. For some reason I suddenly wondered what I looked like to him. What was he *actually* seeing when he saw me? So many times I've asked this of myself, and always the answer is this: a warm, smart woman, yes, but an unattractive one. I sat there in the café and asked myself this old question, and startlingly, for the first time in my life, I had no answer readily prepared. I had not looked in a mirror for so long that I quite simply had no clue as to what I looked like. I studied the man as he spoke; my entire life I had seen my ugliness reflected back to me. But now, as reluctant as I was to admit it, the only indication in my companion's behavior was positive.

And then, that evening in that café, I experienced a moment of the freedom I'd been practicing for behind my Halloween mask all those years ago. But whereas as a child I expected my liberation to come as a result of gaining something, a new face, it came to me now as the result of shedding something, of shedding my image. I once thought that truth was eternal, that when you understood something it was with you forever. I know now that this isn't so, that most truths are inherently unretainable, that we have to work hard all our lives to remember the most basic things. Society is no help; it tells us again and again that we can most be ourselves by looking like someone else, leaving our own faces behind to turn into ghosts that will inevitably resent and haunt us. It is no mistake that in movies and literature the dead sometimes know they are dead only after they can no longer see themselves in the mirror; and as I sat there feeling the warmth of the cup against my palm, this small observation seemed like a great revelation to me. I wanted to tell the man I was with about it, but he was involved in his own topic and I did not want to interrupt him, so instead I looked with curiosity toward the window behind him, its night-darkened glass reflecting the whole café, to see if I could, now, recognize myself.

VICKI HEARNE

Can an Ape Tell a Joke?

FROM HARPER'S MAGAZINE

W. H. AUDEN WROTE that poetry survives in those places where "executives would never want to tamper." Similarly, the knowledge of animals survives in places where academics would never want to tamper, even now that many of them have added their voices to the babble that presently obscures the reality of animals. It survives in the circus, eerily revealed by Mark Twain as a place where truth is guarded by scams — by what most would consider tawdry but which Huckleberry Finn embraced as "gaudy." It lives in the shabbier parts of public parks where dog obedience classes are conducted. And it lives at the racetrack, where the beauty of the horses, glowing as though each were the darling of the infinite god of detail, stands in sharp contrast to the gray faces of the gamblers.

But perhaps the least likely place one would expect to find deep knowledge about animals is in a trained-orangutan act on a Las Vegas stage — specifically, in the act performed for many years by Bobby Berosini and his five orangutans at the Stardust Hotel and Casino. I first saw Bobby Berosini's Vegas act three years ago, shortly after he received an unwelcome dose of national celebrity. Now that I've spent a week with him and his orangutans and watched a dozen of his performances, I'm convinced that he deserves his celebrity, though not for the reasons he has come by it.

I would not ordinarily have ventured to Las Vegas to watch a trained-orangutan show, but Bobby Berosini, who immigrated to the United States from his native Czechoslovakia in 1964, is no ordinary animal trainer. I had heard he'd won numerous comedy awards for his act, and that he had probably done more with orangutans — famously difficult animals to train — than any trainer ever has. But this was not the reason for his sudden notoriety. He had been accused in 1989 of abusing his orangutans by, among others, People for the Ethical Treatment of Animals. This in itself was not unusual: these days animal trainers are regularly attacked by animal-rights activists. What was unusual in this case was that the trainer had fought back, suing PETA for defamation and invasion of privacy. And, most unusual of all, he had won his case: after a five-week trial in which Berosini brought his orangutans into court, a jury found PETA, along with several individual activists, guilty of "reckless disregard of the truth" and awarded Berosini $3.1 million in damages. (The judgment is currently on appeal.)

Berosini did not sue for harassment, but while I was in Las Vegas his Australian-born wife, Joan, described to me the harrowing experience of receiving repeated death threats against themselves and their animals in the middle of the night; of spending six months living with armed security guards twenty-four hours a day; and of being forced to shop at a different supermarket each day, since some of the threats had detailed plans to poison the orangs' food. (Many animal-rights activists believe that wild animals are better off dead than confined in any way by humans.) Even today, the harassment continues: when Berosini recently moved his act to the Five Star Theatre in Branson, Missouri, the PETA picketers followed.

Mad as some of these tactics were, the charges against Bobby Berosini were not ones that could be summarily dismissed. PETA had circulated a videotape, made surreptitiously backstage by a Stardust dancer, that purported to document the abuse. The tape, which was broadcast on *Entertainment Tonight,* is of extremely poor quality, but it appears to show Berosini and his assistants on about a half-dozen occasions preparing the animals to go onstage. In each instance one of the orangutans — it's hard to tell, but it looks like the same orang each time — seems to act up and is then threatened, shaken, or struck by Berosini with a wand or baton of some kind.

Jeanne Roush, then PETA's director of research and investigations, and one of the losing defendants, charged that the orangs were routinely beaten into submission right before going onstage. Berosini said that on each of the occasions videotaped, he had had to correct the orangutan backstage because a dancer was making sounds of distressed animals to rile the orangutans. Before I got to Las Vegas, it was impossible to sort out who was telling the truth, so I decided not to pay too much attention to what was being said on either side.

What I would pay attention to, I decided, was what I saw myself — and what, as an animal trainer, I know about animals. I know, for example, that the "correction" of an animal in training is an intricate and poorly understood subject. Properly applied at the right moment, a correction will cause the animal to stop aggressive behavior and perform happily and well. But a correction that expresses the trainer's anger, impatience, or fear, or that is applied when the animal is honestly confused rather than disobedient, will leave the animal unable to perform. Since no one had said that the orangs muffed their performances after the corrections we see on the tape, I can only assume that Berosini was using good judgment.

I assume this also from the uncontested fact that the animals were performing live, twice a night, six nights a week, at liberty — that is, without any physical restraint on an unguarded stage. Roger Fouts, a primatologist who testified in another performing-ape case, has said that "you can get anyone to do anything if you beat them," but, in fact, this is not so. You can perhaps accomplish a fair amount by beating an animal or person who cannot escape (though you can't thereby engage the victim's higher faculties), but not if you beat an animal or person you then leave at liberty.

These thoughts occurred to me before I had had a chance to watch Berosini work, so I came to Las Vegas prepared to doubt PETA's charges. And after spending a week with Berosini, watching twelve performances and joining him backstage before several of them, I saw nothing to make me think he was a cruel or phony trainer — no thumps, no fists. (Could Berosini have acted differently while I was around? Possibly, but any trainer who behaves differently in public than in private will soon lose the respect of his animals.)

What I did see, there amid the Vegas glitz and against the ugly backdrop of this furious animal-rights battle, was mastery, and even a kind of miracle. Berosini and his orangs are, to be sure, masters of much that is gaudy — his act is a half-hour of animal slapstick and off-color skits sandwiched between the usual Vegas dancing girls and boys; the orangs wear shorts and funny hats and make obscene gestures to the audience. But Bobby Berosini and his orangs are masters of something else as well — of the miracle that was unavailable to Job, who, as the voice in the whirlwind thunderously reminded him, could not engage the wild animals in any fruitful, cooperative enterprise. Bobby Berosini can.

As well as being a gifted trainer, Berosini is a gifted comedian, though by his reckoning he is not the only comedian on the Stardust stage. When I asked him, between shows in the Stardust's coffee shop, what motivates his orangs to work, he said to me, passionately, "We are comedians. *We* are comedians. Do you understand me?"

Comedians? Orangutans? This is not a reasonable remark, from the point of view of either popular or institutionally sanctioned knowledge about animals. If, as many human-rights activists and academics believe, animals are capable of feeling and suffering but not of elaborate intentions and creative thought, then Berosini's orangs *must* be beaten into submission, since food rewards would not be powerful enough to motivate their complex actions. Besides, animals could not possibly know the mood or muse of comedy. They lack the conceptual apparatus to handle the mischievous shifts in meaning required for jokes.

When Berosini told me that his orangutans are comedians, I nodded my head vigorously; the enchantment of the act had not worn off. But what does it mean to say of an animal that he or she is a comedian? This question leads back onstage, to the act itself, and to the sorts of questions Berosini and his orangs toss about, invert, capsize, and rescue, only to turn them on their head, time and time again.

The running theme of the act is "How I Train Them." Berosini keeps saying to the audience, "People ask me how I get them to do things," or "People ask me how I train them," and then he supplies different "answers." At one point the answer is "You have to show them who is boss." He brings Rusty out to show him who is boss, and Rusty not only refuses to jump onto the stool provided for the purpose but tricks his trainer into doing so by pretending incomprehension until Berosini finally demonstrates, jumping onto the stool himself. Once Berosini has dutifully jumped, Rusty invites the audience to applaud.

Berosini goes on to mock much scientific and popular wisdom about operant conditioning — training that relies more on the carrot than on the stick — by demonstrating how he doesn't need to train the orangutans at all because "I have magic orang cookies." A fast and lively slapstick round results from his failed attempts to get Bo to eat a cookie; the cookie is juggled, spit into the audience, hidden, fed to Berosini, but never eaten by the orangutan.

Then there is yet another variation on the theme: "People ask me how I train them. The truth is, I do not have to train them, because I just mesmerize them." Bo is then asked to come forward and be a hypnotic subject. There is much crooning of "You are getting very, very sleepy." Bo drops her shoulders, stands more and more still, and — wonder of wonders — closes her eyes. Pleased with the trance, the "trainer" whispers, "Are you asleep?" All of a sudden Bo grins outrageously, nods her head vigorously, and then immediately droops back into her "mesmerized" posture. The joke, again, is on Berosini — or, rather, on the Berosini character, who, of course, stands for the audience and for our overblown ideas about our superior intelligence and ability to control the world.

As Berosini explains when he is offstage, the way he trains is not "traditional," in that he does not teach his animals "tricks" but rather teaches them through the flow of their intelligence interacting with his. He explains that whereas a suggestion for a move or gesture or gag often originates with him, it is just as likely to come from the orangutan; the trainer must be as adept at picking up cues from the animals as they are at picking up cues from him. And orangutans demand this kind of handling. "I do not train them to do what I know how to do," he told me, "because you just cannot do that. It doesn't work!" According to Berosini, orangutans are the hardest of all the apes to teach a trick to because they are so self-contained, so mentally poised. The same idea is expressed in scholarly literature on orangs with reference to their marked lack of social interaction in the wild. Unlike most other apes, they are not dependent on social support and approval, which vastly complicates the training relationship. An orangutan is irredeemably his or her own person — "the most poetic of the apes," as primate researcher Lyn Miles once told me.

Miles had in mind the difference between orangutans and chimps. Chimps are much admired for their use of tools and their problem-solving relationship with things as they find them. A chimp looks inferential, ingenious, and ever so active while taking the various IQ tests that science presents him with — a hexagonal peg, say, and several holes of different shapes, only one of them hexagonal. Here, the chimp shows his tremendous initiative right away, holding the peg this way and that, trying out this, that, and the other hole; this, that, and the other angle. He *experiments,* he is filled with the inventor's work ethic; he tries, essays, tests, probes, he is full of the integrity of logic, or if not logic then at least something very American: he is so enterprising, so resourceful.

Give your orangutan the hexagonal peg and the several different holes, hide behind the two-way mirror, and watch how he engages the problem. And watch and watch and watch — because he will not engage the problem. He uses the peg to scratch his back, has a look-see at his right wrist, makes a halfhearted and soon abandoned attempt to use his fur for a macramé project, stares dreamily out the window if there is one and at nothing in particular if there is not, and the sun begins to set. (The sun will also set if you are observing a chimp, but the chimp is a lot busier, so you are less likely to mark the moment in your notes. An orangutan observer has plenty of time to be a student of the varieties of sunset.) You watch, and the orang dreams, and your notes perhaps consist of nothing more than memoranda on the behavior of the clock, when casually, and as if thinking of something else, the orangutan slips the hexagonal peg into the hexagonal hole. And continues staring off dreamily.

Professor Miles says that this sort of behavior contradicts the traditional finding that orangs are dumber than chimps. It is rather, she says, that chimps are problem-oriented whereas orangs are insight-oriented, the dreamers and visionaries of the world of the great apes. Which is all well and good, but how do you entertain five hundred people for half an hour twice a night, every night, six nights a week, for seven years, with animals whose forte is meditation, animals who do not do tricks? It's like trying to entertain a Las Vegas audience with five performing poets.

In the wild, too, orangs have not provided ethologists with the glamorous behaviors that, say, Jane Goodall's chimps have given her. I found no reports of orangs doing anything like the equivalent of fashioning special sticks to fish for termites, for instance. Orang observers instead report such exciting phenomena as the "fruit stare," which some people say is a function of the difficulty orangutans have foraging for food in the wild. Orangutans need to develop the fruit stare because trees can be coy about when, where, and how much they fruit, and the fruit is often hidden in the canopy of leaves. The fruit stare is an expression of reverie, but it is a reverie directed outward rather than inward — "like thinking with your eyes," naturalist Sy Montgomery has said. "That's why they are so spaced out."

But all this only explains why there are not many orangutan acts in the world and not how Bobby Berosini manages to put on an orangutan act night after night.

What Berosini says, again and again, is "We are comedians. Do you understand me? Do you realize what I am telling you? We are comedians, my orangs and I." His voice is urgent now, but not frantic the way it is when PETA and the charges of abuse and the harassment are the topic. The act, he explains, is a collaboration: "Rusty will have an idea for a gag, and maybe I don't like his idea, but often I do, so I leave my gag aside and accept his idea, or maybe I sometimes insist that we still do it the other way. Or maybe Tiga insists that the old way was funnier, and then I have to laugh at myself and accept what she says. She has as many ideas as I do. She is an old campaigner, Tiga, she knows what she is doing."

I find the act screamingly funny, not only because the timing is so good but because the content is so intelligent, even if the orang humor can be a bit coarse. There are, for instance, the many sardonic jokes about "monkeys" and "monkey business." These are jokes about the audience, about humanity's ignorance about its fellow primates, because, of course, orangs are not monkeys — they are, along with chimps, gorillas, and humans, great apes. But this is the sort of detail people consistently get wrong. One witness in another performing-ape controversy told me a story about a zookeeper and an animal he referred to as "some sort of monkey." I pressed to discover what sort, and he said, "It doesn't matter. They're all monkeys, aren't they?"

Well, no, they are not, and it does matter, especially when you are claiming to speak with authority about the animals in question. I've listened to anthropologist Daniel Povinelli hold forth passionately about the importance of understanding the differences not only between monkeys and apes but also between different species of ape and different species of monkey. He says that there are pronounced morphological differences between monkeys and apes, and also pronounced psychological differences: "The apes are doing something different." For Povinelli, it is almost as radical a mistake to confuse monkeys with apes as it would be to confuse elephants with pigs or wolves with golden retrievers. "Evolution would be impossible without difference," Povinelli points out. "There can hardly be anything more fundamental than recognizing, studying, and appreciating the enormous differences, especially the psychological differences, among different animals."

Povinelli and Berosini are very different people, with very different relationships to animals, but they have in common a passionate belief that the details about an animal, whether psychological or morphological, are not merely pedantic decorations but should compel our respect. Berosini is a performer and Povinelli is a scientist, so they would probably disagree about what counts as a violation of this code, but they meet in insisting that there is such a code and that it matters. Indeed, when I told Povinelli that in his act Berosini calls his animals "monkeys" and makes no attempt to correct himself, he was somewhat shocked and not entirely reassured by my explanation of the dark comic irony of the usage.

Berosini, however, is nothing if not canny; it means something when he monkeys around. When Bo nods her head vigorously or applauds his "wit" when he makes a "monkey" joke, there is a sophisticated edge here, as if a physicist were joking around by blurring the difference between an atom and a molecule.

You have to know a great deal more than the bulk of the audience knows, or cares to know, about animals and the politics of animals in order to hear the sardonic implications in the reiteration of the "just monkeys" bit. These darker jibes ride on the back of traditional slapstick, but the jokes are, as perhaps true slapstick always is, constructed both from and about our intellectual ineptitude and hubris; every time one of the orangs makes a "monkey" out of Berosini, the joke is on us. Our brutishness and our intellectual incompetence are one.

But the act is comedy, true comedy, and not merely a collection of dark and sardonic jokes. The orangs and the audience and humanity itself, as represented by the character Berosini portrays, are redeemed in the end, in part by the sheer quicksilver beauty of the timing. When the audience laughs, at times with true joy, a joy free of malice, it is, after all, humanity that is being celebrated, since the ability to laugh without malice at one's own failings — and to see in those failings one's connection with everyone else in the room, a connection made through laughter — is no mean ethical feat.

If Berosini's act can be said to have one overriding theme, it is training — obedience — itself. "Obedience" comes from an old French word that means "to hear" or "to heed," "to pay attention to." The great trainers of every kind of animal, from parakeet to dog to elephant, have said for millennia that you cannot get an animal to heed you unless you heed the animal; obedience in this sense is a symmetrical relationship. In a given instance it may start with the human, who perhaps says to the dog, "Joe, sit!" Soon, however, the dog will take the command and turn it, use it to respond, to say something back. The dog might, for example, take to sitting in a sprightly fashion when one gets out a dumbbell, as if to say, "Yes, that's it, let's go!" It is at this moment that true training with any species, including humans, either begins or fails. If the human obeys, hears, heeds, responds to what the animal is now saying, then training begins. If the human "drops" the animal at this point, not realizing that the task has only begun, then the dog or orangutan will disobey.

Animals, like people, are motivated in many ways. Berosini's orangs are motivated offstage in the same way they appear to be motivated onstage: when they make a gesture, they get a response. Their trainer obeys them, unless they are committing mayhem. The intelligent responsiveness of animals is for us one of the most deeply attractive things about them, not only because we are a lonesome and threatened tribe but because intelligent responsiveness is a central, abiding good. The intelligent responsiveness of trainers, which some of them call respect, is what makes trainers attractive to animals, and may be the whole of the secret of "having a way with animals."

In the comic mismatch between the Berosini character's ideas about the orangs and the nature of the orangs themselves as they triumph continually over the would-be lordly "trainer," our fond hopes are mocked, but not cruelly. The world, which is to say the human project, is in trouble, but within the tiny world of Berosini's act a way is found, even if it is a stumbling, awkward way, to true responsiveness between ourselves and animals. Even the audience gets a response, as when Rusty invites us to applaud Berosini or when Tiga gives an audience member one of her "magic orang cookies," and does so gently, though without a hint of subservience.

Berosini also gets laughs by mocking the character of the orangs — Tiga's onstage character has a drinking problem and loose morals — but the "How I Train Them" series of gags is the most intellectually satisfying part of the act. Interestingly, Bo's simulation of the hypnotic trance is a play on the sort of spacy consciousness ethologists have observed in orangutans. There is the same dreaminess, the trance that frames the unpredictable moment of alert intelligence. Bo's eyes are closed, but otherwise she seems to be imitating the fruit stare in much the same way that a dressage horse — one so highly educated that we say he or she "dances" — imitates, with some variations, the postures and gestures of a horse in "nature."

The radical claim being made here is that the animals are "referring to," or at least imitating, these gestures deliberately, with some sense — if not precisely our sense — of the meaning of what they are doing. Berosini says that Bo is in on the joke, or at least on *some* joke, and that it is her interest and pleasure in such monkeying around that make it possible for him to work with her as he does. This is speculative, of course, but it could be argued that Berosini's is a more parsimonious explanation than an explanation based on conditioning would be. Indeed, it's questionable whether any model of conditioning, however elaborate, can explain behavior this complex, particularly since every performance the act changes, with both Berosini and the orangs offering improvisations. Talk of conditioned responses may be helpful in understanding part of a trained animal's development (or, for that matter, a dancer's or a poet's or an actor's or a philosopher's), but animal performance at this level makes more sense when viewed as rudimentary expressions of at least one primeval artistic impulse — the impulse to play with meaning.

Bo's trance-breaking grin is wonderfully timed, a case of high slapstick, if there can be such a thing; it is also, for me at least, an eerie instant of revelation in which I see something fairly exact in Berosini's claim that his orangs are comedians. But how might such an animal joke come about? Let's say that you are teaching the animal to be "mesmerized," and the animal spontaneously adds the mischievous nodding grin. This is a joke about who's in control, though not necessarily a joke about hypnosis. You accept the move and ask for it on purpose next time, and it becomes part of the routine. The animal offers it spontaneously at first, and then continues with it, perhaps for the same reason we repeat a phrase or a joke — because it felt so delicious the first time.

Berosini's act gives the orangs a point of view, one that I find credible as an animal point of view, and it gives their intelligence pride of place, as do other clever disobedience acts in the tradition — an ancient tradition going back to the Greeks, in which the *eiron*, or apparently lowly character, triumphs over the apparently noble character through wit, awareness, quickness of perception. (The word *eiron* gives us our word "irony.") In circus and movie tradition, the most familiar form of such comedy is the disobedient-dog act, in which the trainer character attempts to induce the dogs to display loyalty, nobility, and willing service; instead, they trip the trainer, disgrace the legacy of Rin Tin Tin by stealing a purse from an audience member, "bite" the trainer, and so on.

It is not Lassie and Rin Tin Tin themselves who are mocked by the disobedient-dog act but rather our own self-serving ideas of the selflessness of dogs, such as the pious notion that dogs "want to please" and work "for love of the handler." Berosini's orangs work with this sort of material wonderfully, displaying their intelligence against the backdrop of our ideas of their debasement.

If Berosini's comedy is somewhat dark and sharp-edged when you take a close look at it, that may be in part because of the tradition of comedy he inherits as a Czech, a tradition that has had to learn, over and over again, how to ensure the survival of intelligence in forms that escape the more violent scrutiny of various regimes. At any rate, the act I saw is one kind of shield for the mind, one kind of comic courage by means of which sanity survives amid social and political darkness.

One of Berosini's most famous monkey jokes occurred in court.

During my stay in Las Vegas shortly after the 1990 trial, I heard it at least two dozen times. At one point during Berosini's testimony, PETA's lawyer asked him to tell the audience how he taught Bo to give the finger. He replied, "I'll give you a demonstration of how to give the finger if you want." This is just the way his orangs perform in his act, ragging him, continually foiling him with impudence, back talk, irreverence, impiety. And they give him the finger. In one way or another, most animals do give their trainers the finger — a great deal of animal humor is coarse, to put it mildly. I have long suspected that the real reason it was for so long heresy, an excommunicable offense, to say that animals have souls is that if you say they have souls, then their jokes and comments have meaning, and no bureaucratic or ecclesiastical or philanthropic dignity can survive animal vaudeville.

Joan Berosini told me that one juror, who asked to remain anonymous, said after the case was over, "It would be abuse to take the orangs away from Bobby." Is there anything to this, anything that can be understood without elevating Berosini to Patron Saint of Apes — a position that would destroy his comic art and that is, in any case, already held by Jane Goodall? Or, to turn the question around, what is the source of the improbable idea that the act's flow and liveliness and energy could possibly be achieved by beatings?

I do not think that the orangs mean their antics the way the audience interprets them. But I do think they mean *something* by them, and that they are motivated to stay onstage, rather than run loose in the audience, not by terror — which is a poor motivator — but by an interest in what they are doing.

So what *do* they mean, what are they doing? I am convinced that some animals — quite a few Airedales, for example, and also Border collies — are interested, and take pleasure, in something like the grammar of gesture itself, much as a dancer does. A bird dog in the field intends to retrieve the bird; the same dog cantering gaily after a dumbbell in an obedience ring "means" only that movement — not the retrieving of a bird, but the glorious gestures of retrieving. A Lippizaner means not to display himself before mares (which is what his movements would mean in "nature") but to call attention to the grandeur and intricacy of the display. These gestures are all metaphors, second inheritances of nature, in the same way poetry is a second inheritance of language. To call any of this — or poetry or dance, for that matter — "play," as some are wont to do, misses the point; it is work that is as serious as play, to borrow a phrase from the poet John Hollander. Such work is the highest use and pleasure of the mind, and orangutans plainly do have minds. The mind may remain satisfied in the wild, where the primitive problems of survival overwhelm other impulses, but if the other great apes are as close to us psychologically as some people claim and have minds, then it is a good for those minds to develop.

And yet training in and of itself, apart from questions of abuse, makes people uneasy. In medieval times ecclesiasts believed that trained animals had devils in them — that dancing dogs were dancing satanically. In our time the idea of the "unnatural" has replaced the idea of the demonic, and for some it does not matter whether or not animals are abused, since keeping and training them is itself "unnatural" or "ethologically inappropriate," as though it were unnatural to develop the mind. These days the contemporary horror of the "unnatural" infects visions of life with domestic animals as well, but the possibility of the hearth — by which I mean a place where the human and animal may sit side by side — is much more likely to be denied when wild animals are in question.

Certainly you cannot have the same relationship with a wolf as with a dog, yet it does not follow from this that there can be *no* relationship. Today, at a time when the habitats of wild animals are rapidly disappearing, the terms of this relationship need to be reinvented, not abjured. We need to learn what we can from Berosini and other trainers — but particularly the wild-animal trainers — about how this might be done. A dog and her trainer, or a horse and his trainer, do not have to "meet each other halfway," because they already share the same social space. An orangutan and his trainer, however, must travel some conceptual distance to meet each other and work together. That this is possible, what it means that it is possible, what implications it has for the possibilities of mutual respect between wild animals and humans — this strikes me as a matter of urgent importance.

That is, I believe not only that the training of wild animals is acceptable but that the knowledge trainers have, which has been eschewed by science and philosophy and the church for millennia, may contain clues to imaginative and enlightened ways we might escape our age's violence and sentimentality toward the nonhuman world and thereby genuinely take up the burden of our responsibility toward animals. In the Book of Job, the voice in the whirlwind points out that the wild goat and the unicorn and the ostrich and the warhorse are beyond Job. But the orangutan is not beyond Bobby Berosini, and it behooves us to understand why, to know that there is something to understand and that the prurient contemplation of abuse, so popular in a self-servingly sentimental climate, will not open understanding here. Furthermore, the mongering of irresponsible images of abuse only obscures our views of the real cruelties that do exist.

James Thurber, who defended the intelligence of animals and animal wit as vigorously as anyone ever has, once wrote this about human wit: "The perfect tribute to perfection in comedy is not immediate laughter, but a curious and instantaneous tendency of the eyes to fill." This, I keep thinking, and not weepy displays of ignorant outrage and pity, is the tribute owed to Berosini's orangs. But be careful your vision does not mist too much. Bo and Rusty and Tiga and Niki and Benny are quite clear-eyed. Trainers speak often of how uncannily good animals are at "reading" people, and of training as a humbling activity. That's because when you train an animal you teach yourself and the animal a "language" by means of which the animal can tell you more than you may have wanted to know about what he or she sees in looking at you. If there is a moral to the act that the orangs are in on, it is this: be sure that when Tiga looks into your eyes she finds a clarity and amused intelligence fit to answer her own, lest she turn from you, leaving you in the foolish darkness yet again.

JAMAICA KINCAID

Alien Soil

FROM THE NEW YORKER

WHATEVER IT IS in the character of the English people that leads them to obsessively order and shape their landscape to such a degree that it looks like a painting (tamed, framed, captured, kind, decent, good, pretty), while a painting never looks like the English landscape, unless it is a bad painting — this quality of character is blissfully lacking in the Antiguan people. I make this unfair comparison (unfair to the Antiguan people? unfair to the English people? I cannot tell, but there is an unfairness here somewhere) only because so much of the character of the Antiguan people is influenced by and inherited, through conquest, from the English people. The tendency to shower pity and cruelty on the weak is among the traits the Antiguans inherited, and so is a love of gossip. (The latter, I think, is responsible for the fact that England has produced such great novelists, but it has not yet worked to the literary advantage of the Antiguan people.) When the English were a presence in Antigua — they first came to the island as slaveowners, when a man named Thomas Warner established a settlement there in 1632 — the places where they lived were surrounded by severely trimmed hedges of plumbago, topiaries of willow (casuarina), and frangipani and hibiscus; their grass was green (odd, because water was scarce; the proper word for the climate is not "sunny" but "drought-ridden") and freshly cut; they kept trellises covered with roses, and beds of marigolds and cannas and chrysanthemums.

Ordinary Antiguans (and by "ordinary Antiguans" I mean the Antiguan people, who are descended from the African slaves brought

to this island by Europeans; this turns out to be a not uncommon
way to become ordinary), the ones who had some money and
could live in houses of more than one room, had gardens in which
only flowers were grown. This made it even more apparent that
they had some money, in that all their outside space was devoted
not to feeding their families but to the sheer beauty of things. I
can remember in particular one such family, who lived in a house
with many rooms (four, to be exact). They had an indoor kitchen
and a place for bathing (no indoor toilet, though); they had a
lawn, always neatly cut, and they had beds of flowers, but I can
now remember only roses and marigolds. I can remember those
because once I was sent there to get a bouquet of roses for my
godmother on her birthday. The family also had, in the middle of
their small lawn, a willow tree, pruned so that it had the shape of
a pine tree — a conical shape — and at Christmastime this tree was
decorated with colored lights (which was so unusual and seemed
so luxurious to me that when I passed by this house I would beg
to be allowed to stop and stare at it for a while). At Christmas, all
willow trees would suddenly be called Christmas trees, and for a
time, when my family must have had a small amount of money, I,
too, had a Christmas tree — a lonely, spindly branch of willow
sitting in a bucket of water in our very small house. No one in my
family and, I am almost certain, no one in the family of the people
with the lighted-up willow tree had any idea of the origins of the
Christmas tree and the traditions associated with it. When these
people (the Antiguans) lived under the influence of these other
people (the English), there was naturally an attempt among some
of them to imitate their rulers in this particular way — by rearranging the landscape — and they did it without question. They can't be
faulted for not asking what it was they were doing; that is the way
these things work. The English left, and most of their landscaping
influence went with them. The Americans came, but Americans
(I am one now) are not interested in influencing people directly;
we instinctively understand the childish principle of monkey see,
monkey do. And at the same time we are divided about how we
ought to behave in the world. Half of us believe in and support
strongly a bad thing our government is doing, while the other half
do not believe in and protest strongly against the bad thing. The
bad thing succeeds, and everyone, protester and supporter alike,

enjoys immensely the results of the bad thing. This ambiguous
approach in the many is always startling to observe in the individual. Just look at Thomas Jefferson, a great American gardener and
our country's third president, who owned slaves and strongly sup-
ported the idea of an expanded American border, which meant
the extinction of the people who already lived on the land to be
taken, while at the same time he was passionately devoted to ideas
about freedom — ideas that the descendants of the slaves and the
people who were defeated and robbed of their land would have to
use in defense of themselves. Jefferson, as president, commis-
sioned the formidable trek his former secretary, the adventurer
and botany thief Meriwether Lewis, made through the West, sending plant specimens back to the president along the way. The
Lewisia rediviva, state flower of Montana, which Lewis found in the
Bitterroot River valley, is named after him; the clarkia, not a flower
of any state as far as I can tell, is named for his co-adventurer and
botany thief, William Clark.

What did the botanical life of Antigua consist of at the time
another famous adventurer — Christopher Columbus — first saw
it? To see a garden in Antigua now will not supply a clue. I made
a visit to Antigua this spring, and most of the plants I saw there
came from somewhere else. The bougainvillea (named for another
restless European, the sea adventurer Louis-Antoine de Bougain-
ville, first Frenchman to cross the Pacific) is native to tropical
South America; the plumbago is from southern Africa; the croton
(genus *Codiaeum*) is from Malay Peninsula; the *Hibiscus rosa-sinensis*
is from Asia and the *Hibiscus schizopetalus* is from East Africa; the
allamanda is from Brazil; the poinsettia (named for an American
ambassador, Joel Poinsett) is from Mexico; the bird of paradise
flower is from southern Africa; the Bermuda lily is from Japan; the
flamboyant tree is from Madagascar; the casuarina is from Australia; the Norfolk pine is from Norfolk Island; the tamarind tree is
from Africa; the mango is from Asia. The breadfruit, the most
Antiguan (to me) and starchy food, the bane of every Antiguan
child's palate, is from the East Indies. This food has been the cause
of more disagreement between parents and their children than
anything else I can think of. No child has ever liked it. It was sent
to the West Indies by Joseph Banks, the English naturalist and
world traveler and the head of Kew Gardens, which was then a

clearinghouse for all the plants stolen from the various parts of the world where the English had been. (One of the climbing roses, *Rosa banksiae*, from China, was named for Banks's wife.) Banks sent tea to India; to the West Indies he sent the breadfruit. It was meant to be a cheap food for feeding slaves. It was the cargo that Captain Bligh was carrying to the West Indies on the ship *Bounty* when his crew so rightly mutinied. It's as though the Antiguan child senses intuitively the part this food has played in the history of injustice and so will not eat it. But, unfortunately for her, it grows readily, bears fruit abundantly, and is impervious to drought. Soon after the English settled in Antigua, they cleared the land of its hard-wood forests to make room for the growing of tobacco, sugar, and cotton, and it is this that makes the island drought-ridden to this day. Antigua is also empty of much wildlife natural to it. When snakes proved a problem for the planters, they imported the mongoose from India. As a result there are no snakes at all on the island — nor other reptiles, other than lizards — though I don't know what damage the absence of snakes causes, if any.

What herb of beauty grew in this place then? What tree? And did the people who lived there grow anything beautiful for its own sake? I do not know; I can only make a straightforward deduction: the frangipani, the mahogany tree, and the cedar tree are all native to the West Indies, so these trees are probably indigenous. And some of the botany of Antigua can be learned from medicinal folklore. My mother and I were sitting on the steps in front of her house one day during my recent visit, and I suddenly focused on a beautiful bush (beautiful to me now; when I was a child I thought it ugly) whose fruit I remembered playing with when I was little. It is an herbaceous plant that has a red stem covered with red thorns, and emerald-green, simple leaves, with the same red thorns running down the leaf from the leafstalk. I cannot remember what its flowers looked like, and it was not in flower when I saw it while I was there with my mother, but its fruit is a small, almost trans-parent red berry, and it is this I used to play with. We children sometimes called it "china berry," because of its transparent, glassy look — it reminded us of china dinnerware, though we were only vaguely familiar with such a thing as china, having seen it no more than once or twice — and sometimes "baby tomato," because of its size, and to signify that it was not real; a baby thing was not a real thing. When I pointed the bush out to my mother, she called it something else; she called it cancanberry bush, and said that in the old days, when people could not afford to see doctors, if a child had thrush they would make a paste of this fruit and rub it inside the child's mouth, and this would make the thrush go away. But, she said, people rarely bother with this remedy anymore. The day before, a friend of hers had come to pay a visit, and when my mother offered her something to eat and drink the friend declined, because, she said, she had some six-sixty-six and maiden-blush tea waiting at home for her. This tea is taken on an empty stomach, and it is used for all sorts of ailments, including to help bring on abortions. I have never seen six-sixty-six in flower, but its leaves are a beautiful ovoid shape and a deep green — qualities that are of value in a garden devoted to shape and color of leaf.

People who do not like the idea that there is a relationship between gardening and wealth are quick to remind me of the cottage gardener, that grim-faced English person. Living on land that is not his own, he has put bits and pieces of things together, things from here and there, and it is a beautiful jumble — but just try duplicating it; it isn't cheap to do. And I have never read a book praising the cottage garden written by a cottage gardener. This person — the cottage gardener — does not exist in a place like Antigua. Nor do casual botanical conversation, knowledge of the Latin names for plants, and discussions of the binomial system. If an atmosphere where these things could flourish exists in this place, I am not aware of it. I can remember very well the cruel Englishwoman who was my botany teacher, and that, in spite of her cruelty, botany was one of my two favorite subjects in school. (History was the other.) With this in mind I visited a bookstore (the only bookstore I know of in Antigua) to see what texts are now being used in the schools and to see how their content compares with what was taught to me back then; the botany I had studied was a catalogue of the plants of the British Empire, the very same plants that are now widely cultivated in Antigua and are probably assumed by ordinary Antiguans to be native to their landscape — the mango, for example. But it turns out that botany as a subject is no longer taught in Antiguan schools; the study of plants is now called agriculture. Perhaps that is more realistic, since the awe and poetry of botany cannot be eaten, and the mystery and pleasure in the knowledge of botany cannot be taken to market and sold.

And yet the people of Antigua have a relationship to agriculture that does not please them at all. Their very arrival on this island had to do with the forces of agriculture. When they (we) were brought to this island from Africa a few hundred years ago, it was not for their pottery-making skills or for their way with a loom; it was for the free labor they could provide in the fields. Mary Prince, a nineteenth-century African woman who was born in Bermuda and spent part of her life as a slave in Antigua, writes about this in an autobiographical account, which I found in *The Classic Slave Narratives*, edited by Henry Louis Gates, Jr. She says:

> My master and mistress went on one occasion into the country, to Date Hill, for change of air, and carried me with them to take charge of the children, and to do the work of the house. While I was in the country, I saw how the field negroes are worked in Antigua. They are worked very hard and fed but scantily. They are called out to work before daybreak, and come home after dark; and then each has to heave his bundle of grass for the cattle in the pen. Then, on Sunday morning, each slave has to go out and gather a large bundle of grass; and, when they bring it home, they have all to sit at the manager's door and wait till he come out: often they have to wait there till past eleven o'clock, without any breakfast. After that, those that have yams or potatoes, or fire-wood to sell, hasten to market to buy . . . salt fish, or pork, which is a great treat for them.

Perhaps it makes sense that a group of people with such a wretched historical relationship to growing things would need to describe their current relationship to it as dignified and masterly (agriculture), and would not find it poetic (botany) or pleasurable (gardening).

In a book I am looking at (to read it is to look at it: the type is as tall as a doll's teacup), *The Tropical Garden*, by William Warren, with photographs by Luca Invernizzi Tettoni, I find statements like "the concept of a private garden planted purely for aesthetic purposes was generally alien to tropical countries" and "there was no such tradition of ornamental horticulture among the inhabitants of most hot-weather places. Around the average home there might be a few specimens chosen especially because of their scented flowers or because they were believed to bring good fortune. . . .

Nor would much, if any, attention be paid to attractive landscape design in such gardens: early accounts by travellers in the tropics abound in enthusiastic descriptions of jungle scenery, but a reader will search in vain for one praising the tasteful arrangement of massed ornamental beds and contrasting lawns of well-trimmed grass around the homes of natives." What can I say to that? No doubt it is true. And no doubt contrasting laws and massed ornamental beds are a sign of something, and that is that someone — someone other than the owner of the lawns — has been humbled. To give just one example: on page 62 of this book is a photograph of eight men, natives of India, pulling a heavy piece of machinery used in the upkeep of lawns. They are without shoes. They are wearing the clothing of schoolboys — khaki shorts and khaki short-sleeved shirts. There is no look of bliss on their faces. The caption for the photograph reads, "Shortage of labour was never a problem in the maintenance of European features in large colonial gardens; here a team of workers is shown rolling a lawn at the Gymkhana Club in Bombay."

And here are a few questions that occur to me: what if the people living in the tropics, the ones whose history isn't tied up with and contaminated by slavery and indenturedness, are contented with their surroundings, are happy to observe an invisible hand at work and from time to time laugh at some of the ugly choices this hand makes; what if they have more important things to do than make a small tree large, a large tree small, or a tree whose blooms are usually yellow bear black blooms; what if these people are not spiritually feverish, restless, and fully of envy?

When I was looking at the book of tropical gardens, I realized that the flowers and the trees so familiar to me from my childhood do not now have a hold on me. I do not long to plant and be surrounded by the bougainvillea; I do not like the tropical hibiscus; the corallita (from Mexico), so beautiful when tended, so ugly when left to itself, which makes everything around it look rusty and shabby, is not a plant I like at all. I returned from my visit to Antigua, the place where I was born, to a small village in Vermont, the place where I choose to live. Spring had arrived. The tulips I had planted last autumn were in bloom, and I liked to sit and caress their petals, which felt disgustingly delicious, like scraps of peau de soie. The dizzy-making yellow of dandelions and cowslips was in the fields and riverbanks and marshes. I like these things. (I do not like daffodils, but that's a legacy of the English approach: I was forced to memorize the poem by William Wordsworth when I was a child.) I transplanted to the edge of a grove of pine trees some foxgloves that I grew from seed in late winter. I found some Virginia bluebells in a spot in the woods where I had not expected to find them, and some larches growing grouped together, also in a place I had not expected. On my calendar I marked the day I would go and dig up all the mulleins I could find and replant them in a very sunny spot across from the grove of pine trees. This is to be my forest of mulleins, though in truth it will appear a forest only to an ant. I marked the day I would plant the nasturtiums under the fruit trees. I discovered a clump of Dutchman's-breeches in the wildflower bed that I inherited from the man who built and used to own the house in which I now live, Robert Woodworth, the botanist who invented time-lapse photography. I waited for the things I had ordered in the deep cold of winter to come. They started to come. Mr. Pembroke, who represents our village in the Vermont legislature, came and helped me dig some of the holes where some of the things I wanted to put in were to be planted. Mr. Pembroke is a very nice man. He is never dressed in the clothing of schoolboys. There is not a look of misery on his face; on his face is the complicated look of an ordinary human being. When he works in my garden, we agree on a price; he sends me a bill, and I pay it. The days are growing longer and longer, and then they'll get shorter again. I am now used to that ordered progression, and I love it. But there is no order in my garden. I live in America now. Americans are impatient with memory, which is one of the things order thrives on.

MARK KRAMER

Escape from Moscow

FROM OUTSIDE

THE DOORMAN at the Institute for the Study of the USA and Canada, with whom I'd exchanged nods for five years, stepped into Moscow's morning smog. He poked one of those strong Belomor cigarettes that's half filter (and named after the ship canal built by convicts in the 1920s at a cost of two million lives) between his old dry lips, thumbed open a matchbox, and struck a match that spat and fizzled. He flicked it toward the broken pavement of Khlebny Pereulok (the name translates as "Bread Alley," after the bakeries that thrived there until the revolution shut them) and muttered as it spun away, "Killed two and a half kopeks."

He was talking inflation. Everyone was talking inflation. For decades, a box of fifty matches had cost him five kopeks. That was as much a fact of life as the fixed price of bread, which until 1991 had spent decades steady at ten kopeks. Suddenly matches cost one ruble and twenty-five kopeks; bread, ten rubles. And both prices were rising fast, though they were still low by a Westerner's standards — about a penny for the matches, eight cents for the bread. The doorman's salary had quadrupled since the August 1990 coup, but matches had gone up twenty-five-fold and bread a hundred-fold. He was losing ground.

On the streets, you can overhear conversations about prices all day long. People are skittish. Bounced out of economic never-never land, they've been gripped by the invisible hand of economic necessity. They're rechanneling their society, shovelful by painful shovelful, and day-to-day life for most has gotten tougher.

Russians are desperate to mellow out. Moscow's sour-smelling squares swarm with stay-at-home escapists, absolute drunks who wobble about, scanning the harsh world through slit vodka-eyes. As our Wild West was, Russia remains: sopping in alcohol.

People respond to the pressure by finding themselves out-of-town jaunts, some of them a sight more rugged than an American's idea of vacation. Serge Molotchkov, once adviser on matters Canadian to the now blessedly retired Politburo, fled all the way to backmost Siberia a year after the near coup and floated for a month down the Lena River on a rubber raft, camping and frying fresh-caught salmon.

Mitya Genkin, impelled by the economic transition to shift from electrical engineering to silversmithing, got sick of bureaucratic folderol and headed for the Kola Peninsula as a porter on a geology expedition, hauling hundred-pound loads over the bleak landscape.

My friend Seryozha Sossinsky made an even more elaborate escape. He'd long been a rebel. In the early seventies he'd organized an exhibition of dissident modern artists, shortly after which his Ph.D. thesis bounced, with only this comment on it: "Where are the quotes from Lenin; where are the quotes from Brezhnev?"

Outside the Party, Seryozha had eked out a living translating awful children's stories about Papa Lenin and the like for Progress, the English-language publishing house. Then perestroika muted the call for propaganda. Seryozha's income faded. In the sinking economy, he didn't even look for a job. Like our own post-Vietnam back-to-the-country migrants, Seryozha scouted the outback. He found a cabin in a nearly abandoned village ("nonprospective," authorities under Brezhnev had labeled such villages when they evicted families that had lived there for centuries). He battled bureaucrats for title to the hut and got it (but not the land beneath it, which still hadn't been privatized) for two hundred rubles. He gardened, wrote history, and produced a book of essays called *Letters from the Country*. He subsisted virtually without income.

We went there in midsummer, rolling northward, covering six hundred miles in three days of increasingly hard travel, first by train, then by riding with private drivers willing to bargain, then, after we ran out of paved road, by offering cigarettes to the drivers of passing jeeps and logging trucks. Finally, in the hilly upper reaches of the Kostroma region, we sputtered in Seryozha's cranky old outboard for many miles up the Unzha River.

The Unzha is a beautiful, wild waterway, now sadly scoured,

bottom and banks, by hundreds of huge log rafts shoved by churning river tugs. Few fish survive. We dodged logs, breakaways from
the rafts, some of them submerged. We reached the six-hut village
called Astafyevo in slanting evening light.

We heard the residents — two old women, one a shepherd, one
a cowherd — before we saw them, cussing their animals up and
down the grassy slopes. The women ceaselessly ran at the herd with
sticks, shrieking their curses. Horseflies as big as thumbs spiraled
in a buzzing snarl, stinging the animals' faces. "The women fight
each other, fists and teeth, sometimes," said Seryozha, "and then
they love each other. In winter the sheep move right in with Aunt
Masha. So do her cats."

That evening Aunt Masha was on the subject of her cats when I
sat in the kitchen of her log hut. I had a ginger cat on my lap; she
had two on hers. "They sleep on my bed," she said. "I slug them hard,
but still they climb up." Her thoughts drifted to the uncertain times
— she knew little about politics, but the transition had reached
out to change her life. "How will I live this winter? There's no
transport. Last year they took fifty rubles for a trailer-load of hay.
This year they want one thousand!" Big, basic questions are about
to surface in Astafyevo — who owns the sheep, the land, and the
huts, and eventually whether or not Aunt Masha's small flock is
economical, questions that have had no bearing on her life or work
during all of her sixty years.

A few hours downriver in the town of Kologreve we visited friends
of Seryozha's, a retired high-school shop teacher turned wood-
carver and his wife, who had been a member of the Party administration in town and regretted it. "Now that I've read about the
lies of the Party, I think I wasted my whole life," she said, shaking
her head.

The man spoke of what Russians call "the grief of the country"
in recalling the Unzha: "Practically every village, big or small, was
a separate collective farm when I was a boy," he said. "The Unzha
was navigable then, and big steamships went all summer. People
fished. No logging. The riverbed was all plants, except at the
rapids. Then logging came. That tore the plants out. Crews came
with small motorboats whose big wakes washed away at the riverbanks. Slow tugs used to pull the old barges — no waves. Now boats

rush upriver, even when the water is low. They've destroyed the river. The small boats, the logging, clearing the forests — all this changes the runoff so the forests along the banks of all the tributary streams have been destroyed. Now, no forests even out the water flow. Rain, and up goes the river. Drought, down it goes. Ponga, Veega, Svyatitza Knyajhaya — all these small streams used to be bigger."

Cutting and shipping trees is the work of the River Logging Authority, and on our way home we moored our boat for a time at the authority's base camp. It was in fact a small town — a boozy, Klondike-style log village with bunkrooms for transients and cabins for workers with families, a one-room store (well stocked — this crowd had money), a one-room schoolhouse, a bakery (which turned out boutique-quality sourdough loaves), and a huge bull-dozed arena where hundreds of thousands of logs were yarded, bunched into rafts and just waiting for the spring, when the Unzha would swell and the big tugs would waddle upstream. The River Logging Authority can now export logs for hard currency. The logs will rebuild Russia as they destroy it.

That night a few come-from-aways showed up in Astafyevo — first a retired doctor who'd loved to hunt here with her late husband and felt she was still with him when she hunted alone. Then, in the middle of the night, a whimsical art professor arrived with his lanky mistress, after having bribed a tractor driver from the Chermeninsky Collective Farm with a bottle ("He needed to smell it right away, before we even set out!") to ford the river and churn his way up the convoluted logging road. It was about as complete an escape as one could make from Moscow, and we spent the rest of the midsummer night celebrating.

Then we picked our way back to the city, first by the outboard, then by offering a work crew about $3.50, which inspired them to climb into their smashed-up four-wheel-drive work wagon and bounce over knee-high ruts and potholes like caldrons to the railhead at Manturova. Two days later, we reached Moscow. Inflation in the capital was proceeding normally. The subway fare had doubled since we'd left, up from fifty kopeks to a ruble.

After a week of dreary office work, I made a second escape, in the manner more typical of Muscovites. Stepping around the weekend drunks, my friend Pavel and I headed for his dacha in the hills just out of town. Entire families flee each weekend — babushkas clutching tiny grandkids in shorts, papas mysteriously dressed in suits and fedoras straight from 1930s gangster films, all laden like pack mules with garden tools, bedding, squares of window glass, scavenged boards and tin for cottage repairs, new buckets for wells and outhouses, a few live chickens in crates. They trudge down the steps, dogs tugging on leashes, into the still-grand subways, past old folks hawking Christian newspapers and pornography, gypsies who set pleading toddlers clinging to the legs of passersby, and old ladies kneeling and genuflecting obsessively in catacombed corridors niched with statues of discredited Soviet heroes. The trains, amazingly, have gone on working well.

Dachas are little summerhouses, usually in colonies that ring the city. One didn't have to be rich, or even influential, to get a dacha. They were handed out by the workplace, which before the attempted coup supervised all aspects of employees' lives. Workplace committees decided who could buy a car, take a holiday, get health care. Humorless Leonid Brezhnev had banned freestanding dachas for a while — too much like private homes. So construction crews built duplex and quadruplex dachas across the corners of adjacent lots, joined by just a few feet of common wall. Even then, dachas remained private retreats where bourgeois individualism could be practiced on weekends. Cheap dachas and cheap vodka made misery bearable; they helped keep the lid on for decades.

Most Russians are poorer than ever and have not found jobs linked to hard currency. As cost of production has begun to matter, factory managers are shedding amenities — including dachas and vacations and health care — as fast as the strong labor bosses permit. Twenty years ago, the Institute for the Study of the USA and Canada, where Pavel still works, snared a leasehold on fifteen acres. The managers sliced it into eighty lots, bribed the construction ministry, and distributed the resulting cottages by draw. Pavel got lucky.

He'd always wanted a car, too, but had bad luck in this quest. In Soviet times, money wasn't money, in the basic Western sense that money works equally well for all purchases. To ensure that everything went "to each according to his deserts," and to maximize central control of individual lives, the Soviets required case-by-case permission for major purchases. Only with a permit could one pay out rubles and get a dacha or a car. It was a key mechanism for controlling the ambitious and rewarding the meek.

Pavel's name had risen for a decade until, in 1988, he was first on his institute's list — he'd scoop up the next Lada that came their way. But meanwhile, on the other side of town, perestroika was gathering steam. An executive order declared that scarce goods would henceforth be issued not by seniority but by lottery. For Pavel, it was the earliest pain of the transition.

The nightmare of the car lottery was over after ten minutes in a subdirector's office. A secretary — one Pavel never liked — plucked the short straw and drove away in Pavel's new car. By chance, years before, she had drawn the dacha right across from Pavel's. After she won the car, she moved her cottage's front fence forward a meter — breaking the bylaws of the compound, once enforced by the now-fallen Communists. She parks Pavel's Lada in her widened yard every weekend.

Pavel and I lugged supplies the few kilometers from Kikoshina Station to the dacha compound; the secretary's car across the street was the first thing he pointed out.

His dacha looked good. It was two stories high, with an anteroom and two small bedrooms on each floor. It had taken on real value and had become legally salable. An open market in dachas had sprung up, and one nearby had gone for about $5,000. But the dacha was Pavel's only asset. He'd turned sixty, and savings that should have lasted through a sheltered old age now wouldn't support him for six months. Even his salary suddenly seemed shaky; the institute had fallen a month behind in issuing paychecks.

At 8 P.M. Pavel's wife, Anna, was in the garden compensating for hard times. She hoed and watered and weeded 7,000 square feet of squashes, cucumbers, radishes, tomatoes, onions, potatoes, oregano, mint, watercress, gooseberries, cloudberries, and other berries not found in the Russian-English dictionary, including one sort that dangled on bushes with pale green leaves, waving in the night breeze. The dog crouched and barked at the jerking branches.

It was buggy. Pavel had covered the dacha windows with cheesecloth — Russia is a nation with big mosquitoes and no screens. One of the most valued gifts a Westerner can bring is a few yards of plastic mesh, and I presented him with some.

We scrubbed off city grime and ate sorrel soup and black bread in the freestanding summer kitchen, near the back of the garden. I lazed for an hour, reading in the late sun. A few neighbors drifted in. We poured pepper vodka. The talk was entirely of love — mostly failed love — and it went on until midnight came and the sky was finally in twilight.

Love is an escape this crowd had put to hard use. The only smiles I saw when I walked around Moscow were on the faces of infants and lovers. Pavel told of marrying Anna thirty-eight years earlier, on a dare, a few weeks after they'd met.

Natasha, a neighbor who now sold Western office equipment to foreign embassies, had just bailed out of five years of tragic infatuation — "as pure as in one of those American romance novels," she said — with a Muslim from Tashkent. His parents, on the Communist Party central committee, forbade the relationship. But Natasha had flown there whenever the parents flew up to Moscow. Between illicit visits, the boy's family chauffeur posted letters for the lovers. Near the end, a friendly uncle had taken Natasha aside and said that her only hope of marriage was to conceive a male child and then confront her lover's parents. She'd realized then that she wanted to be loved for herself alone, so she tore herself away. Someone new would turn up.

We toasted the future. Down the road, a family, dining on their porch, shouted out Russian folk songs. "These songs are always sad," Pavel said, "complaining about lost lands, lost family, lost love."

The next morning, blinking in the sunlight, I saw Natasha out in her yard, a few dachas down, hoeing potatoes for the winter while her old dad staked tomatoes. Anna stood by the water spigot, scrubbing her face with whey. "Cold cream's best," she said, "but we haven't any. Whey is second-best. We struggle for everything we find, and that gives it meaning. Maybe it's not so bad to live this way."

A hard winter was coming. These gardens a little way out of town, which had been a Russian hobby, were once more how even the families of the intelligentsia would survive. For the first time, collective farms close to the city had been forced to make plots available to thousands of urban families, who commuted all summer to tend potato patches. The gardens answer the riddle of why Russians aren't in the midst of famine, with the collective farming

system so badly broken and the politics of land privatization stale-
mated. In a sense, everyone in the country had temporarily re-
verted to peasantry. No one was many steps away from a garden
patch. Dacha cellars bulged with potatoes, and Moscow apartments
looked like warehouses, crammed with hoarded food.

During the dark days that followed the light summer nights,
Russians would eat their potatoes with canned fish and plot the
coming summer's escapes. Seryozha and his brother Alyosha, on
a lark, once drove three thousand miles to Lake Baikal in a car the
size of a baby carriage, often on roads like horse paths. They camped
by the shore and wrote up a journal — in English, because it
sounded exotic. One afternoon, the journal records, they watched
wonderingly as a yet more ardent escapist, an Armenian engineer,
worked out his dreams. He'd elaborately but incompetently crafted
a catamaran; he said he'd dreamed of sailing on this deepest and
once purest of inland waters. But in true Soviet fashion he'd paid
little attention to reality. The open pontoons were far too small for
the weight of boat, crew, and supplies. Seryozha and Alyosha
watched as the craft sailed thirty feet into Baikal's choppy waters
and swamped to the gunnels.

WILLIAM LANGEWIESCHE

The Turn

FROM THE ATLANTIC MONTHLY

PEOPLE WHO DISTRUST the sensations of flight, who balk when an airplane banks and turns, are on to something big. I was reminded of this recently while riding in the back of a United Boeing 737 that was departing from San Francisco. Directly over the Golden Gate we rolled suddenly into a steep turn, dropping the left wing so far below the horizon that it appeared to pivot around the bridge's nearest tower. For a moment we exceeded the airline maximum of a thirty-degree bank, which is aerodynamically unimportant but is imposed for passengers' peace of mind. Sightseeing seemed more important now. Our pilots may have thought we would enjoy a dramatic view of the famous bridge and the city beyond. But as the airplane turned, startled passengers looked away from the windows. A collective gasp rippled through the cabin.

The reaction did not surprise me: as an instructor of beginning pilots, I've heard gasps and worse from my students. Pilots are merely trained passengers. They have to be told not to flinch, whimper, or make audible appeals to the Savior. They have to be encouraged to ride the airplane willingly, as they would a horse, to think as it thinks. And they have to be persuaded of the strange logic of the turn. At its core lies the relationship between banking and the resulting flight path, and the fact, difficult at first to accept, that neither can be felt.

Most people — certainly the ones who were sitting next to me over San Francisco — would insist that they can indeed feel the bank. We have all had the experience while reading or dozing on an airliner of feeling a lurch and looking up to see, as expected, that the airplane is tilted. The lurch comes when the airplane dips or raises a wing, starting into a turn or starting out of one. Sometimes we can even give a direction to the bank. But if we then close our eyes, we have no way of telling that we are sitting at an angle. I know from experience how difficult it is to convince people of this. When the bank is visible — for instance, on a clear day — the tilted horizon looks so unusual that the view overpowers other perceptions. But during flight on black nights, or in clouds, the bank is imperceptible, and passengers are heedless. They may feel the odd lurch, but they have no way of guessing the airplane's degree of bank. The inner ear, and with it the sense of balance, is neutralized by the motion of flight. The airplane could be momentarily upside down and passengers would not know.

Of course, none of this matters unless you are the pilot. But historically, pilots have made the same mistakes as passengers. Having been given the airplane, they had to learn to use it. Generations were required. Eventually they admitted that instinct was unreliable in clouds, and that they needed special instruments to tell them what was happening to the plane. Without the instruments they went into mysterious banks and dived out of control. Thus was born the most basic distinction in flying, between conditions in which the turn is visible and conditions in which it must be measured. The ability to fly through weather and in darkness is more important than speed in the conquest of distance. The mastery of the turn is the story of how aviation became practical as a means of transportation. It is the story of how the world became small.

Some definitions are in order. The bank is a condition of tilted wings, and the turn is the change in direction that results. The connection between the two is inexorable: the airplane must bank to turn, and when it is banked, it must turn. The reason is simple. In flight with level wings, the lifting force of the wings is directed straight up, and the airplane does not turn; in a bank, the lifting force is tilted to the side, and the airplane therefore must move to that side. It cannot slide sideways through the air, because it has a vertical fin on the tail, which forces the turn by keeping the tail in line behind the nose. The result is an elegantly curved flight path, created as the airplane lifts itself through the changes in direction.

The turn, however, comes at a price. As the bank steepens, the airplane has greater difficulty holding its altitude. Flown at bank angles approaching ninety degrees — in which the wings point straight up and down — a normal airplane cannot keep from descending. In such "knife-edge" flight, the force that once lifted the wings in a direction perpendicular to the earth's surface is now directed parallel to it, and gravity pulls the airplane down. However, if the pilot controls the airplane carefully and allows it to keep turning, it will happily roll past the vertical, onto its back, and finally right side up again. During such a maneuver San Francisco Bay would momentarily appear above you, and the Golden Gate Bridge would seem to hang from the water. This is fine if you are prepared for it. Full rolls are the purest expression of flight. They are normally flown only in fighters and other acrobatic airplanes, but if you ignore convention, you can fly them in any airplane, including a Boeing 737.

None of this would have comforted the man sitting next to me during that steep turn over the Golden Gate. He was large, sharp-eyed, and alert. When the wing dropped, he said, "Hey!" and grabbed the armrests. Now he rode "above" me in the bank, leaning into the aisle as if he feared toppling into my lap. He need not have worried. If he had dropped his pen, it would have fallen not "down" in the conventional sense — toward me and the earth — but rather toward the tilted carpet at his feet. If he had dangled the pen from a string, it would have hung at a ninety-degree angle with respect to the tilted floor.

A dangled pen is a primitive inclinometer, like a plumb bob or the heel indicator on a sailboat. On land or at sea it will hang toward the center of the planet. But in flight it will hang toward the floor, no matter how steeply the airplane is banked. A carpenter's level would be equally fooled. This peculiar phenomenon is a manifestation of the turn's inherent balance. The earth's gravity acts on an airplane, and of course on objects in an airplane, but so do the forces of inertia, the desire of any mass to keep doing what it has been doing. The neatness of this Newtonian package is beautiful to behold. Bob Hoover, a stunt pilot, mounted a video camera in his cockpit, set an empty glass on the instrument panel, and poured himself a soft drink while flying full rolls. Our United pilots seemed inclined to fly the same way. If they had done so, as we passed inverted above the Golden Gate Bridge and saw it hanging

from the water, my sharp-eyed neighbor could have watched his
pen dangling toward the sky. During the roll the flight attendants
could have walked upside down. And some passengers, too busy
to look outside, wouldn't even have noticed.

The human body is another inclinometer. Undisturbed by the
view, it sits quietly, dangling toward the tilted floor, churning out
memos for the home office. The man next to me was not about
to fall into my lap. He could have relaxed, lowered the tray in front
of him, and called for a coffee. Unlike a table on a sailboat, an
airplane tray requires no gimbals. Flight attendants do not develop
sea legs. They brew coffee on a fixed counter, deliver it without
worrying about the bank angle, and fill cups to their brims. Full
cups make people behave during turns: if they try to hold them
level with the earth, the coffee pours out and scalds their thighs.
If this is hard to believe, imagine the alternative — an airplane in
which "down" was always toward the ground. Bedlam would break
loose in the cabin during turns.

As long as its wings are level, an airplane is well mannered and
slow to anger. If you pull its nose up and then release the controls,
it puts its nose back down; if you push it down, it answers by rearing
up. Like horseback riding, flying consists mostly of leaving the
beast alone. The problem is that this particular beast does not stay
on the trail unguided, and once it strays, it develops a strong
impulse to self-destruct.

Unguided, any airplane will eventually begin to bank. That by
itself would be fine if you didn't mind the resulting turn. But as
the bank tilts the lift force of the wings, reducing their vertical
effectiveness, it erodes the equilibrium that previously countered
the pull of the earth. The airplane responds to the loss by lowering
its nose and accelerating. Sitting in the cockpit with folded arms
and watching it proceed is like letting a temperamental horse
gallop down a steepening slope: it requires steady nerves and a
morbid curiosity. In flight the slope steepens because the acceleration tightens the airplane's turn, which increases its bank angle,
which causes further acceleration. Sooner or later a sort of aero-
dynamic lock-in occurs. The airplane banks to vertical or beyond,
and points its nose straight down.

That's the spiral dive. In its most lethal forms it is called the graveyard spiral. The airplane flies in ever steeper circles and either disintegrates from excessive speed or hits the ground in a screaming descent. Most flights would suffer this end if the pilot (or autopilot) did not intervene. In good weather the intervention is easy. When you see that the airplane has banked, you unbank it. During turns you hold the controls more firmly and keep the nose from dropping.

The increased loading caused by inertia during a well-flown turn is felt within the cabin as a peculiar heaviness. Pilots measure it in "Gs," as a multiple of gravity's normal pull. An airplane that banks to thirty degrees creates a loading of 1.15 Gs: the airplane, and everything in it, temporarily weighs 15 percent more than normal. Fifteen percent is hardly noticeable. But when the bank grows only a bit steeper, to forty-five degrees, the load increases to 1.4 Gs: people feel pressed into their seats, and they might notice that the wings have flexed upward. Technically, it is not important. Airplanes are strong. Pilots shrug off two Gs, and may feel comfortable at twice as much. But passengers are unaccustomed to the sensation. As we pivoted over the Golden Gate, I estimated that my neighbor had gained about eighty pounds. Had he dangled his pen toward the tilted floor, it would have pulled on the string with surprising force. This might not have reassured him. But the extra heaviness is a measure of the pilot's success in resisting the spiral dive. If we had felt "normal" during the turn, it could only have meant that the nose was dropping fast toward the water.

No pilot would make such a mistake on a clear day. The view from the cockpit is dominated by the horizon, the constantly renewing division between the sky and the earth. It forms a line across the windshield, and makes immediate sense of the airplane's movements. In clouds or on black nights, when they cannot see outside, pilots keep their wings level by watching an artificial horizon on the instrument panel. The artificial horizon is a gyroscopically steadied line, which stays level with the earth's surface. The airplane pitches and banks in relation to this steady line, which in spatial terms never moves. Of course, in *airplane* terms it does move — which presents a problem, because pilots are part of the airplane: they fly it from within, strapped to their seats. In clear skies they would never misjudge a bank as the tilting of the earth, but with their view restricted to the abstractions of the instrument panel they sometimes do just that: when the airplane banks, they perceive the motion as a movement of the artificial horizon line across the face of the instrument. This causes them to "fly" the wrong thing — the moving horizon line, rather than the fixed symbolic airplane. For example, as turbulence tilts the airplane to the left, the pilots, tilting with it, notice the artificial horizon line dropping to the right. Reacting instinctively to the indication of motion, they sometimes try to raise the line as if it were a wing. The result of such a reversal in such cases is murderous. Pilots steer to the left just when they should steer to the right, and then in confusion they steer harder. While cruising calmly inside clouds, I have had student pilots suddenly try to flip the airplane upside down. These were perfectly rational people, confronted by the turn.

Airplanes did not shrink the world overnight. The Wrights flew straight and level at Kitty Hawk in December of 1903, and nobody paid much attention. They went home to Dayton, rented a cow pasture, and spent the following year stretching their flights and learning to turn. The first detailed account of their flights appeared in *Gleanings in Bee Culture,* a journal for beekeepers published in nearby Medina. The editor, A. I. Root, traveled to the pasture and on September 20, 1904, saw Wilbur fly the first full circle. Bees, of course, are the great specialists in full-circle flying; they spend their days on round-trip missions, and construct whole worlds out of their ability to turn. I do not know if Root was influenced by these thoughts, but he understood the significance of the Wrights' achievement. The U.S. Army was slower to catch on. Five years later, after much persuading by the Wrights, it reluctantly took delivery of its first airplane. In 1909 horses still seemed more glorious.

The war in Europe changed that. Unsullied by the carnage in the trenches, pilots chased across the sky, turning hard on each other's tails. The war taught them to fly with confidence, and encouraged the myth of instinct. Those who survived made the dangerous discovery that they could feel at home in the sky. They learned to accept the strangeness of a steep bank — the G load and the tilted horizon — and the magic of a full roll. Nonetheless, they still believed in instinctive balance: when they ducked through small clouds and emerged with their wings slightly tilted, they did not appreciate the significance of this small clue — did not suspect the importance of the unfelt bank. Although scientific thinkers on both sides of the Atlantic had, by the end of the war, come to understand the intricacies of the banked turn, pilots, trapped by vanity, paid little heed. And because pilots at the time rarely flew in bad weather or on black nights, they did not expose themselves to the conditions that would have fostered deeper insight.

At the end of the war, regular airmail service started in Europe and the United States. It made airplanes useful to the public for the first time, gave birth to the airlines, and placed pressure on the pilots to operate on schedules. They followed rivers and rail-roads in open-cockpit biplanes, flying under the weather, some-times at extremely low altitude, dodging steeples and oil derricks. Many pilots were killed.

In December of 1925 a young army pilot named Carl Crane got caught in the clouds at 8,000 feet directly over Detroit while trying to fly a congressman's son to Washington, D.C., in a biplane. Crane later became a famous master of the turn. Recalling this particular flight, he said, "In a short time I was losing altitude, completely out of control. I could not fly the airplane at all — it had gotten into a spiral dive. Halfway down I looked around at my boy in the back, and he was enjoying the flight no end. He was shaking his hands and grinning, and I was slowly dying because I knew we were going to crash."

The boy in the rear cockpit was just unaware. Crane had an altimeter and an airspeed indicator. He thought he was dying "slowly" only because of the way experience is compressed when an airplane goes wild. People's minds can work extraordinarily fast. Pilots tend to think not about God or their lives but about solu-tions. Crane searched his training and remembered only vague admonitions to stay out of bad weather. Of course, he was in it now, and couldn't see a thing. He knew he was turning but could make no sense of the compass. It is a notorious problem: because the earth's magnetic field does not lie parallel to the globe's surface but dips down toward the magnetic poles, the compass responds to banks by spinning erratically, jamming, and sometimes showing turns in reverse. Crane did not know which wing was down, let alone by how much. If he tried to level the wings, he was just as likely to roll upside down as right side up. If he tried to raise the nose, the effect would be exactly the opposite: the turn would quicken, steepening the descent. For a pilot these are the central issues of the spiral dive. Crane understood none of it at the time, but he sensed that his situation was hopeless.

In modern times air-traffic control recorded the radio transmissions of an unskilled pilot who, with his family on board, tried to descend through overcast. After he lost control, he began to sob into the microphone, begging the radar controllers to tell him which side was up. But radar shows air traffic as wingless blips on a map, and is incapable of distinguishing banks. Controllers are in the business of keeping airplanes from colliding. Pilots are in the business of flight control. This one had instruments on board by which he could have kept his wings level, but in the milkiness of the clouds he became confused. The controllers listened helplessly to his panic and, in the background, to the screams of his children. The transmission ended when the airplane broke apart.

Crane's biplane was stronger. "Finally it got down to under a thousand feet, and I said, 'Well, here we go. I'm going to look at my boy once more.' And as I turned around to look at him, a sign went by my wing. It said 'Statler Hotel.' I had just missed the top of the Statler Hotel. In all the mist and rain, I could see the buildings and the streets. I flew down the street and got over the Detroit River, and flew about ten feet high all the way to Toledo, shaking all the way."

Shocked by the way intuition had abandoned him, Crane began to ask questions. For years he got no intelligent answers. Veterans of the military and the airmail service still insisted they could fly "by the seat of the pants," and they thought less of those who could not. Their self-deception now seems all the more profound because the solution to the problem of flying in clouds and darkness — a gyroscope adapted to flying — was already widely available.

The gyroscope is a spinning wheel, like a child's top, mounted in gimbals that allow it freedom of movement. It has two important traits: left alone, it maintains a fixed orientation in space (in relation to the stars); and when tilted, it reacts in an odd but predictable way. Elmer Sperry, the great American inventor, started playing with these traits in the early 1900s. As a curiosity, he designed a gyrostabilized "trained wheelbarrow," and he tried, without success, to interest a circus in it. Undiscouraged, Sperry turned to the U.S. Navy instead, and interested it in gyro-compasses and ship stabilizers. Competitors in Europe developed similar devices, and during the buildup to war interested their countries' navies, too.

Airplanes were an intriguing sideline. Sperry built a gyroscopic autopilot in 1910, not to enable blind flight but to stabilize the otherwise unruly early flying machines. In 1915 he began to ponder instrumentation, and with prescient insight into the problems of flight was able after three years to produce the first gyroscopic turn indicator, an instrument still in use today. Its face consisted of a vertical pointer, which indicated turns to the left or right. (Necessarily, it also included a ball like the one in a carpenter's level, an inclinometer that showed not bank but "skid" or "slip" — conditions of imbalance.) Sperry called the instrument a "crutch for the compass." In his patent application he described it as an instrument that would allow pilots to fly indefinitely through clouds, implying that without it they could not.

One of the earliest cloud flights with a turn indicator was made by William Ocker, an army pilot, in 1918. Though he, too, spiraled out of overcast, he concluded correctly that his mistake had been to favor sensation over the instrument's indications. During the 1920s a few post office pilots began to fly by instruments. When Charles Lindbergh crossed the Atlantic in 1927, a turn indicator kept him from spiraling into the sea when he met fog. Two years later Jimmy Doolittle made a "blind" landing, after flying a complete circuit around an airport in a special biplane modified with a domed cockpit from which he could not see outside. The landing itself was a technical dead end. Once Doolittle was over the field, he reduced the power and waited until the biplane plunked into the grass — a technique that would not be practical for the airlines. More significant were the special devices that made the precisely flown circuit possible. The airplane was equipped with navigational radios, an airspeed indicator, an improved altimeter, a turn indicator, and two new gyroscopic instruments from Elmer Sperry — a gyroscopic compass and an artificial horizon. This combination was so effective that it still forms the core of instrument panels today. Doolittle compared the artificial horizon to cutting a porthole through the fog to look at the real horizon.

Devising technology was the easy part. The more stubborn problem of belief remained. As late as 1930 one of the airlines wrote to Sperry complaining about a mysterious problem: the instruments worked fine in clear air, but as soon as they were taken into clouds, they began to indicate turns.

Still worried about his near collision with the Statler Hotel, Carl Crane read with fascination the descriptions of Doolittle's flight. He was now, in 1929, an army instructor at a training base in Texas. Though his superior officers disapproved of instrument flying, Crane was convinced of the need for gyroscopes. He finally got permission to cover over a cockpit and turn one of the biplanes into an instrument trainer. While he was at work on this, William Ocker wandered into the hangar. Ocker didn't look like much of a pilot, with his bifocals and his mournful, puritan face, but he had a powerful mind and the restless soul of a missionary. The truth about instrument flying had come to him in 1926, during a routine medical examination in San Francisco. To demonstrate that the senses could be fooled, a doctor had asked Ocker to close his eyes while being spun in a chair. Ocker felt the chair begin to turn and guessed the direction correctly — but when the chair slowed, he felt it had stopped, and when the chair stopped, he felt it was now turning in the opposite direction. For the doctor, it was a trick on the inner ear, an amusing exercise in vertigo. For Ocker, it was a stunning revelation: the sense of accelerating into a turn is the same as that of decelerating from the opposite turn. The chair induced the same false sensations that led pilots to mistrust their turn indicators. Even those who accepted their inability to feel the bank were losing control. Ocker now knew why. He had found here in the spinning chair the proof that instinct is *worse* than useless in the clouds.

Ocker became so obsessed with the spinning chair that he was hospitalized twice for sanity tests and later banished by the army to Texas. His preaching had become tiresome. Nonetheless, he had discovered the most disturbing limitation of human flight — the feelings that cause people to sway dizzily from wings-level flight into spiral dives. Having gyroscopes is not enough. Pilots must learn to believe them, even though their bodies may have invented phantom turns. And fiction can be compelling. I have seen students break into a sweat in the effort not to submit.

Ocker and Crane began a systematic exploration of flying inside clouds. In 1932 they published *Blind Flight in Theory and Practice,* the first clear analysis of instrument flying. The book had an enormous influence. The authors tried to lay to rest the old faith in flying by instinct. They described the physics of the turn and the confusion experienced by the inner ear, but their most dramatic argument grew out of an experiment with pigeons. From everything pilots had learned, it seemed evident that birds, too, must be unable to fly without a visible horizon. Ocker and Crane blindfolded pigeons, took them up in biplanes, and threw them out. Sure enough, the birds dropped into fluttering emergency descents — they panicked and went down like feathered parachutes. It is possible, of course, that they did not like the blindfolds, which were made of Bull Durham tobacco pouches. But anyway, the experiment was the kind pilots understood. If God had meant birds to fly in the clouds, He would have given them gyroscopes.

Birds are not the perfect flyers that you might expect. They cannot fly through heavy rain. They get sucked up by thunderstorms, frozen by altitude, and burned by lightning. They crash into obstacles, wander offshore, run out of fuel, and die by the millions. They would rather not migrate in bad weather, and usually don't. Nonetheless, it now appears that Ocker and Crane may have been wrong: there is evidence that some birds do occasionally fly inside clouds. This is big news. Word of it appeared in 1972, in the proceedings of a NASA symposium on animal navigation. Hidden among reports like "When the Beachhopper Looks at the Moon" and "Anemomenotactic Orientation in Beetles and Scorpions" (that is, "When a Bug Feels the Wind") was a paper titled "Nocturnal Bird Migration in Opaque Clouds." It was written by Donald Griffin, the Harvard zoologist who discovered the use of sonar by bats. Griffin reported that he had bought a military-surplus radar and on overcast nights in New York had tracked birds that seemed to be flying inside clouds. There were only a few, and Griffin was able to track them only for a couple of miles, but they appeared to be flying straight. Griffin's biggest problem was uncertainty over the flight conditions at the birds' altitude. Were the clouds really as thick as they looked from below? Were the birds really flying blind? Griffin had good reason to believe so, but as a scientist he had to be cautious. His final report, in 1973, reinforced the earlier findings but was more cautiously titled "Oriented Bird Migration in or Between Opaque Cloud Layers." Ornithologists still cite it from memory. To those interested in bird navigation, the difference between "in" and "between" is just a detail; the point is, the birds seemed to know their way without reference to the stars or to the ground. But to birds, whose first job is keeping their wings level and controlling their turns, the distinction might be crucial. Griffin, a former pilot, understands its importance. I recently mentioned to him my impression that some ornithologists seem stuck on the ground, and he laughed. "I keep telling them, 'Gee, birds fly!'"

Assuming they fly in the clouds, the question is how? Ornithologists have no answer, and they shy away from speculation. It is known that birds navigate by watching the ground and the positions of the sun, the moon, and the stars — none of which would help them in clouds. But they may also use a host of nonvisual clues, and may use mental "maps" based on sound, smell, air currents, variations in gravitational pull, and other factors. Experiments have shown that some species are extremely sensitive to magnetic forces. In their heads they have magnetite crystals surrounded by nerves, which may give them intuitive knowledge of their direction (and location) in the earth's magnetic field.

Another possibility is that birds have internal gyroscopes of a primitive sort. This is less farfetched than it seems: the rhythmic flapping of wings could have the effect of Foucault's pendulum, allowing a bird to sense turns without any external cue. A pendulum is more than a hanging weight — it is a hanging weight that has been pushed and is swinging freely. Swinging gives a pendulum its special ability to maintain spatial orientation. Leon Foucault was the French physicist who first used one, in 1851, to demonstrate the rotation of the earth: though the pendulum appeared to change direction as it swung, in fact the plane of its swing remained constant, and the apparent change was caused by the turning of the earth underneath it. If birds rely on the pendulum effect, they are not alone. Flies and mosquitoes (along with more than 85,000 other species of Diptera) use specially adapted vibrating rods to maintain spatial orientation in flight. Not only can they turn sharply, roll upside down, and land on the underside of leaves, but they can do it in fog.

Pilots, too, have relied on pendulums. It is said that an airliner inbound to New York in the 1950s lost all its gyroscopes in heavy weather over Block Island. The captain was a wise old man who had risen with the airlines from the earliest airmail days and was approaching retirement. A lesser pilot might have fallen for the trap of intuition. But the captain simply took out his pocket watch, dangled it from its chain, and began to swing it toward the instrument panel. Flying by the pendulum and the compass, he proceeded the length of Long Island in the clouds. After breaking into the clear near the airport, he landed and wished his passengers a good day.

The story is not impossible. I had it in mind one night when I flew out over the Pacific Ocean in a small airplane. High clouds darkened the sky. The light of a fishing boat drifted close by the coast. Flying a mile above the water, I headed beyond it, into complete blackness.

Nowhere can a person find greater solitude than alone in flight. At night in clouds and over water, the cockpit becomes a world of its own, and the instrument panel another world within it. The instruments glow in a warm light, telling the strange story of the airplane's motion. Enjoying this isolation, I flew on until, behind me, the fishing boat was a distant glimmer. The gyroscopes functioned perfectly. The radios were blissfully silent. I hooked a metal pen to a fishing line and dangled it from a knob on the ceiling. Flying by the artificial horizon, I made a steep turn and watched the pen dangle toward the tilted floor. Then I straightened out, pushed the pen toward the instrument panel, and released it. It swung for almost a minute before requiring another push. Each renewal would, of course, erase the pendulum's spatial memory. Nonetheless, I thought the device might work. After turning parallel to the coast, I covered the gyroscopes with slips of paper.

The night air was smooth. The pen swung rhythmically toward the panel and back. When eventually the airplane banked and therefore turned, the swinging pen, though it continued to swing through a point perpendicular to the floor, maintained a memory of the airplane's original heading, and seemed to have redirected itself to the left. This could only mean that the airplane had banked to the right. I steered left gingerly, hoping to raise the right wing just enough to return to straight flight. The pen seemed to stabilize in its new direction. I renewed the swing, shoving the pen again directly toward the panel. It soon confirmed that the airplane had indeed leveled its wings. After the compass settled, it showed that I had turned twenty degrees to the right. Lowering the left wing cautiously, watching the pen swing to the right, I crept back to my original heading. Later, when I tried to make a large turn, I spiraled and had to peek at the gyroscopes. But with the wings level again I flew on for miles, learning to work with the swinging pen. Trust comes slowly in the indication of turns. It is a peculiar faith that makes the world so small.

JAMES A. MCPHERSON

Ivy Day in the Empty Room

FROM THE IOWA REVIEW

I

ABOUT SIX YEARS AGO, at a time when the issues clustered around race still simmered on the back burners of national consciousness, I had a fierce argument with one of my oldest black friends. He had called me from his home in Lansing, Michigan, to report about a conflict between members of his group, people devoted to the memory of Malcolm X, and a group of black ministers who were partisans of the memory of Martin Luther King, Jr. At issue between the two groups was the naming of a street in Lansing, one of the early homes of Malcolm Little, now known as Malcolm X. My friend's group wanted a certain street in Lansing named for Malcolm X. The black ministers wanted the same street named for Martin Luther King. I responded to the conflict by pointing out what I considered a bizarre contradiction. At a time when drugs, drive-by shootings, teenage pregnancies, unemployment, self-hatred, and racism were decimating whole segments of the group, it seemed of little practical consequence whether a street in Lansing, Michigan, bore the name of either man. I said that it seemed of greater importance for the two opposing groups to unite their energies to advance the causes for which both men stood and for which they gave their lives. I went further, and enraged my friend, by saying that the worship of the images of these two martyrs, during such a bleak and deadly time, was in reality a substitute for meaningful actions, if not the institutionalization of a death wish. My friend and I broke off our communication after this exchange, and I fell to brooding over whether my response to him had grown out of my own insensitivity to the basic needs of unsophisticated people for positive images or role models. Still, the ease with which images were used to obscure substance continued to bother me.

Now, a few years later, the generation of men whose work in early life made the civil rights movement is resurfacing, though they are radically transformed in terms of public image. Vernon Jordan seems to be a Washington insider. Andrew Young seems to be an elder statesman. James Farmer was on television recently, speaking professorily as a repository of historical memory. John Lewis is entrenched in the U.S. Congress. Ralph Abernathy, after publishing a book describing Martin King as a man of flesh and blood and bone, is dead. Malcolm X has been resurrected, more vital in his martyred youth than he probably was in life, by the cinematography of Spike Lee. To someone who lived through that period of transformation, the reappearance of such familiar faces brings back memories of what might be called naive optimism about possibilities, both for oneself and for society. There seems now to be a nostalgia for these icons of a Golden Age, a lust for that Sacred Time. But what is missing from this pantheon of heroes is the human image, and the idiom, of the man who was the moral center of the movement they made.

Because Martin Luther King, Jr., has, through a process of iconization or reification, grown larger than life, he tends to exist on a plane far above the everyday concerns of ordinary people. He has been made to function as a caretaker of the Sacred, and any suggestion that he could have ever partaken of the Profane aspects of human life is viewed as something close to blasphemy. His memory has been democratized and fragmented. He lives on street signs, buildings, postage stamps, in biographies, arguments, vilifications. And on his birthday, which is now a legal holiday in every state. During the downside of the winter, a thriving cottage industry of multiculturalists, diversity sages, merchants of nostalgia, mendicants, and sentimentalists reminds us of the details of his life, and of his dreams. These are, for the most part, devotees of Martin Luther King, Jr., the icon, the public figure, mythologized now out of his birthright as a man of flesh and blood and bone.

It seems inevitable that this same process of iconization will also claim, and much more swiftly and efficiently, the man of flesh and blood and bone named Malcolm X. That aspect of American tradition derived from the ancient Greeks is relentless in its imposition of an ethic, in the case of large-souled men, a mythologizing which ensures survival after death, as one of society's highest rewards. But after the reward has been institutionalized, one basic issue still remains: would the human being at the center of the myth embrace the meaning that has been drawn from his life as the meaning he intended his life to have? Would Jesus of Nazareth, the carpenter's son, accept the version of his life that was filtered through the Greco-Roman perceptions of Paul of Tarsus? Would Martin Luther King, the man of flesh and blood and bone, accept the uses that have been made of *his* life?

It is useful, while considering this, to speculate about what might have happened if Martin King had not died on April 4, 1968. He was then only a public figure who was already losing the interest of the media. But by 1968 he had begun to oppose the war in Vietnam and was attempting to form a coalition of the poor in every racial group. Although he might have been less visible during the years after 1968, his support of the antiwar movement might have brought an end to the war much sooner, and his attempt to appeal to the common condition of all the poor might have energized Lyndon Johnson's War on Poverty. Johnson, in turn, might have been able to negotiate a peaceful end to the war that would allow his domestic programs to continue and allow him to remain in office for another term. Robert Kennedy, that other partisan of the poor, might not have been assassinated. And the death of his brother, John F. Kennedy, earlier in the decade, might have been viewed as an aberration instead of as a signal that absolutely anyone in public life — King, Robert Kennedy, Gerald Ford, Ronald Reagan, John Lennon, George Wallace, even Jimmy Carter (and his rabbit) — was vulnerable. These three men, King, Johnson, and Robert Kennedy, might have maintained for a while longer the moral high point of that cycle of history, and might have brought about the necessary transformations in American life. They might have filled, with their voices and through their actions, what has now become an empty public square. We might not have become such a fear-filled people. We might have trusted longer in something larger than ourselves. We might have become much more human.

If such large-spirited men had remained active in public life, perhaps the right-wing reaction, cultivated by Richard Nixon and his silent/moral majority, might not have come to power with such a sense of vengeance in 1968, or 1972, or 1980, or 1984, or 1988. And the sense of security in the public sphere, dependent in large part on continuance at the highest levels of power, might not have been undermined. Moreover, the evangelical idiom employed by King might have become better democratized, but with a meaning that transcended politics. The cause of civil rights, which began as a point of entry for excluded minorities into the larger society, might have helped to revitalize the American democratic ethos, as King had intended.

If King had remained active, the status of black Americans might not have remained frozen someplace between desegregation and integration, and the word "integration" itself, which is now in extreme disfavor, might have reclaimed its original meaning, moving from the physical or material plane to an ethical or spiritual one ("Integration is genuine intergroup, interpersonal doing . . . based on unenforceable obligations"), as King had anticipated. We might have tried much harder to become a better people, or at least better than we are now.

Of course, no one man could possibly change the course of a nation of people devoted to a variety of different ends, but King's voice, had it lasted, might have counseled modifications in the means we chose toward those ends. Even if I can now imagine King as only a featured guest on talk shows, answering questions about the current state of "race relations," I am confident that, even in such mundane contexts as *Larry King Live* or *Oprah*, he would still be insisting on an ethic that would be a guide to *human* behavior. He would still be speaking a moral language. He would still be speaking confidently about what is *right*.

And as a deeply personal matter, his voice would have helped me to resolve stories that have been stored in my memory for twenty-five years.

April 4, 1968: *My girlfriend, Devorah Watkins, runs into my apartment screaming. She has just heard, in the office of her employer, Robert Coles, the news that King has been shot in Memphis and that riots are beginning in all parts of the country. The Boston police are putting up a blockade around Roxbury, the black section of Boston, while in Cambridge there is the most oppressive silence. We call Devorah's mother in New Jersey.*

She is crying, too, and keeps saying to me, "Take care of my little girl." I decide to take Devorah to her own apartment on Linnaean Street near Porter Square. We leave my apartment with my television set and begin our walk from Harvard Square up Massachusetts Avenue toward Linnaean Street. Ahead of us, in the night, we can see stalled traffic and crowds of silent people. One crowd is moving as a group, a body, seeming to stop and accost other people in cars and on the street. This moving crowd is white. I tell Devorah, "We must keep walking past that crowd. White people are capable of anything! If they try to stop us, I'll throw this television and try to fight them while you run." This becomes our plan. The crowd seems to get larger and larger and whiter and whiter as we approach. We cross Massachusetts Avenue several times to avoid it. Then we are spotted and the crowd crosses after us. Both of us are ready to run when we begin to see, in the streetlights, individual faces. They are all young people, probably students. They follow us and keep saying, as they must have said to individual black people the whole length of Massachusetts Avenue, "We're sorry! We're sorry!" But I am not listening. My mind and my emotions and my imagination have become polarized by now. I am thinking about the police blockade going up around Roxbury. I am thinking, "Suppose they never take it down? Where would I want to be: here in Cambridge, or over there with the majority of black people?" I think and think and think and think all the way to Devorah's place on Linnaean Street . . .

Twenty-five years later, I still have not resolved this issue.

July, 1968: *My employer, the editor of the* Bay State Banner *in Roxbury, Massachusetts, has given his permission for me to do a story for the paper on Resurrection City, a sea of tents occupied by representatives of the nation's poor on the Mall, alongside the Reflecting Pool, in Washington, D.C. Because this black paper is poor and understaffed, I pay my own way to the capital, and take my own pictures. Martin King has been dead since early April, but a decision has been made by his staff that the long-planned in-gathering of the nation's poor from all groups should proceed as planned. There are many hundreds of tents and many thousands of people, most of them poor, camped out alongside the Reflecting Pool under the brooding, squirrel-hunting, narrow eyes of Father Abraham and the oblivious, blinking red eye of the Washington Monument. Jefferson's statue, off at a distance, is not visible. They have come, the nation's orphans and outcasts, to claim their birthright. They are whites from Appalachia, black people from the South and from the cities, poor farmers from the Midwest, Spanish from the cities and from the Southwest and the West, Indians from their reservations. King is dead, but a nervous spiritual solidarity, something close to hope, remains among them. But a white park policeman cautions me not to enter the city. They are savages, he says. They are all poor and angry and looking for something to steal. They may kill me, just to get my camera and my suitcase. And he, the park policeman, can provide me with protection only on* this *side of the picket fence. But my press credentials get me past him and onto the avenues of the vast tent city. Everything around me seems improvised. Ralph Abernathy is there. He is dressed in overalls and is giving a press conference. There are rumors that he sleeps in a luxury hotel and comes to Resurrection City, dressed for that occasion, only to hold press conferences. Jesse Jackson is also there. He is sprawled on the grass, looking elegant in overalls, with a crowd of people clustered around him. He seems to know that a great responsibility is floating in the air, looking for someplace to lodge itself. He speaks cautiously and confidently to the people around him, who are mostly black. He says, "Now, if I were to riot and loot a liquor store, I wouldn't just grab anything. I'd grab the Chivas Regal . . ." A material age is dawning . . .*

Within a few years, these human beings will be relegated to an abstract category called "the underclass." There will be few people left with the language to remind us of who they were, and are. Twenty-five years later, they will no longer knock on the doors of our imaginations except as worrisome symbols of homelessness on the evening news.

II

If Martin King, the man of flesh and blood and bone, were alive today, if he had not died in 1968, I think that he would have tired very soon of his ritual appearances on television talk shows. Like one of his mentors, Mahatma Gandhi, he might have sought out an alternative forum. But instead of an ashram, he might have attempted to reclaim his own meaning from the mythologies that have been imposed on his life. He might have withdrawn from enforced obligation to the persona that has grown up around his name, and he might have discovered that the one place where he could truly be centered again was his old jail cell in Birmingham, Alabama. He might have gone there, reflected back on the goals he had set for himself, and measured these against the image of himself, the iconization, that had grown up around his name.

I imagine him looking back over what he had written, and

bringing to bear on it the wisdom of maturity and deeper understanding of some of the less admirable, or even tragic, aspects of
both human nature and of his own country. I imagine him sifting
through his old writings, discarding some ideas and refining others. He might just write another letter, perhaps because that ancient form of communication has also fallen into disfavor. Perhaps
this letter would be an open one, addressed to everyone, black *and*
white and others, instead of one addressed to only his fellow
clergymen. Perhaps this letter would begin as his own attempt to
reclaim his own basic humanity, his own flesh and blood and bone,
from the abstraction and sterility that results from iconization.
Perhaps he would go on to generalize, and be much more explicit,
about some of the basic moral flaws he criticized in his fellow
clergymen in his first letter from that jail on April 16, 1963. He
wrote then: "One of the basic points in your statement is that our
acts are untimely. Some have asked, 'Why don't you give the new
administration time to act?' . . . For years now I have heard the
word 'Wait!' It rings in the ear of every Negro with a piercing
familiarity. This 'Wait' has always meant 'Never.' It has been a
tranquilizing thalidomide, relieving the emotional stress for a moment, only to give birth to an ill-formed infant of frustration . . ."
Beneath this language, there might have been a broader criticism,
one that his maturity of years might have allowed him to express
much more fully. It might be about what happens when a commitment to an abstraction, like "Wait" or "Time," becomes a substitute
for meaningful action. This new language might say:

There is in human nature a nostalgia for perfection. The source of this
hunger might preexist in the human soul, or it might result from a belief
in Democracy as a substitute for a religious sense, or it might derive from
the romanticism at the basis of Western tradition. Whatever its source, this
hunger for abstract perfection can lead to perverse ends when people, even
the most well-meaning of people, give the nerve-centers of their consent, the
totality of their value-content, over to the quality of an abstract commitment
rather than to the thing to which they profess to be committed. Those who
are seduced into this abstract commitment, this idealization, are personally
challenged by any reality, outside of this specific ideal, that threatens the
purity of their commitment. The perfection of the commitment then, like
Ahab's holy pursuit of the white whale, becomes an idol. And the quality
of the commitment is viewed as of more importance than the reality of the

human community out of which the commitment grows. So Ahab abandons the ship The Rachel *in order not to be distracted from the purity of his pursuit of Moby-Dick. So "liberals" give money to do-gooder organizations so as not to be bothered by the faces and the pleas of homeless people on the streets. So fellow clergymen make an icon of Time, and worship it, and avoid learning of what waiting does to Time's victims.*

This lust for unbothered purity of commitment was the focus of King's letter to his fellow clergymen. They worshipped the God of Time. But the very same critique might also be aimed at many other groups, who have gained the attention of the public square, in the years since King's death: white and black nationalists, feminists, liberals, paleo-conservatives, neo-conservatives, seekers after middle-class status, environmentalists, even those who sing "We Shall Overcome" on January 18th but who do not speak to black people, or white people, on January 19th. King might even apply this critique to the cult that has grown up around his own flesh and blood and bone. To salvage his own personal meaning from the meaning that has been imposed on his life by the processes of iconization, he might have warned, in his mature years, his own partisans of this tragic mistake: "I make my commitment an idol when the quality of commitment itself becomes more important than the thing to which I am committed."

King might also address himself to the current impasse in the black community concerning the issue of civil rights. He might reflect on the reasons why, twenty-five years after his death, the humanly transcendent movement he inspired is still mired in debate over the means toward specific ends; why his beloved community is still stuck in a cycle of desegregation — resegregation — increasing demands for desegregation. During the past twenty-five years of this cycle, advocates of desegregation have been assigned a new category — the Civil Rights Community — and are viewed, sometimes admirably, as creative users of the various laws to break down the racial walls which, somehow, always find ways of reforming themselves — in schools, in neighborhoods, in jobs, and in personal relationships — as soon as the written law looks the other way. The end toward which the strategy of desegregation was only a means, integration, has itself become a kind of category, subject to the control of the rule of law.

The entire affirmative action industry grows out of an effort to apply the technology of law to organic human relationships. It also seeks to achieve some balance in artificial human categories, white and black, which are assumed to be natural and unnatural, superior and inferior, privileged and deprived, if not depraved. Moreover, the focus on affirmative action, the legal protection given to oppressed minorities, has led group after group to retreat from association with what used to be called the universals of life and has encouraged the location of the true, the good, and the beautiful exclusively within the precincts of one's own category or group. To qualify for this special status, one only need prove, in court, that biology, or life, has made one a victim. Over the past twenty-five years the domain of law has all but replaced, or eroded, personal codes of conduct which once had the potential to create a vital human center, a body of shared assumptions about the commonality of human life in its spiritual precincts. In the absence of such a human center, in situations ripe with spiritual hunger, sects, groups, and ideologies provide substitutes for what used to be assumed as basically human.

Martin King, in his letter from his jail cell in Birmingham, Alabama, seemed painfully aware of the limitations of law as a guide to human doings. He cautioned his fellow clergymen: "An unjust law is a code that is out of harmony with the moral law. To put it in the terms of St. Thomas Aquinas, an unjust law is a human law that is not rooted in eternal law and natural law." From his new cell in Birmingham, King might have reflected more on this dilemma. He might have been brave enough to rethink the basic strategy of the entire civil rights movement, which is at the basis of the racial and sexual and group-oriented balkanization of American life.

The movement itself was premised in the language of American law. Its basic strategy, forcing the American legal system to concede that separate could never be equal, assumed a model of white American society as the norm to which black Americans should aspire. This norm was implicit in the legal attack made by the pioneer of the civil rights movement.

Charles Hamilton Houston, born in the shadow of the Supreme Court's 1896 decision in *Plessy* v. *Ferguson,* a *Law Review* graduate of the Harvard Law School, the first black recipient of a Sheldon Traveling Fellowship, studied civil law in Spain following his graduation. During the 1930s, when he took over the Howard Law

School and its students, Houston began to evolve the theories that would lead eventually to a legal challenge of the *Plessy* v. *Ferguson,* separate but equal, precedent. The civil law in Spain that interested Houston was the remnant of old Roman law. It was what the Romans of the empire called *jus gentium* or *jus naturale,* the law of peoples or the law of nature. That is, the ancient Romans, seeing their empire consolidated under Julius Caesar and Augustus, evolved a special body of laws, based on the perceived habits of the foreigners in their ports and in their cities, in order to provide legal remedies for their disputes. This body of law was considered natural to *them,* but had no relation to the body of law, the *jus civile,* reserved for Roman citizens. The Roman jurisconsults, who administered the laws, applied one set of "universal" or "natural" laws to non-Romans and another set of laws, the *jus civile,* to Romans. Jurisconsults would not stoop to applying Roman law, the *jus civile,* to non-Romans.

In one of history's great ironies, Charles Houston's lifelong effort to erode the *Plessy* precedent, which resulted in *Brown* v. *Board of Education* in 1954, succeeded also in resurrecting, within the framework of the U.S. Constitution, a special set of laws which are comparable to the old Roman *jus gentium.* Black Americans, in the almost forty years since the *Brown* decision, still remain separate, and institutionalized, within the special legal category called "civil rights law." One result is that native-born, multigeneration American citizens, and their basic rights under the Constitution, still remain captive to every shift in the political climate, every modification in the nuanced language of each new political administration. A collective shudder runs through the corporate black community each time a new Justice Department (*jurisconsult?*) assumes control of law enforcement. *The issue is always whether protection of civil rights will be extended once again to foreigners. The issue is never whether the alleged foreigners are in reality U.S. citizens, from many generations back, whose basic rights have been in continuous violation over a period of centuries.*

This legal stasis, or limbo, has encouraged a deep cynicism toward the law among black Americans. In the larger American community, it has contributed to an erosion of belief in the applicability of "universal" standards within the context of an American community of citizens equal under *the same set of laws,* a truly American *jus civile.*

One might go further and speculate as to whether this separate category has become the basis of a new civil religion, with every group which perceives itself as outside the scope of traditional law, because of biological fate or personal choice, defining itself into *jus gentium* and the scope of its protections. It also raises the question of whether each new group which claims the virtue of victimization can lay claim to a special category of legal protections that is much more valid than the claims that might be made under a universally applicable common body of laws. If this is indeed the direction in which we are heading, then Martin Luther King, Jr., the icon, has been elected as high priest of the new civic religion named Civil Rights. Also, a brilliant constitutional lawyer and former U.S. Supreme Court justice, Thurgood Marshall, is being remembered as only "Mr. Civil Rights." Monuments and museums are steadily being built to sanctify this special, peculiar status. And the processes of desegregating streets and buildings, and most especially minds and spirits, which were once only a means, have become perpetual ends in themselves.

Meanwhile, while we retreat into a debate over which group is more victimized and deserving of close attention, the larger and more important issue remains: just who, even under the purview of the old Roman *jus gentium,* remains a foreigner, and what is left of the Romans who maintain the remnants of the old *jus civile?* The antagonistic cooperation, the creative tension, between the rule of law and a settled code of conduct could be ripe with human possibilities. The Americans of the coming centuries will emerge, and mature, out of this tension. According to my own thinking, they will be the ones who act, and who encourage others to act, in areas beyond either a fixation on civil rights or the preservation of the more negative and reductive aspects of the white status quo, both of which have produced nothing more than human stasis. They will be the ones who accept the greater challenges and goals of full and equal citizenship, of a higher ethical responsibility toward the human individual, in a space far above and beyond the fires of two radically opposed camps. But after the destruction of most of the country's large-souled men, and during this time of fear, such people, even if they do exist, have no good reason to announce their presence among us, even if they were welcomed.

III

Homo sum nihil a me alienum puto.
I am a man; no other man do I deem a stranger.

Some version of this phrase has always been at the basis of the professed public values of Westerners, of what was once called Christendom. The Latin ancestral voices of the older cultures have always found subtle expression within the American context. It may well be that our current fixation on the law and on legal processes tends to close out alternate means of achieving desired ends. We are witnessing now a dawning realization of the limitations of the law. The hypothetical "reasonable man" of American jurisprudence now confronts a situation that is much too complex to be open to reason alone. Other cultures admit ethical as well as reasonable voices into their jurisprudence. The Japanese, for instance, admit into their law the question "In such a circumstance, what would a human being do?" I believe that this culture has now reached a point at which moral models offer much more vitality and possibility of renewal than legal models.

In his last public address, or essay, published in *Playboy* magazine in January 1969, King attempted to outline what he called "A Testament of Hope." It was fitting that *Playboy* should have been the forum for King's last public words. By 1968, when he died while trying to help garbage men who were on strike in Memphis, King had been all but shut out by the respectable media. The fact that *Playboy* published his last public words, while *The Atlantic Monthly* had published his first, might have confirmed for him the reality of a relation between the Profane and the Sacred.

Almost stripped of all his worldly hopes, King, in the pages of *Playboy,* sandwiched between the nudes and the risqué cartoons, offered his insights into what it would take to revitalize a decadent American democratic ethos. "When Rome began to disintegrate from within," he said,

> it turned to a strengthening of the military establishment, rather than to a correction of the corruption within the society. We are doing the same thing in this country and the result will probably be the same — unless, and here I admit to a bit of chauvinism, the black man in America can provide a new soul force for all Americans, a new expres-

sion of the American dream that need not be realized at the expense of other men around the world, but a dream of opportunity and life that can be shared with the rest of the world. It seems glaringly obvious to me that the development of a humanitarian means of dealing with some of the social problems of the world — *and the correlative revolution in American values that this will entail* — is a much better way of protecting ourselves against the threat of violence than the military means we have chosen. On these grounds, I must indict the Johnson administration . . .

King died shortly after he wrote this testament.

There has emerged no large-souled black American leader since King because the black American community has learned, very, very well, the price that will be exacted for such principled stands. And yet King did call for, in his last Testament, the emergence of such a moral chauvinism on the part of black Americans. I sometimes think that the black American obsession with material gain over the past twenty-five years is only an ironic confidence game. I suspect that most thinking black Americans are really saying, through their actions, "Don't you see? I am only trying to make it. I want to demonstrate my distance from any moral stance that will cause me to be killed. I am not, and never will be, a Martin Luther King, Jr."

And yet we are. And so we name streets after *him,* the better to protect *ourselves.*

Perhaps a fitting resting place for King's legacy, and for his language, should not be within the monuments built to celebrate, or to contain, the spirit of the movement he tried his best to lead. Perhaps he and his language deserve to occupy an integrated room in the national pantheon, a room set aside to honor his basic ethic: "Integration is genuine intergroup, interpersonal doing . . . based on unenforceable obligations." If there ever comes an Ivy Day for those who evolved, and attempted to safeguard, the American sacred language, his roommate should be John Winthrop, who laid the spiritual foundations of the tradition that King tried to follow. Winthrop's language and King's language derived from the same sources. Both men renewed the quality of the moral discourse of their day. John Winthrop said, aboard ship, just before landing at the Massachusetts Bay in 1630, essentially what King repeated all during the 1960s:

Thus stands the cause betweene God and us. Wee are entered into Covenant with him for this worke, wee have taken out a Commission, the Lord hath given us leave to draw our own Articles, wee have professed to enterprise these Accions upon these and these ends, wee have hereupon besought him of favor and blessing: Now if the Lord shall please to heare us, and bring us in peace to the place wee desire, then hath hee ratified this Covenant and sealed our Commission [and] will expect a strickt performance of the Articles contained in it, but if wee shall neglect the observation of these Articles which are the ends wee have propounded, and dissembling with our God, shall fall to embrace this present world and prosecute our carnall intencions seeking great things for our selves and our posterity, the Lord will surely breake out in wrathe against us, be revenged of such a perjured people and make us knowe the price of the breache of such a Covenant.

Now the onely way to avoyde this shipwracke and to provide for our posterity is to followe the Counsell of Micah, to doe Justly, to love mercy, to walke humbly with our God. For this end, wee must be knitt together in this worke as one man, wee must entertain each other in brotherly Affeccion, wee must be willing to abridge our selves of our superfluities, for the supply of others necessities, wee must uphold a familiar Commerce together in all meekness, gentleness, patience and liberality, wee must delight in each other, make others Condicions our owne, rejoyce together, mourne together, labor and suffer together, allwayes haveing before our eyes our Commission and Community in the worke, our Community as members of the same body, soe shall wee keepe the unite of the spirit in the bond of peace, the Lord will be our God and delight to dwell among us as his owne people and will command a blessing upon us in all our wayes, soe that wee shall see much more of his wisdome, power, goodness and truthe than formerly wee have been acquainted with. Wee shall finde that the God of Israel is among us, when tenn of us shall be able to resist a thousand of our enemies, when hee shall make us a prayse and glory, that men shall say of succeeding plantations: the Lord make it like that of New England: for wee must consider that wee shall be as a Citty upon a Hill, the eies of all people are uppon us: soe that if wee shall deal falsely with our God in this worke wee have undertaken and soe cause him to withdrawe his present help from us, wee shall shame the faces of many of Gods worthy servants, and cause theire prayers to be turned into Cursses upon us till wee be consumed out of the good land whither wee are goeing . . .

This is a vision of the Beloved Community that King was trying to create. This was one of the goals of integration. This was one of the sources of the moral language used by Martin Luther King, Jr. It is a language that is in very short supply in these bleak days. If King had lived, he would have made another heroic attempt to reclaim it and to reapply it to our wounded spiritual circumstances.

This effort to try again would have been the true source of his greatness as a man, of flesh and blood and bone.

S. OSO

Lots

FROM ANTIOCH REVIEW

AFTER WORLD WAR II 75 percent of white Philadelphians left the city for the suburbs. Hardly any whites remained in downtown Philly, where I lived with my family over Father's business. Most of the suburban whites had to drive back to Philly for work. Commuting required them to park, and parking brought them into contact with the black men who worked Philly's lots. In the fifties, racial violence had yet to occur, so I could be the only white kid in the fourth grade and on the job, running errands for the men on the lots.

"Whats'ya wan, Jewboy?"

"Need any errands run?"

"Nope."

"Sure?"

"Wha'kina erran y'all think ah nee?"

"How 'bout a sandwich from the deli?"

"Braw one fra' home."

"Howsa 'bout a taste? The old clerk at the liquor store will sell to me if I say I'm gettin' it for you."

"Ga dat too."

I looked around the parking shack's interior. Scrawled on the walls were numbers, usually in three and four digits and often accompanied by a day of the week. "Put your number in yet?"

"Da man be by."

"Not always: he missed a day last month. Suppose six-eighty hits tomorrow, and you ain't in?"

Starting with three lots close to Father's building, I expanded my errand service to thirty other locations. When I bagged school, I hustled errands at lunchtime. If not, I began after school. After five the night shift came on, and I ran errands sometimes until midnight.

Commuters had to park on the lots. In Philly every parkable street was metered, and the meters needed to be fed hourly, demanding that the commuter interrupt his workday eight times; moreover, parking enforcement was the most efficient part of city government. Philly traffic court was nicknamed "no fix." "No fix" did not mean that fixing a ticket was impossible, but rather that fixing a ticket was more trouble than it was worth; furthermore, scofflaws were captured in publicized hunts. Not publicized were the contributions of the Parking Lot Owners Association so this civic function could maintain its high standard.

Public relations for severe parking enforcement was the narrowness of the streets designed by William Penn. Penn's four-hundred-year-old street plan had not anticipated the car. The argument went: if there was a fire, fire trucks wouldn't be able to maneuver the narrow, car-jammed streets. But the downtown had expanded beyond Penn's original design to include wide boulevards. One parking lot sat at the edge of downtown. Traffic was sparse on this wide street, which became a dead end. The lot was full, and the streets were empty. If a car happened to park on the street, the lot's owner called the police to ticket it immediately. The only business nearby was the Philadelphia Board of Education. Since Board of Education workers, being city employees, would have the time to feed hourly meters, the area had No Parking signs.

Behind the public-spirited parking lot owners were the public-spirited real estate interests. Philly proper covers a vast amount of land. Greater Philadelphia, which includes eastern Pennsylvania, south Jersey, and Delaware, is an enormous quantity of land. None of this expanse has ever commanded anything like the prices in D.C. or New York. For the whole area to have a value, the downtown must be able to fetch a respectable price, since real estate appraisal assumes an outlying district close to a metropolis is more valuable than one farther away. For developed downtown land to be valuable, undeveloped downtown property must have a value, since undeveloped downtown land — usually a parking lot — is the alternative to construction. The value of Jersey marsh is contingent upon Philly parking lot values, which are contingent upon the impossibility of parking on the street. Albert M. Greenfield, who owned the most real estate, and Harry Sley, who operated the most lots, were best friends.

In my first few years of errands I got to know the different lots. Some lots were well paved, while others were cracked, exposing portions of Philly's already deteriorating infrastructure. Many surfaces had gullies that made it seem that two same-model cars parked beside one another were not the same, one being lower or higher in the rear. Despite these discrepancies, all lots were much the same: asphalt patches with one tiny structure — the shack.

Sley System lots had prefabricated sheet-metal shacks painted in Christmas colors. ("Sley" became Santa's "sleigh" on the company's ten-foot-by-five-foot flashing neon signs.) Since Sley shacks also had raised wood floors and space for up to five people, they were the Cadillacs of the asphalt. Although some shacks of other companies were cinder block, the average shack was really a shack: odd lengths of salvaged wood held together by massive layers of tarpaper and so small that the car jockey had to sit up against the coal stove. The shacks would have been windowless had it not been necessary to watch the cars. Even though the fifties were comparatively crime-free, cars did occasionally get stolen.

Besides the physical format of the lots, I got to know the car jockeys. Even though civil rights publicity had yet to become prevalent, many of the blacks who worked the lots were as upwardly mobile as any whites from the suburbs. These men were parking as a second job so that their children would have the schooling to join Philly's entrenched black political and professional classes. For the most part these men, though sometimes discriminated against by whites, embraced the dominant society's values. Their errands were for food and, maybe, a newspaper. Very few touched liquor, even at home, and none gambled. They never used slang, much less profanity. Their conversations with me revolved around why I should be interested in public school, religious training, and family matters so that I could have a middle-class future. Frequently they would caution me to stay away from so-and-so since so-and-so was a bad influence.

I didn't crave bad influences so much as influences different from white culture, which I had already found to have more rules than seemed necessary. For example, I never understood why I had to address white adults as "Mr.," "Mrs.," or "Miss" when I could call the car jockeys, who were just as adult, "Slick Willie," "Fat Daddy," and "Deac." Or why I was forced to dress up, cleaned and ironed, to be socially acceptable at school, which I detested, while I could dress any old way to be acceptable for running errands. Although I remained on good terms with the upwardly mobile element, I sought out the black men who spoke jive, got high, and chased mamas. In any case, not one of the upwardly mobile ever would have risked that second paycheck and his children's future by letting a kid work on his lot.

Like most pubescent males, I was fascinated by driving, so it wasn't too long after I became a fixture on the lots that I started bugging the workers to let me park the cars for them. Of course, that met with "Whi'boy, can' leh'you dri' no mathafuckin' car. Gi'me in trouble." But in spite of my not being allowed behind the wheel, many were grateful for my assistance in ticketing cars and collecting money whenever I chanced upon a driveway suddenly overcome with customers. Because of this driveway management skill, I started to earn money watching a lot while the car jockey entertained a lady in the shack. These jobs were late at night, after business had thinned out. I was supposed to direct the customers to their cars and collect from stragglers, who were to be directed to empty spaces and told to "Lock it up and take your keys." During these nights I always had a few cars with the keys in the ignitions and no one to stop me from getting inside to practice what I had watched for several years. Thankfully, automatics had started to become prevalent, so at first I didn't have to try to learn the clutch while trying to teach myself steering and stopping.

Parking a car like a pro is not the hardest trade, but it does require experience. Even someone who drives in the street cannot just show up and start parking, since professional parking requires driving in reverse to be as natural as driving forward. In most locations there are rush periods, usually at the beginning and end of business days. It is at these times that training is necessary. Anybody who can drive can eventually back a car into a row. The pro can put the car into the row in one shot and have the entire row of cars straight and even with one another and with the neighboring rows. There is none of what is called "upping and backing," searching for an elusive alignment as cars and anxious customers wait for service in a gridlocked driveway.

Car jockeying can get tedious day in and day out, so as the workers saw my ability improve, they let me do more and more of their work. When I started parking, I was so happy to be driving a car five years before I could legally that I gave the worker involved the tips I collected. As my maneuvering became more professional and the workers became more dependent upon me to do their jobs, I kept the tips and abandoned errands.

Still too young to drive legally, I began to get regular work on the lots. The parking lot owners had seen me around for several years and assumed I was old enough. When I occasionally turned down shifts because of school, the owners believed "school" was college. Much of this assumption was based on my being very tall and prematurely balding. The owners, every one of whom was Jewish, knew that my parents were members of their tribe. They assumed I shared this tribal allegiance and was therefore more honest than a *shatvos*.

In those days there was hardly a lot where the customer self-parked and took his keys. Self-parking, lock-it-take-your-keys lots were limited in their capacity, since cars could not be in tight rows one after the other. A car owner could show up at any time. There might be an emergency at home or an unforeseen change of schedule. Consequently, self-park lots wasted space; each individual space needed an obvious, unobstructed route of egress, whereas car-jockey lots packed cars into every possible nook and cranny.

The use of car jockeys allowed for the conversion of small, irregular (L- or U-shaped) areas into successful parking lots. An example was Fogel's Garage Corporation. Fogel's had only one decent-size (two-hundred-car capacity) lot. The remaining twenty were irregular or very tiny. These sorts of lots existed in the few really bustling areas in the otherwise sleepy downtown. In almost any other plot of downtown, parking was the most profitable use of land. In these busy areas, not only were there no places on the street, there were few on the lots: here buildings were more profitable than parking. Fogel's lots were therefore highly profitable.

For most lots the daytime pricing structure was so much for the first hour, and so much for the second; over two hours was considered all day and billed at the all-day rate. This structure was devised for commuters, who stayed all day, with provision for the occasional short-termers. In contrast, the Fogel fee structure was so much for the first half-hour and so much for each additional half-hour, ad infinitum. This discouraged commuters and, instead, catered to high turnover there for a sales pitch. Normal parking maximum was then around a buck twenty-five, whereas all day on a Fogel lot could work itself up to six bucks, an unheard-of amount for parking in the late fifties.

Working a Fogel lot honed jockey skills because Fogel's had fifteen- to thirty-space lots that could total ninety to more than two hundred cars a day. At other lots cars were arranged by the times their owners said they would leave — occasionally subject to change. The two o'clock car is in front of the three o'clock car in front of the four o'clock car. In a Fogel lot it was impossible to keep the short-term — less than an hour — cars in front because all the cars were short-term, except for the occasional tourist who hadn't bothered to read the price board. By the time a customer came for his car, it was in the back row with three in front. Digging this car out usually meant taking the three other cars into traffic, sometimes onto the pavement, cutting in and out of moving cars and pedestrians. These cars were double-parked in the street, sometimes with the engines running. Often, between the time that the jockey left one car in the street and the time it took to get the next, a new customer pulled into the row that was being vacated for the last car. This parking, unparking, and rearranging went on for every ten-hour shift. No lunch hour. Piss went into a Coke bottle during a stolen moment in the minuscule aluminum shack. Usually for every hundred cars taken in, a thousand had to be moved. In spite of the hard work, guys would kill for a day shift on a Fogel lot. In the 1960s the average take for a Fogel's jockey was six hundred per week. A grand was not out of the question, even though the salary was minimum wage and management routinely shortchanged pay envelopes.

Rare was the customer who didn't tip. Rarer still was the customer who hadn't tipped after parking a second time at the same lot, even if it was empty, or even at the lot up the street. The first jockey would run up to the second jockey or yell up the street, "Meatball!" Tips then were almost always a quarter. Up front with the big shots earned a bill. At Fogel's the tips were much better because the customer was often impressed with the hustle of the attendant. Besides, because the lot was almost always at legal capacity, it was true to say, "I'll do my best to fit you in."

Car jockeys owned the nearby streets. Owning the street meant parking preferred customers at meters and feeding the meters and/or the meter maids. Generally, equitable arrangements could be made for "No Parking" spaces. The attendants also owned those semilegal car spaces in the lot driveway. Since Fogel lots were in the busiest parts of town, these additional spaces cost slightly less than the all-day charge.

The biggest source of income at Fogel was from "burning," which involved two factors. The first was the Fogel never-ending fee structure. As the car came into the lot the attendant punched a new ticket in the time clock: the clock started before the customer got out of the car. The next half-hour's charge began the second the next half-hour began: thirty-one minutes counted as two half-hours. The second factor was that the customer had difficulty keeping track of parking lot time. It was simple to tell a customer who had stayed, say, twenty-eight minutes that the ticket said thirty-one minutes. It takes a small amount of experience to become accustomed to reading a time stamp calculated in military time, so if the customer looked the slightest bit suspicious, the ticket was immediately shoved into his face with a "see for yourself." He would then pretend to study it before nodding affirmatively with slight embarrassment for disputing the hard-working attendant. "Oh, I must have lost track of time." Even a stay of fifteen minutes computed to thirty-one.

The Fogel lot at Rittenhouse Square, Philly's ritziest area, was the company's flagship. (It had planters around its sides.) Moreover, it was the only Fogel lot that had a majority of steady customers. They visited doctors in the high-rise medical building across the street. All day long folks were moving from the building to the lot as fast as they could to ask, "Did I make it?"

"Ah thin maybe ya'll di."

"BANG," said the time clock.

"Oh no, ya'll miz ahgen. Ah feel ter'ble. Ah pay fal diz time myself. Can'stan ta'see diz happen ta'ya'll ever'week."

"I couldn't let you do that," the customer would say, looking at the parking shack windows covered with snapshots of black children. "The elevator took its time getting there. How can it be your fault?"

"Ahright," the childless jockey would say, "Ah leh ya'pay diz time. Bah nest time it on me. Promise? Now ya'll come and si down here in mah warm shack while Ah geh ya'car."

The car would be running and pointing towards the street.

"Di Ah tell ya'll dassa bootiful ha ya'wearin? . . . A dollah tip? Ah can 'cept dat. Ya'll t'gen'rous."

"It's not for you. It's for all your lovely children."

Fogel's tolerated burning because this was the only large parking operation that didn't have major labor problems. The workers were making too much money stealing from the customers to steal from the company. The owner of Fogel's counted the money and set up locations: he didn't want to know about problems. The operation ran itself with no management input except for the owner or his son stopping by a location to say hello. Everybody made money and minded their own business except for Maurice.

Maurice was rumored to be a French relative of Fogel's owner. That he was a relative was the only reason he could have been hired to be the supervisor, if he was the supervisor. Maurice had trained as an accountant, but given his personality and the management vacuum, he may have simply assumed the position of boss. Being French, Maurice had difficulty understanding American white culture; consequently, it was impossible for him to have any sensitivity to blacks. Since very few Fogel workers aspired to become bourgeois, they were everything Maurice expected niggers to be. Conversely, Maurice, caring only about money, was the stereotypic kike. The difference between the two stereotypes was that the blacks had enough experience to know that not all Jews were alike. In fact, to a man they felt the owner, who made tons of money, was a good Jew because he let them have theirs as well.

Parking lot tickets are perforated into three sections, each of which bears the same number. The numbers — printed by a printer specializing in these tickets — start at one and go to infinity. The difference between the day's starting number and the day's ending number is the number of cars parked for that day. One part of the three-part matching numbered ticket goes under the wiper, one part goes to the customer as a claim check, and the third part stays in the ticket rack in the booth. On this third part entering and exiting times are punched. If management should stop by to check the lot, the numbers of the checks on the rack have to correspond to the numbers of the checks on the windshields. One way for an attendant to cheat a parking company is to reissue windshield stubs and claim checks, charge the customer, and pocket the change. In order to foil this, the rack check and the windshield check have spaces for the attendant to write the license number, make, and color of the car. At Fogel's these spaces were never filled; Maurice decided that they would be.

On paper Maurice's new policy made sense, and at most of the other companies that was the way it was. However, Fogel's was unique in that its lots were almost always at capacity and therefore generated maximum revenue. Even nonaccountants could calculate the take by multiplying each lot's capacity by the hours of operation, then multiplying that sum by the hourly rate. This was the argument made by some of the jockeys most friendly with the owner. They also pointed out that business was so brisk that stopping to write license numbers deprived them of time to stuff the lots. The owner hadn't heard of Maurice's new policy. But after noting that revenue in the weeks that Maurice's policy was in effect came to less than the weekly average before the policy, the owner agreed with his jockeys; moreover, the owner knew his employees had no interest in stealing — from the company, that is. Though this idea was ended, Maurice's innovations continued.

Fogel's had a ten-car lot beside the Forrest Theater, where Barbra Streisand's *Funny Girl* had sold out the entire run. Ten cars was small even for Fogel's. Conveniently, the back led to an alley from which cars could be taken two blocks away to the one large Fogel lot — two hundred capacity. The plan was to charge a high price next to the Forrest, have some of the day men and part-timers come in to drive the cars to the big lot, run two blocks back to the smaller lot, and drive some more.

This was okay with the day guys, even though they would be working for far less than they made at their day operations. All parking companies had similar practices, and it was a chance to be together for a raucous three-hour social while getting extra time on the clock and making good tips for retrieving the cars.

Opening night began as expected: cars were showing up from all over. The one thing out of the ordinary was Maurice cashiering.

Usually in this situation the lot's night jockey cashiered. But no one paid Maurice's presence any mind. There was nothing to hide; moreover, the lot manager was happy to drive cars, for his driving meant more tips for all. But as soon as the rush was over, Maurice sent everyone home with less than an hour on the clock. No fun, and no juicy tips. He even sent the lot's night man home. Maurice stayed by himself and sent the customers two blocks away to the larger lot to get their own cars with the assistance of the guys who worked the larger lot.

Though pissed, everyone showed up the next night. It seemed that what looked like a three-week nightly rip-off would be one of the prices for having a tidy daytime scam. The only difference between this night and the one before was that on this night the big lot filled up on its own.

Having made this discovery well before the anticipated rush had happened, I ran back from the large lot and said to the small lot's regular night man, "The large lot's full. What are we gonna to do with the cars?"

The manager, who already knew this, gave me one of the biggest smiles I had ever seen. "Park da fuckin' cars all over town, anyplace you want. Motherfuck Moreez."

The tiny lot's atmosphere changed from depressed to manic. Prior to learning the news, no one had been moving quickly, and gridlock paralyzed the tiny lot's driveway. After learning the news, we couldn't hustle enough. Bright-eyed and grinning, we caught one another's eyes at times on the lot. We laughed uncontrollably whenever we encountered one another on the street or in an alleyway in which we had just stashed a few more cars.

Since we were abandoning the cars instead of parking them, we were able to return more quickly to take more cars than we had the night before; consequently, Maurice was able to increase the company's take substantially. Not only had the driveway gridlock disappeared, but Maurice could barely keep up with the rush of cars to be ticketed. Greenbacks in one hand and parking checks in the other, Maurice was ecstatic when he dismissed us after less than an hour on the clock.

"Now, Moreez, you sho you don' wan me t'stay? You look awfully tired. Maybe you should ge'some res?" the lot's regular night man asked.

Maurice gave him a knowing smile. "Zou verry 'bout me? Zou

can not fool me. I know zou just vunt more hours. There ess no more cars to move, so vhy should the company pay zou? Zou go home vith zee others."

One of the day men asked, "But, Moreez, why you don' wanna share some o'dose hours wi'us? We worked real har. Look at all da business we ga so y'all kin look good t'da owner."

"I'll verry about how I look to zee owner. As for 'sharing,' zee company gives zou zee job. Dass ess 'sharing' zeenough. Now get going, all of zou."

In the next few days, the owner called each of us in to find out what had happened. Anticipating an investigation, we had prepared a story. Each of us said that we informed Maurice that the big lot was full, but he chose to ignore us. Anyone who knew Maurice could imagine his being so involved taking in money that he would ignore information from those he disdained. Maurice was ordered to remain in the office.

The camaraderie exhibited that night was common among workers not only in the same company but throughout the parking industry. For example, a worker on one company's lot might rely upon a worker at a neighboring lot owned by a different company to watch the lot while he went to the bathroom or entertained a lady friend. And if one jockey was having trouble negotiating with a meter maid, a neighboring jockey would never try to outbid him for street spaces.

Camaraderie's most visible manifestation, however, was the A.F. of L./C.I.O.'s Local 700, which represented the workers at the major parking chains. The owners had the Parking Lot Owners Association to represent their interests, yet most of them hated the fact that the workers had their own representation. Without knowing the intricacies of the industry, one might have reasoned that labor and management have a traditional rivalry: management wants labor to work harder for less, while labor wants more to work less. The parking industry differed from other industries in that labor, never turning away business, worked as hard as possible all the time. The busier the lot, the more tips. The better the lot was run, the more return business, the more tips. Moreover, unlike other unions, such as the Railroad Workers, that opted for featherbedding, Local 700 favored minimal staffing: a parking lot worker did not want to share tips.

Back then the country was recovering from McCarthyism. Organized labor was supposed to have been one of communism's inroads. Even though militancy was often associated with un-Americanism, it would have been impossible to connect Local 700 with communism or anything else un-American. The most militant member of Local 700 was its perennial secretary-treasurer, Bob Keith. Over the years Bob and I discussed many topics, some of which were political. But not only did I never hear him espouse the overthrow of the government, I never heard him mention Marx or anything remotely communistic. He wasn't even a Socialist. Rather he was a traditional Democrat in his campaigns for membership's job security, benefits, and wages.

Recognizing that wages and benefits didn't constitute the bulk of a member's pay, the union never had great expectations at contract time. Disputes tended to be about an extra nickel an hour, the late arrival of winter uniforms, or more coal for shack stoves. The union never demanded a cut anywhere near commensurate with that of the owners'. For Local 700 the concept of "job security" meant that management could terminate a worker only for due cause, such as theft, and that such allegations required evidence. Because, more than any other enterprise, the success of the lot depended upon labor and ownership cooperating, Local 700 felt management should show more concern for the workers by readily granting these minor requests.

In the smaller operations (up to four locations), management did demonstrate concern with bonuses, perks, and, more often than not, compassion. Every small operator that I knew thought nothing of working right beside the workers and sharing the same cramped shack. Even though by working alongside the help, the operator was helping himself, the close contact between employee and employer, black and white, created a rapport, if not a trust, that protected the small operator against theft, worker turnover, and, most importantly, Local 700.

One of the small operators for whom I worked was Marty Kaplan, who was also president of the Parking Lot Owners Association. Like the other small operators, Marty thought nothing of working beside his employees. Unlike most other operators, however, Marty had no fear of the union. "If my men want it, it's fine with me," he often said. "If my men vote for the union's contract, I'll save money. In addition, since I'm planning more locations, I'll save time and hassle by using the union for staffing."

"But, Marty," I asked, "how come the other owners don't feel the way you do?"

At this question Marty smirked off into the distance. "Because they're businessmen second, refugees first. They act like they just got off the boat. They worked hard to get their money so that they wouldn't have to be treated like shit like they were when they and their fathers were employees in the old country. Because their employers treated them like shit, they think they should be able to be dictators on their lots. They won't see that it's to their benefit to give their employees a say. As money-grubbing as they can be, they'd rather have power than money. I was even told to get rid of you because you're a union spy."

"A union spy? That's ridiculous. What is there to spy? On a lot everything is in the open, and everybody knows everybody and everything already. Who told you to get rid of me?"

"Fogel's."

That made sense, since Fogel's was the second largest parking corporation in Philly not to be union. Suddenly one day when I showed up for work at Fogel's I was told there was no work now and in the future. "Nobody'd rock the boat at Fogel's: there's too much money to steal. Whatever made them think I was a spy?" I asked, trying to remember if I had even mentioned the union to anyone during my time there.

"They thought you spent too much time with Bob Keith."

"You spending too much time with me?" Bob said, breaking into a hard chuckle when I told him what Marty had told me. "What kind of information do I need from you that I don't already know?" Bob asked, grinning with self-assurance and shaking his head at such a preposterous thought.

Remembering how he would smile wide-mouthed and bulge his eyes to the edge of their sockets whenever he heard a foolish statement, I could conceive of why the refugees associated Bob and Local 700 with a loss of control. Bob didn't suffer bullshitters. It wasn't hard to imagine chagrin flowing from an owner whose recalcitrance had just been mocked by a flash of Bob's pearly whites against the jet black background. That Bob's face sat on the body of a former heavyweight fighter made him quite intimidating.

The owners were no more ready to negotiate with his level of preparation than with his physical presence. He often came to his lot with a briefcase full of union business to study during slack periods. He divided the papers into stacks that filled up most of his cinder-block, three-person-capacity shack. Working from stack to stack, he compared the various figures, and then, to be certain of the comparisons, he brought out an accounting tablet and small adding machine. "That company can afford this contract. Who they trying to kid?" he would say with his usual mouth and eye expression.

Even though the rumor that I was a union spy limited work opportunities, it didn't really affect me. Several of the small operators knew how preposterous the accusation was; I could get all the work I wanted, especially since at the time of the accusation I was old enough to have a driver's license. If anything, the accusation pleased me. I interpreted it as recognition from the dominant culture that even though I looked white, I was not one of them. That I could be mistaken for a spy made me feel more grown-up than any of my other pseudo-adult behavior. It seemed I had been able to avoid another social guideline — adolescence — and become an adult, a black adult.

Since this was before the sexual revolution, the best part about seeing myself as a black male was that black men didn't need a sexual revolution. One cold and wet Sunday I was working for a small operator. Weekends were extremely slow, so the operator and I split the take. Once in a while business appeared, and I made out, but usually it was a time to keep my feet next to the pot-bellied stove, smoke a joint, and stare out the window at empty, cracked asphalt. On this particular Sunday, while staring out the window, I saw a lady I had seen at several different lots. All dressed up, she was on tiptoes as she tried to negotiate puddles in high heels.

I decided to operate the way I had witnessed many times. "Wanna get in from that chill, sugar?" I said, sticking my head outside the shack.

Moving her gaze from the puddles to me, she said, "Why, thank you. Don't mind if I do."

Had I not declared myself an adult, her acceptance might have astonished me, for she was at least fifteen years older than I. But one of the things I had learned about being a black male was that treating a woman as sex was a foregone conclusion. As soon as this lady entered the shack, I frowned at her and with mock consternation said, "Are you tryin' to catch your death? Your clothes are all wet. Better take 'em off so I can dry 'em by the stove."

Unbuttoning, she asked, "Will you keep me warm?"

But no matter how many trysts I enjoyed, I could never be black — not because of my skin color, but because the black people I knew, no matter how at odds they were with the dominant culture, still related to a culture, whether it was the dominant culture or one they had isolated for themselves. I had been unaware of my compulsion to be intellectually, morally, and emotionally independent of all culture. Unconsciously I had used black street culture as a fulcrum to detach myself from white society, not so I could join the black underclass, but so I could be my own class. I made this discovery about myself toward the end of my time on the lots one afternoon in '63.

I had cut several high school classes to arrive early enough to assist on a lot at Fifteenth and Spruce. The ballroom of the hotel across the way was booked for a large affair. The day man for this lot was Duke Hayes, one of my favorite people. Tall and rock hard, he was covered with knife-fight scars from when he was younger. Almost always with a Pall Mall dangling from his lip, he was skeptical that anyone or any institution would look out for him. "Ah trust me, me, and me," he was fond of saying. A nice mama and a good buzz were his only wants besides being "left da fuck alone."

That afternoon Duke and I were to do a parking lot variation we had done several times before. Instead of merely taking the cars as they entered the lot and backing them into rows, we were to back the cars across Spruce Street — an active thoroughfare — to a larger lot owned by the brother-in-law of the owner of our lot; once there, we were to back the cars into rows. Duke, being my superior, took it upon himself to edge out into traffic first and then block the street enough for me to get across smoothly. Once across the street at the bigger lot, he would zip into a space, and I would pull in right next to him. Then we'd run back across the street to the smaller but slightly better-located lot.

No matter how competently we worked, cars came into the smaller lot faster than we could park them at the larger. The lot owner — a small businessman typically not too proud to handle the money at peak times — had ticketed ten cars in the driveway and was out in the street telling people to leave their cars there. "No problem. I've got a little more room for you."

Now, with cars abandoned on the street, Spruce's pre-rush-hour flow was really congested; Duke, more than ever, was having to muscle our way across. Already inside his car, Duke waited for me to put the next car's tail at his bumper before sticking his tail into the street. The car that had to be taken next still had its driver, who wasn't showing any sign of being ready to get out of it so I could get in. One trick to hasten a slow-moving customer was to open his door with the pretext of courtesy.

Duke got out of his car and folded his arms in front of himself while leaning against his car. I was happy to see mockery in his pissed-off pose. He was playing older and worldlier to my teenage incompetence. "Whi'boy, speed up dis slug." Duke wanted to put as many cars on the lot as he could to maximize tips.

Hanging on the door, I next chose to let the customer know I was there and that his delay was my delay by asking, "So you goin' to the affair at the hotel?"

The guy looked up at me, ashen and wide-eyed. "Somebody shot Kennedy!"

"What?"

Before the guy could repeat his statement, the lot's owner, concerned about the snafu, was in my face. "What's going on?"

As the customer listened to the radio, he repeated, "The president's dead. Somebody shot Kennedy."

"Hey, Duke, the president got shot."

"Stop joshin' wi'me, Jewboy. We gotta move cars," Duke said, this time with amusement gone. When mad, he narrowed to show you the least amount of target in case you wanted to retaliate when he popped you. He could have fun with my incompetence, but frivolity wasn't allowed if it messed with his money. I was certain what the customer had said was true when Duke, after he had come over to the car, stopped narrowing at me.

I detached from the group composed of Duke, the lot owner, and the customer. Seconds later the group around the customer's car had expanded to include a thirty-year-old woman in business clothes, two fifty-year-old men in painter's garb, and an elderly man in a tattered suit. Up and down Spruce and over to Fifteenth similar unlikely groups were forming. People were communicating to people based on proximity instead of prior association.

When the news had spread sufficiently, everyone except me halted in a spontaneous stillness. Alone, I walked about the area, savoring the paralysis. At Fifteenth and Spruce drivers were frozen at the still functioning traffic light. No horns honked at the front drivers to point out light changes. At that moment there must have been at least five hundred other organisms, with whom I was supposed to be sorrowfully in sync. But it seemed I was actually in sync only with the traffic light since I was functioning, oblivious to remorse.

Recovering from the stillness, folks had to decide about the next moment. The affair at the hotel ballroom was canceled. That decision meant that the affair was half in and half out of the lot. Spruce Street was jammed now that rush-hour drivers decided to mourn at home. Things were chaotic, but the customers were somber; calm prevailed while Duke and I unscrambled the mess. After we had emptied the lot, Duke and I went into the shack to close up, as the owner had ordered us to do before he left.

To me, Kennedy was only a reviled authority figure, so during that initial stillness I believed that many were faking grief. Once they stopped dealing with those in their proximity and resumed dealing with those with whom they were familiar, the fakers would ask one another, "Who gives a shit?"

Certainly it never occurred to me that my buddy Duke would give a shit. When he had learned that Kennedy had caused the parking snafu, Duke had doffed his baseball cap and lowered his eyes. That mournful attitude had to be for the white people so that they'd remember him with bigger tips: he wouldn't feel bad about the death of a white, rich, pretty boy. With me he would be truthful.

While Duke was doing the lot's paperwork, I stuck my hands inside my pocket, brought out all my tips, and dumped the change on the counter. "Think we made more or less because of the shooting?"

Duke looked up from the parking stubs. "You don' 'spect nothin', do ya?"

Even boredom stopped for the two official weeks of mourning. Establishments that knew no holidays, like the pinball arcades on Market Street and the waterfront speakeasies, were closed. The news was the only activity: the assassination was recounted endlessly. I was often told that it was disrespectful to walk on the street. But since the streets were empty, I was able to walk to Fifteenth and Spruce, smoke a joint, and commune with the light.

CYNTHIA OZICK

Rushdie in the Louvre

FROM THE NEW YORKER

SOME MONTHS AGO — it was in Paris, in the Louvre — I saw Salman Rushdie plain. He was sitting in a high-backed chair at the foot of an incalculably long banquet table fitted out with two rows of skinny microphones, each poking upward like a knuckly finger. His hands lay on a dark-red leather portfolio stamped with his name in gilt. A gargantuan crystal chandelier, intricately designed, with multiple glinting pendants, hung from a ceiling painted all over with rosy royal nymphs — a ceiling so remote that the climate up there seemed veiled in haze. Who could measure that princely chamber, whether in meters or in history? And, all around, gold, gold, gold.

The day before, in a flood of other visitors, I had penetrated an even more resplendent hall of the Louvre, the Galerie d'Apollon: a long, spooky corridor encrusted with kingly treasures — ewers and reliquaries of jasper and crystal, porphyry vases, scepters of coronations anciently repudiated, and, forlorn in their powerlessness, the crown jewels. All these hide in the gloom of their glass cases, repelling the gray granules of light that drizzle down from above. The filtered light throws a perpetual dusk over the march of regal portraits that once commanded awe and now, in the half-dark, give out a bitter look of faint inner rot. Here, among its glorious leavings, one can feel the death of absolutism. "I can stand a great deal of gold," Henry James once said; and so could the kings of France, and the Napoleons who succeeded them, all devoted to the caressings and lustings of gold — Midas-like objects of gold, soup bowls and spoons, fretwork and garnishings and pilasters of gold, gold as a kind of contagion or irresistible eruption.

James was enchanted; for him that rash of gold hinted at no disease, whether of self-assertion or exposure to the force of dread. He equated the artist's sovereign power with what he had "inhaled little by little" in the Gallery of Apollo: "an endless golden riot and relief, figured and flourished in perpetual revolution, breaking into great high-hung circles and symmetries of squandered picture, opening into deep outward embrasures" — a glory that signified for him "not only beauty and art and supreme design but history and fame and power." On his deathbed, confused by a stroke, he imagined himself to be Napoleon in the midst of a project of renovating the Louvre: "I call your attention," he dictated to his secretary, "to the precious enclosed transcripts of plans and designs for the decoration of certain apartments of the palaces here, of the Louvre and the Tuileries, which you will find addressed in detail to artists and workmen who are to take them in hand."

James's Napoleonic hallucination of 1916 has been realized almost eight decades later. Artists and workmen *have* taken the Louvre and the Tuileries in hand. There are cranes and sandy excavations — a broad tract of these at the end of the gardens of the Tuileries abutting the Louvre — and then, suddenly, there is the great, living, anti-Ozymandian I. M. Pei Pyramid, swarming with visitors, a peaked postmodernist outcropping of glass and steel in the wide square courtyard of this brilliant old palace: a purposeful visual outrage conceived in amazing wit and admirable utility, flanked by a triplet of smaller pyramids like three echoing laughters. The apartments of the Louvre's Richelieu wing, where Rushdie sat — balding, bearded, in sober coat and tie — have been undergoing reconstruction: until recently, visitors' shoes would leave plaster-powder footprints on the red-carpeted grand stair. But visitors were, anyhow, few during the renovation, when the Richelieu was closed to the public. On the day Rushdie came, the entire Louvre was closed, and the Richelieu wing was effectively sealed off by a formidable phalanx of security men in black outfits, with black guns at their hips. Rushdie's arrival was muted, unnoticed: out of the blue, he was there, unobtrusive yet somehow enthroned — ennobled — by the ongoing crisis of terror that is his visible nimbus.

He was attending a seminar of the Académie Universelle des Cultures, the brainchild of President François Mitterrand. The

academy's president, appointed by Mitterrand, is Elie Wiesel, recipient of the Nobel Peace Prize, and there are nine other Nobel-
winning members, among them Wole Soyinka, of Nigeria (in literature), and the Americans Joshua Lederberg (in medicine and
physiology) and Toni Morrison (the 1993 laureate in literature).
The official meeting place of this newborn organization is in the
Richelieu apartments. Unlike the twilight majesties of the Gallery
of Apollo, the academy's space is brightly warmed in sun from
immense windows. Peering out, one sees a bit of courtyard but
mainly the long line of an encircling balcony, ranged with mammoth stone figures in plumed Monte Cristo headgear and buckled
eighteenth-century pumps, the very soles of which seem mountainously tall. It is as if hallucinations could inhabit even daylight. A
low door — low in relation to the ceiling — opens into what might
pass for a giantess's pantry: a series of closets white with plaster
dust and smelling of an unfinished moistness, and then a sort of
gangway leading to just installed toilets. On the day Rushdie came,
it was up to an armed guard to decide whether or not to let one
through to the plumbing.

The other end of this vast sanctum is a threshold to salon after
palatial salon, magnificence serving as vestibule to still more magnificence, everything freshly gilded everywhere: the Napoleonic
dream reimagined for the close of a century that has given new
and sinister vitality to the meaning of absolutism. The gas chambers and the ovens; the Gulag; and, finally, the terror that invents
car bombs, airplane hijackings, ideological stabbings of civilians at
bus stops, the murder of ambassadors and Olympic athletes and
babies in their cribs, the blowing up of an embassy in Buenos Aires,
the World Trade Center in New York, the financial district of
London, a restaurant in Paris, a synagogue in Istanbul. Under the
shadow of this decades-long record, the setting of a price on a
novelist's head is hardly a culmination, though it is surely, in an
era of imaginative atrocity, a new wrinkle, a kind of hallucination
in itself. Hallucination, after all, is make-believe taken literally:
dream assessed as fact.

Long before he dreamed himself the imperial Napoleon ordering the rehabilitation of the Louvre, Henry James had a dream of
limitless terror. The dream was of the Gallery of Apollo, but now
those inhalations of absolutism were wholly altered: what had been

seen as the potency of fame and the absolute rule of beauty and art turned away its sublime face to reveal absolutism's underside, a thing uncompromisingly deadly, brutal, irrational. Artist and dreamer, James in his nightmare is being pursued down the length of the Galerie d'Apollon by an "appalling" shape intent on murdering him. (Note the dreamer's pun: Apollo, appalling. Supremacy transformed into horror.) A door is shut against the powerful assassin; the assassin — "the awful agent, creature or presence, whatever he was" — presses back. And then, all at once, in a burst of opposing power, the dreamer defends himself: "Routed, dismayed, the tables turned upon him by my so surpassing him for straight aggression and dire intention, my visitant was already but a diminished spot in the long perspective, the tremendous, glorious hall . . . over the far-gleaming floor of which, cleared for the occasion of its great line of priceless *vitrines* down the middle, he sped for *his* life, while a great storm of thunder and lightning played through the deep embrasures of high windows on the right."

Not far from the Gallery of Apollo, the Richelieu apartments of the Louvre do not quake with the storm of nightmare, but the members of the academy, discreet, courtly, inhale the appalling breath of the pursuer. The image of routing is dim: what weapon is there against a hidden assassin who may strike a moment from now, or tomorrow, or the day after? The arsenal of intellect — what we mean by the principles or intuitions of culture — is helpless before such willed, wild atrocity: anybody here might overnight become Rushdie. The academy's president, a survivor of Auschwitz, has already *been* Rushdie — a human being pitilessly hunted as prey. No one cranes down the endless table, with its line of microphones, to gape at this new human prey; yet Rushdie's quiet reality is electrifying, a prodigy in itself. It is his first appearance at a meeting since his unanimous election to the academy. His arrival was hinted at, elusively, by President Wiesel the evening before, but would the man who is hunted and stalked actually show up? His plain humanity is a marvel — a fellow sitting in a chair, loosening his tie, taking off his jacket as the afternoon warms. He is no metaphor, no legend, no symbol. His fame, once merely novelist's fame, is now the fame of terror. A writer has been transmuted into a pharaoh, wrapped in hiddenness, mummified in life. It happens that Rushdie nowadays looks more scribbler than pharaoh: a certain scruffiness of falling-out hair and indecisive beard, the telltale fleshiness of the sedentary penman; the recognizable mien of someone who hates wearing a tie. How different from that slender princeling who at the Forty-eighth International PEN Congress, in New York in 1986, stood up to speechify in the aisle! What we saw then was a singularly beautiful young man got up in a bright Indian (or perhaps pseudo-Indian) tunic, black-haired, black-eyed, as ravishing in outline as some gilt Persian miniature. I no longer recollect what he said on that occasion, though I retain something of his point of view: rigidly "Third World," loyally "progressive." A document protesting Middle Eastern terrorism had been circulating through that body for some days; Rushdie did not append his name to it.

The bristling protection that surrounds him now is an offense, an enormity: professional, determined, watchful, admitting no breach; above all, conducted on a kingly scale. There is a twist of corruption — of civilization undone — in Rushdie's necessary retinue, a retinue that shocks: all these sentries, these waiting police cars in the courtyard, dedicated to the preservation of a single human life. Or one could easily, and more justly, claim the opposite: that it is civilization's high humane standard, a society's concrete and routine glory, that so much sheltering force should be dedicated to the protection of one man under threat. But the first response is the sharper one: the sensation of recoil from the stealthily meandering armed men in black — the armed men lurking on the way to the toilet, the squad of armed men churning in this or that passageway or bunched oddly against a wall. When, at the beginning of the year, President Mitterrand came for the official inauguration of the Académie Universelle des Cultures, the crush of television cameras, reporters, ambassadors, distinguished oglers, assorted intellectuals, and the charmed hoopla of fervent French *gloire* brought in the wake of the president's footsteps a troop of security men drumming over the Louvre's burnished floors, but there was nothing grim in that train. It signified honor and festivity. Monarchs and presidents may have to live like targets in danger of being detonated; for their guests at a celebration, though, that busy retinue, however fearsomely occupied, registers as innocently as a march of bridesmaids. Rushdie, by contrast, is tailed by a reminder of death. Whoever is in a room with him, no matter how secured against intruders, remembers that the would-be assassin is on the alert for opportunity, whether for greed or for God.

Rushdie's so-called blasphemy is the fabrication of literalists whose piety can be respected but whose literalism assumes what may not be assumed: that the Creator of the Universe can be diminished by any human agency, that the sacred is susceptible of human soiling. How can a novel blaspheme? How can a work of art (which can also mean a work of dream, play, and irony) blaspheme? Islam, like Judaism, is not an iconic creed (both are famously the opposite), but the philosophers of even such iconic religious expressions as medieval Christianity and classical Hinduism do not locate the divine literally in paint or carving, and know that art, while it may for some kindle reverence, cannot be a medium for the soiling of the sacred. Art cannot blaspheme, because it is not in the power of humankind to demean or besmirch the divine. Can a man's book tarnish God? "Where wast thou when I laid the foundations of the earth?" the Lord rebukes Job. "Knowest thou the ordinances of heaven? canst thou set the dominion thereof in the earth? . . . Who hath put wisdom in the inward parts? or who hath given understanding to the heart?" After which, Job is chastened enough to "lay mine hand upon my mouth."

Men who were not there when the foundations of the earth were laid nevertheless lay their hands on a novelist's mouth. One of Rushdie's translators, the Japanese Hitoshi Igarashi, has been murdered; another, the Italian Ettore Capriolo, was seriously wounded. William Nygaard, Rushdie's Norwegian publisher, shot near Oslo, survived; apparently, an additional motive for the attack was Norway's part in facilitating the Arafat-Rabin peace initiative. The American publishers of the paperback *Satanic Verses* hide behind an anonymous "consortium." And meanwhile Rushdie walks or rides nowhere without his train of guards. After lunching in a dining room of the Pyramid, the other members of the academy stroll the few yards across the Louvre's inner court to return to the Richelieu for the afternoon plenary; but Rushdie, emerging alone from the Pyramid like the pharaonic figure he has been made into, is invisibly placed, alone, in a limousine that moves with glacial languor from one part of the courtyard to the other, accompanied by security men slowly pacing beside it and all around it. Rushdie is the prisoner both of his protectors and of his accusers.

In the eyes of his accusers, his very existence is a blasphemy to be undone and a blemish to be annihilated. Barricaded day and night against fanatic absolutists who look for a chance to kill, who despise reason and discourse, repudiate compromise, and reject amelioration, he has become, in his own person, a little Israel — or, rather, Israel as it felt its circumstances until just recently, before the Arafat-Rabin peace accord. This is something that, in all logic, has cried out to be said aloud ever since the *fatwa* was first promulgated; but Rushdie's defenders, by and large, have not said it — some because they feared to exacerbate his situation (but how could it have been worsened?), some because they have themselves been among Israel's fiercest ideological opponents. But one fact is incontrovertible: for the mullahs of Iran, who oppose both recognition and peace, Rushdie and the Jews of Israel are to be granted the same doom. What can be deduced from this ugly confluence is, it seems to me, also incontrovertible: morally and practically, there is no way to distinguish between the terrorist whose "cause" is pronounced "just" (and whose assaults on civilians are euphemized as political or religious resistance) and the terrorist who seeks to carry out the mullahs' *fatwa* against Rushdie (a call to assassination euphemized as religious duty). One cannot in the past have reasonably exculpated Arafat's Al-Fatah for its longstanding program of bloodshed — not yet wholly suppressed — directed against both Jews and Arabs (the latter for what is termed "collaboration") while at the same time defending Rushdie and deploring his plight. And in one way, after all, Rushdie is better off than women knifed on street corners or bus passengers shot to death: he is at every moment under the surveillance of his security team. On the other hand, individual civilians on their errands, exposed to the brutal lottery of ambush, have their lucky and unlucky days; Rushdie, no longer a civilian, drafted into the unwilling army of victimhood, has drawn the targeted ticket. All his days are unlucky.

Still, like James in the Gallery of Apollo, today in the Louvre Rushdie means to turn the tables. Why link Henry James and Salman Rushdie? They are separated by a century. They were born continents apart. One is a vast and completed library; the other, his ultimate stature unfathomable, is in the middle of the way. Moreover (as for the issue of terror), what threatens Rushdie has a name, *fatwa,* and a habitation, Iran, and all those other places and men and women driven by the mullahs' imaginings of God's imperatives. Whereas what threatened James was no more than his own imagination, an extrusion of the psyche's secrets, nothing enacted in the world of real and ferocious event. What threatened James was a fable of his own making. But a dream, gossamer and ephemeral though it may be, is like a genius loci, which can send out exhalations with the force of ciphers or glyphs that can be decoded or read across centuries. (Is it the Louvre itself that will speak up for Rushdie? Wait and see.) There is, besides, an arresting nexus of situation and temperament. Like James, Rushdie left the country of his birth for England: each sought, and won, a literary London life. Each kept a backward-glancing eye on his native society. As James never abandoned interest, inquisitiveness, sympathy, and the sometimes adversarial passions of kinship with regard to America, so Rushdie retains a familial, historical, and scholarly connection to Islam, warmed by kinship, interest, sympathy. Both men were charged with apostasy: James because near the end of his life, partly out of gratitude to Britain, he gave up his American citizenship; Rushdie more savagely, on account of having written a fable. Both are in thrall to fable; both have an instinct for the intercultural tale of migration, what James called "the international theme." Both are beguiled by notions of assimilation and strangeness, of native and newcomer.

There is more. Rushdie, like James, is secular, history-minded, skeptical, impatient with zealotry. James's father, though harmless enough, was a man metaphysically besotted, a true believer, dogmatically sunk in Swedenborgian fogs. Having been reared in an atmosphere of private fanaticism, James repudiated its public expression wherever he encountered it. He had nothing but contempt for the accusers of Dreyfus. He followed the case day by day. "I sit . . . and read *l'Affaire Dreyfus.* What a bottomless and sinister *affaire* and in what a strange mill it is grinding. . . . I eat and drink, I sleep and dream Dreyfus." He did better than that. He wrote to Zola to congratulate him on the publication of *J'Accuse* — "one of the most courageous things ever done" — for which Zola was brought to trial and convicted. In James's view, if Zola had not fled from his sentencing, "he would have been *torn limb from limb* by the howling mob in the street."

Bottomless and sinister; apostasy and treason; the howling mob in the street. It is all familiar and instantly contemporary. The determination of the anti-Dreyfusards in France, and their fellow-travelers all over Europe, to destroy an innocent and consummately patriotic Frenchman by conspiracy and forgery, and especially by the incitement of mobs, reminds one that the concept of *fatwa* is not held exclusively by mullahs. And Rushdie, too, has been conspired against by a kind of forgery: having written a fable, he is represented as having issued a curse; he is charged with betraying Islam. Dreyfus was charged with betraying France. Millions were avid to believe it, until his champion Zola turned the tables on the persecutors.

It is now clearer than ever that Rushdie is resolved to become his own champion. Though ringed always by his ferocious security apparatus, he ventures more and more into the hot zone of political suasion. His meeting at the White House last month with President Clinton constitutes, for Rushdie, the hottest — the most influential — zone of all. The mullahs, whose denunciations followed immediately, hardly disagree, and the White House visit triggered instant State Department warnings to Americans overseas about possible retaliation. No one forgets the murder of that translator; as the anonymity of Rushdie's paperback publishers shows, it is never easy for others to speak up for him. And among writers' organizations Rushdie's cause was until only recently reduced to a half-yawning obligatory gesture: after a time, even a celebrated crisis grows humdrum and loses the glamour that writers notoriously enjoy. Wole Soyinka points out that standing up for Rushdie is currently out of fashion and looked down on among certain multicultural academics: it is considered an intellectual offense against the mores and sensibilities of another culture — very much in the spirit of the recent World Conference on Human Rights in Vienna, where the idea of the universalism of human rights initially was resisted by some countries either as prejudicial to national sovereignty or else as an objectionable parochial contrivance being foisted on societies that are satisfied with their own standards and values. The danger in defending Rushdie's right to exist is no longer the simple business of turning oneself into one more lightning rod to attract the assassins. Nowadays, standing up for Rushdie brings another sort of risk: it places one among the stereotypes and the "Orientalists," as they are sometimes called, who are accused of denigrating whole peoples. To stand up for Rushdie is to display a colonialist mentality. A man's right to exist is mired in the politics of anticolonialism — and never mind the irony of this, given Rushdie's origins as a Muslim born in India.

Though Iran responded to Rushdie's White House appearance by labeling the president "the most hated man before all the Muslims of the world," and though the majority of other Muslim governments have shown official indifference to Rushdie's situation, not all Muslims have been silent, even in the face of personal endangerment. Remarkably, France this year saw the publication of *For Rushdie,* a volume of poems and essays protesting the *fatwa,* by a hundred Muslim and Arab writers and intellectuals, including the Egyptian Nobel winner Naguib Mahfouz. And in Bangladesh the novelist Taslima Nasrin, herself lately condemned to death as a "blasphemer" in a *fatwa* issued by the fundamentalist Council of Soldiers of Islam, continues to speak out for the emancipation of women, for tolerance, and for secular freedom. "Without freedom," one of the contributors to *For Rushdie* wrote, "there is no creation, no life, no beauty."

In the academy's afternoon plenary session, André Miquel, the president of the Assembly of Professors of the Collège de France and a distinguished specialist in Arabic literature, proposes a resolution condemning the systematic assassination of Algerian intellectuals by fundamentalist extremists. The language of the resolution is plain: "A terrible thing is happening in Algeria — people are being killed simply because they think." This action comes under the heading of Intervention, the academy's chosen topic for its first year of life — a philosophic theme, but spurred on by the urgencies of Bosnia and Somalia. (Marc Kravetz, of the French newspaper *Libération,* and a consultant to this session, counts forty separate conflicts ongoing in the world. How many are cause for intervention, and by whom, and for whom?) Rushdie, who earlier quietly remarked that he hoped "to speak of something besides myself," keeps to his word. Without directly offering himself in illustration, he argues against "the specific thrust of the motion," and suggests that the particular case of Algeria is "typical, part of a larger phenomenon, not just an isolated thing" — that "there is a concentrated program to oppress intellectuals in many countries." Yashar Kemal, a Turkish writer, mentions the killings in southern Turkey by Hezbollah, the Party of God, and the murder of Turkish intellectuals "fighting for lay principles." The resolution is altered. "In many countries, and recently in Algeria," it now begins, "a terrible thing is happening." Someone raises a question of credibility: Is it appropriate for an academy as newly formed as this one to be sending out resolutions? Don't we first have to settle down a little, and acquire a recognizable character? To which Rushdie replies, "We should issue motions even if the academy is newborn. *We* are not newborn."

Luc Ferry, a professor of philosophy at the University of Caen, and another consultant to the plenary, describes Muslim societies, insofar as they fail to separate religion from matters like human rights, as "premodern." Rushdie, scribbling away as Ferry develops this idea, disputes the term. Moral fundamentalism, Rushdie argues, is not premodern but postmodern — in short, decidedly contemporary. Secular ideals, though they may be taken for granted in Europe, are seriously under threat elsewhere. In Saudi Arabia, for instance, modernity has been declared to be against religion, and its practitioners have been denounced as heretical. The concept of human rights is regarded by fundamentalists as an expression of modernity, and is rejected and despised. Moreover, not only are there conflicts between opposing cultures — between, say, fundamentalism and the secularizing West — but the same kind of conflict can occur *within* a culture, and on its own ground. Finally, if intervention means that you set out from home to supply assistance to another people, then what of terror, which leaves its place of origin to seek you out and destroy you in your own country? "Terror," Rushdie finishes, "is a reverse form of intervention."

He had, as he promised, not spoken of himself or of his condition. Though composed and eloquent, he had not spoken much at all. When he was neither speaking nor writing, he sat very still, as immobile as a Buddha statue. One got the impression (but impressions can violate) that he had learned to be still; that he had taught himself to be *that* still. He was, in fact, a magnet of stillness: it was as if that great splendid room were shrinking to a single point of awareness — Rushdie sitting there in his shirt-sleeves.

Come back now to Henry James, and the glyphs he has left behind. In another part of the Louvre on this day, past turnings of corridors, is the darkened Gallery of Apollo, empty but for its portraits and carvings and accretions of gold — as deserted as it was in James's hot imagining, when the appalling pursuer scrabbled after him over those polished floors. The ghosts of the Louvre are many — kings, cardinals, emperors. Add to these the generations of museumgoers; remember also that Emerson walked here when America itself was almost new — Emerson, whose mind James once described as "a ripe unconsciousness of evil." In this fanciful place, it is today not possible to escape the fullest, ripest consciousness of evil; Rushdie's hunted presence draws it out. He is poet, fabulist, ironist; he is the one they want to kill because his intelligence is at play. But these ancient galleries, these tremendous, glorious halls, reverberate with a memory of the tables being turned, the pursuer diminished and in flight. Dream? Hallucination? Rushdie in Paris calls up that old nightmare of panic in the Louvre, and how the stalker was driven to retreat. And Paris itself calls up Dreyfus, who was no dream, and the heroic Zola, who routed evil with reason. Still, there is a difference. The terror of our time is stone-deaf to reason, and it is not enough for the Dreyfus of our time to suffer being Dreyfus. Against all the odds, he must take on being Zola, too.

LAUREN SLATER

Striptease

FROM NEW LETTERS

A PERSONALITY DISORDER is one of the more troubling diagnoses a mental health clinician can give to someone seeking relief from suffering, because unlike a neurosis, viewed as a set of curable symptoms, or a psychosis, increasingly believed to be the result of a trigger-happy brain in need of mere medication, the personality disordered individual is seen as close to hopeless, beyond the reach of either drugs or healing dialogue. The man or woman with such a diagnosis is thought of as a kind of blighted being, the udder of a cow on the belly of a gazelle, flippers on the side of a skunk. What can you do with this mishmash except try to soothe its confused cries?

George came to our clinic in early autumn and was diagnosed by the intake worker with an antisocial personality disorder — in short, a sociopath, a deviant — whom I, a newcomer to the field of psychology, was now assigned to work with in therapy for an undefined period of time. He looked almost ridiculously tough, sitting in a sleeveless leather vest in the clinic's lobby, hair scrunched back in a ponytail, a cigarette dangling from his mouth. Tattoos coiled over his arms, bloomed on his bare chest.

Immediately I felt awkward in his presence. Perhaps I was experiencing some throwback to my high-school days, when I longed to be liked by the cool and vicious popular kids who stared at the world slant-eyed and wagged their Winstons in the teachers' faces. Around such a crowd I have always felt stout and dumpy, the dust of my ancestors' Jewish shtetl still settled on my skin. The day I met George I was wearing my working garb, a sundress, a pair of falling-apart flats, legs stubbly from hair I'd only half shaved, and perhaps a swatch of slip showing from beneath my hem.

As a therapist, I think I should be beyond these silly social embarrassments. I think I should at least be beyond my own bodily insecurities enough to throw my full attention into the client's waiting lap, but I am not. Around George I am not, and the sense of shame he evokes in me, to this day, is part of our treatment story together.

My office at the time was windowless and so small we had to sit with our knees near brushing. I got ready to ask my usual orienting questions. Especially with a client like George, who makes rise in me my own archaic discomforts, these questions are like life rafts I throw myself, bright verbal floats I can cling to.

"Age?" I asked.

Instead of answering me, George gave a dramatic sigh. "Whew," he said, "have I been waiting for this day. I've seen six of you guys and so far no one's worked out. I need a doc who can really push me. I need to be challenged."

In my mind then I pictured a boxing ring, a hefty human in each corner, thick leather mitts poised for the punch.

"Challenged?" I asked. "Like how?"

"I've got my problems," George said, "and I can admit to them. The other six I went to just sat there and stared at me. I want someone who will give me feedback, make me see things in a new way."

"So what are these problems?"

George sat back, ran one hand over a large tattoo on his bicep. "Masturbation," he said gravely. "I can't stop."

"Can't —"

"Nope! Seven, eight, nine times a day. I have a strong drive." He shook his head in wonder. He looked proud, like a little boy opening a toy chest to show his speckled marbles and magnificent seven-sailed ship. Now he pulled a list out of his pocket and began to read. "Masturbation, pornography, aggression, defensiveness, pride, control. These are my character defects. Take porn. I love it, but the truth is I'd rather do it with a videotape than with my girlfriend Joanne. We have huge beefs, huge," George said. "My anger is just —" He paused. "Like I think I could kill her. I've killed a few people before so I wouldn't put it past me." George was staring straight at me when he said this, testing me for my reaction.

"So why do you think you prefer porn to people?" I said, keeping my voice even despite the fact that I suddenly felt like fleeing.

"Don't get me wrong," George said. "I like Joanne. She's a real smoker. But I'll be honest, a picture's just a lot easier. No one you gotta talk to. No one to perform for or try to please. Just a completely quiet and beautiful bod."

I thought of my own "bod" then and felt my breasts beneath my dress burn with shame.

For the rest of that session I gathered background information. George is thirty-five years old, has lived seven of those years on the street, drugging, knife fighting, and stealing. During those years he slept beneath fire escapes and went in and out of prisons, where the beds were warmer, the dope cheaper. He has been clean now for a half-decade, a really remarkable achievement, which he attributes to his spirituality, a weird blend of mysticism and heavy metal. In his apartment, where he lived with Joanne, he has two special cupboards side by side. In one of them he keeps his incense and tarot cards, his books on palm reading; in the other he stores his collection of sadomasochistic videos and magazines. Oddly, this second cupboard is lined with floral contact paper left by a previous tenant.

They bring him satisfaction, these videos. A lot goes on for him each day. Joanne is, as he said, a beautiful woman, but she is also unpredictable and self-absorbed, a series of seismic cycles he cannot control. "Modern woman," he says, shaking his head. He tells me he is from the old school, expects his girl to cook and clean, to have fish on the table by six each night, expects dustless halls and sex where her moans are synchronized to his orgasms. When Joanne lets him down in any of these areas, he gets mad, really red-faced furious, so that he hauls her up against the wall, wallops her across the face; he feels so much sheer and irrational hate that he has to retreat to his room to watch his videos; they soothe him, images of female flesh cut into, female flesh controlled, the man pumping with pride above her.

Just by writing these words I can feel George's anger, his gut lust to control. It is real to me, this hate of the female form. In our first several sessions I tried to find the origins of his hate. For instance, George's father, a stonemason, dead now for ten years. He went to work at six in the morning, returned after eight each night, his face similar to the substances he worked with, features descending like ledges to a jutting chin nicked with a dimple. He would have been a handsome man except his expression was so stern and his breath smelled; when he was drunk, George imagined his father's breath took on the color of the liquor he swallowed, so he exhaled yellow on whiskey nights, neon green on Midora.

His father beat him, but the beatings were not as bad as the humiliation that went along with them. He remembers the strap, the hands that were like hatchets, but the intensity of his tale lies for me in this image: a small boy pressed against a refrigerator, white as a nuptial bedsheet, the man pressing against him, shouting at him; George could feel his father's groin, hot and hard, right in the nook between his thighs. He started to think of himself as having a nook there, a gross, gaping place. One day, when he was outside playing, he had a terrible fantasy. George was twelve years old now; he imagined his body was a girl's. In his mind he took off his buttocks and put them on his flat chest, making breasts. Then he plucked off his penis and, peeling his mouth from his face, carefully placed it between his legs, tweaking the tongue so the red tip lapped over the lips. He could feel his father close by him, possibly right behind him, watching this and getting aroused. George was disgusted, horrified. A sheen of sweat broke out on his forehead. Soon afterward he learned to fight, started to lift weights, running from the softness that is the requisite for all rapes.

I had, at first, a hard time dealing with George because he offended me. I understood his pornography obsession as a deflection of his own anxieties. So he wouldn't have to feel his fear, his memories of helplessness, he tried to control women. He wanted to whittle my sex, and therefore me, down into a tiny teacup he could lift to his suddenly powerful lips and sip. Now understand, I am a woman who has spent much time aiming to please men. I am a woman who, in her adolescent days, denied herself food or threw it all up so I could fit into the airless image this man in my office was both struggling to possess and shed at the same time. I remember the smell of myself as an anorexic, a frail dry odor like scorched grass, my limbs coated with hair. Because of these memories, it was impossible for me to like George, but I did feel deeply for him. After all, hadn't I once striven for his same goals, to control the random, fleshy facets of female life, to eradicate the weak part of the self who hurts and bleeds and feeds? In a sense we were both murderers, and we were both crying out from our crimes.

During the first few weeks of our therapy together I began to feel the old shame about my body returning more strongly than it had in a while. Although George said he wanted help to overcome his pornography obsession (he was sometimes driven to watch five, six films a night), and to learn to understand and diffuse his rages, he used his sessions to vent about Joanne's latest transgressions and from there he would segue into paeans about "the perfect pussy," its size and smell. After a day during which I'd seen George had ended, I would go home and feel my flesh more heavily than ever. I often felt like weeping. And it was during this time I noticed small black pubes growing up around my nipples. On the one hand, I wanted to pluck them out. On the other hand, I wanted them to grow, lush like the marshweed that springs up in swamps.

My prescription was for George to learn, somehow, that being soft does not mean being molested or murdered, necessarily. And also to learn that softness is not only a requisite for rape but also the texture of soil and sheets and the tender, almost melting skin that covers the penis. To that end, I thought he should explore his wounds and weaknesses and thereby gain the knowledge that feeling them now, in a safe place, would not bring the humiliation he feared but the enriched humanity he claimed he wanted. He would have none of it, of course. While he came to therapy stating he ached for change, he remained, in his actions, dedicated to defensiveness. He all but brought rifles to our sessions. He ranted, swore, swung the verbal muzzle left, now right; his neck was almost beautiful, strung with gut, with a trigger moving in his throat.

He told me a story that bowled me over. We had been going at it for about two months.

The woods of his childhood home divided his family's house from Teddy Swayez's, a classmate who lived through several stands of pines. George was nine years old, and that day, Teddy had promised him the use of his new red Tonka toy truck if only George would come over and play.

But when he got there, Teddy went back on his part of the

bargain. The truck, nope, was not to be shared. George had walked all this way, had stumbled over tree roots, had opened himself to hope, only to find he was fooled.

He felt a curious, sick stirring in his stomach and between his legs as he watched that Swayez kid totally ignoring him, moving the truck up and down the pile, treaded tires leaving small slashes and scars in the sand.

So he went home, took his father's knife, some rope from the cellar, and made a gallows in the woods, using branches as a platform. "Boy, have I got the coolest thing to show you," George said to Teddy. "You gotta come."

And then, when they were there, George said, "Look up." It was floating against the sky, the noose, very bright in the sunlight.

"Climb," George said, using the knife to persuade. He remembers this moment as being very fine, clearly etched, shadows cool as corpses on the ground, a cocoon in the niche of a tree, the glaze of snot on Teddy's blubbering lip. He used the blade on the kid's soft skin and had a sudden, jarring image of his mother in the kitchen in the morning, wearing an apron and slicing through a warm bar of butter.

Teddy was up there; George positioned his head in place, kicked away the sticks, so all of a sudden Teddy swung, neck bunched in the noose . . .

I was leaning forward in my seat. I thought I might throw up. "Oh Jesus," I said, "what happened?"

George snorted, sucked back some mucus into his throat. "The rope broke," he said. "I knew it would. It was already ragged as hell. I just wanted to scare him because I wouldn't be had. I *can't* be had; you see what I mean?"

I didn't say anything.

"You see what I mean?" he shouted, shaking his head in agitation.

"Yes, yes, I see what you mean," I said quickly. "It's horrible for you to have to endure any kind of humiliation or helplessness. The only way you know how to deal is by getting the person back even worse."

"That's the only way I know," George agreed. "Otherwise I feel like I'm just a doormat." He took an angry drag off his cigarette and then crushed it out in the ashtray, which was littered with the smushed remains of all George's butts.

"But do you think everyone in the whole world wants to treat you as a doormat? Was Teddy Swayez really trying to humiliate you, or was he just possibly feeling selfish at the moment you arrived? I mean, is everyone in the whole world just waiting for their chance to take advantage of George, abuse George in some way?"

"Absolutely," George said. "I know it."

"God. It must be tiring having to think that. You can never really let down your guard. Have you ever cried in front of someone to show that you're scared, upset?"

George didn't say anything. For a moment I thought he looked sad. I had the urge to reach over, take him by his uptight shoulders, and shake him until I felt his muscles turn sap-soft and sweet, feel the rusty joints and junctures of his body loosen and liquid slip through.

A long silence settled between us; we were a cut cord, a swarm of static.

"George," I said, trying again, "as a kid, feeling anything but vengeful violence was dangerous, because your dad really did abuse you. But do you have to turn the whole world into him now? What would happen if, at this very moment, right here, you let me know what you're feeling? Try."

Silence.

"What's going on, George? My hunch is you won't be diminished by showing yourself, but you'll actually be a lot 'bigger' for allowing yourself to feel more."

"Oh really?" George said. His tone sounded both subtly sarcastic and curious at the same time.

"Why is it unsafe to feel anything but defensiveness or violence in this office? Do you think I'm going to take advantage of you?"

Immediately I realized I'd made a blunder by allowing him the opportunity to sexualize our interaction.

"*You*, take advantage of me? Isn't that supposed to be the other way around?" He leaned back in his chair, lit another cigarette. I saw the smoke slide from his mouth, felt it wrap around me in a blue and gauzy cloud, decking me in the moving material of a see-through dress.

Mistrust is the fuel for so much mental pain, so many mental disorders. I am not here talking about the suspicions we sometimes have of one another, the distant but lurking sense that perhaps our lover lies to us, our best friend whispers behind our back. I am talking about a belief that betrayal inundates the atoms of the universe, is so woven into the workings of the world that every step is treacherous, and below the rich mud lies a mine.

George believed that the bodies outside him were missiles poised and poisonous. His aggressive slit-eyed stance is a typically male phenomenon. My eating disorder, the obsessive desire to be thin thin thin and perfectly poisonously poised, is typically a female phenomenon. But their shared themes must not go unnoticed if the sexes are ever to learn real compassion for one another. George and I were both victims of our culture's fear of the feminine, unable to lay down our system of weapons and spread our legs open to life because we learned that in this posture we will be shamed, not invigorated. We did not know how to trust what we could not dominate. In treating George, I came to remember with eerie clarity the years and years of my own hostile dieting — I am forcing myself to run ten miles under a broiling summer sun; I am climbing the sixty stories of my father's apartment building, footsteps slapping echoes in the clammy concrete stairwell. I believed my body was my enemy, every cell, unless vigilantly starved and stripped by exercise, eager to add layer upon layer of crude fat.

The culture that makes us afraid of the fat, the floppy, the soft and sap-sweet is the culture that kills us. And the recovering anorexic is not only in a particularly good position to articulate these truths, she is also, ironically, in a particularly good position, vis-à-vis therapy, to treat the misogynist male. She understands perhaps better than anyone the urge to whip and dominate, discipline and even delete the female form. I understand. I made my body a whitened bone, a pale blade. Like any real man, for years I lived with my fist and not with my flesh. I was hungry but could not risk the softness of surrender. I dreamt of letting down my guard, sitting at a table on which silver dishes steamed, and ingesting colors. Orange carrots, the soft wombs of tomatoes, the tangy dirt of chocolate cake. But I couldn't dare, couldn't trust enough to let myself go. My head was empty except for the willpower that drove me on, and the fear that I would fall through into life.

These are the memories that came to mind when I looked at George, rigid in his chair, his face set against the seepage of any emotion that wasn't cruel or lewd, his skin so tattooed I couldn't have found a plain limb to touch if I had wanted to. He told me about forcing himself to rise before dawn each morning, working out two hours a day, jogging barefoot in the snow. He told me he made his girlfriend wear a "pussy ring," a tight gold band around her swelling sex. I nodded, yes, having done the same to myself.

You could call my response countertransference. I call it building a bridge.

Of frayed rope and cracked sticks, a rickety bridge no doubt. But nevertheless, I did not feel we were strangers, only estranged. Ours was a lonely therapy. The more deeply I went into it with him, the more difficult he became. Except for the brief stories he had told me early on about his father's beatings, he absolutely refused to make himself vulnerable to me. Our therapy started to evolve so that I played a mostly silent role, while he went on and on — endlessly, it seemed — about Joanne's anatomy, her "tight little box," the "six-hour plow" (I got sore just thinking about that), her sagless "bags" with the nipple always hard in his hand. He spoke of split beavers and sucking dick *ad nauseam*.

"What about me?" I wanted to say to him. "Does it occur to you that I am a woman here, that you just might be *offending* me?" And beneath that another, smaller voice was crying, "What about me; am I not also attractive; do I not measure up to your standards; why not?"

I began to realize our sessions were a lot like porn, in which I, the silent subject, absorbed his fantasies and, in my featurelessness, reflected them back to him so that we both remained trapped in unalterable images of bondage. George let me know clearly what my role in our relationship was, by shifting impatiently whenever I spoke, by the quick brushing motions he made with his hands as though to sweep away my words, by interrupting me and then exploding in a tyrannical temper if I asserted my right to finish my own sentence.

"Quiet," he once roared at me, and I, like a little girl, sank back down in my seat and felt darkness grow up around me. At other times, I imagined myself in sequins, my crotch sprayed silver as I, nude, gyrated to the beat of his voice.

"I wonder if you ever think," I finally burst out to him one day, trying to chase the images of leopard skins and loincloths from my head as he spoke, "that I might be uncomfortable with your sexual talk, with the, uh, kinds of expressions you use."

"But you're a shrink," George said to me. "That's what you're here for, to listen to my expressions. That's your whole job."

"First of all," I said, "my whole job is not simply to sit and listen, but to go with you, as your coworker, codiscoverer, into the issues that make your life difficult, so we can *together* work them out. And second of all" (I felt a snarl creep into my voice), "not even in my office am I just a shrink. I am also a woman and the way you talk about my gender disgusts me." I wanted to reach out and slap him, see my palm, a tiny but powerful print on his white cheek.

"I wouldn't ever talk to a woman I was trying to make it with like that. But you're not supposed to —"

"Supposed to what?"

George looked uncomfortable. "Hallefuckinlujah," I thought. I imagined I saw the colors on his tattoo start to blur and bleed.

"Supposed to mind," he said.

"Surprise," I said. "I mind." Tapping the side of my head. "I have a mind."

George looked up at me, his expression confused. My face felt all red. For one moment then our masks dropped away. The stagnant stereotypes shifted, crumbled. I could tell by the way George was looking at me that he was, for maybe the first time, considering me not as a function but as a feeling. I smiled at him.

He nodded, hello.

Shortly after this encounter George left the state for six weeks to do a series of carpentry jobs in Arizona. During the time he was away I found myself thinking of him in the desert, in the small Indian towns with clumps of blowing tumbleweed. Was he lonely? Lost? I thought of him running his hands over the contours of rock, feeling within it the craggy father face; in my imagination he was there, with wood, long blond planks of it which, as he held them, turned to hanks of soft hair in his hands.

He returned to therapy in late May, deep spring in the North, the rose's red claw beginning to open. It was raining the day we resumed our sessions, and he stepped into my office soaking wet, beaded eyelashes, T-shirt stuck to his chest so the two tiny thorns of his nipples showed. His thick wavy hair was plastered down on a suddenly small skull; his shorts clung to buttocks I, for the first time, recognized as bony.

When I was a child I had a Shih Tzu dog, a high-blown, hairy canine with a fierce temper. I still have a small pale scar on my knee where he once tore out a hunk of my six-year-old skin. The first time my mother gave the dog a bath is etched in my memory as one of the most remarkable metamorphoses I've witnessed in my lifetime. She dunked him, struggling, into a tub of water; and he came up, fluffed hair now wet as a second skin, a thin little animal with the tracings of bone visible beneath his hide. Even his tail, that gorgeous caramel-colored flare of fur, was now no more than a piece of old raveled rope, hanging over a pitifully pink and naked anus.

George shivered in the air-conditioned building and goosebumps, like tiny buds, appeared on all the tattoos. I stared because I had never seen so much spontaneous movement in George's body before, any evidence that he wasn't willing, controlling. Wet George, I thought. I like you.

So it was a moment before I saw his expression. His eyes were hooded with exhaustion, ringed by blue, his face, untouched by the southern sun, too pale. He slumped down in his seat; looked at his lap.

"I was going to call you," he said in a low voice. I had never heard him use that voice before, a raw tone that brought to my mind a sapling branch stripped of its bark, and his voice elicited, for the first time, something gentle and even aching in me.

"What happened?" I asked.

"She left me," George said. He shook his head. "Just like that." He snapped his fingers in the air.

I was torn, surprised. I felt glad for Joanne. I had often worried about her safety with George, especially when he told me stories about shoving her, punching her, once even hauling her toward an open second-story window. I was glad she had finally gathered the courage to strike out on her own — this woman I had never met. But George looked awful.

"I came back from Arizona — the closets are empty, her picture's gone, not even a note. I called her at her parents', and she says it's completely finished. Gonzo. But I'm chasing her, I'm running after her like a goddamn desperate dog." George shook his head in confusion. "Me," he said, "I've never begged a bitch in my life; I can't stop; I'm making a fool of myself, phoning her ten, twenty times a day, bawling in her ear; but she's just wood. It doesn't matter what I do —"

"It doesn't matter what you do," I said. "Tell me more about that."

"I've never not been able to convince someone, to force someone if I needed to, into doing what I wanted. But I've been trying every ploy with this cunt for the past week and I'm —"

"What? You're what?"

"Helpless." His mouth was a bitter line of tension but his eyes were wet.

"I think that's what upsets you the most about Joanne's leaving. That you have no control, that you feel helpless to get her back."

George, to my surprise, nodded in agreement. His own pain had made him flexible, open to vision and suggestion. I also wondered if, having seen me step out of my stereotype in our previous meeting, he now felt freer to step out of his.

"I've never, never felt this way before. I've been stabbed in the neck, but this is way worse. I'm afraid to go home. I'm afraid to be alone. I didn't know I could ever have pain like this. How can it be so bad? *This is not me.*"

"But it is you, only a part of you you've managed, until now, to ignore."

For the first time in six months of treatment I think we really talked. We exchanged. He had opened himself to me with his honest questions. Pain almost always does this, its intensity, like a hot spray, clearing away the dirt of denial. Perhaps this is one reason why, after we cry, we feel cleansed.

During this session, when George asked why and trembled, he brought up a lot of historical material, his relationship with his father, moments of abandonment, and all of this was important, but even more so was the intimacy now building between us, our voices low, our expressions intent, not masked.

"I feel we got something accomplished in this session," George said, "but I'm not sure what or how."

"I think it's that we really connected," I said. "I felt much closer to you in this session than I have before. I know you're really terrified of your openness, or weakness even, because you're afraid of being taken advantage of; but as far as I'm concerned, it's just the opposite. Your willingness to finally talk about your pain lets me see how complicated, and I guess colorful, you really are."

George smiled. "Of course," he said. "I'm no simple Joe Schmo. I'm quite a case, huh?" He looked at me proudly, thumped on his chest.

We laughed a little, and then the hour was up.

The next few weeks brought some changes in George. He found himself facing an emotion he could not defend himself against. No amount of swearing or swaggering could express mourning. The pain of Joanne's leaving so suddenly broke his shield with an intensity neither of us had anticipated, and brought up memories for him, as though, by going into a red wound, he had reached a new layer of his life. I was reminded of being in the Caribbean as a little girl and seeing, after a violent, sobbing storm, a school of dead sharks washed up on the beach, the silver bodies surprisingly lovely, laid out on the sand. George remembered touching his father's face once when the man was sleeping, peddling to a pond in the summer, finding, one winter, a squirrel with something yellow dripping from its mouth, as now something yellow was dripping from his, some courage curdled and soured, some sadness. But to me he was not sour at all. The texture of our sessions altered. In his admission of pain, he was now naked; he had pressed himself against me, and I wanted to celebrate, not violate, this stance.

I was drawn in to George now, and I told him so, told him that for six months I had seen only a posture, and now I was seeing a person, and this person was brave.

"Brave?" George said to me. "I can't believe what a wreck I am. I can't believe that I am falling apart over some bitch. You call that brave?"

"You're a lot braver now than you were before," I said, "when you were too scared to face your own soul. To me," I said, "and these are just my own values, but to me, as a woman, I think of a man as someone who is strong enough to experience himself, not afraid of taking voyages instead of standing stuck in a block of cement."

I think he was a little grateful to me for saying that, for telling him I did find him masculine in the moments he considered his worst.

For the next few weeks George ricocheted between two ways of being. Outside of therapy he was his usual hostile and inappropriate self, fighting with people, threatening Joanne over the phone. But within the office, the combination of his now-surfaced suffering and the deepening level of trust between us made him open. In some moments I think I saw his real face, the flow of emotion across it like wind working on sand. Those days, early summer, the sounds of the city streets drifting up to us — the millions of languages of the modern world, the occasional roar of an airplane in its angle of ascent — we discussed the ancient myths and fairy tales, specifically the voyage of the archetypal hero who must leave his father's structured, cool castle and step into the messy wreckage of woods, the rotting leaves, in order to find a solid and secure authority within himself. It was crucial for George to be able to relate his painful journey to a mythic structure, to see that the rotting leaves of his soul were part of a socially sanctioned male odyssey. And I, well, I grew to love him and love the strength in his slow surrender.

It is August, I am twenty-three years old, I have never met George, I am just out of college. I weigh eighty-eight pounds. The heat of this month is thick as wet angora; the waxy leaves on the trees droop. When I look out my bedroom window I can see tulips; they are the most trusting beings, they with their throats always open, their long gold tongues hanging out. Nothing bad happens to them; the sun doesn't rape them; they don't gag on the rain.

This day is really many months. I watch the world. I watch the natural cycle of things. Cliché as it may be, this is what cures me.

There comes a moment when recovery is religious, when a person says, "All right. I will have faith. I will lay down my sword and shield and see what the world works in me."

It is a dangerous thing for us, we people who grow up suckling the steel nipples of this country's missiles, men who think living in the world is living in a war, women who think their bodies are Molotov cocktails that must be detonated, destroyed, before they are munched up by their own metabolisms. What symbols do we have of safety?

I look away from my bedroom window and go downstairs, out onto the porch. Someone has set a table for me, my sister or an angel I don't know. Sliced strawberries lie like the tongues of maidens on a platter. Wedges of cheese and bread. I put food in my mouth; for the first time in years I swallow the softness of ice cream. I want to see if my body will blow up in disgusting fatness with this slow animal stupidity swelling in my stomach. It doesn't. Letting down my guard, opening my many mouths, does not bring about the ruin, the rape I had feared. On the contrary. Food brings vitality back to me. I feel my hair take on its sheen, grow longer, as though new stalks of thought are springing from my brain; my brain, now nourished, thinks in colors instead of calories. I can run harder, my eyes are moist enough to cry. It takes me years to learn this, but in my memory just a day goes by. A sun sets. Food is fuel, the weakness that makes us want it our greatest strength.

George started to taste — styles, voices, times. He reported allowing himself to sleep late one morning, waking to a room where light quivered on the walls. He started going out some nights without his leather vest or black boots, tried kissing a woman on the neck and "going no farther." He brought wood home with him at the end of working days, stayed up late making small objects without any obvious functions — a box, a mobile, a chiseled plaque. It turned out he was good not only at nailing things together but also at carving out designs, the chisel nuzzling slowly into the pine, yellow shavings like the rinds of lemons littered around him.

One day he came to session and told he had met a woman — Lucky — whom he thought he could fall in love with, "if only I could get over Joanne."

"The other problem is," George said, "she's the greatest person, but she's heavy, maybe thirty pounds overweight. I've never made it with a fat woman before. You know me, I'm used to perfect curves, thighs I can grab ahold of, someone I can flip like a doll." He gave me one of his lewd George smiles.

I was enchanted by the idea of George with a fat woman, although, as often happens in therapy, his changes frightened him, and he retreated back into his shell, which was, nevertheless, not nearly as brittle as before. This leads me to believe that a personality disorder, even the most entrenched, is open to change. I had seen enough of George changed, naked, to imagine how his body would be within a fat woman's arms. I imagined her rocking him, and him kissing her face and mouth. I could not help but see her spread legs on a bed, and he, a little cowed by the sight of so much, trying to touch her, first with his fingers, then with his penis, allowing himself entry into the many layers of her life; he brushes her uterus, goes up past her hip, until he touches the curved rib bone, the hard male bone, taken a long time ago from the man, buried and found only in the full woman's body.

PAUL THEROUX

Chatwin Revisited

FROM GRANTA

WHEN I THINK of Bruce Chatwin, who was my friend, I am always reminded of a particular night, a dinner at the Royal Geographical Society, hearing him speaking animatedly about various high mountains he had climbed. And that struck me as very odd, because I knew he had never been much of a mountaineer.

I was some way down the table but I heard him clearly. He spoke in his usual way, very rapidly and insistently, stuttering and interrupting and laughing, until he had commanded enough attention to begin speechifying. Being Chatwin, he did not stop at the peaks he scaled. He had plans for further assaults and expeditions — all of them one-man affairs, no oxygen, minimum equipment, rush the summit — and as he appeared to be holding his listeners spellbound (they were murmuring, "Of course" and "Extraordinary" and "Quite right"), I peeked over to see their faces. On Chatwin's right was Chris Bonington, conqueror of Nanga Parbat and numerous other twenty-thousand-footers, and on his left, Lord Hunt, leader of the first successful expedition up Everest.

"Chatter, chatter, chatter, Chatwin," a mutual friend once said to me. He was smiling, but you could tell his head still hurt. Bruce had just been his houseguest for a week. "He simply never stops."

This talking was the most striking thing about him, yet there were so many other aspects of him that made an immediate impression. He was handsome, he had piercing eyes; he was very quick — full of nervous gestures, a rapid walker; he was often surprisingly mocking of the English. Of course, Bruce talks a lot, people said. It's because he's alone so much of the time. It was

true that he was intensely solitary — he was given to sudden disappearances, that is, and everyone assumed he was alone. But even
so, I believe he talked to himself, probably yakked nonstop, re-
hearsing his stories and practicing funny accents and mimicry: it
is a habit of many writers and travelers. I am sorry I never asked
him whether he did this. I am sure he would have let out his
screeching laugh and said, "Constantly!"

He was such a darter he seldom stayed still long enough for
anyone to sum him up, but when he died many people published
their memories of him — and the portraits were so different. It
was amazing how many people, old and young, many of them
distinguished, a number of them glamorous, gathered to mourn
him, in a Greek Orthodox church in London. Salman Rushdie sat
in the pew in front of me with his then wife. It was Valentine's Day
1989, the day after the ayatollah condemned Salman to death —
I thought it was a hollow condemnation, and I joked about it.
Judging from the congregation, Bruce had known everyone in
London. But he had flitted from one to another, keeping people
separate, making a point of not introducing them to each other,
but often dropping their names.

He did not only drop Francis Bacon's name: he went one better
and mimicked him — which suggested just how well he knew him.
"Oh, dear," he would say, with an epicene hiss, "a million quid for
one of my paintings — I'll just spend it on champagne." He could
get two or three boasts into a single statement, as in "Werner
Herzog and I just hiked two hundred miles in Dahomey," or "David
Hockney told me that his favorite painter is Liotard, a seventeenth-
century Swiss. He's brilliant. I often go to the Rijksmuseum just to
look at his work." (This must have been true, because one day in
Amsterdam, Bruce showed me a Liotard painting.)

Postcards are the preferred medium for many boasters, combin-
ing vividness, cheapness, and an economy of effort — something
like a miniature billboard. Bruce was a great sender of postcards. He
sent them to me from France, from China, from Australia, and from
the artists' colony Yaddo — *Feverish lesbian sculptors doing vulvaic
iconography in plastic.* He encapsulated a theory about an Italian
writer in Yunnan. From Australia he wrote, *You must come here. The
men are awful, like bits of cardboard, but the women are splendid.* And
on another postcard (this one of a bushranger), *Have become inter-*

ested in an extreme situation — of Spanish monks in an Aboriginal mis-
sion and am about to start sketching an outline. Anyway the crisis of the
"shall-never-write-another-line" sort is now over.

In terms of writing, he was in a state of permanent crisis. Perhaps
he had started to write too late in his life, perhaps he lacked
confidence. A writer talking to another writer about the difficulty
of writing is hardly riveting. Bruce was at his least interesting
bemoaning his writer's block, and I often felt that he was not really
bemoaning it at all, but rather boasting about the subtlety of his
special gift, the implication being that it was so finely tuned it
occasionally emitted a high-pitched squeal and seemed to go dead;
but no, it was still pulsing like a laser — it had simply drifted an
instant from his sights. I had no such story to tell — I was produc-
ing a book a year, turning the big wooden crank on my chomping
meatgrinder. How could I talk about a literary crisis, when all I
had to do was grab the crank and give it a spin?

He did write like an angel most of the time, but he is never more
Chatwinesque than when he is yielding to his conceit. In *The
Songlines* he mentions being in Vienna speaking with Konrad Lorenz (in itself something of a boast) on the subject of aggression.
Considering that Lorenz is the author of *On Aggression,* this was
audacious of Bruce, but he was unfazed in the presence of the
master, and went further, cheerfully adumbrating his own theories
of aggression ("But surely," he asked pointedly, "haven't we got the
concepts of 'aggression' and 'defense' mixed up?"), implying that
Konrad Lorenz had been barking up the wrong tree in sixty-odd
years of scientific research. Bruce then sketches his Beast Theory:
mankind needing to see his enemy as a beast in order to overcome
him; or needing to be a "surrogate beast" in order to see men as prey.

It seems astonishing that the renowned zoologist and philosopher did not find Bruce's theory conventional and obvious (as it
sounds to me). Instead, "Lorenz tugged at his beard, gave me a
searching look and said, ironically or not I'll never know: 'What
you have just said is totally new.'"

Chatwin claimed to have the usual English disdain for flattery
and praise, which is odd, because he adored it, and of course —
praise is cheap and plentiful — it was lavished upon him. To need
praise is human enough. Bruce solicited it by circulating to his
friends bound proof copies of his books. We would read them and

scribble remarks in the margin. I remember the scribbled-over copy of *The Viceroy of Ouidah*. My remarks were anodyne, but some other snippets of marginalia were shrieks of derision: "Ha! Ha!" or "Rubbish" or "Impossible!" He said he didn't care.

Here he is in Dahomey, speaking to an African soldier, in his sketch "A Coup":

> "You are English?"
> "Yes."
> "But you speak excellent French."
> "Passable," I said.
> "With a Parisian accent I should have said."
> "I have lived in Paris."

Much of his reading was in French, usually obscure books. It would be something like Rousseau's *Des rêveries du promeneur solitaire*, Gide's *Nourritures terrestres*, Rimbaud's *Les Illuminations* or — one of the strangest travel books ever written — *Voyage au tour de ma chambre*. When he found a book that few other people had read he tended to overpraise it. He might dismiss a book precisely because it was popular.

His ability to speak French well was of course part of his gift for mimicry, and it delighted me, though it irritated many who felt Bruce was showing off. When he appeared on the Parisian literary television show *Apostrophe*, he was interviewed in French and he replied with complete fluency, talking a mile a minute.

He was full of theories. One was highly complex and concerned the origin of the color red as the official color of Marxism. This theory took you across the ocean to Uruguay. It involved butchers in Montevideo, peasants on horseback, Garibaldi and the Colorado Party. I think I've got that right. The theory then whisked you back to Europe, to Italy, to Germany, to Russia, and to the adoption of — was it an apron? was it a flag? It was all very confusing, though Chatwin told the story with precision, and always the same way. I know this because I heard him explain the theory at least four times. He told it to everyone. It was tiresome to hear this theory repeated, but it was even more annoying to realize that he had not remembered that he had told you before.

That was something his friends had to endure. If he couldn't recall that he was repeating something to you verbatim — shrieking each predictable thing and looking eager and hopeful — that seemed to indicate that he cared more about the monologuing itself than about you. The worst aspect of bores — even part-timers like Bruce — is their impartiality, their utter lack of interest in whoever they happen to be drilling into. Because it hardly matters who they are with, they victimize everyone, great and small.

Bruce was a fairly bad listener. If you told him something he would quickly say that he knew it already; and he would go on talking. Usually he was such a good talker that it hardly mattered.

But while most of us knew his stories, there were always great gaps in between them. There is an English saying which expresses befuddlement, *Who's he when he's at home?* Exactly. Everyone knew Bruce was married — we had met his wife, Elizabeth. But what sort of marriage was this? *"A mariage blanc,"* a friend once said to me, pursing his lips. Bruce was in his way devoted to his wife, but the very fact of Bruce having a wife was so improbable that no one quite believed it.

One night at dinner, just before he left the table, I heard Bruce distinctly speak of his plans for the near future and say, "I'm going to meet my wife in Tibet." Afterwards, one of the people present said, "Did he say his wife was dead?" and another replied, "No. He said his wife's in bed."

He kept so much to himself. We heard the colorful stories of a born raconteur. But what of the rest of it? We wondered what his private life was really like, and sometimes we speculated. His first book, *In Patagonia*, embodied all his faults and virtues. It was highly original, courageous, and vividly written. He inscribed a copy to me, writing generously, *To Paul Theroux, who unwittingly triggered this off* (and he explained that a book of mine had inspired him). But his book was full of gaps. How had he traveled from here to there? How had he met this or that person? Life was never so neat as Bruce made out. What of the other, small, telling details, which to me give a book reality?

I used to look for links between the chapters, and between two conversations or pieces of geography. Why hadn't he put them in?

"Why do you think it matters?" he said to me.

"Because it's interesting," I said. "And because I think when you're writing a travel book you have to come clean."

This made him laugh, and then he said something that I have

always taken to be a pronouncement that was very near to being his motto. He said — he screeched — "I don't believe in coming clean!"

We had a mutual friend, an older and distinguished writer who felt that Bruce was trying to live down the shame of being the son of a Birmingham lawyer. I challenged this.

The man said, "No. You're wrong. Look at Noel Coward. His mother kept a lodging house. And he pretended to be so grand — that theatrical English accent. All that posturing. He knew he was common. It was all a pretense. Think of his pain."

This might have been true in a small way of Bruce, but I think that he was secretive by nature. It kept him aloof. It helped him in his flitting around. He never revealed himself totally to anyone, as far as I know, and in this way he kept his personality intact. In any case, he never struck me as being thoroughly English. He was more cosmopolitan — liking France, feeling liberated in America, being fascinated by Russia and China, something of a cultural exile.

I am skirting the subject of his sexual preference because it does not seem to me that it should matter. Yet it was obvious to anyone who knew him that in speaking tenderly of marital bliss he was always suppressing a secret and more lively belief in homosexuality. That he was homosexual bothered no one; that he never spoke about it was rather disturbing.

In an ungracious memoir, the writer David Plante refused to see Bruce's sense of fun and perhaps even deeper sense of insecurity. Plante wrote at length about how they had gone to a gay disco in London called Heaven, but it is characteristic of the memoir's dark hints and hypocrisy that Bruce's behavior is regarded as sneaky and insincere, while Plante himself never discloses his own motive for going to the gay hangout.

I wanted to know more about his homosexual life, not because I am prurient but because if I like someone I want to know everything. And while Bruce was exasperated by others who kept their secrets, he was secretive himself. He never wrote about his sexuality, and some of us have laid our souls bare.

When he called me he always did so out of the blue. I liked that. I liked the suddenness of it — it suited my life and my writing. I

hated making plans for the future. I might not be in the mood
that far-off day; I might be trying to write something. If he called
in the morning, it was always a proposal to meet that afternoon or
evening. And then I might not hear from him for six months or a
year.

It surprised me that he had agreed to give a lecture for the Royal
Geographical Society, but he had done it on one condition — that
it be a duet. Would I agree? I said O.K., and I quickly realized we
were both doing it so as to seem respectable among all these
distinguished explorers and travelers.

Working together with him to prepare the lecture, I realized how
little I knew him and what an odd fish he was. He was insecure, I
knew that, and it had the effect of making him seem domineering.
"I can't believe you haven't read Pigafetta," he would say, and he
would put the book in my hand and insist I read it by tomorrow;
and the next day he would say, "Our talk's going to be awful, it's
hopeless, I don't know why we agreed to do this"; and later on
would say, "By the way, I've invited Sally, Duchess of Westminster."

I found this maddening. I felt it was a task we had to perform,
and that we would do it well if we were decently prepared. Bruce's
moods ranged from rather tiresome high spirits to days of belit-
tling gloom. "No one's going to come," he said. "I'm certainly not
inviting anyone."

We got in touch with a dozen members of the RGS who had
photographs of Patagonia, and we assembled eighty or a hundred
beautiful pictures of the plains, of glaciers, of penguins, of snow
and storms.

When the day came it turned out that Bruce had invited many
people, including his parents — his big beefy-faced father had the
look of a Dickensian solicitor — and he was miffed that the duchess hadn't been able to make it. The lecture itself I thought was
splendid — not so much for the text but for the atmosphere, the
oddity. We gave it in the wooden amphitheater, where so many
distinguished explorers had reported back to the society; and we
stood in the dark — a little light shining on our notes, while big
beautiful pictures of Patagonia flashed on the screen behind us.
This was thrilling — just our voices and these vivid Patagonian
sights.

There was loud applause afterwards. Bruce, who would have

been a wonderful actor, was flushed with pleasure. He had been brilliant, and I realized that he had needed me to encourage him and get him through it.

And when I heard him at dinner regaling Lord Hunt and Chris Bonington with his mountaineering exploits I thought: He's flying!

He traveled. We ran into each other in various places — in America, in Amsterdam. When he wanted to meet someone I knew well he simply asked me to introduce him. Graham Greene he particularly wanted to meet. But Bruce was disappointed. He thought Greene was gaga. He could not understand the mystique. He loved Borges. Later he needed glamour. He let himself be courted by Robert Mapplethorpe. He liked the thought of his portrait appearing in Mapplethorpe's notorious exhibition, along with photographs of women weightlifters and strange flowers and even stranger sexual practices.

He went to China — just a magazine assignment, but Bruce made it seem as though he had been sent on an expedition by the Royal Geographical Society. I admired that in him. He took his writing assignments seriously, no matter who he was writing for. He was the opposite of a hack, which is to say something of a pedant, but a likable one, who was fastidious and truly knowledgeable.

When he fell deathly ill soon after his China trip, the word spread that he had been bitten by a fruit bat in Yunnan and contracted a rare blood disease. Only two other people in the entire world had ever had it, so the story went, and both had died. Bruce was near death, but he fought back and survived. And he had another story to tell at dinner parties — of being bitten by a Chinese bat. He recovered. A friend said to me, "I just saw Bruce walking through Eaton Square carrying a white truffle."

But the blood disease returned. "I was warned that it might pop up again," Bruce explained. What kind of bat was this exactly? Bruce was vague, and he became very ill. Seeing him was like looking at the sunken cheeks and wasted flesh of a castaway. That image came to me again and again, the image of an abandoned traveler — the worst fate for travelers is that they become lost, and instead of reveling in oblivion, they fret and fall ill.

When I visited his bedroom in Oxfordshire — a pretty, homely farmhouse that Elizabeth kept ticking over — his hands would fly to his face, covering his hollow cheeks.

"God, you're healthy," he would say sadly. But later he would cheer up, making plans. "I'm going to California to see Lisa Lyon. She's fabulous. The woman weightlifter? You'd love her." And when I prepared to go, he would say, "I'm not ready for *The Tibetan Book of the Dead* yet."

"He expected to get better, and when he got worse he was demoralized and just let go," Elizabeth told me. "He was in terrible pain, but at the height of it he lapsed into a coma, and that was almost a blessing."

Hovering in this fragile state of health he died suddenly. He had been handsome, calculating, and demanding; he was famous for his disappearances. His death was like that, just as sudden, like Bruce on another journey. We were used to his vanishings — his silences could be as conspicuous as his talk. It seems strange, but not unlike him, that he has been gone so long.

JOHN UPDIKE

The Disposable Rocket

FROM MICHIGAN QUARTERLY REVIEW

INHABITING A MALE BODY is much like having a bank account;
as long as it's healthy, you don't think much about it. Compared
to the female body, it is a low-maintenance proposition: a shower
now and then, trim the fingernails every ten days, a haircut once
a month. Oh yes, shaving — scraping or buzzing away at your face
every morning. Byron, in *Don Juan*, thought the repeated nuisance
of shaving balanced out the periodic agony, for females, of child-
birth. Women are, his lines tell us,

> Condemn'd to child-bed, as men for their sins
> Have shaving too entail'd upon their chins, —

> A daily plague, which in the aggregate
> May average on the whole with parturition.

From the standpoint of reproduction, the male body is a delivery
system, as the female is a mazy device for retention. Once the
delivery is made, men feel a faint but distinct falling-off of interest.
Yet against the enduring female heroics of birth and nurture
should be set the male's superhuman frenzy to deliver his goods:
he vaults walls, skips sleep, risks wallet, health, and his political
future all to ram home his seed into the gut of the chosen woman.
The sense of the chase lives in him as the key to life. His body is,
like a delivery rocket that falls away in space, a disposable means.
Men put their bodies at risk to experience the release from gravity.
    When my tenancy of a male body was fairly new — of six or so
years' duration — I used to jump and fall just for the joy of it.

Falling — backwards, downstairs — become a specialty of mine, an attention-getting stunt I was practicing into my thirties, at suburban parties. Falling is, after all, a kind of flying, though of briefer duration than would be ideal. My impulse to hurl myself from high windows and the edges of cliffs belongs to my body, not my mind, which resists the siren call of the chasm with all its might; the interior struggle knocks the wind from my lungs and tightens my scrotum and gives any trip to Europe, with its Alps, castle parapets, and gargoyled cathedral lookouts, a flavor of nightmare. Falling, strangely, no longer figures in my dreams, as it often did when I was a boy and my subconscious was more honest with me. An airplane, that necessary evil, turns the earth into a map so quickly the brain turns aloof and calm; still, I marvel that there is no end of young men willing to become jet pilots.

Any accounting of male-female differences must include the male's superior recklessness, a drive not, I think, toward death, as the darker feminist cosmogonies would have it, but to test the limits, to see what the traffic will bear — a kind of mechanic's curiosity. The number of men who do lasting damage to their young bodies is striking; war and car accidents aside, secondary-school sports, with the approval of parents and the encouragement of brutish coaches, take a fearful toll of skulls and knees. We were made for combat, back in the post-simian, East African days, and the bumping, the whacking, the breathlessness, the pain-smothering adrenaline rush, form a cumbersome and unfashionable bliss, but bliss nevertheless. Take your body to the edge, and see if it flies.

The male sense of space must differ from that of the female, who has such interesting, active, and significant inner space. The space that interests men is outer. The fly ball high against the sky, the long pass spiraling overhead, the jet fighter like a scarcely visible pinpoint nozzle laying down its vapor trail at forty thousand feet, the gazelle haunch flickering just beyond arrow-reach, the uncountable stars sprinkled on their great black wheel, the horizon, the mountaintop, the quasar — these bring portents with them, and awaken a sense of relation with the invisible, with the empty. The ideal male body is taut with lines of potential force, a diagram extending outward; the ideal female body curves around centers of repose. Of course, no one is ideal, and the sexes are somewhat androgynous subdivisions of a species: Diana the huntress is a more trendy body-type nowadays than languid, overweight Venus, and polymorphous Dionysus poses for more underwear ads than Mars. Relatively, though, men's bodies, however elegant, are designed for covering territory, for moving on.

An erection, too, defies gravity, flirts with it precariously. It extends the diagram of outward direction into downright detachability — objective in the case of the sperm, subjective in the case of the testicles and penis. Men's bodies, at this juncture, feel only partly theirs; a demon of sorts has been attached to their lower torsos, whose performance is erratic and whose errands seem, at times, ridiculous. It is like having a (much) smaller brother toward whom you feel both fond and impatient; if he is you, it is you in curiously simplified and ignoble form. This sense, of the male body being two of them, is acknowledged in verbal love play and erotic writing, where the penis is playfully given its own name, an individuation not even the rarest rapture grants a vagina. Here, where maleness gathers to a quintessence of itself, there can be no insincerity, there can be no hiding; for sheer nakedness, there is nothing like a hopeful phallus; its aggressive shape is indivisible from its tender-skinned vulnerability. The act of intercourse, from the point of view of a consenting female, has an element of mothering, of enwrapment, of merciful concealment, even. The male body, for this interval, is tucked out of harm's way.

To inhabit a male body, then, is to feel somewhat detached from it. It is not an enemy, but not entirely a friend. Our essence seems to lie not in cells and muscles but in the traces our thoughts and actions inscribe on the air. The male body skims the surface of nature's deep, wherein the blood and pain and mysterious cravings of women perpetuate the species. Participating less in nature's processes than the female body, the male body gives the impression — false — of being exempt from time. Its powers of strength and reach descend in early adolescence, along with acne and sweaty feet, and depart, in imperceptible increments, after thirty or so. It surprises me to discover, when I remove my shoes and socks, the same paper-white hairless ankles that struck me as pathetic when I observed them on my father. I felt betrayed when, in some tumble of touch football twenty years ago, I heard my tibia snap; and when, between two reading engagements in Cleveland, my appendix tried to burst; and when, the other day, not for the first time, there arose to my nostrils out of my own body the musty attic smell my grandfather's body had.

A man's body does not betray its tenant as rapidly as a woman's. Never as fine and lovely, it has less distance to fall; what rugged beauty it has is wrinkle-proof. It keeps its capability of procreation indecently long. Unless intense athletic demands are made on it, the thing serves well enough to sixty, which is my age now. From here on, it's chancy. There are no breasts or ovaries to admit cancer to the male body, but the prostate, that awkwardly located little source of seminal fluid, shows the strain of sexual function with fits of hysterical cell replication, and all that beer and potato chips add up in the coronary arteries. A writer, whose physical equipment can be minimal, as long as it gets him to the desk, the lectern, and New York City once in a while, cannot but be grateful to his body, especially to his eyes, those tender and intricate sites where the brain extrudes from the skull, and to his hands, which hold the pen or tap the keyboard. His body has been, not himself exactly, but a close pal, pot-bellied and balding like most of his other pals now. A man and his body are like a boy and the buddy who has a driver's license and the use of his father's car for the evening; he goes along, gratefully, for the ride.

Biographical Notes

NICHOLSON BAKER has published four novels — *The Mezzanine* (1988), *Room Temperature* (1990), *Vox* (1992), and *The Fermata* (1994) — as well as a book-length autobiographical-critical essay about John Updike entitled *U and I* (1991). He has written for *The New Yorker, The Atlantic Monthly, The New York Review of Books,* and *Esquire.* He is married, with two children.

TED CONOVER is the author of the books *Rolling Nowhere: A Young Man's Adventures Riding the Rails with America's Hoboes; Coyotes: A Journey Through the Secret World of America's Illegal Aliens;* and *Whiteout: Lost in Aspen.* Raised in Colorado, he graduated from Amherst Colleqe and was a Marshall Scholar at Cambridge University. Much of his work combines journalism with the teachings of anthropology. "Trucking Through the AIDS Belt," first published in *The New Yorker,* and "Christy Picks a Mother," from the *New York Times Magazine,* are part of a planned series of writings about HIV disease.

DAVID DENBY is the film critic for *New York* magazine. "Does Homer Have Legs?" is part of a book he is writing that chronicles the experience of going back to Columbia and retaking the college's two required core curriculum courses, in classic Western literary and philosophic texts.

ANDRE DUBUS III is the author of a collection of short fiction, *The Cage Keeper and Other Stories,* and *Bluesman,* a novel. His stories have appeared in *Playboy, Yankee, Crazyhorse, The Crescent Review, Epoch,* and *Image.* He is a winner of the 1985 National Magazine Award for Fiction and was a 1994 finalist for the Rome Prize Fellowship from the American Academy and Institute of Arts and Letters. A carpenter and part-time writing teacher, he is married to the actress-dancer Fontaine Dollas Dubus. They live in Massachusetts with their son, Austin.

STANLEY ELKIN is Merle King Professor of Modern Letters at Washington University, in St. Louis. This is his fourth appearance in *The Best American Essays*. A member of the American Academy and Institute of Arts and Letters, he has published a dozen works of fiction, including *The MacGuffin, The Living End, The Dick Gibson Show, The Franchiser, The Magic Kingdom,* and *George Mills,* which won the 1982 National Book Critics Circle Award. *Van Gogh's Room at Arles* was published in 1993. His new novel, *Mrs. Ted Bliss,* is scheduled to be published in 1995.

LOUISE ERDRICH has written two books of poetry and four novels, including *The Bingo Palace,* published in 1994. "Skunk Dreams" is included in a nonfictional book about art and motherhood scheduled to be published in the winter of 1995.

IAN FRAZIER is the author of the nonfiction *Great Plains* and two books of essays. His work appears in *The New Yorker* and other magazines. He lives in Brooklyn, New York.

DARCY FREY is a regular contributor to *Harper's Magazine* and the *New York Times Magazine.* The essay in this volume won the National Magazine Award and the Livingston Award and is the basis for his forthcoming book about inner-city basketball, *The Last Shot,* to be published in the fall of 1994.

ADAM GOPNIK has been a staff writer at *The New Yorker* since 1987. In the spring of 1995, he will deliver the Oxford University Press lectures at the New York Public Library.

STEPHEN JAY GOULD teaches biology, geology, and the history of science at Harvard University. He is the author of *Ontogeny and Phylogeny, The Mismeasure of Man, Wonderful Life,* and six collections of essays: *Ever Since Darwin, The Panda's Thumb, Hen's Teeth and Horse's Toes, The Flamingo's Smile, An Urchin in the Storm,* and *Bully for Brontosaurus.* A MacArthur Prize Fellow, he writes a monthly scientific essay for *Natural History* magazine.

LUCY GREALY is an award-winning poet. Her work has appeared, among other places, in *The Paris Review* and the London *Times Literary Supplement.* She has received a fellowship from the Bunting Institute, been a guest of the Yaddo Corporation, and been a fellow at the Fine Arts Work Center in Provincetown. Her memoir, *Autobiography of a Face,* is based on the essay in this book, which won a National Magazine Award. She lives in Manhattan.

VICKI HEARNE is the author of three volumes of poetry — *Nervous Horses, In the Absence of Horses,* and *The Parts of Light* — and three books of essays — *Adam's Task: Calling Animals by Name, Bandit: Dossier of a Dangerous Dog,* and *Animal Happiness.* An active professional dog trainer, she is at Yale University.

JAMAICA KINCAID is the author of *Annie John, A Small Place,* and *Lucy.* Her first book, *At the Bottom of the River,* received the Morton Dauwen Zabel Award of the American Academy and Institute of Arts and Letters. A staff writer for *The New Yorker,* she was born in Antigua and lives with her husband, her daughter, and her son in Vermont.

MARK KRAMER is writer-in-residence (and professor) at Boston University's Journalism Department and taught for a decade at Smith College. He has written for *The Atlantic Monthly,* the *New York Times Magazine, National Geographic, Yankee,* and *Outside.* His books include *Three Farms: Making Milk, Meat, and Money from the American Soil* and *Invasive Procedures: A Year in the World of Two Surgeons.* He is on the home stretch of *Travels with a Hungry Bear,* a wanderer's account of rural Russia during and after perestroika.

WILLIAM LANGEWIESCHE, a contributing editor of *The Atlantic Monthly,* is the author of *Cutting for Sign* (1994). His second book, *On the Sahara,* will be published in 1995. He first flew an airplane at the age of five and began working as a professional pilot while a student at Stanford University, from which he graduated in 1977.

JAMES A. McPHERSON is the author of *Hue and Cry, Railroad,* and *Elbow Room.* His articles and short stories have appeared in numerous periodicals, including *The Atlantic Monthly, Esquire, The Nation, Ploughshares,* and *The Iowa Review.* A graduate of Morris Brown College and Harvard Law School, he has received a Guggenheim Fellowship, a Pulitzer Prize, and a MacArthur Prize Fellows Award. He is a professor of English at the University of Iowa.

S. OSO currently resides in California. "Lots" is part of the collection *Misconceptions.* His work has appeared in *The Hudson Review* and *Antioch Review.*

CYNTHIA OZICK is the author of four novels — *Trust, The Cannibal Galaxy, The Shawl,* and *The Messiah of Stockholm* — and several collections, including *The Pagan Rabbi and Other Stories, Bloodshed and Three Novellas,* and *Levitation: Five Fictions.* She has published two collections of essays, *Art and Ardor* and *Metaphor and Memory.* Two more collections of essays will appear in 1994: *What Henry James Knew, and Other Essays on Writers* and *Portrait of the Artist as a Bad Character, and Other Essays on Writing.* She has also written *Blue Light,* a play scheduled to open in the summer of 1994.

LAUREN SLATER has published fiction and essays in *One Meadway, Iowa Woman, New Letters, The Belletrist Review, Fireweed,* and *Salamander.* She was a first-place winner of both the 1993 New Letters Literary Award and the 1993 Belletrist Review Fiction Competition. In addition, her fiction was nominated for a 1994 Pushcart Prize. Ms. Slater has recently completed both a novel and a doctoral dissertation in psychology, and she is currently in practice at After Care Services, an inner-city mental health clinic, where she works primarily with male sex-abuse perpetrators and schizophrenics. Her therapeutic work revolves around the oral or written construction of narrative, and she is in the process of publishing a literary magazine representing the poetry and prose poems of eleven institutionalized schizophrenic clients, in the hope that their marginalized voices can become a valid part of our culture.

PAUL THEROUX was born in Massachusetts in 1941 and published his first novel in 1967. His prolific fiction output includes *Picture Palace, Mosquito Coast, My Secret History,* and *Chicago Loop;* he has also written a number of travel books, among them *The Great Railway Bazaar, The Old Patagonian Express,* and *Riding the Iron Rooster.* He now divides his time between Massachusetts and Hawaii. His most recent novel is *Millroy the Magician.*

JOHN UPDIKE was born in 1932 in Shillington, Pennsylvania. After graduation from Harvard in 1954 and a year at an English art school, he worked for two years for *The New Yorker's* "Talk of the Town" department. Since 1957 he has lived in Massachusetts as a free-lance writer. His most recent books are a novel, *Brazil,* and a collection of short stories, *The Afterlife.*

Notable Essays of 1993

Selected by Robert Atwan